THE POLITICS OF WOMEN'S BODIES

THE POLITICS OF WOMEN'S BODIES

Sexuality, Appearance, and Behavior

FOURTH EDITION

Rose Weitz
Arizona State University
Samantha Kwan
University of Houston

New York Oxford
OXFORD UNIVERSITY PRESS

Oxford University Press is a department of the University of Oxford.
It furthers the University's objective of excellence in research,
scholarship, and education by publishing worldwide.

Oxford New York
Auckland Cape Town Dar es Salaam Hong Kong Karachi
Kuala Lumpur Madrid Melbourne Mexico City Nairobi
New Delhi Shanghai Taipei Toronto

With offices in
Argentina Austria Brazil Chile Czech Republic France Greece
Guatemala Hungary Italy Japan Poland Portugal Singapore
South Korea Switzerland Thailand Turkey Ukraine Vietnam

For titles covered by Section 112 of the US Higher Education Opportunity Act, please visit www.oup.com/us/he for the latest information about pricing and alternate formats.

Published by Oxford University Press
198 Madison Avenue, New York, New York 10016
http://www.oup.com

Library of Congress Cataloging-in-Publication Data

The politics of women's bodies: sexuality, appearance, and behavior / [edited by] Rose Weitz, Arizona State University, Samantha Kwan, University of Houston. -- Fourth edition.
pages cm
ISBN 978-0-19-934379-9
1. Women--Psychology. 2. Women--Physiology. 3. Women--Social conditions. 4. Human body--Social aspects. 5. Human body--Political aspects. I. Weitz, Rose, 1952- II. Kwan, Samantha.
HQ1206.P56 2014
305.4--dc23
2013033939

Printing number: 9 8 7 6 5 4 3 2 1

Printed in the United States of America
on acid-free paper

Contents

* = *New to this edition*
Preface *xi*

PART I THE SOCIAL CONSTRUCTION OF WOMEN'S BODIES *1*

1 A History of Women's Bodies *3*
Rose Weitz

Weitz delineates how ideas about the female body have changed—or not—over time, as well as the very real impact those ideas have had on women's lives.

2 Believing Is Seeing: Biology as Ideology *13*
Judith Lorber

Lorber argues that binary sex differences are a social construction: they appear to be natural and real only because our cultural practices *make* them real.

3 Becoming a Gendered Body: Practices of Preschools *27*
Karin A. Martin

Martin explores how preschools teach young children to "perform gender" and to develop embodied selves that are "properly" gendered.

4 Medicalization, Natural Childbirth, and Birthing Experiences* *49*
Sarah Jane Brubaker and Heather E. Dillaway

Brubaker and Dillaway take a critical look at "natural" and "medical" childbirth and examine women's subjective experiences of medical childbirth.

5 Foucault, Femininity, and the Modernization of Patriarchal Power *64*
Sandra Lee Bartky

Bartky describes how women internalize social expectations regarding female appearance and behavior and then attempt to meet those expectations by adopting various "disciplinary practices."

6 Integrating Disability, Transforming Feminist Theory* *86*
Rosemarie Garland-Thomson

Garland-Thomson argues that feminist theories of the body could be strengthened by incorporating key ideas from disability studies.

PART II THE POLITICS OF SEXUALITY *105*

7 Breasted Experience: The Look and the Feeling *107*
Iris Marion Young

Young explores women's relationships with their breasts; women sometimes view their breasts as objects to be used and other times act as subjects whose breasts are part of their essential selves.

8 Daring to Desire: Culture and the Bodies of Adolescent Girls *120*
Deborah L. Tolman

Tolman describes how teenage girls think about sexual desire and explores how their ideas are shaped by both the promise of sexual pleasure and the threat of sexual danger.

9 A Tale of Two Technologies: HPV Vaccination, Male Circumcision, and Sexual Health* *143*
Laura M. Carpenter and Monica J. Casper

Carpenter and Casper illustrate how discourses of gender, sexuality, race, age, and nationality shape the use and cultural meanings of body technologies.

10 "Get Your Freak On": Sex, Babies, and Images of Black Femininity *164*
Patricia Hill Collins

Hill Collins explores contemporary images of African American women, discusses how these images reinforce racism, and shows how African American women use these images to assert control over their bodies and lives.

11 Brain, Brow, and Booty: Latina Iconicity in U.S. Popular Culture *176*
Isabel Molina Guzmán and Angharad N. Valdivia

Molina Guzmán and Valdivia analyze the gendered and racialized media portrayals of Jennifer Lopez, Salma Hayek, and Frida Kahlo.

12 "So Full of Myself as a Chick": Goth Women, Sexual Independence, and Gender Egalitarianism *184*
Amy C. Wilkins

Wilkins shows how Goth women are exempted from dominant cultural norms for sexuality and appearance; their post-feminist assumptions, however, camouflage gender and sexual inequality within Goth culture.

PART III THE POLITICS OF APPEARANCE *199*

13 Designing Women: Cultural Hegemony and the Exercise of Power among Women Who Have Undergone Elective Mammoplasty *201*
Patricia Gagné and Deanna McGaughey

Gagné and McGaughey show how women actively choose cosmetic surgery, but do so in the context of hegemonic cultural norms that make it difficult for them to consider not doing so.

14 Women and Their Hair: Seeking Power through Resistance and Accommodation *223*
Rose Weitz

Weitz uses women's experiences with their hair to illustrate how resistance and accommodation are interwoven in women's everyday bodily experiences.

15 Navigating Public Spaces: Gender, Race, and Body Privilege in Everyday Life* *241*
Samantha Kwan

Kwan examines weight-based stigma and illustrates how "body privilege" is distinctly patterned by gender and race/ethnicity.

16 The Moral Underpinnings of Beauty: A Meaning-Based Explanation for Light and Dark Complexions in Advertising* *258*
Shyon Baumann

Baumann argues that the portrayal of men and women with different skin tones in print advertisements reflects cultural ideas about gender and about the meaning of lightness and darkness.

17 Reclaiming the Female Body: Women Body Modifiers and Feminist Debates *277*
Victoria Pitts

Pitts analyzes how women use body modification to take control of their bodies, as well as the benefits and limitations of this particular type of embodied resistance.

PART IV THE POLITICS OF BEHAVIOR *291*

18 From the "Muscle Moll" to the "Butch" Ballplayer: Mannishness, Lesbianism, and Homophobia in U.S. Women's Sport *293*
Susan K. Cahn

Cahn traces the modern history of women in sport and shows how gendered and racial stereotypes stigmatized women athletes, first as heterosexually "loose" and later as presumed lesbians.

19 Branded with Infamy: Inscriptions of Poverty and Class in the United States *309*
Vivyan C. Adair

Adair describes how poverty and its stigma are physically marked on the bodies of poor women and how that stigma both supports public policies that discipline poor women's bodies and encourages poor women to discipline their own bodies.

20 Backlash and Continuity: The Political Trajectory of Fetal Rights *322*
Rachel Roth

Roth describes how the battle over reproductive rights has led to the recent push for "fetal rights"—an idea she believes has served more to punish women for nontraditional behavior than to protect their children.

21 *Hijab* and American Muslim Women: Creating the Space for Autonomous Selves* *331*
Rhys H. Williams and Gira Vashi

Williams and Vashi explore the multiple meanings of veiling for college-age, second-generation Muslim American women.

22 Compulsive Heterosexuality: Masculinity and Dominance *346*
C. J. Pascoe

Pascoe describes how male high school students demonstrate their heterosexuality and their dominance over girls' bodies—sometimes violently—in order to claim masculine power and identity for themselves.

23 Being Undocumented and Intimate Partner Violence (IPV): Multiple Vulnerabilities through the Lens of Feminist Intersectionality* *357*
Margaret E. Adams and Jacquelyn Campbell

Adams and Campbell explore how gender, ethnicity, and legal status intersect and leave undocumented immigrant women who experience intimate partner violence at risk of further violence and health problems.

Appendix *373*

Preface

Since the start of the modern feminist movement, many writers and scholars have examined how the female body and ideas about the female body affect women's lives. They have produced a large and diverse literature, spread across many academic disciplines and using many theoretical approaches, on topics ranging from the nature of lesbianism, to the sources of eating disorders, to the consequences of violence against women. Taken together, this literature forms the nucleus of a new field, the politics of women's bodies. At the time the first edition of this book was published, however, no monograph or anthology had brought this literature together and demonstrated its coherence. Thus, that book aimed to cast a new light on this growing field and bring it the attention it deserved. The current edition continues in this tradition.

Three themes unite the readings in this anthology: How ideas about women's bodies are socially constructed, how these social constructions can be used to control women's lives, and how women can resist these forces.

The social construction of women's bodies refers to the process through which cultural ideas (including scientific ideas) about women's bodies develop and become accepted. As this anthology demonstrates, this is a political process which reflects, reinforces, or challenges the distribution of power between men and women.

Like all other political processes, the social construction of women's bodies develops through battles between groups with competing political interests and with differential access to power and resources. For example, doctors have presented their ideas about the existence, nature, and consequences of "premenstrual syndrome" (PMS) as objective medical truths. Yet those ideas reflect both a particular context—in which women are increasingly willing to speak up about their anger and dissatisfaction—and a particular set of cultural rather than scientific ideas regarding the frailty and dangerousness of the female body. Doctors' ability to convince the public to accept these ideas has depended both on their economic and social power and on the support they have received from women who believe they have PMS and want validation for and treatment of their symptoms.

The social construction of women's bodies often serves as a powerful tool in the social control of women's lives by fostering material changes in women's lives and bodies. Again, we can use PMS as an example. The existence of this diagnostic category gives employers an excuse to not hire or promote women—regardless of whether they have PMS—on the grounds that women's menstrual cycles make them physically and emotionally unreliable. Similarly, when a woman acts or speaks in ways that others find threatening, those others may dismiss her actions or remarks as symptoms of PMS—regardless of whether the woman herself believes she experiences such a syndrome and even regardless of whether she is at that moment premenstrual. Finally, this social construction of PMS encourages medical practices (including the use of sedatives, hormones, and hysterectomies) that materially change and control women's bodies, while encouraging women to police their own behaviors more closely during their premenstrual days.

As Michel Foucault has so vividly described, a powerful array of disciplinary practices—both internalized and external—are used to produce "docile bodies" that willingly accede to their own social control. Yet women are not always passive victims of these disciplinary practices. Rather, they may collaborate in or resist their creation and maintenance. For example, many women fought for the social construction of PMS because they believed it would provide medical legitimation for behaviors and emotions that were otherwise socially unacceptable. Conversely, many other women have fought against this social construction. Similarly, some women resist pressures to conform to social norms of female appearance by refusing to get breast implants following mastectomies, while other women live a lesbian life despite the social construction of lesbianism as deviant and the social control of lesbians through stigma, discrimination, and physical violence. Consequently, this volume also examines the possibilities for and limits on women's resistance.

Unfortunately, given the burgeoning nature of the field, no one volume—or at least no volume of reasonable size and price—can do justice to the full range of topics that touch on the politics of women's bodies. Consequently, despite the growing and important literature on how men's bodies are also gendered, political, and socially constructed, this edition continues to focus solely on women's bodies. Similarly, rather than barely touch on international issues by adding a few articles based in other countries, *The Politics of Women's Bodies* focuses only on women's lives within the United States. For better or worse, the United States disproportionately affects other countries due to its broad cultural, economic, and political impact, and so ideas about women's bodies in this country are particularly important.

Changes to This Edition

This edition of *The Politics of Women's Bodies* retains the basic structure of the previous edition but brings on a second editor, Samantha Kwan, who offers new perspectives and insights. Seven of the 23 articles are new to this edition.

Important new topics include child birth, disability, human papillomavirus (HPV) vaccination, fat stigma, skin tone, veiling, and intimate partner violence experienced by undocumented immigrants.

To increase accessibility, we continue to include brief introductions for each article. These introductions are designed to help readers put the articles in context and understand their general viewpoints. In addition, this edition includes a new appendix with several discussion questions for each article.

Overview of Volume

Part I of this volume looks at the social construction of women's bodies. The first article (written specifically for this anthology) provides a context for the rest of the anthology by providing a broad overview of the history of social ideas about women's bodies and demonstrating how changes in these ideas can either challenge or reinforce women's position in society. The other articles draw on both poststructuralist and traditional social scientific theoretical traditions to provide a framework for questioning our most basic ideas about the female body, examining the political process through which those ideas develop, and exploring how and why women accept or resist those ideas.

The remainder of the volume looks in more detail at how the politics of women's bodies affects women's lives. These readings are somewhat arbitrarily divided into three parts: the politics of sexuality, the politics of appearance, and the politics of bodily behavior. (Obviously, these three parts overlap, as, for example, to present a culturally acceptable appearance, women must engage in certain behaviors, with certain consequences for how their sexuality is perceived by others.)

Part II, on the politics of sexuality, addresses how women are socialized toward a Euro-American, heterosexual norm that emphasizes male pleasure and female restraint. Two articles discuss cultural attitudes toward the sexuality of African-American and Latina women, as well as the price these women pay for those attitudes. Another considers how new medical technologies reproduce beliefs about young women's sexuality. The remaining articles examine norms of heterosexual romance and the social consequences experienced by those who resist these norms.

Part III explores the politics of appearance. The articles in this part explore the myriad cultural norms regarding female appearance. Several examine the ways that women are taught to adopt these norms and the dilemmas faced by those who cannot meet them. This section also explores the ways in which appearance norms restrict women's lives and raises questions regarding the possibilities for, and limits on, resistance to these norms.

Part IV, on the politics of behavior, examines how social institutions have attempted to define and shape women's bodies and bodily behaviors. It opens with a history of women's participation in sport and the impact of homophobia on women athletes. This is followed by readings about how the state stigmatizes poor women's bodies and the meanings of religious veiling.

The remaining readings look at reproductive rights and violence against women.

The readings included in this volume were selected to cover a wide range of topics related to women and the body. All the readings are intellectually stimulating but written in a fashion accessible to any literate audience. The articles present theoretical concepts as well as data, but avoid the sort of convoluted "academese" and complex statistical techniques that nonacademic readers might find difficult to comprehend.

Our other goal in choosing readings was to find readings relevant to a diverse population of women and reflecting diverse academic perspectives. Readings were selected with attention to issues of diversity with regard to class, ethnicity, age, and sexual orientation. The articles also represent a range of disciplines, including communications, history, literature, nursing, political science, philosophy, and sociology. Seven articles, including two classic pieces, were first published before 2000; the rest are all more recent.

To increase accessibility, we have shortened most of the articles, deleting some of the more tangential issues. (Deleted text is marked with ellipses.) This editing also allowed for greater coverage of many topics while restricting the book's size and, consequently, price. We have also edited the readings to regularize spelling and style, to further increase accessibility. Finally, and as noted earlier, we have included brief introductions and discussion questions for each article.

Acknowledgments

Earlier editions of this anthology were developed by Rose, and benefited greatly from the many conversations she had with Georganne Scheiner, Mary Logan Rothschild, and Myra Dinnerstein. Rose also remains grateful to Judith Lorber, Beth Rushing, and Wendy Simonds for their comments on the original book manuscript.

Samantha Kwan thanks Alberto Mancillas, Luana Da Silva, and Scott Lee for their research assistance, as well as T. Xavia Karner, Mary Nell Trautner, and Scott V. Savage for their ongoing support throughout the project.

Both Rose and Samantha are delighted to have this opportunity to also thank our editor, Sherith Pankratz. Sherith has been a delight to work with, and has consistently made our task easier.

Finally, we would like to thank the reviewers of this edition who helped us continue to improve this book: Angela Aujla, Humber College; Amy Hudec, University of Redlands; Winifred Poster, Washington University; Erynn Masi de Casanova, University of Cincinnati; Claudia Schippert, University of Central Florida; Karyn Valerius, Hofstra University; Kimberly Williams, Mount Royal University.

I

THE SOCIAL CONSTRUCTION OF WOMEN'S BODIES

The articles in this part provide the historical and theoretical underpinnings for analyzing social ideas about women's bodies. The central theme of this section is the social construction of women's bodies. "Social construction" refers to the process through which ideas become culturally accepted. As the following articles illustrate, this is an intensely political process, reflecting different groups' competing vested interests and differential access to power. This section also explores how these socially constructed ideas are reinforced both through the actions of teachers, doctors, and others in positions of power, as well as by each of us, as we come to internalize these ideas and to police our own bodies and actions.

The first article, "A History of Women's Bodies," by Rose Weitz, explores how throughout Western history, ideas about women's bodies embedded in law, culture, and medicine have both reflected and affected women's position in society. After this, in "Believing Is Seeing: Biology as Ideology," Judith Lorber looks at how the everyday structure of our society not only reinforces the idea that there are two and only two sexes, but also reinforces the differences between those two sexes. Karin A. Martin provides an example of how this process occurs among very young children in her article "Becoming a Gendered Body: Practices of Preschools."

In "Medicalization, Natural Childbirth, and Birthing Experiences," Sarah Jane Brubaker and Heather E. Dillaway examine the medical profession's role in controlling women's bodies during childbirth, as well as feminist responses to both "medicalized" and "natural" childbirth. Then, in "Foucault, Femininity, and the Modernization of Patriarchal Power," Sandra Lee Bartky explores how society trains women to discipline themselves to fit cultural ideas about proper female appearance and behavior. Finally, Rosemarie Garland-Thomson argues in "Integrating Disability, Transforming Feminist Theory" that feminist understandings of the social construction of women's bodies could be strengthened by incorporating key ideas from disability studies.

1

A History of Women's Bodies

Rose Weitz

"A History of Women's Bodies," by Rose Weitz, provides an outline history of the politics of women's bodies. In this article, Weitz delineates how ideas about the female body have changed over time, as well as the very real impact those ideas have had on women's lives. As she illustrates, three ideas about women's bodies recur periodically: that women's bodies are mentally and physically inferior to men's, that women's bodies are (and should be) men's property, and that women's bodies make them dangerous sexual seductresses who threaten men's bodies and souls.

At the same time, as Weitz describes, throughout Western history these general ideas about women's bodies have been applied in different ways to women of different social classes and ethnic, racial, or religious groups. So, for example, whereas U.S. law in the 1820s treated white women more or less like property (refusing them the right to vote, assigning their earnings to their husbands, and so on), enslaved black women were literally regarded as property to be bought and sold. Similarly, whereas cultural belief in the physical and mental frailty *of middle-class white women made it impossible for most to seek higher education, cultural belief in the animal-like physical* strength *of poor women allowed factory owners to expose these women workers to dangerous conditions without any moral qualms or risk of legal sanction.*

Finally, this brief history illustrates how, whenever women have fought to change ideas about their bodies and to improve their situations, others have fought to keep them in their places. This battle continues to this day.

Women's Bodies, Women's Lives

Throughout history, ideas about the nature of women's bodies have played a dramatic role in either challenging or reinforcing power relationships between men and women. As such, we can regard these ideas as political tools and can regard the battle over these ideas as a political struggle. This article presents a brief history of women's bodies, looking at how ideas about the female body have changed over time in western law and biological theory.

Beginning with the earliest recorded western legal system, the Babylonian Code of Hammurabi, and continuing nearly to the present day, western law typically has defined women's bodies as men's property. In ancient societies, women who were not slaves belonged to their fathers before marriage and to their husbands thereafter. For this reason, Babylonian law, for example, treated rape as a form of property damage, requiring a rapist to pay a fine to the husband or father of the raped woman, but nothing to the woman herself. Similarly, marriages in ancient societies typically were contracted between prospective husbands and prospective fathers-in-law, with the potential bride playing little if any role.

Women's legal status as property reflected the belief that women's bodies were inherently different from men's in ways that made women both defective and dangerous. These ideas come through clearly in the writings of Aristotle, whose ideas about women's bodies would form the basis for "scientific" discussion of this topic from the fourth century B.C. through the eighteenth century (Martin 1987; Tuana 1993). Aristotle's biological theories centered around the concept of heat. According to Aristotle, only embryos that had sufficient heat could develop into fully human form. The rest became female. In other words, woman was, in Aristotle's words, a "misbegotten man" and a "monstrosity"—less than fully formed and literally half-baked. Based on this premise, Galen, a highly influential Greek doctor, would later declare that women's reproductive organs were virtually identical to men's, but were located internally because female embryos lacked the heat needed for those organs to develop fully and externally. This view would remain common among doctors until well into the eighteenth century.

Lack of heat, classical scholars argued, also produced a plethora of other deficiencies in women, including a smaller stature, frailer constitution, less developed brain, and emotional and moral weaknesses that could endanger any men who came under their spell. These ideas later would resonate with ideas about women embedded in Christian interpretations of Mary and Eve. Christian theologians argued that Eve had caused the fall from divine grace and the expulsion from the Garden of Eden by succumbing when the snake tempted her with the forbidden fruit. This "original sin" had occurred, these theologians argued, because women's nature made them inherently more susceptible to sexual desire and other passions of the flesh, blinding them to reason and morality and making them a constant danger to men's souls. Mary, meanwhile, had avoided this fate only by remaining virginal.

Such ideas later would play a large role in fueling the witchcraft hysteria in early modern Europe and colonial America. Women formed the vast majority of the tens of thousands executed as witches during these centuries because both Protestants and Catholics assumed that women were less intelligent than men, more driven by sexual passions, and hence more susceptible to the Devil's blandishments (Barstow 1994).

By the beginnings of the modern era, women's legal and social position had changed little. When the famous English legal theorist, Sir William Blackstone, published his encyclopedic codification of English law in 1769, non-slave women's legal status still remained closer to that of property than to that of non-slave men. According to Blackstone, "By marriage, the husband and wife are one person in the law; that is, the very being and legal existence of the woman is suspended during the marriage, or at least is incorporated into that of her husband under whose wing, protection and cover she performs everything" (1904, 432). In other words, upon marriage a woman experienced "civil death," losing any rights as a citizen, including the right to own or bestow property, make contracts or sue for legal redress, hold custody over minor children, or keep any wages she earned. Moreover, as her "protector," a husband had a legal right to beat her if he believed it necessary, as well as a right to her sexual services. These principles would form the basis of marital law in the United States from its founding.

Meanwhile, both in colonial America and in the United States for its first 89 years, slave women *were* property. Moreover, both the law and contemporary scientific writings often described African-American women (and men) as animals, rather than humans. Consequently, neither slave women nor slave men held any of these rights of citizenship. By the same token, African-American women slaves were completely subject to their white masters. Rape was common, both as a form of "entertainment" for white men and as a way of breeding more slaves, since the children of slave mothers were automatically slaves, regardless of their fathers' race. Nor did African-American women's special vulnerability to rape end when slavery ended.

Both before and after the Civil War, the rape of African-American women was explained, if not justified, by an ideology that defined African-Americans, including African-American women, as animalistically hypersexual, and thus blamed them for their own rapes (Gilman 1985; Giddings 1995). For example, an article published by a white southern woman on March 17, 1904 in the popular periodical, the *Independent*, declared:

> Degeneracy is apt to show most in the weaker individuals of any race; so Negro women evidence more nearly the popular idea of total depravity than the men do. They are so nearly lacking in virtue that the color of a Negro woman's skin is generally taken (and quite correctly) as a guarantee of her immorality. . . . I sometimes read of a virtuous Negro woman, hear of them, but the idea is absolutely inconceivable to me . . .

These ideas about sexuality, combined with ideas about the inherent inferiority of African Americans, are vividly reflected in the 1861 Georgia penal code. That code left it up to the court whether to fine or imprison men who raped African-American women, recommended two to twenty years imprisonment for white men convicted of raping white women, and mandated the death penalty for African-American men convicted of raping white women (Roberts 1990, 60). Moreover, African-American men typically were lynched before being brought to trial if suspected of raping a white woman, while white men were rarely convicted for raping white women and probably never convicted for raping African-American women.

For both free and slave women in the United States, the legal definition of women's bodies as men's property experienced its first serious challenges during the nineteenth century. In 1839, Mississippi passed the first Married Women's Property Act. Designed primarily to protect family farms and property from creditors rather than to expand the rights of women (Speth 1982), the law gave married women the right to retain property they owned before marriage and any wages they earned outside the home. By the end of the nineteenth century, similar laws had passed in all the states.

Also during the nineteenth century, both white and African-American women won the right to vote in Wyoming, Utah, Colorado, and Idaho, and a national suffrage campaign took root. Meanwhile, beginning with Oberlin College in 1833, a growing number of colleges began accepting women students, including free African-American women, with more than 5,000 women graduating in 1900 alone (Flexner 1974, 232). At the same time, the industrial revolution prompted growing numbers of women to seek paid employment. By 1900, the U.S. census would list more than 5 million women gainfully employed outside the home (Flexner 1974, 250). This did not reflect any significant changes in the lives of African-American women—who had worked as much as men when slaves and who often worked full-time post-slavery (Jones 1985)—but was a major change for white women.

Each of these changes challenged the balance of power between men and women in American society. In response to these challenges, a counterreaction quickly developed. This counterreaction combined new "scientific" ideas with older definitions of women's bodies as ill or fragile to argue that white middle-class women were unable to sustain the responsibilities of political power or the burdens of education or employment.

Ideas about middle-class women's frailty drew heavily on the writings of Charles Darwin, who had published his groundbreaking *On the Origin of the Species* in 1872 (Tuana 1993). As part of his theory of evolution, Darwin argued that males compete for sexual access to females, with only the fittest succeeding and reproducing. As a result, males continually evolve toward greater "perfection." Females, on the other hand, need not compete for males, and therefore are not subject to the same process of natural selection. Consequently, in any species, males will be more evolved than females. In addition, Darwin argued, females must expend so much energy on reproduction that they retain little energy for either physical or mental development. As a result, women remain subject to their emotions and passions: nurturing, altruistic, and child-like, but with little sense of either justice or morality.

These ideas meshed well with Victorian ideas about middle-class white women's sexuality, which depicted women as the objects of male desire, emphasized romance and downplayed female sexual desire, and reinforced a sexual double standard. Middle-class women were expected to have passionate and even romantic attachments to other women, but these attachments were assumed to be emotional, rather than physical. Most women who had "romantic friendships" with other women were married to men, and only those few who adopted male clothing or behavior were considered lesbians (Faderman 1981). Lesbianism only became more broadly identified and stigmatized in the early twentieth century, when women's entry into higher education and the workforce enabled some women to survive economically without marrying, and lesbianism therefore became more of a threat to male power.

With women's increasing entry into education and employment, ideas about the physical and emotional frailty of women—with their strong echoes of both Christian and Aristotelian disdain for women and their bodies—were adopted by nineteenth century doctors as justification for keeping women uneducated and unemployed. So, for example:

> The president of the Oregon State Medical Society, F. W. Van Dyke, in 1905, claimed that hard study killed sexual desire in women, took away their beauty, and brought on hysteria, neurasthenia [a mental disorder], dyspepsia [indigestion], astigmatism [a visual disorder], and dysmenorrhea [painful menstruation]. Educated women, he added, could not bear children with ease because study arrested the development of the pelvis at the same time it increased the size of the child's brain, and therefore its head. The result was extensive suffering in childbirth by educated women. (Bullough and Voght 1984, 32)

Belief in the frailty of middle-class women's bodies similarly fostered the epidemic rise during the late nineteenth century in gynecological surgery (Barker-Benfield 1976; Longo 1984). Many doctors routinely performed surgery to remove healthy ovaries, uteruses, and clitorises, from women who experienced an extremely wide range of physical and mental symptoms—including symptoms such as rebelliousness or malaise which reflected women's constrained social circumstances more than their physical health. These operations were not only unnecessary but dangerous, with mortality rates up to 33 percent (Longo 1984).

Paradoxically, at the same time that scientific "experts" emphasized the frailty of middle-class white women, they emphasized the robustness of poorer women, both white and non-white. As Jacqueline Jones (1985, 15) explains:

> Slaveholders had little use for sentimental platitudes about the delicacy of the female constitution. . . . There were enough women like Susan Mabry of Virginia, who could pick 400 or 500 pounds of cotton a day (150 to 200 pounds was considered respectable for an average worker) to remove from a master's mind all doubts about the ability of a strong, healthy woman field worker. As a result, he conveniently discarded his time-honored Anglo-Saxon notions about the type of work best suited for women.

Similar attitudes applied toward working-class white women. Thus, Dr. Lucien Warner, a popular medical authority, could in 1874 explain how middle-class women were made frail by their affluence, while "the African negress, who toils beside her husband in the fields of the south, and Bridget [the Irish maid], who washes, and scrubs and toils in our homes at the north, enjoy for the most part good health, with comparative immunity from uterine disease" (cited in Ehrenreich and English 1973, 12–13).

At any rate, despite the warnings of medical experts, women continued to enter both higher education and the paid workforce. However, although education clearly benefited women, entering the workforce endangered the life and health of many women due to hazardous working conditions.

Although male workers could hope to improve their working conditions through union agitation, this tactic was far less useful for women, who more often worked in non-unionized jobs, were denied union membership, or were uninterested in joining unions. As a result, some feminists began lobbying for protective labor laws that would set maximum working hours for women, mandate rest periods, and so on (Erickson 1982). In 1908, the U.S. Supreme Court first upheld such a law in *Muller v. Oregon*. Unfortunately, it soon became clear that protective labor laws hurt women more than they helped, by bolstering the idea that women workers were inherently weaker than men.

Twelve years after the *Muller* decision, in 1920, most female U.S. citizens finally won the right to vote in national elections. (Most Asian-born and Native American women, however, were ineligible for citizenship, and most African-American women—like African-American men—were kept from voting through both legal and illegal means.) Unfortunately, suffrage largely marked the close of decades of feminist activism rather than the start of any broader reforms in women's legal, social, or economic position.

By the 1960s, little had changed in women's status. For example, although the fourteenth amendment (passed in 1868) guaranteed equal protection under the law for all U.S. citizens, not until 1971, in *Reed v. Reed*, would the Supreme Court rule that differential treatment based on sex was illegal. Similarly, based still on Blackstone's interpretation of women's legal position and the concept of women as men's property, until the 1970s courts routinely refused to prosecute wife batterers unless they killed their wives, and not until 1984 did any court convict a man for raping a woman to whom he was married and with whom he still legally resided.

Recognition of these and other inequities led to the emergence of a new feminist movement beginning in the second half of the 1960s (Evans 1979). In its earliest days, this movement adopted the rhetoric of liberalism and the civil rights movement, arguing that women and men were morally and intellectually equal and that women's bodies were essentially similar to men's bodies. The (unsuccessful) attempts to pass the Equal Rights Amendment, which stated that "equality of rights under the law shall not be denied or abridged by the United States or any state on account of sex," reflected this strain of thinking about gender.

The goal of these liberal feminists was to achieve equality with men within existing social structures—for example, to get men to do a fair share of child care. Soon, however, some feminists began questioning whether achieving equality within existing social structures would really help women, or whether women would be served better by radically restructuring society to create more humane social arrangements—for example, establishing communal living arrangements in which child care could be more broadly shared. Along with this questioning of social arrangements came questions about the reality not only of sex differences but also of the categories "male" and "female."

In contrast, a more recent strand of feminist thought, known as "cultural feminism," has reemphasized the idea of inherent differences between men and women. Unlike those who made this argument in the past, however, cultural feminists argue that women and their bodies are *superior* to men's. From this perspective, women's ability to create human life has made women (especially mothers) innately more pacifistic, loving, moral, creative, and life-affirming than men (e.g., Daly 1978). For the same reason, some feminists, such as Susan Griffin (1978), now argue that women also have an inherently deeper connection than men to nature and to ecological concerns. (Ironically, many in the anti-abortion movement and on the far right use rhetoric similar to that of cultural feminists to argue that women belong at home.)

Despite the differences among feminists in ideology and tactics, all share the goal of challenging accepted ideas about women's bodies and social position. Not surprisingly, as the modern feminist movement has grown, a backlash has developed that has attempted to reinforce more traditional ideas (Faludi 1991). This backlash has taken many forms, including (*1*) increasing pressure on women to control the shape of their bodies, (*2*) attempts to define premenstrual and postmenopausal women as ill, and (*3*) the rise of the anti-abortion and "fetal rights" movements.

Throughout history, women have experienced social pressures to maintain acceptable appearances. However, as Susan Faludi (1991), Naomi Wolf (1991), and many others have demonstrated, the backlash against modern feminism seems to have increased these pressures substantially. For example, since 1978, a steady 70% of *Playboy* centerfolds have been significantly underweight, while the average weight of Miss America winners has decreased sharply, even though average height has increased (Rubinstein and Caballero 2000; Katzmarzyk and Davis 2001).

Current appearance norms call for women to be not only painfully thin, but muscular and buxom—qualities that only can occur together if women spend vast amounts of time on exercise, money on cosmetic surgery, and emotional energy on diet (Seid 1989).

The backlash against feminism also has affected women's lives by stimulating calls for the medical control of premenstrual women. Although first defined in the 1930s, the idea of a "premenstrual syndrome" (PMS) did not garner much attention either inside or outside medical circles until the 1970s. Since then, innumerable popular and medical articles have argued that to function at work or school, women with PMS (or the more serious PMDD—premenstrual dysphoric disorder) need medical treatment to control their anger and discipline their behaviors. Similarly, many doctors now believe that menopausal women need drugs to maintain their sexual attractiveness and to control their behavior and emotions.

Finally, the backlash against feminism has restricted women's lives through facilitating the rise of the anti-abortion and "fetal rights" movements. Prior to the twentieth century, abortion was generally considered both legally and socially acceptable, although dangerous. By the midtwentieth century, abortion had become a safe medical procedure, but legal only when deemed medically necessary. Doctors were deeply divided, however, regarding when it was necessary, with some performing abortions only to preserve women's lives and others doing so to preserve women's social, psychological, or economic well-being (Luker 1984). To protect themselves legally, beginning in the 1960s, those doctors who favored more lenient indications for abortion, along with women who considered abortion a right, lobbied heavily for broader legal access to abortion. This lobbying culminated in 1973 when the U.S. Supreme Court ruled, in *Roe v. Wade*, that abortion was legal in most circumstances. However, subsequent legislative actions and Court decisions (including the 1976 Hyde Amendment and the Supreme Court's 1992 decision in *Planned Parenthood v. Casey*) have reduced legal access to abortion substantially, especially for poor and young women.

Embedded in the legal battles over abortion is a set of beliefs about the nature of women and of the fetus (Luker 1984). On the one side stand those who argue that unless women have an absolute right to control their own bodies, including the right to abortion, they will never attain fully equal status in society. On the other side stand those who argue that the fetus is fully human and that women's rights to control their bodies must be subjugated to the fetus's right to life.

This latter belief also underlays the broader social and legal pressure for "fetal rights." For example, pregnant women around the country—almost all of them non-white and poor—have been arrested for abusing alcohol or illegal drugs while pregnant, on the grounds that they had no right to expose their fetuses to harmful substances. Others—again, mostly poor and nonwhite—have been forced to have cesarean sections against their will. In these cases, the courts have ruled that the fetus's interests are more important than women's right to determine what will happen to their bodies—in this case, the right to refuse invasive, hazardous surgery—and that doctors know better than mothers what is in a fetus's best interests. Still other women have been refused jobs by employers who have argued that hazardous work conditions might endanger a pregnant worker's fetus; these employers have ignored evidence that the same conditions would also damage men's sperm and thus any resulting fetuses.

Conclusions

Throughout history, ideas about women's bodies have centrally affected the strictures within which women live their lives. Only by looking at the embodied experiences of women, as well as at how those experiences are socially constructed, can we fully understand women's lives, women's position in society, and the possibilities for resistance against that position.

References

Barker-Benfield, G. J. 1976. *The Horrors of the Half-known Life: Male Attitudes Towards Women and Sexuality in 19th Century America.* New York: Harper.

Barstow, Anne Llewellyn. 1994. *Witchcraze: A New History of the European Witch Hunts.* San Francisco: Pandora.

Blackstone, Sir William. 1904. *Commentaries on the Laws of England in Four Books.* Volume I, edited by George Sharswood. Philadelphia: Lippincott.

Bullough, Vern, and Martha Voght. 1984. Women, Menstruation, and Nineteenth Century Medicine. In *Women and Health in America: Historical Readings*, edited by Judith Walzer Leavitt. Madison: University of Wisconsin Press.

Daly, Mary. 1978. *Gyn/Ecology: The Metaethics of Radical Feminism.* Boston: Beacon.

Darwin, Charles. 1872. *On the Origin of the Species.* Akron, OH: Werner.

Ehrenreich, Barbara, and Deirdre English. 1973. *Complaints and Disorders: The Sexual Politics of Sickness.* Old Westbury, NY: Feminist Press.

Erickson, Nancy S. 1982. Historical Background of "Protective" Labor Legislation: Muller v. Oregon. In *Women and the Law: A Social Historical Perspective.* Volume II, edited by D. Kelly Weisberg. Cambridge, MA: Schenkman.

Evans, Sara M. 1979. *Personal Politics: The Roots of Women's Liberation in the Civil Rights Movement and the New Left.* New York: Vintage Books.

Faderman, Lillian. 1981. *Surpassing the Love of Men: Romantic Friendship and Love Between Women from the Renaissance to the Present.* New York: Morrow.

Faludi, Susan. 1991. *Backlash: The Undeclared War Against American Women.* New York: Crown.

Flexner, Eleanor. 1974. *Century of Struggle: The Women's Rights Movement in the United States.* New York: Atheneum.

Giddings, Paula. 1995. The last taboo. In *Words of Fire: An Anthology of African American Feminist Thought*, edited by Beverly Guy-Sheftall. New York: New Press.

Gilman, Sander. 1985. Black bodies, white bodies: Toward an iconography of female sexuality in late nineteenth century art, medicine, and literature. In *"Race," Writing and Difference*, edited by Henry Louis Gates. Chicago: University of Chicago Press.

Griffin, Susan. 1978. *Woman and Nature: The Roaring Inside Her.* New York: Harper.

Jones, Jacqueline. 1985. *Labor of Love, Labor of Sorrow: Black Women, Work, and the Family from Slavery to the Present.* New York: Basic.

Katzmarzyk, P. T., and C. Davis. 2001. Thinness and body shape of *Playboy* centerfolds from 1978 to 1998. *International Journal of Obesity* 25:590–92.

Longo, Lawrence D. 1984. The Rise and Fall of Battey's Operation: A Fashion in Surgery. In *Woman and Health in America*, Judith Walzer Leavitt. Madison: University of Wisconsin Press.

Luker, Kristin. 1984. *Abortion and the Politics of Motherhood.* Berkeley: University of California Press.

Martin, Emily. 1987. *The Woman in the Body.* Boston: Beacon.

Roberts, Dorothy E. 1990. The future of reproductive choice for poor women and women of color. *Women's Rights Law Reporter* 12(2):59–67.

Rubinstein, Sharon, and Benjamin Caballero. 2000. Is Miss America an undernourished role model? *JAMA* 283:1569.

Seid, Roberta Pollack. 1989. *Never Too Thin: Why Women Are at War with Their Bodies.* New York: Prentice Hall.

Speth, Linda E. 1982. The married women's property acts, 1839–1865: Reform, reaction, or revolution? In *Women and the Law: A Social Historical Perspective.* Volume II, edited by D. Kelly Weisberg. Cambridge, MA: Schenkman.

Tuana, Nancy. 1993. *The Less Noble Sex: Scientific, Religious, and Philosophical Conceptions of Woman's Nature.* Bloomington: Indiana University Press.

Wolf, Naomi. 1991. *The Beauty Myth: How Images of Beauty Are Used Against Women.* New York: W. Morrow.

2

Believing Is Seeing

Biology as Ideology

JUDITH LORBER

Judith Lorber's article, "Believing is Seeing: Biology as Ideology," attacks head on our assumptions about men's and women's nature. Like other scholars, she uses the term sex *to refer to the* biological *categories of male and female (to which we are assigned based on our chromosomal structure, genitalia, hormones, and the like) and uses the term* gender *to refer to the* social *categories of masculine and feminine and to social expectations regarding masculinity and femininity. Most if not all feminist scholars agree that gender is a social construction (that is, that our ideas about what is properly masculine and feminine is a product of culture, not biology). Lorber goes one step further and argues that sex, too, is a social construction.*

First, Lorber argues, there is no definition of the word female *that could include everyone we label as female. Some individuals whom we label female have a uterus, others don't. Some have XX chromosomes, others don't. And so on. Thus our definition of femaleness glides over evidence that this sex category is based on social expectations, not on clear biological evidence. Similarly, Lorber argues, we can treat sex as a binary concept (i.e., a concept that has only two possible categories, male and female)—only by ignoring (or hiding) the evidence regarding intermediate sexes. Sociologists call this a self-fulfilling prophesy—something we believe to be true is then, through our actions, made into a truth. In this case, because we expect all humans to be either male or female, we then as a society do everything necessary (including sex assignment surgery of intersex newborns) to make sure everyone appears to be either male or female.*

Lorber further argues that our assumptions about the biological differences between men and women have led us to construct a world that heightens (or even creates) those differences. For example, in women's basketball the size of the ball and the rules of the game result in a style of play that is slower and less intense than in men's basketball. For this reason, women's basketball games are often considered less athletic and exciting compared to their male counterparts. This supposedly natural difference is intensified by disparate media coverage; researchers repeatedly find that men's baseball, basketball, and football dominate television sports coverage thus reinforcing the idea that women's sports are inferior and unimportant.

Finally, Lorber argues, in a society in which men and women are assumed to be innately different, and in which men overall have more power than women, it should not surprise us that the human-built environment is designed to fit male bodies. For example, the fact that tables in corporate conference rooms are permanently fixed at a height too tall for most women reflects and reinforces male power, even while it disadvantages both most women and *shorter men.*

Until the eighteenth century, Western philosophers and scientists thought that there was one sex and that women's internal genitalia were the inverse of men's external genitalia: the womb and vagina were the penis and scrotum turned inside out (Laqueur 1990). Current Western thinking sees women and men as so different physically as to sometimes seem two species. The bodies, which have been mapped inside and out for hundreds of years, have not changed. What has changed are the justifications for gender inequality. When the social position of all human beings was believed to be set by natural law or was considered God-given, biology was irrelevant; women and men of different classes all had their assigned places. When scientists began to question the divine basis of social order and replaced faith with empirical knowledge, what they saw was that women were very different from men in that they had wombs and menstruated. Such anatomical differences destined them for an entirely different social life from men.

In actuality, the basic bodily material is the same for females and males, and except for procreative hormones and organs, female and male human beings have similar bodies (Naftolin and Butz 1981). Furthermore, as has been known since the middle of the nineteenth century, male and female genitalia develop from the same fetal tissue, and so infants can be born with ambiguous genitalia (Money and Ehrhardt 1972). When they are, biology is used quite arbitrarily in sex assignment. Suzanne Kessler (1990) interviewed six medical specialists in pediatric intersexuality and found that whether an infant with XY chromosomes and anomalous genitalia was categorized as a boy or a girl depended on the size of the penis—if a penis was very small, the child was categorized as a girl, and sex-change surgery was used to make an artificial vagina. In the late nineteenth century, the presence or absence of ovaries was the determining criterion of gender assignment for hermaphrodites because a woman who could not procreate was not a complete woman (Kessler 1990, 20).

Yet in Western societies, we see two discrete sexes and two distinguishable genders because our society is built on two classes of people, "women" and "men." Once the gender category is given, the attributes of the person are also gendered: Whatever a "woman" is has to be "female," whatever a "man" is has to be "male." Analyzing the social processes that construct the categories we call "female and male," "women and men," and "homosexual and heterosexual" uncovers the ideology and power differentials congealed in these categories (Foucault 1978). This article will use two familiar areas of social life—sports and technological competence—to show how myriad physiological differences are transformed into similar-appearing, gendered social bodies. My perspective goes beyond accepted feminist views that gender is a cultural overlay that modifies physiological sex differences. That perspective assumes either that there are two fairly similar sexes distorted by social practices into two genders with purposefully different characteristics or that there are two sexes whose essential differences are rendered unequal by social practices. I am arguing that bodies differ in many ways physiologically, but they are completely transformed by social practices to fit into the salient categories of a society, the most pervasive of which are "female" and "male" and "women" and "men."

Neither sex nor gender are pure categories. Combinations of incongruous genes, genitalia, and hormonal input are ignored in sex categorization, just as combinations of incongruous physiology, identity, sexuality, appearance, and behavior are ignored in the social construction of gender statuses. Menstruation, lactation, and gestation do not demarcate women from men. Only some women are pregnant and then only some of the time; some women do not have a uterus or ovaries. Some women have stopped menstruating temporarily, others have reached menopause, and some have had hysterectomies. Some women breast-feed some of the time, but some men lactate (Jaggar 1983, 165 fn). Menstruation, lactation, and gestation are individual experiences of womanhood (Levesque-Lopman 1988), but not determinants of the social category "woman," or even "female." Similarly, "men are not always sperm-producers, and in fact, not all sperm producers are men. A male-to-female transsexual, prior to surgery, can be socially a woman, though still potentially (or actually) capable of spermatogenesis" (Kessler and McKenna [1978] 1985, 2).

When gender assignment is contested in sports, where the categories of competitors are rigidly divided into women and men, chromosomes are now used to determine in which category the athlete is to compete. However, an anomaly common enough to be found in several women at every major international sports competition are XY chromosomes that have not produced male anatomy or physiology because of a genetic defect. Because these women are women in every way significant for sports competition, the prestigious International Amateur Athletic Federation has urged that sex be determined by simple genital inspection (Kolata 1992). Transsexuals would pass this test, but it took a lawsuit for Renée Richards, a male-to-female transsexual, to be able to play tournament tennis as a woman, despite his male sex chromosomes (Richards 1983). Oddly, neither basis for gender categorization—chromosomes nor genitalia—has anything to do with sports prowess (Birrell and Cole 1990).

In the Olympics, in cases of chromosomal ambiguity, women must undergo "a battery of gynecological and physical exams to see if she is 'female enough' to compete. Men are not tested" (Carlson 1991, 26). The purpose is not to categorize women and men accurately, but to make sure men don't enter women's competitions, where, it is felt, they will have the advantage of size and strength. This practice sounds fair only because it is assumed that all men are similar in size and strength and different from all women. Yet in Olympics boxing and wrestling matches, men are matched within weight classes. Some women might similarly successfully compete with some men in many sports. Women did not run in marathons until about twenty years ago. In twenty years of marathon competition, women have reduced their finish times by more than one-and-one-half hours; they are expected to run as fast as men in that race by 1998 and might catch up with men's running times in races of other lengths within the next 50 years because they are increasing their fastest speeds more rapidly than are men (Fausto-Sterling 1985, 213–18).

The reliance on only two sex and gender categories in the biological and social sciences is as epistemologically spurious as the reliance on chromosomal or genital tests to group athletes. Most research designs do not investigate whether physical skills or physical abilities are really more or less common in women and men (Epstein 1988). They start out with two social categories ("women," "men"), assume they are biologically different ("female," "male"), look for similarities among them and differences between them, and attribute what they have found for the social categories to sex differences (Gelman et al. 1986). These designs rarely question the categorization of their subjects into two and only two groups, even though they often find more significant within-group differences than between-group differences (Hyde 1990). The social construction perspective on sex and gender suggests that instead of starting with the two presumed dichotomies in each category—female, male; woman, man—it might be more useful in gender studies to group patterns of behavior and only then look for identifying markers of the people likely to enact such behaviors.

What Sports Illustrate

Competitive sports have become, for boys and men, as players and as spectators, a way of constructing a masculine identity, a legitimated outlet for violence and aggression, and an avenue for upward mobility (Dunning 1986; Kemper 1990, 167–206; Messner 1992). For men in Western societies, physical competence is an important marker of masculinity (Fine 1987; Glassner

1992; Majors 1990). In professional and collegiate sports, physiological differences are invoked to justify women's secondary status, despite the clear evidence that gender status overrides physiological capabilities. Assumptions about women's physiology have influenced rules of competition; subsequent sports performances then validate how women and men are treated in sports competitions.

Gymnastic equipment is geared to slim, wiry, prepubescent girls and not to mature women; conversely, men's gymnastic equipment is tailored for muscular, mature men, not slim, wiry prepubescent boys. Boys could compete with girls, but are not allowed to; women gymnasts are left out entirely. Girl gymnasts are just that—little girls who will be disqualified as soon as they grow up (Vecsey 1990). Men gymnasts have men's status. In women's basketball, the size of the ball and rules for handling the ball change the style of play to "a slower, less intense, and less exciting modification of the 'regular' or men's game" (Watson 1987, 441). In the 1992 Winter Olympics, men figure skaters were required to complete three triple jumps in their required program; women figure skaters were forbidden to do more than one. These rules penalized artistic men skaters and athletic women skaters (Janofsky 1992). For the most part, Western sports are built on physically trained men's bodies:

> Speed, size, and strength seem to be the essence of sports. Women *are* naturally inferior at "sports" so conceived.
>
> But if women had been the historically dominant sex, our concept of sport would no doubt have evolved differently. Competitions emphasizing flexibility, balance, strength, timing, and small size might dominate Sunday afternoon television and offer salaries in six figures. (English 1982, 266, emphasis in original)

Organized sports are big businesses and, thus, who has access and at what level is a distributive or equity issue. The overall status of women and men athletes is an economic, political, and ideological issue that has less to do with individual physiological capabilities than with their cultural and social meaning and who defines and profits from them (Messner and Sabo 1990; Slatton and Birrell 1984). Twenty years after the passage of Title IX of the U.S. Civil Rights Act, which forbade gender inequality in any school receiving federal funds, the goal for collegiate sports in the next five years is 60 percent men, 40 percent women in sports participation, scholarships, and funding (Moran 1992).

How access and distribution of rewards (prestigious and financial) are justified is an ideological, even moral, issue (Birrell 1988, 473–76; Hargreaves 1982). One way is that men athletes are glorified and women athletes ignored in the mass media. Messner and his colleagues found that in 1989, in TV sports news in the United States, men's sports got 92 percent of the coverage and women's sports 5 percent, with the rest mixed or gender-neutral

(Messner, Duncan, and Jensen 1993). In 1990, in four of the top-selling newspapers in the United States, stories on men's sports outnumbered those on women's sports 23 to 1. Messner and his colleagues also found an implicit hierarchy in naming, with women athletes most likely to be called by first names, followed by Black men athletes, and only white men athletes routinely referred to by their last names. Similarly, women's collegiate sports teams are named or marked in ways that symbolically feminize and trivialize them—the men's team is called Tigers, the women's Kittens (Eitzen and Baca Zinn 1989).

Assumptions about men's and women's bodies and their capacities are crafted in ways that make unequal access and distribution of rewards acceptable (Hudson 1978; Messner 1988). Media images of modern men athletes glorify their strength and power, even their violence (Hargreaves 1986). Media images of modern women athletes tend to focus on feminine beauty and grace (so they are not really athletes) or on their thin, small, wiry androgenous bodies (so they are not really women). In coverage of the Olympics,

> loving and detailed attention is paid to pixie-like gymnasts; special and extended coverage is given to graceful and dazzling figure skaters; the camera painstakingly records the fluid movements of swimmers and divers. And then, in a blinding flash of fragmented images, viewers see a few minutes of volleyball, basketball, speed skating, track and field, and alpine skiing, as television gives its nod to the mere existence of these events. (Boutilier and SanGiovanni 1983, 190)

Extraordinary feats by women athletes who were presented as mature adults might force sports organizers and audiences to rethink their stereotypes of women's capabilities, the way elves, mermaids, and ice queens do not. Sports, therefore, construct men's bodies to be powerful: women's bodies to be sexual. As Connell (1987, 85) says,

> The meanings in the bodily sense of masculinity concern, above all else, the superiority of men to women, and the exaltation of hegemonic masculinity over other groups of men which is essential for the domination of women.

In the late 1970s, as women entered more and more athletic competitions, supposedly good scientific studies showed that women who exercised intensely would cease menstruating because they would not have enough body fat to sustain ovulation (Brozan 1978). When one set of researchers did a yearlong study that compared 66 women—21 who were training for a marathon, 22 who ran more than an hour a week, and 23 who did less than an hour of aerobic exercise a week—they discovered that only 20 percent of the women in any of these groups had "normal" menstrual cycles every month (Prior et al. 1990). The dangers of intensive training for women's fertility therefore were exaggerated as women began to compete successfully in arenas formerly closed to them.

Given the association of sports with masculinity in the United States, women athletes have to manage a contradictory status. One study of women college basketball players found that although they "did athlete" on the court—"pushing, shoving, fouling, hard running, fast breaks, defense, obscenities and sweat" (Watson 1987, 441), they "did woman" off the court, using the locker room as their staging area:

> While it typically took fifteen minutes to prepare for the game, it took approximately fifteen minutes after the game to shower and remove the sweat of an athlete, and it took another thirty minutes to dress, apply makeup and style hair. It did not seem to matter whether the players were going out into the public or getting on a van for a long ride home. Average dressing time and rituals did not change. (Watson 1987, 443)

Another way women manage these status dilemmas is to redefine the activity or its result as feminine or womanly (Mangan and Park 1987). Thus women bodybuilders claim that "flex appeal is sex appeal" (Duff and Hong 1984, 378).

Such a redefinition of women's physicality affirms the ideological subtext of sports that physical strength is men's prerogative and justifies men's physical and sexual domination of women (Hargreaves 1986; Messner 1992, 164–72; Olson 1990; Theberge 1987; Willis 1982). When women demonstrate physical strength, they are labeled unfeminine:

> It's threatening to one's takeability, one's rapeability, one's femininity, to be strong and physically self-possessed. To be able to resist rape, not to communicate rapeability with one's body, to hold one's body for uses and meanings other than that can transform what *being a woman means.* (MacKinnon 1987, 122, emphasis in original)

Resistance to that transformation, ironically, was evident in the policies of American women physical education professionals throughout most of the twentieth century. They minimized exertion, maximized a feminine appearance and manner, and left organized sports competition to men (Birrell 1988, 461–62; Mangan and Park 1987).

Dirty Little Secrets

As sports construct gendered bodies, technology constructs gendered skills. Meta-analysis of studies of gender differences in spatial and mathematical ability have found that men have a large advantage in ability to mentally rotate an image, a moderate advantage in a visual perception of horizontality and verticality and in mathematical performance, and a small advantage in ability to pick a figure out of a field (Hyde 1990). It could be argued that these advantages explain why, within the short space of time that computers have become ubiquitous in offices, schools, and homes, work on them and with them has become gendered: Men create, program, and market computers, make war and produce science and art with them; women microwire them in computer factories and enter data in computerized offices; boys play games, socialize, and commit crimes with computers; girls are rarely seen in computer clubs, camps, and classrooms. But women were hired as computer programmers in the 1940s because

> the work seemed to resemble simple clerical tasks. In fact, however, programming demanded complex skills in abstract logic, mathematics, electrical circuitry, and machinery, all of which . . . women used to perform in their work. Once programming was recognized as "intellectually demanding," it became attractive to men. (Donato 1990, 170)

A woman mathematician and pioneer in data processing, Grace M. Hopper, was famous for her work on programming language (Perry and Greber 1990, 86). By the 1960s, programming was split into more and less skilled specialties, and the entry of women into the computer field in the 1970s and 1980s was confined to the lower-paid specialties. At each stage, employers invoked women's and men's purportedly natural capabilities for the jobs for which they were hired (Cockburn 1983, 1985; Donato 1990; Hartmann 1987; Hartmann et al. 1986; Kramer and Lehman 1990; Wright et al. 1987; Zimmerman 1983).

It is the taken-for-grantedness of such everyday gendered behavior that gives credence to the belief that the widespread differences in what women and men do must come from biology. To take one ordinarily unremarked scenario: In modern societies, if a man and woman who are a couple are in a car together, he is much more likely to take the wheel than she is, even if she is the more competent driver. Molly Haskell calls this taken-for-granted phenomenon "the dirty little secret of marriage: the husband-lousy-driver syndrome" (1989, 26). Men drive cars whether they are good drivers or not because men and machines are a "natural" combination (Scharff 1991). But the ability to drive gives one mobility; it is a form of social power.

In the early days of the automobile, feminists co-opted the symbolism of mobility as emancipation: "Donning goggles and dusters, wielding tire irons and tool kits, taking the wheel, they announced their intention to move beyond the bounds of women's place" (Scharff 1991, 68). Driving enabled them to campaign for women's suffrage in parts of the United States not served by public transportation, and they effectively used motorcades and speaking from cars as campaign tactics (Scharff 1991, 67–88). Sandra Gilbert also notes that during World War I, women's ability to drive was physically, mentally, and even sensually liberating:

> For nurses and ambulance drivers, women doctors and women messengers, the phenomenon of modern battle was very different from that experienced by entrenched combatants. Finally given a chance to take the wheel, these

> post-Victorian girls need motorcars along foreign roads like adventurers exploring new lands, while their brothers dug deeper into the mud of France. . . . Retrieving the wounded and the dead from deadly positions, these once-decorous daughters had at last been allowed to prove their valor, and they swooped over the wastelands of the war with the energetic love of Wagnerian Valkyries, their mobility alone transporting countless immobilized heroes to safe havens. (1983, 438–39)

Not incidentally, women in the United States and England got the vote for their war efforts in World War I.

Social Bodies and the Bathroom Problem

People of the same racial ethnic group and social class are roughly the same size and shape—but there are many varieties of bodies. People have different genitalia, different secondary sex characteristics, different contributions to procreation, different orgasmic experiences, different patterns of illness and aging. Each of us experiences our bodies differently, and these experiences change as we grow, age, sicken, and die. The bodies of pregnant and nonpregnant women, short and tall people, those with intact and functioning limbs, and those whose bodies are physically challenged are all different. But the salient categories of a society group these attributes in ways that ride roughshod over individual experiences and more meaningful clusters of people.

I am not saying that physical differences between male and female bodies don't exist, but that these differences are socially meaningless until social practices transform them into social facts. West Point Military Academy's curriculum is designed to produce leaders, and physical competence is used as a significant measure of leadership ability (Yoder 1989). When women were accepted as West Point cadets, it became clear that the tests of physical competence, such as rapidly scaling an eight-foot wall, had been constructed for male physiques—pulling oneself up and over using upper-body strength. Rather than devise tests of physical competence for women, West Point provided boosters that mostly women used—but that lost them test points in the case of the wall, a platform. Finally, the women themselves figured out how to use their bodies successfully. Janice Yoder describes this situation:

> I was observing this obstacle one day, when a woman approached the wall in the old prescribed way, got her fingertips grip, and did an unusual thing: she walked her dangling legs up the wall until she was in a position where both her hands and feet were atop the wall. She then simply pulled up her sagging bottom and went over. She solved the problem by capitalizing on one of women's physical assets: lower-body strength. (1989, 530)

In short, if West Point is going to measure leadership capability by physical strength, women's pelvises will do just as well as men's shoulders.

The social transformation of female and male physiology into a condition of inequality is well illustrated by the bathroom problem. Most buildings that have gender-segregated bathrooms have an equal number for women and for men. Where there are crowds, there are always long lines in front of women's bathrooms but rarely in front of men's bathrooms. The cultural, physiological, and demographic combinations of clothing, frequency of urination, menstruation, and child care add up to generally greater bathroom use by women than men. Thus, although an equal number of bathrooms seems fair, equity would mean more women's bathrooms or allowing women to use men's bathrooms for a certain amount of time (Molotch 1988).

The bathroom problem is the outcome of the way gendered bodies are differentially evaluated in Western cultures: Men's social bodies are the measure of what is "human." Gray's *Anatomy*, in use for 100 years, well into the twentieth century, presented the human body as male. The female body was shown only where it differed from the male (Laqueur 1990, 166–67). Denise Riley says that if we envisage women's bodies, men's bodies, and human bodies "as a triangle of identifications, then it is rarely an equilateral triangle in which both sexes are pitched at matching distances from the apex of the human" (1988, 197). Catharine MacKinnon also contends that in Western society, universal "humanness" is male because

> virtually every quality that distinguishes men from women is already affirmatively compensated in this society. Men's physiology defines most sports, their needs define auto and health insurance coverage, their socially defined biographies define workplace expectations and successful career pattens, their perspectives and concerns define quality in scholarship, their experiences and obsessions define merit, their objectification of life defines art, their military service defines citizenship, their presence defines family, their inability to get along with each other—their wars and rulerships—define history, their image defines god, and their genitals define sex. For each of their differences from women, what amounts to an affirmative action plan is in effect, otherwise known as the structure and values of American society. (1987, 36)

The Paradox of Human Nature

Gendered people do not emerge from physiology or hormones but from the exigencies of the social order, mostly, from the need for a reliable division of the work of food production and the social (not physical) reproduction of new members. The moral imperatives of religion and cultural representations reinforce the boundary lines among genders and ensure that what is demanded, what is permitted, and what is tabooed for the people in each gender is well-known and followed by most. Political power, control of scarce resources, and, if necessary, violence uphold the gendered social order in the face of resistance and rebellion. Most people, however, voluntarily go along with their society's prescriptions for those of their gender status because the norms and expectations get built into their sense of worth and identity as a certain kind of human being and because they believe their society's way is the natural way. These beliefs emerge from the imagery that pervades the way we think, the way we see and hear and speak, the way we fantasize, and the way we feel. There is no core or bedrock human nature below these endlessly looping processes of the social production of sex and gender, self and other, identity and psyche, each of which is a "complex cultural construction" (Butler 1990, 36). The paradox of "human nature" is that it is always a manifestation of cultural meanings, social relationships, and power politics—"not biology, but culture, becomes destiny" (Butler 1990, 8).

Feminist inquiry has long questioned the conventional categories of social science, but much of the current work in feminist sociology has not gone beyond adding the universal category "women" to the universal category "men." Our current debates over the global assumptions of only two categories and the insistence that they must be nuanced to include race and class are steps in the direction I would like to see feminist research go, but race and class are also global categories (Collins 1990; Spelman 1988). Deconstructing sex, sexuality, and gender reveals many possible categories embedded in the social experiences and social practices of what Dorothy Smith calls the "everyday/everynight world" (1990, 31–57). These emergent categories group some people together for comparison with other people without prior assumptions about who is like whom. Categories can be broken up and people regrouped differently into new categories for comparison. This process of discovering categories from similarities and differences in people's behavior or responses can be more meaningful for feminist research than discovering similarities and differences between "females" and "males" or "women" and "men" because the social construction of the conventional sex and gender categories already assumes differences between them and similarities among them. When we rely only on the conventional categories of sex and gender, we end up finding what we looked for—we see what we believe, whether it is that "females" and "males" are essentially different or that "women" and "men" are essentially the same.

References

Birrell, Susan J. 1988. Discourses on the gender/sport relationship: From women in sport to gender relations. In *Exercise and Sport Science Reviews*, Vol. 16, edited by Kent Pandolf. New York: Macmillan.

Birrell, Susan J., and Sheryl L. Cole. 1990. Double fault: Renée Richards and the construction and naturalization of difference. *Sociology of Sport Journal* 7:1–21.

Boutilier, Mary A., and Lucinda SanGiovanni. 1983. *The Sporting Woman.* Champaign, IL: Human Kinetics.

Brozan, Nadine. 1978. Training linked to disruption of female reproductive cycle. *New York Times*, 17 April.

Butler, Judith. 1990. *Gender Trouble: Feminism and the Subversion of Identity.* New York and London: Routledge & Kegan Paul.

Carlson, Alison. 1991. When is a woman not a woman? *Women's Sport and Fitness*, March:24–29.

Cockburn, Cynthia. 1983. *Brothers: Male Dominance and Technological Change*. London: Pluto.

——— 1985. *Machinery of Dominance: Women, Men and Technical Know-how*. London: Pluto.

Collins, Patricia Hill. 1990. *Black Feminist Thought: Knowledge, Consciousness, and the Politics of Empowerment*. Boston: Unwin Hyman.

Connell, R. W. 1987. *Gender and Power*. Stanford, CA: Stanford University Press.

Donato, Katharine M. 1990. Programming for change? The growing demand for women systems analysts. In *Job Queues, Gender Queues: Explaining Women's Inroads into Male Occupations*, edited by Barbara F. Reskin and Patricia A. Roos. Philadelphia: Temple University Press.

Duff, Robert W., and Lawrence K. Hong. 1984. Self-images of women bodybuilders. *Sociology of Sport Journal* 2:374–80.

Dunning, Eric. 1986. Sport as a male preserve: Notes on the social sources of masculine identity and its transformations. *Theory, Culture and Society* 3:79–90.

Eitzen, D. Stanley, and Maxine Baca Zinn. 1989. The deathleticization of women: The naming and gender marking of collegiate sport teams. *Sociology of Sport Journal* 6:362–70.

English, Jane. 1982. Sex equality in sports. In *Femininity, Masculinity, and Androgyny*, edited by Mary Vetterling-Braggin. Boston: Littlefield, Adams.

Epstein, Cynthia Fuchs. 1988. *Deceptive Distinctions: Sex, Gender and the Social Order*. New Haven, CT: Yale University Press.

Fausto-Sterling, Anne. 1985. *Myths of Gender: Biological Theories about Women and Men*. New York: Basic Books.

Fine, Gary Alan. 1987. *With the Boys: Little League Baseball and Preadolescent Culture*. Chicago: University of Chicago Press.

Foucault, Michel. 1978. *The History of Sexuality: An Introduction*, translated by Robert Hurley. New York: Pantheon.

Gelman, Susan A., Pamela Collman, and Eleanor E. Maccoby. 1986. Inferring properties from categories versus inferring categories from properties: The case of gender. *Child Development* 57:396–404.

Gilbert, Sandra M. 1983. Soldier's heart: Literary men, literary women, and the Great War. *Signs: Journal of Women in Culture and Society* 8:422–50.

Glassner, Barry. 1992. Men and muscles. In *Men's Lives*, edited by Michael S. Kimmel and Michael A. Messner. New York: Macmillan.

Hargreaves, Jennifer A., ed. 1982. *Sport, Culture, and Ideology*. London: Routledge & Kegan Paul.

———. 1986. Where's the virtue? Where's the grace? A discussion of the social production of gender relations in and through sport. *Theory, Culture, and Society* 3:109–21.

Hartmann, Heidi I., ed. 1987. *Computer Chips and Paper Clips: Technology and Women's Employment*. Vol. 2. Washington, DC: National Academy Press.

Hartmann, Heidi I., Robert E. Kraut, and Louise A. Tilly, eds. 1986. *Computer Chips and Paper Clips: Technology and Women's employment*. Vol. 1. Washington, DC: National Academy Press.

Haskell, Molly. 1989. Hers: He drives me crazy. *New York Times Magazine*, 24 September, 26, 28.

Hudson, Jackie. 1978. Physical parameters used for female exclusion from law enforcement and athletics. In *Women and Sport: From Myth to Reality*, edited by Carole A Oglesby. Philadelphia: Lea and Febiger.

Hyde, Janet Shibley. 1990. Meta-analysis and the psychology of gender differences. *Signs: Journal of Women in Culture and Society* 16:55–73.

Jaggar, Alison M. 1983. *Feminist Politics and Human Nature*. Totowa, NJ: Rowman & Allanheld.

Janofsky, Michael. 1992. Yamaguchi has the delicate and golden touch. *New York Times*, 22 February.

Kemper, Theodore D. 1990. *Social Structure and Testosterone: Explorations of the Socio-biosocial Chain*. New Brunswick, NJ: Rutgers University Press.

Kessler, Suzanne J. 1990. The medical construction of gender: Case management of intersexed infants. *Signs: Journal of Women in Culture and Society* 16:3–26.

Kessler, Suzanne J., and Wendy McKenna. [1978] 1985. *Gender: An Ethnomethodological Approach*. Chicago: University of Chicago Press.

Kolata, Gina. 1992. Track federation urges end to gene test for femaleness. *New York Times*, 12 February.

Kramer, Pamela E., and Sheila Lehman. 1990. Mismeasuring women: A critique of research on computer ability and avoidance. *Signs: Journal of Women in Culture and Society* 16:158–72.

Laqueur, Thomas. 1990. *Making Sex: Body and Gender from the Greeks to Freud*. Cambridge, MA: Harvard University Press.

Levesque-Lopman, Louise. 1988. *Claiming Reality: Phenomenology and Women's Experience*. Totowa, NJ: Rowman & Littlefield.

MacKinnon, Catherine. 1987. *Feminisms Unmodified*. Cambridge, MA: Harvard University Press.

Majors, Richard. 1990. Cool pose: Black masculinity in sports. In *Sport, Men and the Gender Order: Critical Feminist Perspectives*, edited by Michael A. Messner and Donald F. Sabo. Champaign, IL: Human Kinetics.

Mangan, J. A., and Roberta J. Park. 1987. *From Fair Sex to Feminism: Sport and the Socialization of Women in the Industrial and Post-industrial Eras*. London: Frank Cass.

Messner, Michael A. 1988. Sports and male domination: The female athlete as contested ideological terrain. *Sociology of Sport Journal* 5:197–211.

———. 1992. *Power at Play: Sports and the Problem of Masculinity*. Boston: Beacon Press.

Messner, Michael A., Margaret Carlisle Duncan, and Kerry Jensen. 1993. Separating the men from the girls: The gendered language of television sports. *Gender & Society* 7:121–37.

Messner, Michael A., and Donald F. Sabo, eds., 1990. *Sport, Men, and the Gender Order: Critical Feminist Perspectives*. Champaign, IL: Human Kinetics.

Molotch, Harvey. 1988. The restroom and equal opportunity. *Sociological Forum* 3:128–32.

Money, John, and Anke A. Ehrhardt. 1972. *Man & Woman, Boy & Girl*. Baltimore, MD: Johns Hopkins University Press.

Moran, Malcolm. 1992. Title IX: A 20-year search for equity. *New York Times*, sports section, 21, 22, 23 June.

Naftolin, F., and E. Butz, eds. 1981. Sexual dimorphism. *Science* 211:1263–1324.

Olson, Wendy. 1990. Beyond Title IX: Toward an agenda for women and sports in the 1990s. *Yale Journal of Law and Feminism* 3:105–51.

Perry, Ruth, and Lisa Greber. 1990. Women and computers: An introduction. *Signs: Journal of Women in Culture and Society* 16:74–101.

Prior, Jerilynn C., Yvette M. Yigna, Martin T. Shechter, and Arthur E. Burgess. 1990. Spinal bone loss and ovulatory disturbances. *New England Journal of Medicine* 323:1221–27.

Richards, Renée, with Jack Ames. 1983. *Second Serve*. New York: Stein and Day.

Riley, Denise. 1988. *Am I That name? Feminism and the Category of Women in History*. Minneapolis: University of Minnesota Press.

Scharff, Virginia. 1991. *Taking the Wheel: Women and the Coming of the Motor Age*. New York: Free Press.

Slatton, Bonnie, and Susan Birrel. 1984. The politics of women's sport. *Arena Review* 8 (July):entire issue.

Smith, Dorothy E. 1990. *The Conceptual Practices of Power: A Feminist Sociology of Knowledge*. Toronto: University of Toronto Press.

Spelman, Elizabeth. 1988. *Inessential Woman: Problems of Exclusion in Feminist Thought*. Boston: Beacon Press.

Theberge, Nancy. 1987. Sport and women's empowerment. *Women Studies International Forum* 10:387–93.

Vecsey, George. 1990. Cathy Rigby, unlike Peter, did grow up. *New York Times*, sports section, 19 December.

Watson, Tracey. 1987. Women athletes and athletic women: The dilemmas and contradictions of managing incongruent identities. *Sociological Inquiry* 57:431–46.

Willis, Paul. 1982. Women in sport in ideology. In *Sport, Culture, and Ideology*, edited by Jennifer A. Hargreaves. London: Routledge & Kegan Paul.

Wright, Barbara Drygulski, et al., eds. 1987. *Women, Work, and Technology: Transformations*. Ann Arbor: University of Michigan Press.

Yoder, Janice D. 1989. Women at West Point: Lessons for token women in male-dominated occupations. In *Women: A Feminist Perspective*, edited by Jo Freeman, 4th ed. Palo Alto, CA: Mayfield.

Zimmerman, Jan, ed. 1983. *The Technological Woman: Interfacing with Tomorrow*. New York: Praeger.

3

Becoming a Gendered Body

Practices of Preschools

KARIN A. MARTIN

The previous article laid the theoretical groundwork for understanding how both sex and gender are socially constructed. In "Becoming a Gendered Body: Practices of Preschools" Karin A. Martin uses her in-depth observations of preschools to illustrate how this process works in practice. Challenging our typical image of preschools as places where children freely play and explore, Martin illustrates how preschools serve as places where children learn bodily discipline. As she shows, preschool teachers use subtle (and not so subtle) rewards and punishments to teach girls to dress up, sit quietly, restrain their voice, and otherwise act "feminine," while encouraging boys to reject femininity and to act "masculine."

Through these actions, Martin argues, children from very young ages learn to "do gender" or to "perform gender"—two terms used more or less interchangeably by scholars to refer to the (somewhat) conscious actions individuals take to mark their selves and their bodies as "properly" masculine or feminine. For example, women "do gender" whenever they put on lipstick and men "do gender" whenever they refrain from crying during sad movies. Similarly, Martin notes, in part through preschool training, gender becomes embodied *in both girls and boys. By this she means that our gender comes to seem as much part of our bodies and our very selves as does our skin or our feelings about chocolate. By molding children at such young ages to conform to gender norms, Martin argues, preschools help to convince the rest of us that the differences between girls and boys, men and women, are natural, rather than socially constructed.*

Originally published as Karin A. Martin. 1998. "Becoming a Gendered Body: Practices of Preschools." *American Sociological Review* 63(4): 494–511.

Social science research about bodies often focuses on women's bodies, particularly the parts of women's bodies that are most explicitly different from men's—their reproductive capacities and sexuality (E. Martin 1987; K. Martin 1996; but see Connell 1987, 1995). Men and women in the United States also hold and move their bodies differently (Birdwhistell 1970; Henley 1977; Young 1990); these differences are sometimes related to sexuality (Haug 1987) and sometimes not. On the whole, men and women sit, stand, gesture, walk, and throw differently. Generally, women's bodies are confined, their movements restricted. For example, women take smaller steps than men, sit in closed positions (arms and legs crossed across the body), take up less physical space than men, do not step, twist, or throw from the shoulder when throwing a ball, and are generally tentative when using their bodies (Birdwhistell 1970; Henley 1977; Young 1990). Some of these differences, particularly differences in motor skills (e.g., jumping, running, throwing) are seen in early childhood (Thomas and French 1985). Of course, within gender, we may find individual differences, differences based on race, class, and sexuality, and differences based on size and shape of body. Yet, on average, men and women move differently.

Such differences may seem trivial in the large scheme of gender inequality. However, theoretical work by social scientists and feminists suggests that these differences may be consequential. Bodies are (unfinished) resources (Shilling 1993, 103) that must be "trained, manipulated, cajoled, coaxed, organized and in general disciplined" (Turner 1992, 15). We use our bodies to construct our means of living, to take care of each other, to pleasure each other. According to Turner, ". . . social life depends upon the successful presenting, monitoring and interpreting of bodies" (p. 15). Similarly, according to Foucault (1979), controlled and disciplined bodies do more than regulate the individual body. A disciplined body creates a context for social relations. Gendered (along with "raced" and "classed") bodies create particular contexts for social relations as they signal, manage, and negotiate information about power and status. Gender relations depend on the successful gender presentation, monitoring, and interpretation of bodies (West and Zimmerman 1987). Bodies that clearly delineate gender status facilitate the maintenance of the gender hierarchy.

Our bodies are also one *site* of gender. Much postmodern feminist work (Butler 1990, 1993) suggests that gender is a performance. Microsociological work (West and Zimmerman 1987) suggest that gender is something that is "done." These two concepts, "gender performance" and "doing gender," are similar—both suggest that managed, adorned, fashioned, properly comported and moving bodies establish gender and gender relations.

Other feminist theorists (Connell 1987, 1995; Young 1990) argue that gender rests not only on the surface of the body, in performance and doing, but becomes ***embodied***—becomes deeply part of whom we are physically and psychologically. According to Connell, gender becomes embedded in body postures, musculature, and tensions in our bodies.

> The social definition of men as holders of power is translated not only into mental body-images and fantasies, but into muscle tensions, posture, the feel and texture of the body. This is one of the main ways in which the power of men becomes naturalized. . . . (Connell 1987, 85)

Connell (1995) suggests that masculine gender is partly a feel to one's body and that bodies are often a source of power for men. Young (1990), however, argues that bodies serve the opposite purpose for women—women's bodies are often sources of anxiety and tentativeness. She suggests that women's lack of confidence and agency are embodied and stem from an inability to move confidently in space, to take up space, to use one's body to its fullest extent. Young (1990) suggests "that the general lack of confidence that we [women] frequently have about our cognitive or leadership abilities is traceable in part to an original doubt of our body's capacity" (p. 156). Thus, these theorists suggest that gender differences in minute bodily behaviors like gesture, stance, posture, step, and throwing are significant to our understanding of gendered selves and gender inequality. This feminist theory, however, focuses on adult bodies.

Theories of the body need gendering, and feminist theories of gendered bodies need "childrening" or accounts of development. How do adult gendered bodies become gendered, if they are not naturally so? Scholars run the risk of continuing to view gendered bodies as natural if they ignore the processes that produce gendered adult bodies. Gendering of the body in childhood is the foundation on which further gendering of the body occurs throughout the life course. The gendering of children's bodies makes gender differences feel and appear natural, which allows for such bodily differences to emerge throughout the life course.

I suggest that the hidden school curriculum of disciplining the body is gendered and contributes to the embodiment of gender in childhood, making gendered bodies appear and feel natural. Sociologists of education have demonstrated that schools have hidden curriculums (Giroux and Purpel 1983; Jackson 1968). Hidden curriculums are covert lessons that schools teach, and they are often a means of social control. These curriculums include teaching about work differentially by class (Anyon 1980; Bowles and Gintis 1976; Carnoy and Levin 1985), political socialization (Wasburn 1986), and training in obedience and docility (Giroux and Purpel 1983). More recently, some theorists and researchers have examined the curriculum that disciplines the body (Carere 1987; Foucault 1979; McLaren 1986). This curriculum demands the practice of bodily control in congruence with the goals of the school as an institution. It reworks the students from the outside in on the presumption that to shape the body is to shape the mind (Carere 1987).

In such a curriculum teachers constantly monitor kids' bodily movements, comportment, and practices. Kids begin their day running wildly about the school grounds. Then this hidden curriculum funnels the kids into line, through the hallways, quietly into a classroom, sitting upright at their desks, focused at the front of the room, "ready to learn" (Carere 1987; McLaren 1986). According to Carere (1987), this curriculum of disciplining the body serves the curriculums that seek to shape the mind and renders children physically ready for cognitive learning.

I suggest that this hidden curriculum that controls children's bodily practices serves also to turn kids who are similar in bodily comportment, movement, and practice into girls and boys, children whose bodily practices are different. Schools are not the only producers of these differences. While the process ordinarily begins in the family, the schools' hidden curriculum further facilitates and encourages the construction of bodily differences between the genders and makes these physical differences appear and feel natural. Finally, this curriculum may be more or less hidden depending on the particular preschool and particular teachers. Some schools and teachers may see teaching children to behave like "young ladies" and "young gentlemen" as an explicit part of their curriculums.

Data and Method

The data for this study come from extensive and detailed semistructured field observations of five preschool classrooms of three to five-year-olds in a midwestern city. Four of the classrooms were part of a preschool (Preschool A) located close to the campus of a large university. A few of the kids were children of faculty members, more were children of staff and administrators, and many were not associated with the university. Many of the kids who attended Preschool A attended part-time. Although teachers at this school paid some attention to issues of race and gender equity, issues of diversity were not as large a part of the curriculum as they are at some preschools (Jordan and Cowan 1995; Van Ausdale and Feagin 1996). The fifth classroom was located at Preschool B, a preschool run by a Catholic church in the same city as Preschool A. The kids who attended Preschool B were children of young working professionals, many of whom lived in the vicinity of the preschool. These children attended preschool "full-time"—five days a week for most of the day. . . .

A total 112 children and fourteen different teachers (five head teachers and nine aides) were observed in these classrooms. All teachers were female. . . .

A research assistant and I observed in these classrooms about three times a week for eight months. Our observations were as unobtrusive as possible, and we interacted little with the kids. . . . We observed girls and boys for equal amounts of time, and we heeded Thorne's (1993) caution about the "big man bias" in field research and were careful not to observe only the most active, outgoing, "popular" kids. . . .

Results

Children's bodies are disciplined by schools. Children are physically active, and institutions like schools impose disciplinary controls that regulate children's bodies and prepare children for the larger social world. While this disciplinary control produces docile bodies (Foucault 1979), it also produces gendered bodies. As these disciplinary practices operate in different contexts, some bodies become more docile than others. I examine how the following practices contribute to a gendering of children's bodies in preschool: the effects of dressing-up or bodily adornment, the gendered nature of formal and relaxed behaviors, how the different restrictions on girls' and boys' voices limit their physicality, how teachers instruct girls' and boys' bodies, and the gendering of physical interactions between children and teachers and among the children themselves.

Bodily Adornment: Dressing Up

Perhaps the most explicit way that children's bodies become gendered is through their clothes and other bodily adornments. Here I discuss how parents gender their children through their clothes, how children's dress-up play experiments with making bodies feminine and masculine, and how this play, when it is gender normative, shapes girls' and boys' bodies differently, constraining girls' physicality.

DRESSING UP (1). The clothes that parents send kids to preschool in shape children's experiences of their bodies in gendered ways. Clothes, particularly their color, signify a child's gender; gender in preschool is in fact color-coded. On average, about 61 percent of the girls wore pink clothing each day. Boys were more likely to wear primary colors, black, florescent green, and orange. Boys never wore pink.

> The teacher is asking each kid during circle (the part of the day that includes formal instruction by the teacher while the children sit in a circle) what their favorite color is. Adam says black. Bill says "every color that's not pink." (Five-year-olds)

Fourteen percent of three-year-old girls wore dresses each day compared to 32 percent of five-year-old girls. Wearing a dress limited girls' physicality in preschool. However, it is not only the dress itself, but knowledge about how to behave in a dress that is restrictive. Many girls already knew that some behaviors were not allowed in a dress. This knowledge probably comes from the families who dress their girls in dresses.

> Vicki, wearing leggings and a dress-like shirt, is leaning over the desk to look into a "tunnel" that some other kids have built. As she leans, her dress/shirt rides up exposing her back. Jennifer (another child) walks by Vicki and as she does she pulls Vicki's shirt back over her bare skin and gives it a pat to keep it in place. It looks very much like something one's mother might do. (Five-year-olds)

> Four girls are sitting at a table—Cathy, Kim, Danielle, and Jesse. They are cutting play money out of paper. Cathy and Danielle have on overalls and Kim and Jesse have on dresses. Cathy puts her feet up on the table and crosses her legs at the ankle; she leans back in her chair and continues cutting her money. Danielle imitates her. They look at each other and laugh. They put their shoulders back, posturing, having fun with this new way of sitting. Kim and Jesse continue to cut and laugh with them, but do not put their feet up. (Five-year-olds)

Dresses are restrictive in other ways as well. They often are worn with tights that are experienced as uncomfortable and constraining. I observed girls constantly pulling at and rearranging their tights, trying to untwist them or pull them up. Because of their discomfort, girls spent much time attuned to and arranging their clothing and/or their bodies.

Dresses also can be lifted up, an embarrassing thing for five-year-olds if done purposely by another child. We witnessed this on only one occasion—a boy pulled up the hem of a girl's skirt. The girl protested and the teacher told him to stop and that was the end of it. Teachers, however, lifted up girls' dresses frequently—to see if a child was dressed warmly enough, while reading a book about dresses, to see if a child was wet. Usually this was done without asking the child and was more management of the child rather than an interaction with her. Teachers were much more likely to manage girls and their clothing this way—rearranging their clothes, tucking in their shirts, fixing a ponytail gone astray. Such management often puts girls' bodies under the control of another and calls girls' attentions to their appearances and bodily adornments.

DRESSING UP (2). Kids like to *play* dress-up in preschool, and all the classrooms had a dress-up corner with a variety of clothes, shoes, pocketbooks, scarves, and hats for dressing up. Classrooms tended to have more women's clothes than men's, but there were some of both, as well as some genderneutral clothes—capes, hats, and vests that were not clearly for men or women—and some items that were clearly costumes, such as masks of cats and dogs and clip-on tails. Girls tended to play dress-up more than boys—over one-half of dressing up was done by girls. Gender differences in the amount of time spent playing dress-up seemed to increase from age three to age five. We only observed the five-year-old boys dressing up or using clothes or costumes in their play three times, whereas three-year-old boys dressed up almost weekly. Five-year-old boys also did not dress up elaborately, but used one piece of clothing to animate their play. Once Phil wore large, men's winter ski gloves when he played monster. Holding up his now large, chiseled looking hands, he stomped around the classroom making monster sounds. On another occasion Brian, a child new to the classroom who attended only two days a week, walked around by himself for a long time carrying a silver pocketbook and hovering first at the edges of girls' play and then at the edges of boys' play. On the third occasion, Sam used ballet slippers to animate his play in circle.

When kids dressed up, they played at being a variety of things from kitty cats and puppies to monsters and superheroes to "fancy ladies." Some of this play was not explicitly gendered. For example, one day in November I observed three girls wearing "turkey hats" they had made. They spent a long time gobbling at each other and playing at being turkeys, but there was nothing explicitly gendered about their play. However, this kind of adornment was not the most frequent type. Children often seemed to experiment with both genders when they played dress-up. The three-year-olds tended to be more experimental in their gender dress-up than the five-year-olds, perhaps because teachers encouraged it more at this age.

> Everett and Juan are playing dress-up. Both have on "dresses" made out of material that is wrapped around them like a toga or sarong. Everett has a pocketbook and a camera over his shoulder and Juan has a pair of play binoculars on a strap over his. Everett has a scarf around his head and cape on. Juan has on big, green sunglasses. Pam (teacher) tells them, "You guys look great! Go look in the mirror." They shuffle over to the full-length mirror and look at themselves and grin, and make adjustments to their costumes. (Three-year-olds)

The five-year-old children tended to dress-up more gender normatively. Girls in particular played at being adult women.

> Frances is playing dress-up. She is walking in red shoes and carrying a pocketbook. She and two other girls, Jen and Rachel, spend between five and ten minutes looking at and talking about the guinea pigs. Then they go back to dress-up. Frances and Rachel practice walking in adult women's shoes. Their body movements are not a perfect imitation of an adult woman's walk in high heels, yet it does look like an attempt to imitate such a walk. Jen and Rachel go back to the guinea pigs, and Frances, now by herself, is turning a sheer, frilly lavender shirt around and around and around trying to figure out how to put it on. She gets it on and looks at herself in the mirror. She adds a sheer pink and lavender scarf and pink shoes. Looks in the mirror again. She walks, twisting her body—shoulders, hips, shoulders, hips—not quite a (stereotypic) feminine walk, but close. Walking in big shoes makes her take little bitty steps, like walking in heels. She shuffles in the too big shoes out into the middle of the classroom and stops by a teacher. Laura (a teacher) says, "don't you look fancy, all pink and purple." Frances smiles up at her and walks off, not twisting so much this time. She goes back to the mirror and adds a red scarf. She looks in the mirror and is holding her arms across her chest to hold the scarf on (she can't tie it) and she is holding it with her chin too. She shuffles to block area where Jen is and then takes the clothes off and puts them back in dress-up area. (Five-year-olds)

I observed not only the children who dressed up, but the reaction of those around them to their dress. This aspect proved to be one of the most interesting parts of kids' dress-up play. Children interpreted each others' bodily adornments as gendered, even when other interpretations were plausible.

For instance, one day just before Halloween, Kim dressed up and was "scary" because she was dressed as a woman:

> Kim has worn a denim skirt and tights to school today. Now she is trying to pull on a ballerina costume–pink and ruffly—over her clothes. She has a hard time getting it on. It's tight and wrinkled up and twisted when she gets it on. Her own clothes are bunched up under it. Then she puts on a mask—a woman's face. The mask material itself is a clear plastic so that skin shows through, but is sculpted to have a very Anglo nose and high cheek bones. It also has thin eyebrows, blue eye shadow, blush, and lipstick painted on it. The mask is bigger than Kim's face and head. Kim looks at herself in the mirror and spends the rest of the play time with this costume on. Intermittently she picks up a plastic pumpkin since it is Halloween season and carries that around too. Kim walks around the classroom for a long time and then runs through the block area wearing this costume. Jason yells, "Ugh! There's a woman!" He and the other boys playing blocks shriek and scatter about the block area. Kim runs back to the dress-up area as they yell. Then throughout the afternoon she walks and skips through the center of the classroom, and every time she comes near the block boys one of them yells, "Ugh, there's the woman again!" The teacher even picks up on this and says to Kim twice, "Woman, slow down." (Five-year-olds)

The boys' shrieks indicated that Kim was scary, and this scariness is linked in their comments about her being a woman. It seems equally plausible that they could have interpreted her scary dress as a "trick-or-treater," given that it was close to Halloween and she was carrying a plastic pumpkin that kids collect candy in, or that they might have labeled her a dancer or ballerina because she was wearing a tutu. Rather, her scary dress-up was coded for her by others as "woman."

Other types of responses to girls dressing up also seemed to gender their bodies and to constrain them. For example, on two occasions I saw a teacher tie the arms of girls' dress-up shirts together so that the girls could not move their arms. They did this in fun, of course, and untied them as soon as the girls wanted them to, but I never witnessed this constraining of boys' bodies in play.

Thus, how parents gender children's bodies through dressing them and the ways children experiment with bodily adornments by dressing up make girls' and boys' bodies different and seem different to those around them. Adorning a body often genders it explicitly—signifies that it is a feminine or masculine body. Adornments also make girls' movements smaller, leading girls to take up less space with their bodies and disallowing some types of movements.

Formal and Relaxed Behaviors

Describing adults, Goffman (1959) defines front stage and backstage behavior:

> The backstage language consists of reciprocal first-naming, co-operative decision making, profanity, open sexual remarks, elaborate gripping, smoking,

> rough informal dress, "sloppy" sitting and standing posture, use of dialect or substandard speech, mumbling and shouting, playful aggressivity and "kidding," inconsiderateness for the other in minor but potentially symbolic acts, minor physical self-involvements such as humming, whistling, chewing, nibbling, belching, and flatulence. The front stage behavior language can be taken as the absence (and in some sense the opposite) of this. (p. 128)

Thus, one might not expect much front stage or formal behavior in preschool, and often, especially during parents' drop-off and pick-up time, this was the case. But a given region of social life may sometimes be a backstage and sometimes a front stage. I identified several behaviors that were expected by the teachers, required by the institution, or that would be required in many institutional settings, as formal behavior. Raising one's hand, sitting "on your bottom" (not on your knees, not squatting, not lying down, not standing) during circle, covering one's nose and mouth when coughing or sneezing, or sitting upright in a chair are all formal behaviors of preschools, schools, and to some extent the larger social world. Crawling on the floor, yelling, lying down during teachers' presentations, and running through the classroom are examples of relaxed behaviors that are not allowed in preschool, schools, work settings, and many institutions of the larger social world (Henley 1977). Not all behaviors fell into one of these classifications. When kids were actively engaged in playing at the water table, for example, much of their behavior was not clearly formal or relaxed. I coded as formal and relaxed behaviors those behaviors that would be seen as such if done by adults (or children in many cases) in other social institutions for which children are being prepared.

In the classrooms in this study, boys were allowed and encouraged to pursue relaxed behaviors in a variety of ways that girls were not. Girls were more likely to be encouraged to pursue more formal behaviors. Eighty-two percent of all formal behaviors observed in these classrooms were done by girls, and only 18 percent by boys. However, 80 percent of the behaviors coded as relaxed were boys' behaviors.

These observations do not tell us *why* boys do more relaxed behaviors and girls do more formal behaviors. Certainly many parents and others would argue that boys are more predisposed to sloppy postures, crawling on the floor, and so on. However, my observations suggest that teachers help construct this gender difference in bodily behaviors. Teachers were more likely to reprimand girls for relaxed bodily movements and comportment. Sadker and Sadker (1994) found a similar result with respect to hand-raising for answering teachers' questions—if hand raising is considered a formal behavior and calling out a relaxed behavior, they find that boys are more likely to call out without raising their hands and demand attention:

> Sometimes what they [boys] say has little or nothing to do with the teacher's questions. Whether male comments are insightful or irrelevant, teachers respond

> to them. However, when girls call out, there is a fascinating occurrence: Suddenly the teacher remembers the rule about raising your hand before you talk. (Sadker and Sadker 1994, 43)

This gendered dynamic of hand-raising exists even in preschool, although our field notes do not provide enough systematic recording of hand-raising to fully assess it. However, such a dynamic applies to many bodily movements and comportment:

> The kids are sitting with their legs folded in a circle listening to Jane (the teacher) talk about dinosaurs. ("Circle" is the most formal part of their preschool education each day and is like sitting in class.) Sam has the ballet slippers on his hands and is clapping them together really loudly. He stops and does a half-somersault backward out of the circle and stays that way with his legs in the air. Jane says nothing and continues talking about dinosaurs. Sue, who is sitting next to Sam, pushes his leg out of her way. Sam sits up and is now busy trying to put the ballet shoes on over his sneakers, and he is looking at the other kids and laughing, trying to get a reaction. He is clearly not paying attention to Jane's dinosaur story and is distracting the other kids. Sam takes the shoes and claps them together again. Jane leans over and tells him to give her the shoes. Sam does, and then lies down all stretched out on the floor, arms over his head, legs apart. Adam is also lying down now, and Keith is on Sara's (the teacher's aide) lap. Rachel takes her sweater off and folds it up. The other children are focused on the teacher. After about five minutes, Jane tells Sam "I'm going to ask you to sit up." (She doesn't say anything to Adam.) But he doesn't move. Jane ignores Sam and Adam and continues with the lesson. Rachel now lies down on her back. After about ten seconds Jane says, "Sit up, Rachel." Rachel sits up and listens to what kind of painting the class will do today. (Five-year-olds)

Sam's behavior had to be more disruptive, extensive, and informal than Rachel's for the teacher to instruct him and his bodily movements to be quieter and for him to comport his body properly for circle. Note that the boys who were relaxed but not disruptive were not instructed to sit properly. It was also common for a teacher to tell a boy to stop some bodily behavior and for the boy to ignore the request and the teacher not to enforce her instructions, although she frequently repeated them.

The gendering of body movements, comportment, and acquisitions of space also happens in more subtle ways. For example, often when there was "free" time, boys spent much more time in child-structured activities than did girls. In one classroom of five-year-olds, boys' "free" time was usually spent building with blocks, climbing on blocks, or crawling on the blocks or on the floor as they worked to build with the blocks whereas girls spent much of their free time sitting at tables cutting things out of paper, drawing, sorting small pieces of blocks into categories, reading stories, and so on. Compared to boys, girls rarely crawled on the floor (except when they played kitty cats). Girls and boys did share some activities. For example, painting and reading were frequently shared, and the three-year-olds often played at fishing from a play bridge together. Following is a list from my field notes of the most common activities boys and girls did during the child-structured activity periods of the day during two randomly picked weeks of observing:

Boys: played blocks (floor), played at the water table (standing and splashing), played superhero (running around and in play house), played with the car garage (floor), painted at the easel (standing).

Girls: played dolls (sitting in chairs and walking around), played dress-up (standing), coloring (sitting at tables), read stories (sitting on the couch), cut out pictures (sitting at tables).

Children sorted themselves into these activities and also were sorted (or not unsorted) by teachers. For example, teachers rarely told the three boys that always played with the blocks that they had to choose a different activity that day. Teachers also encouraged girls to sit at tables by suggesting table activities for them—in a sense giving them less "free" time or structuring their time more.

> It's the end of circle, and Susan (teacher) tells the kids that today they can paint their dinosaur eggs if they want to. There is a table set up with paints and brushes for those who want to do that. The kids listen and then scatter to their usual activities. Several boys are playing blocks, two boys are at the water table. Several girls are looking at the hamsters in their cage and talking about them, two girls are sitting and stringing plastic beads. Susan says across the classroom, "I need some painters, Joy, Amy, Kendall?" The girls leave the hamster cage and go to the painting table. Susan pulls out a chair so Joy can sit down. She tells them about the painting project. (Five-year-olds)

These girls spent much of the afternoon enjoying themselves painting their eggs. Simon and Jack joined them temporarily, but then went back to activities that were not teacher-structured.

Events like these that happen on a regular basis over an extended period of early childhood serve to gender children's bodies—boys come to take up more room with their bodies, to sit in more open positions, and to feel freer to do what they wish with their bodies, even in relatively formal settings. Henley (1977) finds that among adults men generally are more relaxed than women in their demeanor and women tend to have tenser postures. The looseness of body-focused functions (e.g., belching) is also more open to men than to women. In other words, men are more likely to engage in relaxed demeanors, postures, and behaviors. These data suggest that this gendering of bodies into more formal and more relaxed movements, postures, and comportment is (at least partially) constructed in early childhood by institutions like preschools.

Controlling Voice

Speaking (or yelling as is often the case with kids) is a bodily experience that involves mouth, throat, chest, diaphragm, and facial expression. Thorne (1993) writes that an elementary school teacher once told her that kids "reminded her of bumblebees, an apt image of swarms, speed, and constant motion" (p. 15). Missing from this metaphor is the buzz of the bumblebees, as a constant hum of voices comes from children's play and activities. Kids' play that is giggly, loud, or whispery makes it clear that voice is part of their bodily experiences.

Voice is an aspect of bodily experience that teachers and schools are interested in disciplining. Quiet appears to be required for learning in classrooms. Teaching appropriate levels of voice, noise, and sound disciplines children's bodies and prepares them "from the inside" to learn the school's curriculums and to participate in other social institutions.

The disciplining of children's voices is gendered. I found that girls were told to be quiet or to repeat a request in a quieter, "nicer" voice about three times more often than were boys. This finding is particularly interesting because boys' play was frequently much noisier. However, when boys were noisy, they were also often doing other behaviors the teacher did not allow, and perhaps the teachers focused less on voice because they were more concerned with stopping behaviors like throwing or running.

Additionally, when boys were told to "quiet down" they were told in large groups, rarely as individuals. When they were being loud and were told to be quiet, boys were often in the process of enacting what Jordan and Cowan (1995) call warrior narratives:

> A group of three boys is playing with wooden doll figures. The dolls are jumping off block towers, crashing into each other. Kevin declares loudly, "I'm the grown up." Keith replies, "I'm the police." They knock the figures into each other and push each other away. Phil grabs a figure from Keith. Keith picks up two more and bats one with the other toward Phil. Now all three boys are crashing the figures into each other, making them dive off towers. They're having high fun. Two more boys join the group. There are now five boys playing with the wooden dolls and the blocks. They're breaking block buildings; things are crashing; they're grabbing each other's figures and yelling loudly. Some are yelling "fire, fire" as their figures jump off the block tower. The room is very noisy. (Five-year-olds)

Girls as individuals and in groups were frequently told to lower their voices. Later that same afternoon:

> During snack time the teacher asks the kids to tell her what they like best in the snack mix. Hillary says, "Marshmallows!" loudly, vigorously, and with a swing of her arm. The teacher turns to her and says, "I'm going to ask you to say that quietly," and Hillary repeats it in a softer voice. (Five-year-olds)

These two observations represent a prominent pattern in the data. The boys playing with the wooden figures were allowed to express their fun and enthusiasm loudly whereas Hillary could not loudly express her love of marshmallows. Girls' voices are disciplined to be softer and in many ways less physical—toning down their voices tones down their physicality. Hillary emphasized "marshmallows" with a large swinging gesture of her arm the first time she answered the teacher's question, but after the teacher asked her to say it quietly she made no gestures when answering. Incidents like these that are repeated often in different contexts restrict girls' physicality.

It could be argued that context rather than gender explains the difference in how much noise is allowed in these situations. Teachers may expect more formal behavior from children sitting at the snack table than they do during semistructured activities. However, even during free play girls were frequently told to quiet down:

> Nancy, Susan, and Amy are jumping in little jumps, from the balls of their feet, almost like skipping rope without the rope. Their mouths are open and they're making a humming sound, looking at each other and giggling. Two of them keep sticking their tongues out. They seem to be having great fun. The teacher's aide sitting on the floor in front of them turns around and says, "Shhh, find something else to play. Why don't you play Simon Says?" All three girls stop initially. Then Amy jumps a few more times, but without making the noise. (Five-year-olds)

By limiting the girls' voices, the teacher also limits the girls' jumping and their fun. The girls learn that their bodies are supposed to be quiet, small, and physically constrained. Although the girls did not take the teacher's suggestion to play Simon Says (a game where bodies can be moved only quietly at the order of another), they turn to play that explores quietness yet tries to maintain some of the fun they were having:

> Nancy, Susan, and Amy begin sorting a pile of little-bitty pieces of puzzles, soft blocks, Legos, and so on into categories to "help" the teacher who told them to be quiet and to clean up. The three of them and the teacher are standing around a single small desk sorting these pieces. (Meanwhile several boys are playing blocks and their play is spread all over the middle of the room.) The teacher turns her attention to some other children. The girls continue sorting and then begin giggling to each other. As they do, they cover their mouths. This becomes a game as one imitates the other. Susan says something nonsensical that is supposed to be funny, and then she "hee-hees" while covering her mouth and looks at Nancy, to whom she has said it, who covers her mouth and "hee-hees" back. They begin putting their hands/fingers cupped over their mouths and whispering in each others' ears and then giggling quietly. They are intermittently sorting the pieces and playing the whispering game. (Five-year-olds)

Thus, the girls took the instruction to be quiet and turned it into a game. This new game made their behaviors smaller, using hands and mouths rather than legs, feet, and whole bodies. Whispering became their fun, instead of jumping and humming. Besides requiring quiet, this whispering game also was gendered in another way: The girls' behavior seemed to mimic sterotypical female gossiping. They whispered in twos and looked at the third girl as they did it and then changed roles. Perhaps the instruction to be quiet, combined with the female role of "helping," led the girls to one of their understandings of female quietness—gossip—a type of feminine quietness that is perhaps most fun.

Finally, by limiting voice teachers limit one of girls' mechanisms for resisting others' mistreatment of them. Frequently, when a girl had a dispute with another child, teachers would ask the girl to quiet down and solve the problem nicely. Teachers also asked boys to solve problems by talking, but they usually did so only with intense disputes and the instruction to talk things out never carried the instruction to talk *quietly*.

> Keith is persistently threatening to knock over the building that Amy built. He is running around her with a "flying" toy horse that comes dangerously close to her building each time. She finally says, "Stop it!" in a loud voice. The teacher comes over and asks, "How do we say that, Amy?" Amy looks at Keith and says more softly, "Stop trying to knock it over." The teacher tells Keith to find some place else to play. (Five-year-olds)

> Cheryl and Julie are playing at the sand table. Cheryl says to the teacher loudly, "Julie took mine away!" The teacher tells her to say it more quietly. Cheryl repeats it less loudly. The teacher tells her, "Say it a little quieter." Cheryl says it quieter, and the teacher says to Julie, "Please don't take that away from her." (Three-year-olds)

We know that women are reluctant to use their voices to protect themselves from a variety of dangers. The above observations suggest that the denial of women's voices begins at least as early as preschool, and that restricting voice, usually restricts movement as well.

Finally, there were occasions when the quietness requirement did not restrict girls' bodies. One class of three-year-olds included two Asian girls, Diane and Sue, who did not speak English. Teachers tended to talk about them and over them but rarely to them. Although these girls said little to other children and were generally quiet, they were what I term body instigators. They got attention and played with other children in more bodily ways than most girls. For example, Sue developed a game with another girl that was a sort of musical chairs. They'd race from one chair to another to see who could sit down first. Sue initiated this game by trying to squeeze into a chair with the other girl. Also, for example,

> Diane starts peeking into the play cardboard house that is full of boys and one girl. She looks like she wants to go in, but the door is blocked and the house is crowded. She then goes around to the side of the house and stands with her back to it and starts bumping it with her butt. Because the house is

> cardboard, it buckles and moves as she does it. The teacher tells her, "Stop—no." Diane stops and then starts doing it again but more lightly. All the boys come out of the house and ask her what she's doing. Matt gets right in her face and the teacher tells him, "Tell her no." He does, but all the other boys have moved on to other activities, so she and Matt go in the house together. (Three-year-olds)

Thus, Diane and Sue's lack of voice in this English-speaking classroom led to greater physicality. There may be other ways that context (e.g., in one's neighborhood instead of school) and race, ethnicity, and class shape gender and voice that cannot be determined from these data (Goodwin 1990).

Bodily Instructions

Teachers give a lot of instructions to kids about what to do with their bodies. Of the explicit bodily instructions recorded 65 percent were directed to boys, 26 percent to girls, and the remaining 9 percent were directed to mixed groups. These numbers suggest that boys' bodies are being disciplined more than girls. However, there is more to this story—the types of instructions that teachers give and children's responses to them are also gendered.

First, boys obeyed teachers' bodily instructions about one-half of the time (48 percent), while girls obeyed about 80 percent of the time. Boys may receive more instructions from teachers because they are less likely to follow instructions and thus are told repeatedly. Frequently I witnessed a teacher telling a boy or group of boys to stop doing something—usually running or throwing things—and the teacher repeated these instructions several times in the course of the session before (if ever) taking further action. Teachers usually did not have to repeat instructions to girls—girls either stopped on their own with the first instruction, or because the teacher forced them to stop right then. Serbin (1983) finds that boys receive a higher proportion of teachers' ". . . loud reprimands, audible to the entire group. Such patterns of response, intended as punishment, have been repeatedly demonstrated to reinforce aggression and other forms of disruptive behavior" (p. 29).

Second, teachers' instructions directed to boys' bodies were less substantive than those directed to girls. That is, teachers' instructions to boys were usually to stop doing something, to end a bodily behavior with little suggestion for other behaviors they might do. Teachers rarely told boys to change a bodily behavior. A list of teachers' instructions to boys includes: stop throwing, stop jumping, stop clapping, stop splashing, no pushing, don't cry, blocks are not for bopping, don't run, don't climb on that. Fifty-seven percent of the instructions that teachers gave boys about their physical behaviors were of this undirected type, compared with 15 percent of their instructions to girls. In other words, teachers' instructions to girls generally were more substantive and more directive, telling girls to do a bodily behavior rather than to stop one. Teachers' instructions to girls suggested that they alter their behaviors.

A list of instructions to girls includes: talk to her, don't yell, sit here, pick that up, be careful, be gentle, give it to me, put it down there. Girls may have received fewer bodily instructions than did boys, but they received more directive ones. This gender difference leaves boys a larger range of possibilities of what they might choose to do with their bodies once they have stopped a behavior, whereas girls were directed toward a defined set of options.

Physical Interaction between Teachers and Children

Teachers also physically directed kids. For example, teachers often held kids to make them stop running, tapped them to make them turn around and pay attention, or turned their faces toward them so that they would listen to verbal instructions. One-fourth of all physical contacts between teachers and children was to control children's physicality in some way, and 94 percent of such contacts were directed at boys.

Physical interaction between teachers and children was coded into three categories: positive, negative, or neutral. Physical interaction was coded as positive if it was comforting, helpful, playful, or gentle. It was coded as negative if it was disciplining, assertive (not gentle), restraining, or clearly unwanted by the child (e.g., the child pulled away). Physical interaction was coded as neutral if it seemed to have little content (e.g., shoulders touching during circle, legs touching while a teacher gave a group of kids directions for a project). About one-half of the time, when teachers touched boys or girls, it was positive. For example, the teacher and child might have bodily contact as she tied a shoe, wiped away tears, or tickled a child, or if a child took the teacher's hand or got on her lap. For girls, the remaining physical interactions included 15 percent that were disciplining or instructing the body and about one-third that were neutral (e.g., leaning over the teacher's arm while looking at a book). For boys, these figures were reversed: Only 4 percent of their physical interactions with teachers were neutral in content, and 35 percent were negative and usually included explicit disciplining and instructing of the body.

This disciplining of boys' bodies took a particular form. Teachers usually attempted to restrain or remove boys who had "gone too far" in their play or who had done something that could harm another child:

> Irving goes up to Jack, who is playing dress-up, and puts his arms up, makes a monster face and says, "Aaarhhh!" Jack looks startled. Irving runs and jumps in front of Jack again and says "Aaarrhh!" again. Marie (teacher) comes from behind Irving and holds him by the shoulders and arms from behind. She bends over him and says, "Calm down." He pulls forward, and eventually she lets him go. He runs up to Jack again and growls. Marie says, "He doesn't want you to do that." (Three-year-olds)

As Serbin (1983) suggests, frequent loud reprimands of boys may increase their disruptive behavior; more frequent physical disciplining interactions between teachers and boys may do so as well. Because boys more frequently than girls experienced interactions in which their bodies were physically restrained or disciplined by an adult who had more power and was angry, they may be more likely than girls to associate physical interaction with struggle and anger, and thus may be more likely to be aggressive or disruptive.

Physical Interaction among Children

Thorne (1993) demonstrates that children participate in the construction of gender differences among themselves. The preschool brings together large groups of children who engage in interactions in which they cooperate with the hidden curriculum and discipline each others' bodies in gendered ways, but they also engage in interactions in which they resist this curriculum.

Girls and boys teach their same-sex peers about their bodies and physicality. Children in these observations were much more likely to imitate the physical behavior of a same-sex peer than a cross-sex peer. Children also encourage others to imitate them. Some gendered physicality develops in this way. For example, I observed one boy encouraging other boys to "take up more space" in the same way he was.

> James (one of the most active boys in the class) is walking all over the blocks that Joe, George, and Paul have built into a road. Then he starts spinning around with his arms stretched out on either side of him. He has a plastic toy cow in one hand and is yelling, "Moo." He spins through half of the classroom, other children ducking under his arms or walking around him when he comes near them. Suddenly he drops the cow and still spinning, starts shouting, "I'm a tomato! I'm a tomato!" The three boys who were playing blocks look at him and laugh. James says, "I'm a tomato!" again, and Joe says, "There's the tomato." Joe, George, and Paul continue working on their block road. James then picks up a block and lobs it in their direction and then keeps spinning throughout this half of the classroom saying he's a tomato. Joe and George look up when the block lands near them and then they get up and imitate James. Now three boys are spinning throughout much of the room, shouting that they are tomatoes. The other children in the class are trying to go about their play without getting hit by a tomato. (Five-year-olds)

The within-gender physicality of three-year-old girls and boys was more similar than it was among the five-year-olds. Among the three-year-old girls there was more rough and tumble play, more physical fighting and arguing among girls than there was among the five-year-old girls.

> During clean up, Emily and Sara argue over putting away some rope. They both pull on the ends of the rope until the teacher comes over and separates them. Emily walks around the classroom then, not cleaning anything up. She sings to herself, does a twirl, and gets in line for snack. Sara is behind her

> in line. Emily pushes Sara. Sara yells, "Aaahh," and hits Emily and pushes her. The teacher takes both of them out of line and talks to them about getting along and being nice to each other. (Three-year-olds)

> Shelly and Ann have masks on. One is a kitty and one is a doggy. They're crawling around on the floor, and they begin play wrestling—kitties and doggies fight. The teacher says to them, "Are you ok?" They stop, lift up their masks, and look worried. The teacher says, "Oh, are you wrestling? It's ok, I just wanted to make sure everyone was ok." The girls nod; they're ok. Then, they put their masks back on and crawl on the floor some more. They do not resume wrestling. (Three-year-olds)

From lessons like these, girls have learned by age five that their play with each other should not be "too rough." The physical engagement of girls with each other at age five had little rough-and-tumble play:

> Two girls are playing with the dishes and sitting at a table. Keisha touches Alice under the chin, tickles her almost, then makes her eat something pretend, then touches the corners of her mouth, telling her to smile. (Five-year-olds)

I do not mean to suggest that girls' physical engagement with each other is the opposite of boys' or that all of boys' physical contacts were rough and tumble. Boys, especially in pairs, hugged, gently guided, or helped each other climb or jump. But often, especially in groups of three or more and especially among the five-year-olds, boys' physical engagement was highly active, "rough," and frequent. Boys experienced these contacts as great fun and not as hostile or negative in any way. . . .

The physical engagement of boys and girls *with each other* differed from same-sex physical engagement. Because girls' and boys' play is semi-segregated, collisions (literal and figurative) in play happen at the borders of these gender-segregated groups (Maccoby 1988; Thorne 1993). As Thorne (1993) demonstrates, not all borderwork is negative—40 percent of the physical interactions observed between girls and boys were positive or neutral.

> Ned runs over to Veronica, hipchecks her and says "can I be your friend?" and she says "yes." Ned walks away and kicks the blocks again three to four times. (Five-year-olds)

However, cross-gender interactions were more likely to be negative than same-sex interactions. In fact, physical interactions among children were twice as likely to be a negative interaction if they were between a girl and boy than if they were among same-gender peers. Approximately 30 percent of the interactions among girls and among boys were negative (hostile, angry, controlling, hurtful), whereas 60 percent of mixed-gender physical interactions were negative. Sixty percent of 113 boy-girl physical interactions were initiated by boys, 39 percent were initiated by girls, and only 1 percent of these interactions were mutually initiated.

At the borders of semi-segregated play there are physical interactions about turf and toy ownership:

> Sylvia throws play money on the floor from her play pocketbook. Jon grabs it up. She wrestles him for it and pries it from his hands. In doing this she forces him onto the floor so that he's hunched forward on his knees. She gets behind him and sandwiches him on the floor as she grabs his hands and gets the money loose. Then, two minutes later, she's giving money to kids, and she gives Jon some, but apparently not enough. He gets right close to her face, inches away and loudly tells her that he wants more. He scrunches up his face, puts his arms straight down by his sides and makes fists. She steps back; he steps up close again to her face. She turns away. (Five-year-olds)

Negative interactions occur when there are "invasions" or interruptions of play among children of one gender by children of another:

> Courtney is sitting on the floor with the girls who are playing "kitties." The girls have on their dress-up clothes and dress-up shoes. Phil puts on big winter gloves and then jumps in the middle of the girls on the floor. He lands on their shoes. Courtney pushes him away and then pulls her legs and clothes and stuff closer to her. She takes up less space and is sitting in a tight ball on the floor. Phil yells, "No! Aaarrhh." Julie says, "It's not nice to yell." (Five-year-olds)

As Thorne (1993) suggests, kids create, shape, and police the borders of gender. I suggest that they do so physically. In this way, they not only sustain gender segregation, but also maintain a sense that girls and boys are physically different, that their bodies are capable of doing certain kinds of things. This sense of physical differences may make all gender differences feel and appear natural.

Conclusion

Children also sometimes resist their bodies being gendered. For example, three-year-old boys dressed up in women's clothes sometimes. Five-year-old girls played with a relaxed comportment that is normatively (hegemonically) masculine when they sat with their feet up on the desk and their chairs tipped backward. In one classroom when boys were at the height of their loud activity—running and throwing toys and blocks—girls took the opportunity to be loud too as the teachers were paying less attention to them and trying to get the boys to settle down. In individual interactions as well, girls were likely to be loud and physically assertive if a boy was being unusually so:

> José is making a plastic toy horse fly around the room, and the boys playing with the blocks are quite loud and rambunctious. José flies the toy horse

> right in front of Jessica's face and then zooms around her and straight toward her again. Jessica holds up her hand and waves it at him yelling, "Aaaarrrh." José flies the horse in another direction. (Five-year-olds)

These instances of resistance suggest that gendered physicalities are not natural, nor are they easily and straightforwardly acquired. This research demonstrates the many ways that practices in institutions like preschools facilitate children's acquisition of gendered physicalities.

Men and women and girls and boys fill social space with their bodies in different ways. Our everyday movements, postures, and gestures are gendered. These bodily differences enhance the seeming naturalness of sexual and reproductive differences, that then construct inequality between men and women (Butler 1990). As MacKinnon (1987) notes, "Differences are inequality's post hoc excuse . . ." (p. 8). In other words, these differences create a context for social relations in which differences confirm inequalities of power.

This research suggests one way that bodies are gendered and physical differences are constructed through social institutions and their practices. Because this gendering occurs at an early age, the seeming naturalness of such differences is further underscored. In preschool, bodies become gendered in ways that are so subtle and taken-for-granted that they come to feel and appear natural. Preschool, however, is presumably just the tip of the iceberg in the gendering of children's bodies. Families, formal schooling, and other institutions (like churches, hospitals, and workplaces) gender children's physicality as well.

Many feminist sociologists (West and Zimmerman 1987) and other feminist scholars (Butler 1990, 1993) have examined how the seeming naturalness of gender differences underlies gender inequality. They have also theorized that there are no meaningful natural differences (Butler 1990, 1993). However, how gender differences come to feel and appear natural in the first place has been a missing piece of the puzzle.

Sociological theories of the body that describe the regulation, disciplining, and managing that social institutions do to bodies have neglected the gendered nature of these processes (Foucault 1979; Shilling 1993; Turner 1984). These data suggest that a significant part of disciplining the body consists of gendering it, even in subtle, micro, everyday ways that make gender appear natural. It is in this sense that the preschool as an institution genders children's bodies. Feminist theories about the body (Bordo 1993; Connell 1995; Young 1990), on the other hand, tend to focus on the adult gendered body and fail to consider how the body becomes gendered. This neglect may accentuate gender differences and make them seem natural. This research provides but one account of how bodies become gendered. Other accounts of how the bodies of children and adults are gendered (and raced, classed, and sexualized) are needed in various social contexts across the life course.

References

Anyon, Jean. 1980. Social class and the hidden curriculum of work. *Journal of Education* 162:67–92.

Birdwhistell, Ray. 1970. *Kinesics and Contexts.* Philadelphia: University of Pennsylvania Press.

Bordo, Susan. 1993. *Unbearable Weight.* Berkeley: University of California Press.

Bowles, Samuel, and Herbert Gintis. 1976. *Schooling in Capitalist America.* New York: Basic Books.

Butler, Judith. 1990. *Gender Trouble.* New York: Routledge.

———. 1993. *Bodies That Matter.* New York: Routledge.

Carere, Sharon. 1987. Lifeworld of restricted behavior. *Sociological Studies of Child Development* 2:105–38.

Carnoy, Martin, and Henry Levin. 1985. *Schooling and Work in the Democratic State.* Stanford, CA: Stanford University Press.

Connell, R. W. 1987. *Gender and Power.* Stanford, CA: Stanford University Press.

———. 1995. *Masculinities.* Berkeley: University of California Press.

Foucault, Michel. 1979. *Discipline and Punish: The Birth of the Prison.* New York: Vintage Books.

Giroux, Henry, and David Purpel. 1983. *The Hidden Curriculum and Moral Education.* Berkeley, CA: McCutchan.

Goffman, Erving. 1959. *The Presentation of Self in Everyday Life.* Garden City, NY: Doubleday.

Goodwin, Marjorie Harness. 1990. *He-Said-She-Said: Talk as Social Organization among Black Children.* Bloomington: Indiana University Press.

Haug, Frigga. 1987. *Female Sexualization: A Collective Work of Memory.* London: Verso.

Henley, Nancy. 1977. *Body Politics.* New York: Simon and Schuster.

Jackson, Philip W. 1968. *Life in Classrooms.* New York: Holt, Rinehart and Winston.

Jordan, Ellen, and Angela Cowan. 1995. Warrior narratives in the kindergarten classroom: Renegotiating the social contract. *Gender and Society* 9:727–43.

Maccoby, Eleanor. 1988. Gender as a social category. *Developmental Psychology* 24:755–65.

MacKinnon, Catharine. 1987. *Feminism Unmodified.* Cambridge, MA: Harvard University Press.

Martin, Emily. 1987. *The Woman in the Body.* Boston: Beacon Press.

Martin, Karin. 1996. *Puberty, Sexuality, and the Self: Boys and Girls at Adolescence.* New York: Routledge.

McLaren, Peter. 1986. *Schooling as a Ritual Performance: Towards a Political Economy of Educational Symbols and Gestures.* London: Routledge and Kegan Paul.

Sadker, Myra, and David Sadker. 1994. *Failing at Fairness: How America's Schools Cheat Girls.* New York: Charles Scribner and Sons.

Serbin, Lisa. 1983. The hidden curriculum: Academic consequences of teacher expectations. In *Sex Differentiation and Schooling*, edited by M. Marland. London: Heinemann Educational Books.

Shilling, Chris. 1993. *The Body and Social Theory.* London: Sage.

Thomas, Jerry, and Karen French. 1985. Gender differences across age in motor performance: A meta-analysis. *Psychological Bulletin* 98:260–82.

Thorne, Barrie. 1993. *Gender Play: Girls and Boys in School.* New Brunswick, NJ: Rutgers University Press.

Turner, Bryan S. 1984. *The Body and Society: Explorations in Social Theory.* New York: Basil Blackwell.

———. 1992. *Regulating Bodies: Essays in Medical Sociology.* London: Routledge.

Van Ausdale, Debra, and Joe R. Feagin. 1996. Using racial and ethnic concepts: The critical case of very young children. *American Sociological Review* 61:779–93.

Wasburn, Philo C. 1986. The political role of the American school. *Theory and Research in Social Education* 14:51–65.

West, Candace, and Don Zimmerman. 1987. Doing gender. *Gender and Society* 1:127–51.

Young, Iris. 1990. *Throwing Like a Girl.* Bloomington: Indiana University Press.

4

Medicalization, Natural Childbirth, and Birthing Experiences

SARAH JANE BRUBAKER AND HEATHER E. DILLAWAY

Medicalization is the process by which human behaviors and conditions take on medical meanings. It involves defining a problem in medical terms, understanding it through a medical framework, and treating it with medical interventions. Although men's bodies can also be medicalized (as evidenced in medical diagnoses and treatments for male pattern baldness and erectile dysfunction), the gendered nature of medicalization makes it imperative that feminist scholars pay close attention to the medicalization of women's bodies.

In "Medicalization, Natural Childbirth, and Birthing Experiences," Sarah Jane Brubaker and Heather E. Dillaway examine the medicalization of the birthing experience. They maintain that one of the consequences of medicalization, particularly in regards to childbirth, is a conceptual dichotomy between "natural" and "medical." This shift has fed the idea that natural childbirth allows women to retain greater control over the birthing process, and that medicalized childbirth usurps women's choices during childbirth. Yet, as Brubaker and Dillaway illustrate, a natural childbirth that takes place in a home or a birthing center without invasive technologies also has the potential to deny women choices. Moreover, it can essentialize women and birth as "natural," reflect class and racial biases, and even expand medical surveillance over women's bodies. Because the vast majority of women in the United States continue to birth in hospitals, Brubaker and Dillaway stress the need to examine the medical birthing experiences of women across multiple social landscapes.

Medicalization is a major concept within the subfield of medical sociology. Much of the early analysis of medicalization focused on the constructions of women's reproductive health experiences, such as pregnancy and childbirth (Oakley 1984, 1993; Riessman 1983; Rothman 1989, 1991). Attention has moved away from childbirth over time, however, as new conditions have become subject to the medicalization process, including many that are specific to men's experiences such as erectile dysfunction, male pattern baldness, and andropause (Conrad 2007). Although medicalization continues to be of interest to sociologists, some of the basic concepts within this analytical framework—for instance, the dichotomy of "natural" versus "medical"—have not been sufficiently problematized over time. In this article, we suggest that there is a continued and, in some ways, renewed need to critically examine the medicalization of experiences such as childbirth from a critical perspective, one that is informed by but does not presuppose feminist perspectives, or those of privileged groups of women. As suggested by the literature reviewed here, the prominent conceptual dichotomy between "natural" and "medical" birth that frames much of the criticism of medicalization, particularly that of childbirth, has not proven to be meaningful to all women, and the meanings of natural and medical childbirth have changed over time. Furthermore, the more that medicalization has taken hold over U.S. society (and the more that sociologists write about medicalization), the more unclear "natural" experiences (especially experiences like "natural" birth) become. What does "natural" really mean, and what does the "natural" versus "medical" dichotomy truly signify? Moreover, how do various processes of medicalization shape women's childbirth experiences, and how do those experiences challenge medicalization and assumptions about its effects? . . .

Medicalization

The sociological interest in medicalization spans a wide range of areas of emphasis, but in general, two prominent issues are the expansion of medical jurisdiction and its use as a mechanism of social control through the medical gaze and surveillance (Conrad 2007; Foucault 1975; Riessman 1983; Zola 1972, 1981, 2005). Indeed, Loe (2004, 12) states that, "In the age of medical 'progress,' scientific knowledge and medical answers are generally unquestioned as the best, most efficient, most legitimate solutions. Technology, as an applied science, is similarly constructed and championed. However, the history of science, medicine, and technology is also a history of attempting to solve social problems and control populations."

Conrad (2007) suggests that a key to medicalization is definition—that is, that "a problem is defined in medical terms, described using medical language, understood through the adoption of a medical framework, or 'treated' with medical intervention" (p. 5). Similarly, Riessman (1983, 4) defines "medicalization" as the process by which behaviors or conditions take on medical meanings—"that is, defined in terms of health and illness" (see also Martin 1992). Like Conrad and Loe, Riessman suggests that medicalization is a process in which "medical practice becomes a vehicle for eliminating or controlling problematic experiences that are defined as deviant, for the purpose of securing adherence to social norms" (Riessman 1983, 4).

Although employed routinely by medical sociologists, the concepts "medicalization" and "medical model" have not been clearly defined and employed by theorists or researchers (Van Teijlingen 2005). For example, Riessman (1983) suggests that medicalization can be (1) conceptual, in that medical vocabulary is used to define a problem; (2) institutional, when medical providers legitimate a program or problem; and (3) interactional, at the level of doctor-patient encounters, when actual diagnosis and treatment of a problem occurs. Similarly, and specifically as applied to childbirth, Van Teijlingen (2005) suggests that the medical model can be understood as practical, ideological, or analytical. Riessman (1983, 4) suggests that on a practical level, a consequence of medicalization is the "deskilling of the populace" as experts begin to "manage" and "mystify" human experiences. After medicalization occurs, then, for instance, birthing women must consult "experts" to understand experiences that historically women themselves understood better (Davis-Floyd 1992; Kitzinger 2006; Leavitt 1986; E. Martin 1992; Oakley 1984; Riessman 1983; Rothman 1989; Wertz and Wertz 1977).

Conrad further suggests that there are various degrees of medicalization, and that some conditions, such as homosexuality, have experienced demedicalization and/or remedicalization. Some scholars, in fact, believe that "although some expansion of medical jurisdiction has occurred, the medicalization problem is overstated. They contend that we recently have witnessed a considerable demedicalization" (Conrad 2005, 430). If this is true, there is little empirical evidence to complete this argument, and we propose that considerable research could be done on childbirth experiences to perhaps argue this point. Especially with competing birth settings and birth providers in contemporary times, there is much room to explore whether birth has swung from "natural" to "medical" to slightly more "natural" and now perhaps back toward "medical." To our knowledge, there is a lack of analysis of this dichotomy in birth experiences over time. . . .

Natural vs. Medical

One of the constant components or consequences of medicalization, particularly with regard to childbirth, is the conceptual dichotomy between "natural" and "medical," as well as specific values associated with each. Lupton (2006) describes how early conceptualizations of nature were negative; for example, Henri de Mandeville, surgeon to French King Philip the Fair, between 1306 and 1320, promoted a metaphor of disease as an "invasion of Nature" (Lupton 2006). Continuing the devaluation of nature, in the eighteenth and nineteenth centuries, amidst the beginnings of formal medicine, biomedical science discourse linked nature with women and culture with men. According to Jordanova (1989), "the discourses of science and medicine employed sexual metaphors to describe their endeavours: 'for example by designating nature as a woman to be unveiled, unclothed and penetrated by masculine science'" (1989, 24; quoted in Lupton 2006, 73). As Lupton suggests,

> The women-as-nature and men-as-culture dichotomies became key terms in struggles around child-care and midwifery in the period. Women as mothers and as midwives were represented as irrational and irresponsible, their knowledge based on tradition rather than experience, needing the guidance of men who possessed scientific knowledge. (p. 73)

According to Rostosky and Travis (1996, 293), "conditions and experiences with specific relevance to females are often strongly characterized by their biological [or 'natural'] correlates." Because clinical researchers have had difficulty defining it, childbirth (along with, for example, pregnancy, conception, menstruation, menopause, and breastfeeding) is reduced to a biological or physiological event (Fausto-Sterling 1992; Rostosky and Travis 1996), which has meant that women and their reproductive experiences are reduced to "nature." Over time, men's control of the practice of science, their development of technology, and their establishment of modern medicine caused women's ["healthy," "normal," "natural"] reproductive processes to be socially constructed as "pathological," "abnormal," and "unnatural," or at least in need of continual monitoring (Martin 1992; Riessman 1983). If a "natural" female biological process can be seen as an "illness," then its "deviance" or "difference" gains legitimacy (Riessman 1983). This happens through medicalization, and these are the reasons why many of women's reproductive processes such as childbirth were some of the first to be medicalized.

More recently, however, some of the cultural valuation of "natural" has become more positive. For example, growing interest in biomedical enhancement has been promoted based on the use of "natural" products. According to Conrad (2007), "The term 'natural' is often taken as a proxy for 'good'" (p. 91). He goes on to suggest, however, that "[t]here is no necessary moral value to being natural, nor is the unnatural intrinsically inauthentic or second-rate" (p. 91). Similarly, Lupton argues that the cultural value given to the "natural" reflects politically and morally contested terrain:

> [C]ritics argue that the use of the symbol "nature" in alternative therapies is selective; for example, defining synthesized drugs as "artificial" and "chemicals" (and, thus, bad for health), while herbs are represented as natural and non-chemical, and therefore safe, even though many naturally occurring substances can be toxic, and many chemicals are derived from naturally occurring substances. (Coward 1989, 20–21; quoted in Lupton 2006, 136)

The selectivity of placing a positive value on "natural" goes beyond the use of supplements. For example, groups who refuse medical treatment and allow illness or disease to run its natural course often are viewed negatively, as well as those who would opt for a home birth as a more natural approach.

Similarly, many women reject the "natural" practice of breastfeeding as uncomfortable, embarrassing, or otherwise negative (Schmied and Lupton 2001). Clearly, the cultural valuation of "natural" with respect to health and illness, and particularly women's reproduction, remains unresolved.

To truly understand medicalization, and designations of "medical" versus "natural" experiences, it is important to revisit one of the original health processes that became medicalized: women's childbirth experiences. . . .

Feminist Perspectives on the Medicalization of Childbirth

. . . For the purposes of this article, we focus on three major themes of the feminist critique of medicalized childbirth and how it contrasts with a more natural approach (Macdonald 2006), often referred to as the "midwifery" or "holistic model" (Simonds, Rothman, and Norman 2007). Specifically, we examine the issues of control, the birth setting, and the use of medical technology.

Control

Consistent with the general sociological framework of medicalization, second-wave feminists have viewed the medicalization of childbirth as medical authority's usurpation of authority, choice, and control over women's reproduction, requiring women to consult medical experts for what has been traditionally and naturally women's domain (Arney 1982; Davis-Floyd 1992; Kaufman 1993; Keirse 1993; Kitzinger 2006; Leavitt 1986; E. Martin 1992; Oakley 1984; Rothman 1989, 1993; Wertz and Wertz 1977). Under this perspective, women are viewed as the natural, normal experts in childbirth, and their control over the labor process and their choices for how it progresses are deemed preferable to the authority and control of medical experts (for example, see Macdonald 2006). In contrast, as Lupton (2006) suggests, women giving birth under medical authority are expected to fit into given ideologies and comply with doctors' instructions as well as the use of their technologies, and the emphasis becomes more on the needs of baby than on the needs of the mother. . . .

Setting

Many scholars address the connection between the amount and extent of control a woman experiences regarding her birth experience and the birth setting. Existing literature contends that physicians and those in the medical field feel the need to actively "manage" labor and delivery for fear of this "pathological potential" (Arney 1982; Oakley 1993). It has been hypothesized by many authors that women who seek to manage or control their own labors must birth outside of the hospital and have a midwife in attendance (Harper 1994; Kahn 1995; Leavitt 1986; Simonds et al. 2007; Wertz and Wertz 1977). Others have explored the possibility that women have begun to use alternative settings for birth specifically because they want to regain control over their bodies and the birth process. The increasing medicalization of childbirth likely limits the amount of control a birthing woman experiences. For example, Jordan (1980, 33) proposes that when a birthing woman is admitted to a hospital, "decision-making power and responsibility for her state pass from her to hospital personnel and the physician in charge." Studies show that merely by going to a hospital, a woman often hands over control (Baldwin 1992; Fullerton and Severino 1992; Harper 1994; E. Martin 1992; K. Martin 2003; Rothman 1991; Simonds et al. 2007). The transfer of power and responsibility for birth from a woman to her doctor is seen as normal (almost "natural"?) in most cases, if the consensus is that childbirth has "pathological potential" (Conrad 2005). In the United States, handing over power and responsibility for birth to a doctor is an accepted cultural act. . . .

Some studies and scholars maintain that the "natural" process of childbirth is disrupted in the hospital (Baldwin 1992; Simonds et al. 2007). Many of the typical rituals of hospital routine, for example episiotomies or cesareans often carried out by staff who truly want to help a birthing woman, nevertheless "erode her confidence in the dependable process of birth and disrupt her ability to listen to and follow the inherent rhythm of her labor" (Baldwin 1992). Normal hospital routine presumably interrupts birth as a natural, physiological process, and therefore the woman needs subsequent obstetrical intervention to assure that the birth is carried out successfully (Simonds et al. 2007). In other words, a cyclical pattern of doctors' intervention and women's loss of control develops once the natural physiological process is interrupted. In comparison, the natural process of birth is interrupted less often in a birthing center and almost never in the home (Simonds et al. 2007). Furthermore, very rarely does a birthing woman hand total control of the birth experience over to medical practitioners in these latter two settings (Baldwin 1992; Fullerton and Severino 1992; Schimmel, Lee, Benner, and Schimmel 1994).

"Unlike the medical model, the midwifery model [here, the more 'natural' model] consistently sees the needs of the mother and the fetus as being in harmony, the two as one organic unit" and posits that both pregnancy and childbirth are "health and entirely normal condition[s]" (Simonds et al. 2007, 47). Care in the latter model is woman-centered and holistic, with no attempt by health care providers to take over control of the birth process. Simonds et al. (2007, 9) suggest that the "natural" "home birth" or "midwifery model" was developed in response to the rise of the medical model, thus as a reaction to the increase in medicalization. However, midwives and others "worked to redefine birth and to offer a different place to stand, a new—and maybe a very old—perspective on pregnancy, birth, mothers, and babies" (Simonds et al. 2007, 9).

The Use of Medical Technology

A related distinction in feminist literature is made between childbirth with and without the use of medical technology and intervention. For example, Davis-Floyd (1992, 162) suggests that "natural" birth includes the "conscious participation of the mother in her own birthing process." "Midwife" means "with the woman," and therefore its very meaning illustrates that this model would not take over or disturb the reproductive process except in the case of emergency. Rather, it is geared toward helping the woman let her body do the work (Kitzinger 2006; Leavitt 1986; Simonds et al. 2007; Wertz and Wertz 1977). For traditional feminists, the use of medical technology (and even the potential for the use of technology) destroys the chance for truly "natural" birth because it does not allow women to maintain this control over and participation in their own bodily processes (Davis-Floyd 1992; Kitzinger 2006; Simonds et al. 2007). "Even those medical attendants who lean more toward the wholistic [natural] model of birth often have as much difficulty as pregnant women when they attempt within the hospital to redefine an individual birth experience as natural" (Davis-Floyd 1992, 159; see also Simonds et al. 2007). Thus, in most cases, the very use of a hospital setting for birth is also characterized as destroying the chance for "natural" birth in feminists' writings, as this setting prompts the use of a range of medical technologies and outside control of women's reproductive processes (Davis-Floyd 1992; Kitzinger 2006; Simonds et al. 2007). The hospital, while providing a "cozy, comfortable," and even respectful atmosphere for some women in recent years, is still the "institution that produces that 70% epidural rate and that 29% cesarean section rate" (Simonds et al. 2007, 285). This is exactly why Simonds et al. (2007) suggest that the "natural" birth model is the "home birth model" or "midwifery model." According to feminist literature, medical technology usurps the birthing process once birth is moved to the hospital because there is a tendency to trust the accomplishments of this technology over the accomplishments of women and their bodies when this technology is readily available. This is why Davis-Floyd (1992) terms birth in the hospital setting to be "technocratic birth."

In sum, the feminist critique of the medicalization of childbirth emphasizes the expansion of medical jurisdiction and control over women's natural domain of childbirth through the use of the hospital setting and medical technology. In contrast, they define "natural" and "holistic" birth through women's maintenance of control and authority over their own births.

The Dominance of the Medical Model and Critiques of Feminist and "Natural" Approaches

Gullette (1997) and Lyons and Griffin (2003) suggest that the medical model is the "master narrative" or "discourse" for how to understand women's reproductive health because it represents the only "fully constituted" perspective, and thus women have no choice but to follow it and adhere to it in their own views. This means that the more "natural" model for birth may not be understandable to most, as they do not know how to even talk about what it includes. There is no clear framework in contemporary times for understanding why and how a "natural" birth might take place. The majority of women themselves, then, currently define childbirth as a process that needs medical supervision and control (Arney 1982; Jordan 1980; E. Martin 1992; Oakley 1984, 1993; Simonds et al. 2007). In this case, medicalized birth may make more sense to individual women because it is definable, visible, and unquestioned by most others around them.

One reflection of this cultural dominance of the medical model is that there are a number of criticisms of the traditional feminist or "natural" approach to childbirth. . . .

[For example,] proponents of the natural childbirth movement seek to re-establish the importance of pain to the childbirth experience and argue that pain should be defined by women themselves based on their personal relationships, attitudes, etc., but some of its critics question its complete rejection of medical technology. Critics argue that recently, this movement has influenced some shift in the discourse of obstetricians and hospitals to accommodate women's needs and desires to demedicalize childbirth and make it more "natural" [eliminating or limiting pain medication], but this shift ultimately has not increased women's freedom and agency. Rather, "[T]he emphasis on 'natural' childbirth, involving as little drug intervention as possible, has resulted in a situation in which women feel constrained to request pain relief" (Porter 1990, 192; cited in Lupton 2006, 160). Within this framework, there is little opportunity for women to relax and relinquish control. Karin Martin (2003) even suggests that women report feeling as if they should maintain control and appear passive in the contemporary birth setting, and pain medication may help them do so.

Bokat (1995) has suggested that "'natural childbirth' has become a catch phrase; one that appeals to the 'good mother' in us. What has been lost is the message of the women's movement: Every woman should be free to make her own choices about pregnancy and motherhood without being judged" (p. 36; see also Cohen 2006). . . .

An additional criticism of the natural childbirth movement is that it essentializes women and birth as "natural." This approach places greater pressure on women to be "natural" mothers, as if it were biologically inherent. This framework distinguishes between "natural" and "artificial" childbirth, ultimately recreating and presenting the historical view of women as simple, instinctive, and close to nature, and men as rational and scientific. This paves the way for interpreting (female) midwife-assisted natural birth as inferior to (male) physician-guided medicalized birth, placing greater cultural value on hospital birth and less on home birth.

Critics argue that the natural childbirth discourse reflects class and race biases (Nestel 1994/1995). These approaches are based on middle-class rationalist economic ideology that emphasizes control over birth and informed consumer choice (Lupton 2006) and require access to cultural and material resources available only to privileged women. [For example,]

> [Emily] Martin (1990, 310) points to a social class difference in the attitudes of women to control in childbirth. She suggests that middle-class

> women tend to value personal control over all spheres of life, which translates into resisting medical control, . . . including refusing pain relief during labour. Some working-class women, in contrast, are less concerned about engaging in "out-of-control" behaviour during labour, perhaps resisting the middle-class ideology about the desirability of always being in control. (Lupton 2006, 161; see also Zadoroznyj 1999)

These ideologies of childbirth and control are consistent with other related middle-class attitudes such as support for nontraditional sex roles and greater marital closeness that can translate into more spousal support during labor and contribute to women reporting less pain and [more] enjoyment of childbirth (Norr, Block, Charles, Meyering, and Meyers 1977). Relatedly, Bowler (1993) found that in Britain, even midwives used racist stereotypes of Asian women to guide their prenatal care and birthing interactions. Thus, alternative approaches to childbirth do not necessarily guarantee more fair or compassionate treatment.

Finally, some critics (e.g., Lupton 2006) suggest that rather than awarding women increased control, the shift toward more "natural" childbirth (i.e., as the medical profession has moved away from medical intervention such as anesthesia and attempted to provide more support through childbirth classes) has resulted in an increase in the medical gaze and medical surveillance over women's experiences. Specifically, such a shift furthers medical dominance by directing intense medical attention on individual women's behaviors and emphasizing self-control during labor. Moreover, Mardorossian (2003) argues that the trend toward hospitals' attempts to implement more holistic elements often includes the model of husband-as-coach, which not only retains the hospital's authority, but also creates "'natural' childbirth as a site for the production and reproduction of patriarchal and capitalist power" (p. 113). This could be a case of slight demedicalization on some levels over time, at least within the hospital setting, as more "naturalized" elements are implemented in the hospital setting. On the other hand, this trend could reflect both expanded medical jurisdiction and an extended medical gaze, since medical practitioners control the use of such elements in a medical setting, but this does not mean that rates of technological interventions have necessarily decreased (Conrad 2005, 2007). Thus, the incorporation of "natural" aspects of birth into the hospital setting do not further an actual expansion of or increase in "natural" birth as defined by feminist or midwifery literature. . . .

Women's Subjective Experiences of Birth

Given that the vast majority of women in the United States continue to birth in hospitals and experience medical interventions and, therefore, acquiesce to "medical" childbirth according to feminists' perspectives, some scholars have begun to examine more closely women's experiences of medical birth.

Some recent feminist research suggests that women experience medicalized birth in ways that challenge the traditional, negative, feminist stance and a strict medical-versus-natural dichotomy (Bokat 1995; Cohen 2006; Davis-Floyd 1992; Fox and Worts 1999; K. Martin 2003); yet, the conclusions of this research do not always go this far. From this research, we can infer that most women adhere closely to a medical model for birth and do not question the use of particular procedures in the hospital setting, perhaps not knowing or thinking that technological interventions might not be "natural." In fact, medical birth is so commonplace to women in contemporary times that it may seem "natural" to individual women. Yet, from our reading of existing literature, there is little systematic analysis of how the "medical" becomes "natural" in individual women's lives, or how the "natural" becomes foreign and "abnormal" for most. Individual women may operationalize "medical" and "natural" birth in very particular ways—ways that feminist scholars, activists, midwives, or doctors might not.

Studies in countries outside the United States have suggested that decision-making authority is important to birthing women. For example, Macdonald's (2006) study of contemporary midwifery in Canada suggests that midwives themselves may define "natural" differently from feminist scholars. Specifically, she found that some midwives defined a birth as "natural" even when it involved medical intervention, as long as the birthing woman made the decision regarding its use. She suggests that

> what constitutes natural birth is reconceived and relived in ways that are more individual, contextual and contingent. Given that midwifery philosophy stresses that every birth is different, individual meanings of what is natural are derived more from the perspectives of birthing women themselves rather than from any rigid criteria. (2006, 251)

Similarly, in a recent study in the United Kingdom, McCourt (2006) found that midwives were able to employ a caseload model that is structured around a partnership between the midwife and birthing mother in the hospital setting. Her research suggests that even within the same institutional setting, midwives can offer care that is distinct from that of traditional medical providers and that allows birthing women to exercise more autonomy and control. These two studies' findings suggest that for birthing women, control over decision making may be more important than the birth setting or whether or not medical interventions were used.

In contrast, some sociological scholarship on childbirth does seem to suggest that rather than focus on the concepts of control or authority or the actual effects of various medical interventions (like feminist writers have), many women seem to differentiate between natural and medicalized birth based on the absence or presence of analgesia or anesthesia (Davis-Floyd 1992; Dillaway and Brubaker 2006; Fox and Worts 1999). Women often regard this decision of whether to avoid pain or pain-relief medications as the only choice they have in the hospital birth setting (ibid.).

Dillaway and Brubaker (2006) argue that findings about how individual women define and value specific aspects of "medical" or "natural" birth can illustrate the embeddedness of medicalized or "medical" childbirth in U.S. culture, since women do not typically question the use of other technologies during birth. . . .

As Nichols (1996) reports, a number of factors can contribute to women's assessments of their birth experiences, and although the absence or presence of pain can be important, it is not the only measure. Based on her (albeit dated) review of the literature, Nichols identifies "constant" (those unaffected by the physician) factors that influence women's birth experience, as well as those that can be influenced by the heath care provider. Constant factors include cultural and spiritual beliefs, age, social economic status, personality, and parity; those influenced by the provider include stress and anxiety, self-esteem, women's own personal feelings of mastery and control and expectations for the birth, and the birth environment. Her review suggests that there are myriad influences on how women give meaning to the childbirth experience, many of which may have little to do with whether it is defined as "natural" or "medical." . . .

Davis-Floyd (1992) examined the dichotomy between "natural" and "medical" birth through qualitative research with women, focusing broadly on how they themselves define birth vis-à-vis medical options. She identifies three distinct groups of birthing women. First, there are those who fully accept the technocratic ["medical"] model . . . [where] birth is done not by mothers, but by physicians . . . [and characterized by] complete and unquestioning acceptance of physicians' authority and hospital routine, with little or no sense of themselves as active agents in the process (1992, 189). Davis-Floyd describes these women as passive, and as either afraid of the birth and expecting the doctor to take responsibility for the process, or approaching the event intellectually, determined to manage and control the birth rather than experience it with joy.

Davis-Floyd's second group's approach reflects "full acceptance of the holistic model of birth," where women usually give birth at home (1992, 199). These women typically viewed birth from a politically liberal or New Age ideological approach, where birth is a "natural" or spiritual process. The last group Davis-Floyd identifies as "women in-between," those who feel that they make their own choices but give birth in the hospital. Some of these women chose "natural" birth (i.e., birth without drugs) and others accepted this medical intervention as a personal choice or right.

While Davis-Floyd's work takes us toward an understanding of the variation in women's ideological approaches to childbirth and their subjective experiences, she does little to explore the specific medicalization processes and how they shape those experiences. And while Davis-Floyd cites data from interviews with women that suggest a wide array of definitions of natural and medical (especially in her third group of women), she does not complete a full analysis of these variations. In addition, she does not discuss how women's social locations may affect how they define *natural* or *medical* because her sample is reportedly "middle class" (1992, 3) and also presumably white women of similar ages and life stages. Davis-Floyd's work, almost 20 years old, hints at the importance of looking at the value of a "natural" versus "medical" dichotomy and the diversity in women's experiences but never fully completes this job.

Simonds et al. (2007) and Cohen (2006) also begin to examine the variation in women's birth experiences, but do not go so far as to analyze exactly how changes in the medicalization of childbirth shape those experiences, or how they reframe a "natural" versus "medical" dichotomy. In Davis-Floyd's (1992) and Simonds et al.'s (2007) work, it is clear that the authors still uphold feminist ideals of "natural" being intervention-free, non-hospital birth that somewhat color their analysis of how individual women may define their own experience. This is partially because these authors aim to critique an entire system of maternity care, rather than describe individual experiences (even if they use individual women's experiences as examples). . . .

Brubaker and Dillaway (2008) provide an example, based on empirical qualitative research, of how to explore the commonalities and differences among differently located women as they defined "natural" and "medical" childbirth and the notions of choice and control in childbirth. Comparing interview data gathered from three distinct groups of mothers—poor African American teens giving birth in a hospital, middle-class Caucasian adult women giving birth in a hospital, and middle-class Caucasian adult women giving birth in a birthing clinic, as well as existing literature, the authors suggest that "most contemporary birthing women do not expect to have a strictly 'medical' or 'natural' birth, rather something somewhere in the middle," and they "suggest a need to re-conceptualize 'natural' and 'medical' birth as existing on a continuum rather than within a dichotomy" (Brubaker and Dillaway 2008, 239). . . .

Discussion and Future Directions

This review suggests that the medical approach to birth (i.e., that it is a medical event that should take place in the hospital) remains the dominant cultural view. Although many feminists continue to argue for a more natural approach, their critiques remain largely within academic philosophical discourse, as well as among natural childbirth advocates. Additionally, and perhaps more importantly, what constitutes "natural" childbirth continues to be debated and redefined by both practitioners and women themselves. Both feminists and natural childbirth advocates continue to speak to and reflect experiences of privileged women. Sociologists have fallen short of a critical analysis of the factors driving the medicalization of childbirth, how they shape women's subjective experiences at a variety of social locations, and how women themselves define "natural" and "medical" birth.

As Koeske (1983, 12) warned two decades ago, "feminists must be clear about their role. Their perspective is not a simple adjunct to biomedicine.

Neither should it be a repudiation of the role of biological factors in women's experiences or an exclusive focus on psychological and sociocultural factors as these have been traditionally defined." Scholars have not fully responded to Koeske's and others' calls for more complex biosocial analyses of gendered reproductive processes like childbirth, menstruation, and menopause. While this critique could be made about almost any topic (in that most research topics are not fully explored), the study of women's childbirth experiences in contemporary times may allow us to understand better how a dichotomy of "medical" versus "natural" birth remains important, and whether, and how, medicalization is still the key for understanding how women birth babies today. . . .

References

Arney, William Ray. 1982. *Power and the Profession of Obstetrics.* Chicago, IL: The University of Chicago Press.

Baldwin, Rahima. 1992. Homebirth as the standard of care. *Special Delivery* (spring):1–2.

Bokat, Nicole. 1995. Natural Childbirth: From Option to Orthodoxy. *On The Issues* 4(1):36.

Bowler, Isobel. 1993. "They're not the same as us": Midwives' stereotypes of South Asian descent maternity patients. *Sociology of Health and Illness* 15(2):157–78.

Brubaker, Sarah Jane, and Heather Dillaway. 2008. Re-examining the meanings of childbirth: Beyond gender and the "natural" v. "medical" dichotomy. In *Advancing Gender Research from the Nineteenth to the Twenty-First Centuries: Advances in Gender Research*, Vol. 12, edited by Marcia Texler Segal and Vasilikie Demos. Bingley, UK: Emerald Group Publishing Limited.

Cohen, Marisa. 2006. *Deliver This! Make the Childbirth Choice That's Rights for You No Matter What Everyone Else Thinks.* Emeryville, CA: Seal Press.

Conrad, Peter, ed. 2005. *The Sociology of Health and Illness: Critical Perspectives*, 7th ed. New York, NY: Worth Publishers.

Conrad, Peter. 2007. *The Medicalization of Society: On the Transformation of Human Conditions into Treatable Disorders.* Baltimore, MD: Johns Hopkins University Press.

Coward, Rosalind. 1989. *The Whole Truth: The Myth of Alternative Health.* London, UK: Faber and Faber.

Davis-Floyd, Robbie. 1992. *Birth as an American Rite of Passage.* Berkeley, CA: University of California Press.

Dillaway, Heather, and Sarah Jane Brubaker. 2006. Intersectionality and childbirth: How women from different social locations discuss epidural use. *Race, Gender and Class* 13(3–4):16–41.

Fausto-Sterling, Anne. 1992. *Myths of Gender* (rev. ed.). New York, NY: Basic Books.

Foucault, Michel. 1975. *The Birth of the Clinic: An Archeology of Medical Perception.* New York, NY: Vintage Books.

Fox, Bonnie, and Diana Worts. 1999. Revisiting the critique of medicalized childbirth: A contribution to the sociology of birth. *Gender & Society* 13(3):326–46.

Fullerton Judith, and Richard Severino. 1992. In-hospital care for low-risk childbirth. *Journal of Nurse Midwifery* 37:331–47.

Gullette, Margaret M. 1997. Menopause as magic marker: Discursive consolidation in the United States, and strategies for cultural combat. In *Reinterpreting Menopause:*

Cultural and Philosophical Issues, edited by Paul A. Komesaroff, Philipa Rothfield, and Jeanne Daly. New York, NY: Routledge.

Harper, Barbara. 1994. *Gentle Birth Choices*. Rochester, VT: Healing Arts Press.

Jordan, Brigitte. 1980. *Birth in Four Cultures*. Montreal, Quebec, Canada: Eden Press.

Jordanova, Ludmilla. 1989. *Sexual Visions: Images of Gender in Science and Medicine between the Eighteenth and Twentieth Centuries*. London, UK: Harvester Wheatsheaf.

Kahn, Robbie P. 1995. *Bearing Meaning: The Language of Birth*. Chicago, IL: University of Illinois.

Kaufman, Karyn. 1993. Effective control or effective care? *Birth* 20(3):156–58.

Keirse, Marc. 1993. A final comment . . . Managing the uterus, the woman, or whom? *Birth* 20(3):159–62.

Kitzinger, Sheila. 2006. *Birth Crisis*. London, UK: Routledge.

Koeske, Randi D. 1983. Lifting the curse of menstruation: Toward a feminist perspective on the menstrual cycle. *Women & Health* 8:1–15.

Leavitt, Judith W. 1986. *Brought to Bed*. New York, NY: Oxford University Press.

Loe, Meika. 2004. *The Rise of Viagra: How the Little Blue Pill Changed Sex in America*. New York, NY: New York University Press.

Lupton, Deborah. 2006. *Medicine as Culture*. Thousand Oaks, CA: Sage Publications.

Lyons, Antonia C., and Christine Griffin. 2003. Managing menopause: A qualitative analysis of self-help literature for women at midlife. *Social Science and Medicine* 56:1629–42.

Macdonald, Margaret. 2006. Gender expectations: Natural bodies and natural births in the new midwifery in Canada. *Medical Anthropology Quarterly* 20(2):235–56.

Mardorossian, Carine M. 2003. Laboring women, coaching men: Masculinity and childbirth education in the contemporary United States. *Hypatia* 18(3):113–134.

Martin, Emily. 1990. The ideology of reproduction: The reproduction of ideology. In *Uncertain Terms: Negotiating Gender in American Culture*, edited by Faye Ginsburg and Anna Tsing. Boston, MA: Beacon Press.

———. 1992. *The Woman in the Body: A Cultural Analysis of Reproduction* (2nd ed.). Boston, MA: Beacon Press.

Martin, Karin. 2003. Giving Birth Like a Girl. *Gender & Society* 17(1):54–72.

McCourt, Christine. 2006. Supporting Choice and Control? Communication and Interaction between Midwives and Women at the Antenatal Booking Visit. *Social Science & Medicine* 62:1307–18.

Nestel, Sheryl. 1994/1995. "Other" mothers: Race and representation in natural childbirth discourse. *Resources for Feminist Research* 23(4):5.

Nichols, Francine H. 1996. The meaning of the childbirth experience: A review of the literature. *The Journal of Perinatal Education* 5(4):71–77.

Norr, Kathleen L, Carolyn R. Block, Allan Charles, Suzanne Meyering, and Ellen Meyers. 1977. Explaining pain and enjoyment in childbirth. *Journal of Health and Social Behavior* 18(3):260–75.

Oakley, Ann. 1984. *The Captured Womb: A History of the Medical Care of Pregnant Women*. New York, NY: Basil Blackwell, Inc.

———. 1993. *Essays on Women, Medicine, and Health*. Edinburgh, UK: Edinburgh University Press.

Porter, Maureen. 1990. Professional-client relationships and women's reproductive health care. In *Readings in Medical Sociology*, edited by Sarah Cunningham-Burley and Neil P. McKeganey. London, UK: Routledge.

Riessman, Catherine K. 1983. Women and medicalization: A new perspective. *Social Policy* 14(1):3–18.

Rostosky, Sharon, and Cheryl Travis. 1996. Menopause research and the dominance of the biomedical model 1984–1994. *Psychology of Women Quarterly* 20:285–312.

Rothman, Barbara K. 1989. *Recreating Motherhood: Ideology and Technology in a Patriarchal Society.* New York, NY: W.W. Norton & Co.

———. 1991. *In Labor: Woman and Power in the Birthplace.* New York, NY: W.W. Norton.

———. 1993. The active management of physicians. *Birth* 20(3):158–59.

Schimmel, Lynn, Kathy Lee, Patricia Benner, and Leon Schimmel. 1994. A comparison of outcomes between joint and physician only obstetric practices. *Birth* 21:197–203.

Schmied, Virginia, and Deborah Lupton. 2001. Blurring the boundaries: Breastfeeding and maternal subjectivity. *Sociology of Health and Illness* 23:234–50.

Simonds, Wendy, Barbara K. Rothman, and Bari M. Norman. 2007. *Laboring On: Birth in Transition in the United States.* New York, NY: Routledge.

Van Teijlingen, E. 2005. A critical analysis of the medical model as used in the study of pregnancy and childbirth. *Sociological Research Online* 10(2). http://www.socresonline.org.uk/ 10/2/teijlingen.html#porter1999.

Wertz, Robert W., and Dorothy C. Wertz. 1977. *Lying-in: A History of Childbirth in America.* New Haven, CT: Yale University Press.

Zadoroznyj, Maria. 1999. Social class, social selves and social control in childbirth. *Sociology of Health and Illness* 21(3):267–89.

Zola, Irving K. 1972. Medicine as an institution of social control. *Sociological Review* 20(November):487–504.

———. 1981. Medicine as an institution of social control. In *The Sociology of Health and Illness: Critical Perspectives*, edited by Peter Conrad. New York, NY: St. Martin's Press.

———. 2005. Medicine as an institution of social control. In *The Sociology of Health and Illness: Critical Perspectives,* 7th ed., edited by Peter Conrad. New York, NY: Worth Publishers.

5

Foucault, Femininity, and the Modernization of Patriarchal Power

Sandra Lee Bartky

Early feminist scholars often emphasized how social organizations and institutions such as the Church, family, police, schools, and medicine controlled women's behavior by rewarding girls and women who conformed to social expectations and punishing those who did not. In contrast, philosopher Michel Foucault emphasized how modern society instead creates "docile bodies"—bodies that meet social expectations without complaint or resistance—not through punishment, but by teaching individuals to accept those expectations as their own and to live as if they might *be punished at any moment.*

Foucault developed his ideas about the social creation of docile bodies through his research on the history of prisons. In the premodern world, kings and churches instilled obedience in the population by gruesomely and publicly torturing criminals and burning heretics at the stake. In contrast, according to Foucault, modern societies use a very different approach to instilling obedience. Specifically, obedience results from a "micro-physics of power" that fragments the body's time, space, and movement. This is evident in the modern prison timetable, for which every moment of the day—from morning roll call to evening lights-out—is marked and controlled. This approach is also encapsulated in the idea of the Panopticon. Designed by philosopher Jeremy Bentham, the Panopticon was a proposed "modern" prison design in which a single prison guard, out of sight of the prisoners, would staff a central guard tower. Because the guard could see anywhere in the prison, but the prisoners could never tell if the guard was watching them, the prisoners (at least in theory) would never dare to revolt. Similarly, Foucault argues, workers in factories and students in schools—institutions with highly regimented spaces—come to believe that they are always under surveillance and therefore come to accept the rules and to discipline themselves.

In "Foucault, Femininity, and the Modernization of Patriarchal Power," philosopher Sandra Lee Bartky extends Foucault's ideas to female bodies. She describes how women internalize men's social expectations regarding female appearance and behavior and then strive to meet those expectations, through such "disciplinary practices" as dieting, sitting with knees together, and wearing high heels. Although Bartky wrote this article over two decades ago, these disciplinary practices remain evident today. For example, surveys, such as the National Eating Trends survey, find that about a quarter of U.S. women report being on a weight-loss diet at any one point in time.

Bartky further argues that these disciplinary practices, or "disciplines of femininity," keep women smaller, weaker, less powerful, and constantly struggling with shame when they cannot meet impossible appearance goals (especially if they are poor or minority). As a result, these disciplines not only reflect women's subordination to men's expectations but also reinforce that subordination. Yet because women seem to accept these disciplines willingly—as she writes, "no one is ever marched off for electrolysis at gunpoint"—we rarely recognize the subtle process through which women are pressed to accept those disciplines. Nevertheless, Bartky suggests, the clash between women's increasing economic and social freedom, on the one hand, and their increasing bodily disciplines, on the other, may eventually lead more women to resist their subordination and the disciplines of femininity.

I.

In a striking critique of modern society, Michel Foucault (1979) has argued that the rise of parliamentary institutions and of new conceptions of political liberty was accompanied by a darker counter-movement, by the emergence of a new and unprecedented discipline directed against the body. More is required of the body now than mere political allegiance or the appropriation of the products of its labor: the new discipline invades the body and seeks to regulate its very forces and operations, the economy and efficiency of its movements.

The disciplinary practices Foucault describes are tied to peculiarly modern forms of the army, the school, the hospital, the prison, and the manufactory; the aim of these disciplines is to increase the utility of the body, to augment its forces:

> What was then being formed was a policy of coercions that act upon the body, a calculated manipulation of its elements, its gestures, its behaviour. The human body was entering a machinery of power that explores it, breaks it down and rearranges it. A "political anatomy," which was also a "mechanics of power," was being born; it defined how one may have a hold over others'

> bodies, not only so that they may do what one wishes, but so that they may operate as one wishes, with the techniques, the speed and the efficiency that one determines. Thus, discipline produces subjected and practiced bodies, "docile" bodies. (1979, 138)

The production of "docile bodies" requires that an uninterrupted coercion be directed to the very processes of bodily activity, not just their result; this "micro-physics of power" fragments and partitions the body's time, its space, and its movements (Foucault 1979, 28).

The student, then, is enclosed within a classroom and assigned to a desk he cannot leave; his ranking in the class can be read off the position of his desk in the serially ordered and segmented space of the classroom itself. Foucault (1979, 147) tells us that "Jean-Baptiste de la Salle dreamt of a classroom in which the spatial distribution might provide a whole series of distinctions at once, according to the pupil's progress, worth, character, application, cleanliness and parent's fortune." The student must sit upright, feet upon the floor, head erect; he may not slouch or fidget; his animate body is brought into a fixed correlation with the inanimate desk.

The minute breakdown of gestures and movements required of soldiers at drill is far more relentless:

> Bring the weapon forward. In three stages. Raise the rifle with the right hand, bringing it close to the body so as to hold it perpendicular with the right knee, the end of the barrel at eye level, grasping it by striking it with the right hand, the arm held close to the body at waist height. At the second stage, bring the rifle in front of you with the left hand, the barrel in the middle between the two eyes, vertical, the right hand grasping it at the small of the butt, the arm outstretched, the triggerguard resting on the first finger, the left hand at the height of the notch, the thumb lying along the barrel against the moulding. At the third stage. . . . (Foucault 1979, 153)[1]

These "body-object articulations" of the soldier and his weapon, the student and his desk effect a "coercive link with the apparatus of production." We are far indeed from older forms of control that "demanded of the body only signs or products, forms of expression or the result of labour" (Foucault 1979, 153).

The body's time, in these regimes of power, is as rigidly controlled as its space: the factory whistle and the school bell mark a division of time into discrete and segmented units that regulate the various activities of the day. The following timetable, similar in spirit to the ordering of my grammar school classroom, is suggested for French "écoles mutuelles" of the early nineteenth century:

> 8:45 entrance of the monitor, 8:52 the monitor's summons, 8:56 entrance of the children and prayer, 9:00 the children go to their benches, 9:04 first slate, 9:08 end of dictation, 9:12 second slate, etc. (Foucault 1979, 150)

Control this rigid and precise cannot be maintained without a minute and relentless surveillance.

Jeremy Bentham's design for the Panopticon, a model prison, captures for Foucault the essence of the disciplinary society. At the periphery of the Panopticon, a circular structure; at the center, a tower with wide windows that opens onto the inner side of the ring. The structure on the periphery is divided into cells, each with two windows, one facing the windows of the tower, the other facing the outside, allowing an effect of backlighting to make any figure visible within the cell. "All that is needed, then, is to place a supervisor in a central tower and to shut up in each cell a madman, a patient, a condemned man, a worker or a schoolboy" (Foucault 1979, 200). Each inmate is alone, shut off from effective communication with his fellows, but constantly visible from the tower. The effect of this is "to induce in the inmate a state of conscious and permanent visibility that assures the automatic functioning of power"; each becomes to himself his own jailer (Foucault 1979, 201). This "state of conscious and permanent visibility" is a sign that the tight, disciplinary control of the body has gotten a hold on the mind as well. In the perpetual self-surveillance of the inmate lies the genesis of the celebrated "individualism" and heightened self-consciousness that are hallmarks of modern times. For Foucault (1979, 228), the structure and effects of the Panopticon resonate throughout society: Is it surprising that "prisons resemble factories, schools, barracks, hospitals, which all resemble prisons"?

Foucault's account in *Discipline and Punish* of the disciplinary practices that produce the "docile bodies" of modernity is a genuine *tour de force*, incorporating a rich theoretical account of the ways in which instrumental reason takes hold of the body with a mass of historical detail. But Foucault treats the body throughout as if it were one, as if the bodily experiences of men and women did not differ and as if men and women bore the same relationship to the characteristic institutions of modern life. Where is the account of the disciplinary practices that engender the "docile bodies" of women, bodies more docile than the bodies of men? Women, like men, are subject to many of the same disciplinary practices Foucault describes. But he is blind to those disciplines that produce a modality of embodiment that is peculiarly feminine. To overlook the forms of subjection that engender the feminine body is to perpetuate the silence and powerlessness of those upon whom these disciplines have been imposed. Hence, even though a liberatory note is sounded in Foucault's critique of power, his analysis as a whole reproduces that sexism which is endemic throughout Western political theory.

We are born male or female, but not masculine or feminine. Femininity is an artifice, an achievement, "a mode of enacting and reenacting received gender norms which surface as so many styles of flesh" (Butler 1985, 11). In what follows, I shall examine those disciplinary practices that produce a body which in gesture and appearance is recognizably feminine. I consider three categories of such practices: those that aim to produce a body of a certain size and general configuration; those that bring forth from this body a specific repertoire of gestures, postures, and movements; and those that are directed toward the display of this body as an ornamented surface. I shall examine the nature of these disciplines, how they are imposed and by whom. I shall probe the effects of the imposition of such discipline on female identity and subjectivity. In the final section I shall argue that these disciplinary practices must be understood in the light of the modernization of patriarchal domination, a modernization that unfolds historically according to the general pattern described by Foucault.

II.

Styles of the female figure vary over time and across cultures: they reflect cultural obsessions and preoccupations in ways that are still poorly understood. Today, massiveness, power, or abundance in a woman's body is met with distaste. The current body of fashion is taut, small-breasted, narrow-hipped, and of a slimness bordering on emaciation; it is a silhouette that seems more appropriate to an adolescent boy or a newly pubescent girl than to an adult woman. Since ordinary women have normally quite different dimensions, they must of course diet.

Mass-circulation women's magazines run articles on dieting in virtually every issue. The *Ladies' Home Journal* of February 1986 carries a "Fat Burning Exercise Guide," while *Mademoiselle* offers to "Help Stamp Out Cellulite" with "Six Sleek-Down Strategies." After the diet-busting Christmas holidays and, later, before summer bikini season, the titles of these features become shriller and more arresting. The reader is now addressed in the imperative mode: Jump into shape for summer! Shed ugly winter fat with the all-new Grapefruit Diet! More women than men visit diet doctors, while women greatly outnumber men in such self-help groups as Weight Watchers and Overeaters Anonymous—in the case of the latter, by well over 90 percent (Millman 1980, 46).

Dieting disciplines the body's hungers: appetite must be monitored at all times and governed by an iron will. Since the innocent need of the organism for food will not be denied, the body becomes one's enemy, an alien being bent on thwarting the disciplinary project. Anorexia nervosa, which has now assumed epidemic proportions, is to women of the late twentieth century what hysteria was to women of an earlier day: the crystallization in a pathological mode of a widespread cultural obsession (Bordo 1985–86). A survey taken recently at UCLA is astounding: of 260 students interviewed, 27.3 of women but only 5.8 percent of men said they were "terrified" of getting fat; 28.7 percent of women but only 7.5 percent of men said they were obsessed or "totally preoccupied" with food. The body images of women and men are strikingly different as well: 35 percent of women but only 12.5 percent of men said they felt fat though other people told them they were thin. Women in the survey wanted to weigh ten pounds less than their average weight; men felt they were within a pound of their ideal weight. A total of 5.9 percent of women and no men met the psychiatric criteria for anorexia or Bulimia (*USA Today* 1985).

Dieting is one discipline imposed upon a body subject to the "tyranny of slenderness"; exercise is another (Chernin 1981). Since men as well as women exercise, it is not always easy in the case of women to distinguish what is done for the sake of physical fitness from what is done in obedience to the requirements of femininity. Men as well as women lift weights and do yoga, calisthenics, and aerobics, though "jazzercise" is largely a female pursuit. Men and women alike engage themselves with a variety of machines, each designed to call forth from the body a different exertion: there are Nautilus machines, rowing machines, ordinary and motorized exercycles, portable hip and leg cycles, belt massagers, trampolines, treadmills, and arm and leg pulleys. However, given the widespread female obsession with weight, one suspects that many women are working out with these apparatuses in the health club or at the gym with an aim in mind and in a spirit quite different from men's.

But there are classes of exercises meant for women alone, these designed not to firm or reduce the body's size overall, but to resculpture its various parts on the current model. M. J. Saffon (1981), "international beauty expert," assures us that his twelve basic facial exercises can erase frown lines, smooth the forehead, raise hollow cheeks, banish crow's feet, and tighten the muscles under the chin. There are exercises to build the breasts and exercises to banish "cellulite," said by "figure consultants" to be a special type of female fat. There is "spot-reducing," an umbrella term that covers dozens of punishing exercises designed to reduce "problem areas" like thick ankles or "saddlebag" thighs. The very idea of "spot-reducing" is both scientifically unsound and cruel, for it raises expectations in women that can never be realized—the pattern in which fat is deposited or removed is known to be genetically determined.

It is not only her natural appetite or unreconstructed contours that pose a danger to woman: the very expressions of her face can subvert the disciplinary project of bodily perfection. An expressive face lines and creases more readily than an inexpressive one. Hence, if women are unable to suppress strong emotions, they can at least learn to inhibit the tendency of the face to register them. Sophia Loren (1984, 57) recommends a unique solution to this problem: a piece of tape applied to the forehead or between the brows will tug at the skin when one frowns and act as a reminder to relax the face. The tape is to be worn whenever a woman is home alone.

III.

There are significant gender differences in gesture, posture, movement, and general bodily comportment: women are far more restricted than men in their manner of movement and in their spatiality. In her classic paper on the subject, Iris Young (1980) observes that a space seems to surround women in imagination that they are hesitant to move beyond: this manifests itself both in a reluctance to reach, stretch, and extend the body to meet resistances of matter in motion—as in sport or in the performance of physical tasks—and in a typically constricted posture and general style of movement. Woman's space is not a field in which her bodily intentionality can be freely realized but an enclosure in which she feels herself positioned and by which she is confined (Wex 1979). The "loose woman" violates those norms: her looseness is manifest not only in her morals, but in her manner of speech and quite literally in the free and easy way she moves.

In an extraordinary series of over two thousand photographs, many candid shots taken in the street, the German photographer Marianne Wex (1979) has documented differences in typical masculine and feminine body posture. Women sit waiting for trains with arms close to the body, hands folded together in their laps, toes pointing straight ahead or turned inward, and legs pressed together. The women in these photographs make themselves small and narrow, harmless; they seem tense; they take up little space. Men, on the other hand, expand into the available space; they sit with legs far apart and arms flung out at some distance from the body. Most common in these sitting male figures is what Wex calls the "proffering position": the men sit with legs thrown wide apart, crotch visible, feet pointing outward, often with an arm and a casually dangling hand resting comfortably on an open, spread thigh.

In proportion to total body size, a man's stride is longer than a woman's. The man has more spring and rhythm to his step; he walks with toes pointed outward, holds his arms at a greater distance from his body and swings them farther; he tends to point the whole hand in the direction he is moving. The woman holds her arms closer to her body, palms against her sides; her walk is circumspect. If she has subjected herself to the additional constraint of high-heeled shoes, her body is thrown forward and off balance: the struggle to walk under these conditions shortens her stride still more.

But women's movement is subjected to a still finer discipline. Feminine faces, as well as bodies, are trained to the expression of deference. Under male scrutiny, women will avert their eyes or cast them downward; the female gaze is trained to abandon its claim to the sovereign status of seer. The "nice" girls learns to avoid the bold and unfettered staring of the "loose" woman who looks at whatever and whomever she pleases. Women are trained to smile more than men, too. In the economy of smiles, as elsewhere, there is evidence that women are exploited, for they give more than they receive in return; in a smile elicitation study, one researcher found that the rate of smile return by women was 93 percent, by men only 67 percent (Henley 1977, 176). In many typical women's jobs, graciousness, deference, and the readiness to serve are part of the work; this requires the worker to fix a smile on her face for a good part of the working day, whatever her inner state (Hochschild 1983). The economy of touching is out of balance, too: men touch women more often and on more parts of the body than women touch men: female secretaries, factory workers, and waitresses report that such liberties are taken routinely with their bodies (Henley 1977, 108).

Feminine movement, gesture, and posture must exhibit not only constriction, but grace and a certain eroticism restrained by modesty: all three. Here is field for the operation for a whole new training: a woman must stand with stomach pulled in, shoulders thrown slightly back and chest out, this to display her bosom to maximum advantage. While she must walk in the confined fashion appropriate to women, her movements must, at the same time, be combined with a subtle but provocative hip-roll. But too much display is taboo: women in short, low-cut dresses are told to avoid bending over at all, but if they must, great care must be taken to avoid an unseemly display of breast or rump. From time to time, fashion magazines offer quite precise instructions on the proper way of getting in and out of cars. These instructions combine all three imperatives of women's movements: a woman must not allow her arms and leg to flail about in all directions, she must try to manage her movements with the appearance of grace—no small accomplishment when one is climbing out of the back seat of a Fiat—and she is well-advised to use the opportunity for a certain display of leg.

All the movements we have described so far are self-movements; they arise from within the woman's own body. But in a way that normally goes unnoticed, males in couples may literally steer a woman everywhere she goes: down the street, around corners, into elevators, through doorways, into her chair at the dinner table, around the dance floor. The man's movement "is not necessarily heavy and pushy or physical in an ugly way; it is light and gentle but firm in the way of the most confident equestrians with the best trained horses" (Henley 1977, 149).

IV.

We have examined some of the disciplinary practices a woman must master in pursuit of a body of the right size and shape that also displays the proper styles of feminine motility. But woman's body is an ornamented surface too, and there is much discipline involved in this production as well. Here, especially in the application of makeup and the selection of clothes, art and discipline converge, though, as I shall argue, there is less art involved than one might suppose.

A woman's skin must be soft, supple, hairless, and smooth; ideally, it should betray no sign of wear, experience, age, or deep thought. Hair must be removed not only from the face but from large surfaces of the body as well, from legs and thighs, an operation accomplished by shaving, buffing with fine sandpaper, or applying foul-smelling depilatories. With the new high-leg bathing suits and leotards, a substantial amount of pubic hair must be removed too. The removal of facial hair can be more specialized. Eyebrows are plucked out by the roots with a tweezers. Hot wax is sometimes poured onto the mustache and cheeks and then ripped away when it cools. The woman who wants a more permanent result may try electrolysis: this involves the killing of hair root by the passage of an electric current down a needle that has been inserted into its base. The procedure is painful and expensive.

The development of what one "beauty expert" calls "good skincare habits" requires not only attention to health, the avoidance of strong facial expressions, and the performance of facial exercises, but the regular use of skincare preparations, many to be applied more often than once a day: cleansing lotions (ordinary soap and water "upsets the skin's acid and alkaline balance"), wash-off cleansers (milder than cleansing lotions), astringents, toners, makeup removers, night creams, nourishing creams, eye creams, moisturizers, skin balances, body lotions, hand creams, lip pomades, suntan lotions, sunscreens, and facial masks. Provision of the proper facial mask is complex: there are sulfur masks for pimples; oil or hot masks for dry areas; if these fail, then tightening masks; conditioning masks; peeling masks; cleansing masks made of herbs, cornmeal, or almonds; and mudpacks. Black women may wish to use "fade creams" to "even skin tone." Skincare preparations are never just sloshed onto the skin, but applied according to precise rules: eye cream is dabbed on gently in movements toward, never away from, the nose; cleansing cream is applied in outward directions only, straight down the nose and up and out on the cheeks (Klinger and Rowes 1978).

The normalizing discourse of modern medicine is enlisted by the cosmetics industry to gain credibility for its claims. Dr. Christian Barnard lends his enormous prestige to the Glycel line of "cellular treatment activators"; these contain "glycosphingolipids" that can "make older skin behave and look like younger skins" (ads in *Chicago Magazine*, March 1986). The Clinique computer at any Clinique counter will select a combination of preparations just right for you. Ultima II contains "procollagen" in its anti-aging eye cream that "provides hydration" to "demoralizing lines." "Biotherm" eye cream dramatically improves the "biomechanical properties of the skin" (*Chicago Magazine* 1986). The Park Avenue clinic of Dr. Zizmor, "chief of dermatology at one of New York's leading hospitals," offers not only such medical treatment as derma-brasion and chemical peeling, but "total deep skin cleansing" as well (ad in *Essence* magazine, April 1986, 25).[2]

Really good skincare habits require the use of a variety of aids and devices: facial steamers, faucet filters to collect impurities in the water, borax to soften it, a humidifier for the bedroom, electric massagers, backbrushes, complexion brushes, loofahs, pumice stones, and blackhead removers. I will not detail the implements or techniques involved in the manicure or pedicure.

The ordinary circumstances of life as well as a wide variety of activities cause a crisis in skincare and require a stepping-up of the regimen as well as an additional laying-on of preparations. Skincare discipline requires a specialized knowledge: a woman must know what to do if she has been skiing, taking medication, doing vigorous exercise, boating, or swimming in chlorinated pools; or if she has been exposed to pollution, heated rooms, cold, sun, harsh weather, the pressurized cabins on airplanes, saunas or steam rooms, fatigue, or stress. Like the schoolchild or prisoner, the woman mastering good skincare habits is put on a timetable: Georgette Klinger requires that a shorter or longer period of attention be paid to the complexion at least four times a day (Klinger and Rowes 1978, 137–40). Haircare, like skincare, requires a similar investment of time, the use of a wide variety of preparations, the mastery of a set of techniques, and, again, the acquisition of a specialized knowledge.

The crown and pinnacle of good haircare and skincare is, of course, the arrangement of the hair and the application of cosmetics. Here the regimen of haircare, skincare, manicure, and pedicure is recapitulated in another mode. A woman must learn the proper manipulation of a large number of devices—the blow dryer, styling brush, eyelash curler, and mascara brush. And she must learn to apply a wide variety of products—foundation, toner, covering stick, mascara, eyeshadow, eyegloss, blusher, lipstick, rouge, lip gloss, hair dye, hair rinse, hair lightener, hair "relaxer," and so on.

In the language of fashion magazine and cosmetic ads, making-up is typically portrayed as an aesthetic activity in which a woman can express her individuality. In reality, while cosmetic styles change every decade or so, and while some variation in makeup is permitted depending on the occasion, making-up the face is, in fact, a highly stylized activity that gives little rein to self-expression. Painting the face is not like painting a picture; at best, it might be described as painting the same picture over and over again with minor variations. Little latitude is permitted in what is considered appropriate makeup for the office and for most social occasions; indeed, the woman who used cosmetics in a genuinely novel and imaginative way is liable to be seen not as an artist but as an eccentric. Furthermore, since a properly made-up face is, if not a card of entree, at least a badge of acceptability in most social and professional contexts, the woman who chooses not to wear cosmetics at all faces sanctions of a sort that will never be applied to someone who chooses not to paint a watercolor.

V.

Are we dealing in all this merely with sexual *difference*? Scarcely. The disciplinary practices I have described are part of the process by which the ideal body of femininity—and hence the feminine body-subject—is constructed; in doing this, they produce a "practiced and subjected" body, that is, a body on which an inferior status has been inscribed. A woman's face must be made-up, that is to say, made-over, and so must her body: she is ten pounds overweight; her lips must be made more kissable, her complexion dewier, her eyes more mysterious. The "art" of makeup is the art of disguise, but this presupposes that a woman's face, unpainted, is defective. Soap and water, a shave, and routine attention to hygiene may be enough for *him*; for *her* they are not. The strategy of much beauty-related advertising is to suggest to women that their bodies are deficient; but even without such more or less explicit teaching, the media images of perfect female beauty that bombard us daily leave no doubt in the minds of most women that they fail to measure up. The technologies for femininity are taken up and practiced by women against the background of a pervasive sense of bodily deficiency; this accounts for what is often their compulsive or even ritualistic character.

The disciplinary project of femininity is a "setup": it requires such radical and extensive measures of bodily transformation that virtually every woman who gives herself to it is destined in some degree to fail. Thus, a measure of shame is added to a woman's sense that the body she inhabits is deficient: she ought to take better care of herself; she might after all have jogged that last mile. Many women are without the time or resources to provide themselves with even the minimum of what such a regimen requires, for example, a decent diet. Here is an additional source of shame for poor women, who must bear what our society regards as the more general shame of poverty. The burdens poor women bear in this regard are not merely psychological, since conformity to the prevailing standards of bodily acceptability is a known factor in economic mobility.

The larger disciplines that construct a "feminine" body out of a female one are by no means race or class-specific. There is little evidence that women of color or working-class women are in general less committed to the incarnation of an ideal femininity than their more privileged sisters: this is not to deny the many ways in which factors of race, class, locality, ethnicity, or personal taste can be expressed within the kinds of practices I have described. The rising young corporate executive may buy her cosmetics at Bergdorf-Goodman, while the counter-server at McDonald's gets her at the K-Mart; the one may join an expensive "upscale" health club, while the other may have to make do with the $9.49 GFX Body-Flex II Home-Gym advertised in the *National Enquirer*: both are aiming at the same general result.

In the regime of institutionalized heterosexuality, woman must make herself "object and prey" for the man: it is for him that these eyes are limpid pools, this cheek baby-smooth (de Beauvoir 1968, 642). In contemporary patriarchal culture, a panoptical male connoisseur resides within the consciousness of most women: they stand perpetually before his gaze and under his judgment. Woman lives her body as seen by another, by an anonymous patriarchal Other. We are often told that "women dress for other women." There is some truth in this: who but someone engaged in a project similar to my own can appreciate the panache with which I bring it off? But women know for whom this game is played: they know that a pretty young woman is likelier to become a flight attendant than a plain one, and that a well-preserved older woman has a better chance of holding onto her husband than one who has "let herself go."

Here it might be objected that performance for another in no way signals the inferiority of the performer to the one for whom the performance is intended: the actor, for example, depends on his audience but is in no way inferior to it; he is not demeaned by his dependency. While femininity is surely something enacted, the analogy to theater breaks down in a number of ways. First, as I argued earlier, the self-determination we think of as requisite to an artistic career is lacking here: femininity as spectacle is something in which virtually every woman is required to participate. Second, the precise nature of the criteria by which women are judged, not only the inescapability of judgment itself, reflects gross imbalances in the social power of the sexes that do not mark the relationship of artists and their audiences. An aesthetic of femininity, for example, that mandates fragility and a lack of muscular strength produces female bodies that can offer little resistance to physical abuse, and the physical abuse of women by men, as we know, is widespread. It is true that the current fitness movement has permitted women to develop more muscular strength and endurance than was heretofore allowed; indeed, images of women have begun to appear in the mass media that seem to eroticize this new muscularity. But a woman may by no means develop more muscular strength than her partner; the bride who would tenderly carry her groom across the threshold is a figure of comedy, not romance.

Under the current "tyranny of slenderness" women are forbidden to become large or massive; they must take up as little space as possible. The very contours a woman's body takes on as she matures—the fuller breasts and rounded hips—have become distasteful. The body by which a women feels herself judged and which by rigorous discipline she must try to assume is the body of early adolescence, slight and unformed, a body lacking flesh or substance, a body in whose very contours the image of immaturity has been inscribed. The requirement that a woman maintain a smooth and hairless skin carries further the theme of inexperience, for an infantilized face must accompany her infantilized body, a face that never ages or furrows its brow in thought. The face of the ideally feminine woman must never display the marks of character, wisdom, and experience that we so admire in men.

To succeed in the provision of a beautiful or sexy body gains a woman attention and some admiration but little real respect and rarely any social power. A woman's effort to master feminine body discipline will lack importance just because she does it: her activity partakes of the general depreciation of everything female. In spite of unrelenting pressure to "make the most of what she has," women are ridiculed and dismissed for their interest in such "trivial" things as clothes and makeup. Further, the narrow identification of woman with sexuality and the body in a society that has for centuries displayed profound suspicion toward both does little to raise her status. Even the most adored female bodies complain routinely of their situation in ways that reveal an implicit understanding that there is something demeaning in the kind of attention they receive. Marilyn Monroe, Elizabeth Taylor, and Farrah Fawcett have all wanted passionately to become actresses-artists—and not just "sex objects."

But it is perhaps in their more restricted motility and comportment that the inferiorization of women's bodies is most evident. Women's typical bodylanguage, a language of relative tension and constriction, is understood to be a language of subordination when it is enacted by men in male status hierarchies. In groups of men, those with higher status typically assume looser and more relaxed postures: the boss lounges comfortably behind the desk, while the applicant sits tense and rigid on the edge of his seat. Higher status individuals may touch their subordinates more than they themselves get touched; they initiate more eye contact and are smiled at by their inferiors more than they are observed to smile in return (Henley 1977). What is announced in the comportment of superiors is confidence and ease, especially ease of access to the Other. Female constraint in posture and movement is no doubt overdetermined: the fact that women tend to sit and stand with legs, feet, and knees close or touching may well be a coded declaration of sexual circumspection in a society that still maintains a double standard, or an effort, albeit unconscious, to guard the genital area. In the latter case, a woman's tight and constricted posture must be seen as the expression of her need to ward off real or symbolic sexual attack. Whatever proportions must be assigned in the final display to fear or deference, one thing is clear: woman's body language speaks eloquently, though silently, of her subordinate status in a hierarchy of gender.

VI.

If what we have described is a genuine discipline—a system, in Foucault's words (1979, 222), of "micro-power" that is "essentially non-egalitarian and asymmetrical"—who then are the disciplinarians? Who is the top sergeant in the disciplinary regime of femininity? Historically, the law has had some responsibility for enforcement: in times gone by, for example, individuals who appeared in public in the clothes of the other sex could be arrested. While cross-dressers are still liable to some harassment, the kind of discipline we are considering is not the business of the police or the courts. Parents and teachers, of course, have extensive influence, admonishing girls to be demure and ladylike, to "smile pretty," to sit with their legs together. The influence of the media is pervasive, too, constructing as it does an image of the female body as spectacle, nor can we ignore the role played by "beauty experts" or by emblematic public personages such as Jane Fonda and Lynn Redgrave.

But none of these individuals—the skincare consultant, the parent, the policeman—does in fact wield the kind of authority that is typically invested in those who manage more straightforward disciplinary institutions. The disciplinary power that inscribes femininity in the female body is everywhere and it is nowhere; the disciplinarian is everyone and yet no one in particular. Women regarded as overweight, for example, report that they are regularly admonished to diet, sometimes by people they scarcely know. These intrusions are often softened by reference to the natural prettiness just waiting to emerge: "People have always said that I had a beautiful face, and 'if you'd only lose weight you'd be really beautiful'" (Millman 1980, 80). Here, "people"—friends and casual acquaintances alike—act to enforce prevailing standards of body size.

Foucault tends to identify the imposition of discipline upon the body with the operation of specific institutions, for example, the school, the factory, the prison. To do this, however, is to overlook the extent to which discipline can be institutionally *unbound* as well as institutionally bound.[3] The anonymity of disciplinary power and its wide dispersion have consequences that are crucial to a proper understanding of the subordination of women. The absence of a formal institutional structure and of authorities invested with the power to carry out institutional directives creates the impression that the production of femininity is either entirely voluntary or natural. The several senses of "discipline" are instructive here. On the one hand, discipline is something imposed on subjects of an "essentially nonegalitarian and asymmetrical" system of authority. Schoolchildren, convicts, and draftees are subject to discipline in this sense. But discipline can be sought voluntarily as well—for example, when an individual seeks initiation into the spiritual discipline of Zen Buddhism. Discipline can, of course, be both at once: the volunteer may seek the physical and occupational training offered by the army without the army's ceasing in any way to be the instrument by which he and other members of his class are kept in disciplined subjection. Feminine bodily discipline has this dual character: on the one hand, no one is marched off for electrolysis at gunpoint, nor can we fail to appreciate the initiative and ingenuity displayed by countless women in an attempt to master the rituals of beauty. Nevertheless, insofar as the disciplinary practices of femininity produce a "subjected and practiced," an inferiorized, body, they must be understood as aspects of a far larger discipline, an oppressive and inegalitarian system of sexual subordination. This system aims at turning women into the docile and compliant companions of men just as surely as the army aims to turn its raw recruits into soldiers.

Now the transformation of oneself into a properly feminine body may be any or all of the following: a rite of passage into adulthood, the adoption and celebration of a particular aesthetic, a way of announcing one's economic level and social status, a way to triumph over other women in the competition for men or jobs, or an opportunity for massive narcissistic indulgence (Bartky 1982). The social construction of the feminine body is all these things, but at its base it is discipline, too, and discipline of the inegalitarian sort. The absence of formally identifiable disciplinarians and of a public schedule of sanctions only disguises the extent to which the imperative to be "feminine" serves the interest of domination. This is a lie in which all concur: making-up is merely artful play; one's first pair of high-heeled shoes is an innocent part of growing up, not the modern equivalent of foot-binding.

Why aren't all women feminists? In modern industrial societies, women are not kept in line by fear of retaliatory male violence; their victimization is not that of the South African black [under the former system of apartheid]. Nor will it suffice to say that a false consciousness engendered in women by patriarchal ideology is at the basis of female subordination. This is not to deny that women are often subject to gross male violence or that women and men alike are ideologically mystified by the dominant gender arrangements. What I wish to suggest instead is that an adequate understanding of women's oppression will require an appreciation of the extent to which not only women's lives but their very subjectivities are structured within an ensemble of systematically duplicitous practices. The feminine discipline of the body is a case in point: the practices that construct this body have an overt aim and character far removed, indeed, radically distinct, from their overt function. In this regard, the system of gender subordination, like the wage-bargain under capitalism, illustrates in its own way the ancient tension between what-is and what-appears: the phenomenal forms in which it is manifested are often quite different from the real relations that form its deeper structure.

VII.

The lack of formal public sanctions does not mean that a woman who is unable or unwilling to submit herself to the appropriate body discipline will face no sanctions at all. On the contrary, she faces a very severe sanction indeed in a world dominated by men: the refusal of male patronage. For the heterosexual woman, this may mean the loss of a badly needed intimacy; for both heterosexual women and lesbians, it may well mean the refusal of a decent livelihood.

As noted earlier, women punish themselves too for the failure to conform. The growing literature on women's body size is filled with wrenching confessions of shame from the overweight:

> I felt clumsy and huge. I felt that I would knock over furniture, bump into things, tip over chairs, not fit into VW's especially when people were trying to crowd into the back seat. I felt like I was taking over the whole room. . . . I felt disgusting and like a slob. In the summer I felt hot and sweaty and I knew people saw my sweat as evidence that I was too fat.

> I feel so terrible about the way I look that I cut off connection with my body. I operate from the neck up. I do not look in mirrors. I do not want to spend time buying clothes. I do not want to spend time with make-up because it's painful for me to look at myself. (Millman 1980, 80, 195)

> I can no longer bear to look at myself. . . . Whenever I have to stand in front of a mirror to comb my hair I tie a large towel around my neck. Even at night I slip my nightgown on before I take off my blouse and pants. But all this has only made it worse and worse. It's been so long since I've really looked at my body. (Chernin 1981, 53)

The depth of these women's shame is a measure of the extent to which all women have internalized patriarchal standards of bodily acceptability. A fuller examination of what is meant here by "internalization" may shed light on a question posed earlier: Why isn't every woman a feminist?

Something is "internalized" when it gets incorporated into the structure of the self. By "structure of the self" I refer to those modes of perception and of self-perception that allow a self to distinguish itself both from other selves and from things that are not selves. I have described elsewhere (Bartky 1982) how a generalized male witness comes to structure woman's consciousness of herself as a bodily being. This, then, is one meaning of "internalization." The sense of oneself as a distinct and valuable individual is tied not only to the sense of how one is perceived, but also to what one knows, especially to what one knows how to do; this is a second sense of "internalization." Whatever its ultimate effect, discipline can provide the individual upon whom it is imposed with a sense of mastery as well as a secure sense of identity. There is a certain contradiction here: while its imposition may promote a larger disempowerment, discipline may bring with it a certain development of a person's powers. Women, then, like other individuals, have a stake in the perpetuation of their skills, whatever it may have cost to acquire them and quite apart from the question whether, as a gender, they would have been better off had they never had to acquire them in the first place. Hence, feminism, especially a genuinely radical feminism that questions the patriarchal construction of the female body, threatens women with a certain de-skilling, something people normally resist: beyond this, it calls into question that aspect of personal identity that is tied to the development of a sense of competence.

Resistance from this source may be joined by a reluctance to part with the rewards of compliance; further, many women will resist the abandonment of an aesthetic that defines what they take to be beautiful. But there is still another source of resistance, one more subtle, perhaps, but tied once again to questions of identity and internalization. To have a body felt to be "feminine"—a body socially constructed through the appropriate practices—is in most cases crucial to a woman's sense of herself as female and, since persons currently can *be* only as male or female, to her sense of herself as an existing individual. To possess such a body may also be essential to her sense of herself as a sexually desiring and desirable subject. Hence, any political project that aims to dismantle the machinery that turns a female body into a feminine one may well be apprehended by a woman as something that threatens her with desexualization, if not outright annihilation.

The categories of masculinity and femininity do more than assist in the construction of personal identities; they are critical elements in our informal social ontology. This may account to some degree for the otherwise puzzling phenomenon of homophobia and for the revulsion felt by many at the sight of female bodybuilders; neither the homosexual nor the muscular woman can be assimilated easily into the categories that structure everyday life. The radical feminist critique of femininity, then, may pose a threat not only to a woman's sense of her own identity and desirability but to the very structure of her social universe.

Of course, many women *are* feminists, favoring a program of political and economic reform in the struggle to gain equality with men. But many "reform," or liberal, feminists (indeed, many orthodox Marxists) are committed to the idea that the preservation of a woman's femininity is quite compatible with her struggle for liberation (Markovic 1976). These thinkers have rejected a normative femininity based upon the notion of "separate spheres" and the traditional sexual division of labor, while accepting at the same time conventional standards of feminine body display. If my analysis is correct, such a feminism is incoherent. Foucault has argued that modern bourgeois democracy is deeply flawed in that it seeks political micropowers that lie beyond the realm of what is ordinarily defined as the "political." "The man described for us whom we are invited to free," he says, "is already in himself the effect of a subjection much more profound than himself" (Foucault 1979, 30). If, as I have argued, female subjectivity is constituted in any significant measure in and through the disciplinary practices that construct the feminine body, what Foucault says here of "man" is perhaps even truer of "woman." Marxists have maintained from the first the inadequacy of a purely liberal feminism: we have reached the same conclusion through a different route, casting doubt at the same time on the adequacy of traditional Marxist prescriptions for women's liberation as well. Liberals call for equal rights for women, traditional Marxists for the entry of women into production on an equal footing with men, the socialization of housework, and proletarian revolution; neither calls for the deconstruction of the categories of masculinity and femininity. [Some radical feminists such as Wittig (1976), however, have called for just such a deconstruction.] Femininity as a certain "style of the flesh" will have to be surpassed in the direction of something quite different—not masculinity, which is in many ways only its mirror opposite, but a radical and as yet unimagined transformation of the female body.

VIII.

Foucault (1979, 44) has argued that the transition from traditional to modern societies has been characterized by a profound transformation in the exercise of power, by what he calls "a reversal of the political axis of individualization." In older authoritarian systems, power was embodied in the person of the monarch and exercised upon a largely anonymous body of subjects; violation of the law was seen as an insult to the royal individual. While the methods employed to enforce compliance in the past were often quite brutal, involving gross assaults against the body, power in such a system operated in a haphazard and discontinuous fashion; much in the social totality lay beyond its reach.

By contrast, modern society has seen the emergence of increasingly invasive apparatuses of power: these exercise a far more restrictive social and psychological control than was heretofore possible. In modern societies, effects of power "circulate through progressively finer channels, gaining access to individuals themselves, to their bodies, their gestures and all their daily actions" (Foucault 1980, 151). Power now seeks to transform the minds of those individuals who might be tempted to resist it, not merely to punish or imprison their bodies. This requires two things: a finer control of the body's time and of its movements—a control that cannot be achieved without ceaseless surveillance and a better understanding of the specific person, of the genesis and nature of his "case." The power these new apparatuses seek to exercise requires a new knowledge of the individual: modern psychology and sociology are born. Whether the new modes of control have charge of correction, production, education, or the provision of welfare, they resemble one another; they exercise power in a bureaucratic mode—faceless, centralized, and pervasive. A reversal has occurred: power has now become anonymous, while the project of control has brought into being a new individuality. In fact, Foucault believes that the operation of power constitutes the very subjectivity of the subject. Here, the image of the Panopticon returns: knowing that he may be observed from the tower at any time, the inmate takes over the job of policing himself. The gaze that is inscribed in the very structure of the disciplinary institution is internalized by the inmate: modern technologies of behavior are thus oriented toward the production of isolated and self-policing subjects (Dews 1984, 77).

Women have their own experience of the modernization of power, one that begins later but follows in many respects the course outlined by Foucault. In important ways, a woman's behavior is less regulated now than it was in the past. She has more mobility and is less confined to domestic space. She enjoys what to previous generations would have been an unimaginable sexual liberty. Divorce, access to paid work outside the home, and the increasing secularization of modern life have loosened the hold over her of the traditional family and, in spite of the current fundamentalist revival, of the church. Power in these institutions was wielded by individuals known to her. Husbands and fathers enforced patriarchal authority in the family. As in the ancient regime, a woman body was subject to sanctions if she disobeyed. Not Foucault's royal individual but the Divine Individual decreed that her desire be always "unto her husband," while the person of the priest made known to her God's more specific intentions concerning her place and duties. In the days when civil and ecclesiastical authority were still conjoined, individuals formally invested with power were charged with the correction of recalcitrant women whom the family had somehow failed to constrain.

By contrast, the disciplinary power that is increasingly charged with the production of a properly embodied femininity is dispersed and anonymous; there are no individuals formally empowered to wield it; it is, as we have seen, invested in everyone and in no one in particular. This disciplinary power is peculiarly modern: it does not rely upon violent or public sanctions, nor does it seek to restrain the freedom of the female body to move from place to place. For all that, its invasion of the body is well-nigh total: the female body enters "a machinery of power that explores it, breaks it down and rearranges it" (Foucault 1979, 138). The disciplinary techniques through which the "docile bodies" of women are constructed aim at a regulation that is perpetual and exhaustive—a regulation of the body's size and contours, its appetite, posture, gestures and general comportment in space, and the appearance of each of its visible parts.

As modern industrial societies change and as women themselves offer resistance to patriarchy, older forms of domination are eroded. But new forms arise, spread, and become consolidated. Women are no longer required to be chaste or modest, to restrict their sphere of activity to the home, or even to realize their properly feminine destiny in maternity: normative femininity is coming more and more to be centered on woman's body—not its duties and obligations or even its capacity to bear children, but its sexuality, more precisely, its presumed heterosexuality and its appearance. There is, of course, nothing new in women's preoccupation with youth and beauty. What is new is the growing power of the image in a society increasingly oriented toward the visual media. Images of normative femininity, it might be ventured, have replaced the religiously oriented tracts of the past. New too is the spread of this discipline to all classes of women and its deployment throughout the life cycle. What was formerly the specialty of the aristocrat or courtesan is now the routine obligation of every woman, be she a grandmother or a barely pubescent girl.

To subject oneself to the new disciplinary power is to be up-to-date, to be "with it"; as I have argued, it is presented to us in ways that are regularly disguised. It is fully compatible with the current need for women's wage labor, the cult of youth and fitness, and the need of advanced capitalism to maintain high levels of consumption. Further, it represents a saving in the economy of enforcement: since it is women themselves who practice this discipline on and against their own bodies, men get off scott-free.

The woman who checks her makeup half a dozen times a day to see if her foundation has caked or her mascara has run, who worries that the wind or the rain may spoil her hairdo, who looks frequently to see if her stockings have bagged at the ankle or who, feeling fat, monitors everything she eats, has become, just as surely as the inmate of the Panopticon, a self-policing subject, a self committed to a relentless self-surveillance. This self-surveillance is a form of obedience to patriarchy. It is also the reflection in woman's consciousness of the fact that *she* is under surveillance in ways that *he* is not, that whatever else she may become, she is importantly a body designed to please or to excite. There has been induced in many women, then, in Foucault's words (1979, 201), "a state of conscious and permanent visibility that assures the automatic functioning of power." Since the standards of female bodily acceptability are impossible fully to realize, requiring as they do a virtual transcendence of nature, a woman may live much of her life with a pervasive feeling of bodily deficiency. Hence a tighter control of the body has gained a new kind of hold over the mind.

Foucault often writes as if power constitutes the very individuals upon whom it operates:

> The individual is not to be conceived as a sort of elementary nucleus, a primitive atom, a multiple and inert material on which power comes to fasten or against which it happens to strike. . . . In fact, it is already one of

> the prime effects of power that certain bodies, certain gestures, certain discourses, certain desires, come to be identified and constituted as individuals. (Foucault 1980, 98)

Nevertheless, if individuals were wholly constituted by the power-knowledge regime Foucault describes, it would make no sense to speak of resistance to discipline at all. Foucault seems sometimes on the verge of depriving us of a vocabulary in which to conceptualize the nature and meaning of those periodic refusals of control that, just as much as the imposition of control, mark the course of human history.

Peter Dews (1984, 92) accuses Foucault of lacking a theory of the "libidinal body," that is, the body upon which discipline is imposed and whose bedrock impulse toward spontaneity and pleasure might perhaps become the locus of resistance. Do women's "libidinal" bodies, then, not rebel against the pain, constriction, tedium, semistarvation, and constant self-surveillance to which they are currently condemned? Certainly they do, but the rebellion is put down every time a woman picks up her eyebrow tweezers or embarks upon a new diet. The harshness of a regime alone does not guarantee its rejection, for hardships can be endured if they are thought to be necessary or inevitable.

While "nature," in the form of a "libidinal" body, may not be the origin of a revolt against "culture," domination (and the discipline it requires) are never imposed without some cost. Historically, the forms and occasions of resistance are manifold. Sometimes, instances of resistance appear to spring from the introduction of new and conflicting factors into the lives of the dominated: the juxtaposition of old and new and the resulting incoherence or "contradiction" may make submission to the old ways seem increasingly unnecessary. In the present instance, what may be a major factor in the relentless and escalating objectification of women's bodies—namely, women's growing independence—produces in many women a sense of incoherence that calls into question the meaning and necessity of the current discipline. As women (albeit a small minority of women) begin to realize an unprecedented political, economic, and sexual self-determination, they fall ever more completely under the dominating gaze of patriarchy. It is this paradox, not the "libidinal body," that produces, here and there, pockets of resistance.

In the current political climate, there is no reason to anticipate either widespread resistance to currently fashionable modes of feminine embodiment or joyous experimentation with new "styles of the flesh"; moreover, such novelties would face profound opposition from material and psychological sources identified earlier in this essay (see section VII). In spite of this, a number of oppositional discourses and practices have appeared in recent years. An increasing number of women are "pumping iron," a few with little concern for the limits of body development imposed by current canons of femininity. Women in radical lesbian communities have also rejected hegemonic images of femininity and are struggling to develop a new female aesthetic.

A striking feature of such communities is the extent to which they have overcome the oppressive identification of female beauty and desirability with youth: here, the physical features of aging—"character" lines and graying hair—not only do not diminish a woman's attractiveness, they may even enhance it. A popular literature of resistance is growing, some of it analytical and reflective, like Kim Chernin's [1981 book] *The Obsession*, some oriented toward practical self-help, like Marcia Hutchinson's (1985) *Transforming Body Image, Learning to Love the Body You Have.* This literature reflects a mood akin in some ways to that other and earlier mood of quiet desperation to which Betty Friedan gave voice in *The Feminine Mystique.* Nor should we forget that a mass-based women's movement is in place in this country that has begun a critical questioning of the meaning of femininity, if not yet in the corporeal presentation of self, then in other domains of life. We women cannot begin the re-vision of our own bodies until we learn to read the cultural messages we inscribe upon them daily and until we come to see that even when the mastery of the disciplines of femininity produces a triumphant result, we are still only women.

Notes

An earlier version of this paper was read to the Southwestern Philosophical Society, November 1985. Subsequent versions were read to the Society of Women in Philosophy, March 1986, and to the American Philosophical Association, May 1986. Many people in discussion at those meetings offered incisive comments and criticisms. I would like to thank in particular the following persons for their critiques of earlier drafts of this paper: Nancy Fraser; Alison Jaggar; Jeffner Allen; Laurie Shrage; Robert Yanal; Martha Gimenez; Joyce Trebilcot, Rob Crawford, and Iris Young.

1. Foucault is citing an eighteenth-century military manual, "Ordonnance du Ier janvier 1766 . . . , title XI, article 2."
2. I am indebted to Laurie Shrage for calling this to my attention and for providing most of these examples.
3. I am indebted to Nancy Fraser for the formulation of this point.

References

Bartky, Sandra Lee. 1982. Narcissism, femininity and alienation. *Social Theory and Practice* 8:127–43.

Bordo, Susan. 1985–86. Anorexia nervosa: Psychopathology as the crystallization of culture. *Philosophical Forum* 17:73–104.

Butler, Judith. 1985. Embodied identity in de Beauvoir's *The Second Sex.* Paper presented at the American Philosophical Association, Pacific Division, March 22, 1985.

Chernin, Kim. 1981. *The Obsession: Reflections on the Tyranny of Slenderness.* New York: Harper and Row.

de Beauvoir, Simone. 1968. *The Second Sex.* New York: Bantam Books.

Dews, Peter. 1984. Power and subjectivity in Foucault. *New Left Review* 144 (March–April):17.

Foucault, Michel. 1979. *Discipline and Punish: The Birth of the Prison*. New York: Vintage.

———. 1980. *Power/Knowledge: Selected Interviews and Other Writings, 1972–1977*, edited by Colin Gordon. New York: Pantheon.

Henley, Nancy. 1977. *Body Politics*. Englewood Cliffs, NJ: Prentice Hall.

Hochschild, Arlie. 1983. *The Managed Heart: The Commercialization of Human Feeling*. Berkeley: University of California Press.

Hutchinson, Marcia. 1985. *Transforming Body Image: Learning to Love the Body You Have*. Trumansburg, NY: Crossing Press.

Klinger, Georgette, and Barbara Rowes. 1978. *Georgette Klinger's Skincare*. New York: William Morrow.

Loren, Sophia. 1984. *Women and Beauty*. New York: William Morrow.

Markovic, Mihailo. 1976. Women's liberation and human emancipation. In *Women and Philosophy*, edited by Carol C. Gould and Marx W. Wartofsky. New York: G. P. Putnam.

Millman, Marcia. 1980. *Such a Pretty Face: Being Fat in America*. New York: W. W. Norton.

Saffon, M. J. 1981. *The 15-Minute-A-Day Natural Face Life*. New York: Warner Books.

USA Today. 1985. 30, May.

Wex, Marianne. 1979. *Let's Take Back Our Space: "Female" and "Male" Body Language as a Result of Patriarchal Structures*. Berlin: Frauenliteraturverlag Hermine Fees.

Wittig, Monique. 1976. *The Lesbian Body*. New York: Avon Books.

Young, Iris. 1980. Throwing like a girl: A phenomenology of feminine body comportment, motility and spatiality. *Human Studies* 3:137–56.

6

Integrating Disability, Transforming Feminist Theory

ROSEMARIE GARLAND-THOMSON

Approximately 20 percent of women in the United States live with disability, and almost all of us will eventually develop a disability if we live long enough. This is the backdrop for Rosemarie Garland-Thomson's "Integrating Disability, Transforming Feminist Theory."

Feminist scholars have long recognized the importance of examining how gender intersects with multiple oppressive systems including those based on class, sexuality, and race/ethnicity. In her article, Garland-Thomson argues that to fully understand the social construction of women's bodies we must also examine the impact of disability and social reactions to it.

According to Garland-Thomson, feminist theory has a lot to learn from disability studies. Like gender, disability is a concept that pervades all aspects of culture, including social structures, social identities, and experiences of embodiment. And like "femaleness," disability is not a natural state of corporeal inferiority but rather, as she states, a culturally fabricated narrative of the body. Thus, in the same way that feminist scholars have destabilized social constructions of women's bodies as deviant and inferior, Garland-Thomson argues that feminist disability theory can unseat similar assumptions about disabled bodies—especially female disabled bodies. As she observes, because disability *is a broad term that includes many culturally devalued labels such as* sick, ugly, *and* debilitated, *it plays a key role in preserving and validating privileged designations such as* healthy, beautiful, *and* competent. *Combining feminist and disability theory, she says, can help us to denaturalize disability and challenge the negative labels that come with it, thus helping us to better understand the world around us.*

Garland-Thomson, Rosemarie. "Integrating Disability, Transforming Feminist Theory." *NWSA Journal (now Feminist Formations)* 14:3 (2002), 1–32.

Over the last several years, disability studies has moved out of the applied fields of medicine, social work, and rehabilitation to become a vibrant new field of inquiry within the critical genre of identity studies. Charged with the residual fervor of the civil rights movement, women's studies and race studies established a model in the academy for identity-based critical enterprises that followed, such as gender studies, queer studies, disability studies, and a proliferation of ethnic studies, all of which have enriched and complicated our understandings of social justice, subject formation, subjugated knowledges, and collective action.

Even though disability studies is now flourishing in disciplines such as history, literature, religion, theater, and philosophy in precisely the same way feminist studies did twenty-five years ago, many of its practitioners do not recognize that disability studies is part of this larger undertaking that can be called identity studies. Indeed, I must wearily conclude that much of current disability studies does a great deal of wheel reinventing. This is largely because many disability studies scholars simply do not know either feminist theory or the institutional history of women's studies. . . .

Conversely, feminist theories all too often do not recognize disability in their litanies of identities that inflect the category of woman. Repeatedly, feminist issues that are intricately entangled with disability—such as reproductive technology, the place of bodily differences, the particularities of oppression, the ethics of care, the construction of the subject—are discussed without any reference to disability. Like disability studies practitioners who are unaware of feminism, feminist scholars are often simply unacquainted with disability studies' perspectives. . . .

Disability studies can benefit from feminist theory, and feminist theory can benefit from disability studies. Both feminism and disability studies are comparative and concurrent academic enterprises. Just as feminism has expanded the lexicon of what we imagine as womanly, and has sought to understand and destigmatize what we call the subject position of woman, so has disability studies examined the identity *disabled* in the service of integrating people with disabilities more fully into our society. As such, both are insurgencies that are becoming institutionalized, underpinning inquiries outside and inside the academy. A feminist disability theory builds on the strengths of both.

Feminist Disability Theory

My title here, "Integrating Disability, Transforming Feminist Theory," invokes and links two notions, integration and transformation, both of which are fundamental to the feminist project and to the larger civil rights movement that informed it. Integration suggests achieving parity by fully including that which has been excluded and subordinated. Transformation suggests re-imagining established knowledge and the order of things. By alluding to integration and transformation, I set my own modest project of integrating disability into feminist theory in the politicized context of the civil rights movement in order to gesture toward the explicit relation that feminism supposes between intellectual work and a commitment to creating a more just, equitable, and integrated society.

This essay aims to amplify feminist theory by articulating and fostering feminist disability theory. . . . [T]he goal of feminist disability studies, as I lay it out in this essay, is to augment the terms and confront the limits of the ways we understand human diversity, the materiality of the body, multiculturalism, and the social formations that interpret bodily differences. The fundamental point I will make here is that integrating disability as a category of analysis and a system of representation deepens, expands, and challenges feminist theory.

. . . Feminist theory is a collaborative, interdisciplinary inquiry and a self-conscious cultural critique that interrogates how subjects are multiply interpellated: in other words, how the representational systems of gender, race, ethnicity, ability, sexuality, and class mutually construct, inflect, and contradict one another. These systems intersect to produce and sustain ascribed, achieved, and acquired identities—both those that claim us and those that we claim for ourselves. A feminist disability theory introduces the ability/disability system as a category of analysis into this diverse and diffuse enterprise. It aims to extend current notions of cultural diversity and to more fully integrate the academy and the larger world it helps shape.

A feminist disability approach fosters complex understandings of the cultural history of the body. By considering the ability/disability system, feminist disability theory goes beyond explicit disability topics such as illness, health, beauty, genetics, eugenics, aging, reproductive technologies, prosthetics, and access issues. Feminist disability theory addresses such broad feminist concerns as the unity of the category *woman*, the status of the lived body, the politics of appearance, the medicalization of the body, the privilege of normalcy, multiculturalism, sexuality, the social construction of identity, and the commitment to integration. To borrow Toni Morrison's notion that blackness is an idea that permeates American culture, disability too is a pervasive, often unarticulated, ideology informing our cultural notions of self and other (1992). Disability—like gender—is a concept that pervades all aspects of culture: its structuring institutions, social identities, cultural practices, political positions, historical communities, and the shared human experience of embodiment.

Integrating disability into feminist theory is generative, broadening our collective inquiries, questioning our assumptions, and contributing to feminism's intersectionality. Introducing a disability analysis does not narrow the inquiry, limit the focus to only women with disabilities, or preclude engaging other manifestations of feminisms. Indeed, the multiplicity of foci we now call feminisms is not a group of fragmented, competing subfields, but rather a vibrant, complex conversation. In talking about feminist disability theory, I am not proposing yet another discrete feminism, but suggesting instead some ways that thinking about disability transforms feminist theory. Integrating disability does not obscure our critical focus on the registers of race, sexuality, ethnicity, or gender, nor is it additive. Rather, considering disability shifts the conceptual framework to strengthen our understanding of how these multiple systems intertwine, redefine, and mutually constitute one another. Integrating disability clarifies how this aggregate of systems operates together, yet distinctly, to support an imaginary norm and structure the relations that grant power, privilege, and status to that norm. Indeed, the cultural function of the disabled figure is to act as a synecdoche for all forms that culture deems non-normative.

We need to study disability in a feminist context to direct our highly honed critical skills toward the dual scholarly tasks of unmasking and reimagining disability, not only for people with disabilities, but for everyone. As Simi Linton puts it, studying disability is "a prism through which one can gain a broader understanding of society and human experience" (1998, 118). It deepens our understanding of gender and sexuality, individualism and equality, minority group definitions, autonomy, wholeness, independence, dependence, health, physical appearance, aesthetics, the integrity of the body, community, and ideas of progress and perfection in every aspect of cultures. A feminist disability theory introduces what Eve Sedgwick has called a "universalizing view" of disability that will replace an often persisting "minoritizing view." Such a view will cast disability as "an issue of continuing, determinative importance in the lives of people across the spectrum" (1990, 1). In other words, understanding how disability operates as an identity category and cultural concept will enhance how we understand what it is to be human, our relationships with one another, and the experience of embodiment. The constituency for feminist disability studies is all of us, not only women with disabilities: Disability is the most human of experiences, touching every family and—if we live long enough—touching us all.

The Ability/Disability System

Feminist disability theory's radical critique hinges on a broad understanding of disability as a pervasive cultural system that stigmatizes certain kinds of bodily variations. At the same time, this system has the potential to incite a critical politics. The informing premise of feminist disability theory is that disability, like femaleness, is not a natural state of corporeal inferiority, inadequacy, excess, or a stroke of misfortune. Rather, disability is a culturally fabricated narrative of the body, similar to what we understand as the fictions of race and gender. The disability/ability system produces subjects by differentiating and marking bodies. Although this comparison of bodies is ideological rather than biological, it nevertheless penetrates into the formation of culture, legitimating an unequal distribution of resources, status, and power within a biased social and architectural environment. As such, disability has four aspects: First, it is a system for interpreting and disciplining bodily variations; second, it is a relationship between bodies and their environments;

third, it is a set of practices that produce both the able-bodied and the disabled; fourth, it is a way of describing the inherent instability of the embodied self. The disability system excludes the kinds of bodily forms, functions, impairments, changes, or ambiguities that call into question our cultural fantasy of the body as a neutral, compliant instrument of some transcendent will. Moreover, *disability* is a broad term within which cluster ideological categories as varied as "sick," "deformed," "crazy," "ugly," "old," "maimed," "afflicted," "mad," "abnormal," or "debilitated"—all of which disadvantage people by devaluing bodies that do not conform to cultural standards. Thus, the disability system functions to preserve and validate such privileged designations as "beautiful," "healthy," "normal," "fit," "competent," "intelligent"—all of which provide cultural capital to those who can claim such statuses, who can reside within these subject positions. It is, then, the various interactions between bodies and world that materialize disability from the stuff of human variation and precariousness.

A feminist disability theory denaturalizes disability by unseating the dominant assumption that disability is something that is wrong with someone. By this I mean, of course, that it mobilizes feminism's highly developed and complex critique of gender, class, race, ethnicity, and sexuality as exclusionary and oppressive systems rather than as the natural and appropriate order of things. To do this, feminist disability theory engages several of the fundamental premises of critical theory: (1) that representation structures reality, (2) that the margins define the center, (3) that gender (or disability) is a way of signifying relationships of power, (4) that human identity is multiple and unstable, and (5) that all analysis and evaluation have political implications.

In order to elaborate on these premises, I discuss here four fundamental and interpenetrating domains of feminist theory and suggest some of the kinds of critical inquiries that considering disability can generate within these theoretical arenas. These domains are: (1) representation, (2) the body, (3) identity, and (4) activism. . . .

Representation

The first domain of feminist theory that can be deepened by a disability analysis is representation. Western thought has long conflated femaleness and disability, understanding both as defective departures from a valued standard. Aristotle, for example, defined women as "mutilated males." Women, for Aristotle, have "improper form"; we are "monstrosit[ies]" (1944, 27–28, 8–9). As what Nancy Tuana calls "misbegotten men," women thus become the primal freaks in Western history, envisioned as what we might now call congenitally deformed as a result of what we might now term genetic disability (1993, 18). More recently, feminist theorists have argued that female embodiment is a disabling condition in sexist culture. Iris Marion Young, for instance, examines how enforced feminine comportment delimits women's sense of embodied agency, restricting them to "throwing like a girl" (1990, 141). Young concludes that, "Women in a sexist society are physically handicapped" (1990, 153). Even the general American public associates femininity with disability. A recent study on stereotyping showed that housewives, disabled people, blind people, so-called retarded people, and the elderly were all judged as being similarly incompetent. Such a study suggests that intensely normatively feminine positions—such as a housewife—are aligned with negative attitudes about people with disabilities (Fiske, Cuddy, and Glick 2001).[1]

Recognizing how the concept of disability has been used to cast the form and functioning of female bodies as non-normative can extend feminist critiques. Take, for example, the exploitation of Saartje Bartmann, the African woman exhibited as a freak in nineteenth-century Europe (Fausto-Sterling 1995; Gilman 1985). Known as the Hottentot Venus, Bartmann's treatment has come to represent the most egregious form of racial and gendered degradation. What goes unremarked in studies of Bartmann's display, however, are the ways that the language and assumptions of the ability/disability system were implemented to pathologize and exoticize Bartmann. Her display invoked disability by presenting as deformities or abnormalities the characteristics that marked her as raced and gendered. I am not suggesting that Bartmann was disabled, but rather that the concepts of disability discourse framed her presentation to the Western eye. Using disability as a category of analysis allows us to see that what was normative embodiment in her native context became abnormal to the Western mind. More important, rather than simply supposing that being labeled as a freak is a slander, a disability analysis presses our critique further by challenging the premise that unusual embodiment is inherently inferior. The feminist interrogation of gender since Simone de Beauvoir ([1952]1974) has revealed how women are assigned a cluster of ascriptions, like Aristotle's, that mark us as Other. What is less widely recognized, however, is that this collection of interrelated characterizations is precisely the same set of supposed attributes affixed to people with disabilities.

The gender, race, and ability systems intertwine further in representing subjugated people as being pure body, unredeemed by mind or spirit. This sense of embodiment is conceived of as either a lack or an excess. Women, for example, are considered castrated, or to use Marge Piercy's wonderful term, "penis-poor" (1969). They are thought to be hysterical or have overactive hormones. Women have been cast as alternately having insatiable appetites in some eras and as pathologically self-denying in other times. Similarly, disabled people have supposedly extra chromosomes or limb deficiencies. The differences of disability are cast as atrophy, meaning degeneration, or hypertrophy, meaning enlargement. People with disabilities are described as having aplasia, meaning absence or failure of formation, or hypoplasia, meaning underdevelopment. All these terms police variation and reference a hidden norm from which the bodies of people with disabilities and women are imagined to depart.

Female, disabled, and dark bodies are supposed to be dependent, incomplete, vulnerable, and incompetent bodies. Femininity and race are performances of disability. Women and the disabled are portrayed as helpless, dependent, weak, vulnerable, and incapable bodies. Women, the disabled, and people of color are always ready occasions for the aggrandizement of benevolent rescuers, whether strong males, distinguished doctors, abolitionists, or Jerry Lewis hosting his telethons. For example, an 1885 medical illustration of a pathologically "love deficient" woman, who fits the cultural stereotype of the ugly woman or perhaps the lesbian, suggests how sexuality and appearance slide into the terms of disability. This illustration shows that the language of deficiency and abnormality simultaneously devalue women who depart from the mandates of femininity by equating them with disabled bodies. Such an interpretive move economically invokes the subjugating effect of one oppressive system to deprecate people marked by another system of representation.

Subjugated bodies are pictured as either deficient or profligate. For instance, what Susan Bordo describes as the too-muchness of women also haunts disability and racial discourses, marking subjugated bodies as ungovernable, intemperate, or threatening (1993). The historical figure of the monster, as well, invokes disability, often to serve racism and sexism. Although the term has expanded to encompass all forms of social and corporeal aberration, *monster* originally described people with congenital impairments. As departures from the normatively human, monsters were seen as category violations or grotesque hybrids. The semantics of monstrosity are recruited to explain gender violations such as Julia Pastrana, for example, the Mexican Indian "bearded woman," whose body was displayed in nineteenth-century freak shows both during her lifetime and after her death. Pastrana's live and later her embalmed body spectacularly confused and transgressed established cultural categories. Race, gender, disability, and sexuality augmented one another in Pastrana's display to produce a spectacle of embodied otherness that is simultaneously sensational, sentimental, and pathological (Garland-Thomson 1999). Furthermore, much current feminist work theorizes figures of hybridity and excess such as monsters, grotesques, and cyborgs to suggest their transgressive potential for a feminist politics (Braidotti 1994; Haraway 1991; Russo 1994). However, this metaphorical invocation seldom acknowledges that these figures often refer to the actual bodies of people with disabilities. Erasing real disabled bodies from the history of these terms compromises the very critique they intend to launch and misses an opportunity to use disability as a feminist critical category.

Such representations ultimately portray subjugated bodies not only as inadequate or unrestrained but at the same time as redundant and expendable. Bodies marked and selected by such systems are targeted for elimination by varying historical and cross-cultural practices. Women, people with disabilities or appearance impairments, ethnic Others, gays and lesbians, and people of color are variously the objects of infanticide, selective abortion, eugenic programs, hate crimes, mercy killing, assisted suicide, lynching, bride burning, honor killing, forced conversion, coercive rehabilitation, domestic violence, genocide, normalizing surgical procedures, racial profiling, and neglect. All these discriminatory practices are legitimated by systems of representation, by collective cultural stories that shape the material world, underwrite exclusionary attitudes, inform human relations, and mold our senses of who we are. Understanding how disability functions along with other systems of representation clarifies how all the systems intersect and mutually constitute one another.

The Body

The second domain of feminist theory that a disability analysis can illuminate is the investigation of the body: its materiality, its politics, its lived experience, and its relation to subjectivity and identity. Confronting issues of representation is certainly crucial to the cultural critique of feminist disability theory. But we should not focus exclusively on the discursive realm. What distinguishes a feminist disability theory from other critical paradigms is that it scrutinizes a wide range of material practices involving the lived body. Perhaps because women and the disabled are cultural signifiers for the body, their actual bodies have been subjected relentlessly to what Michel Foucault calls "discipline" (1979). Together, the gender, race, ethnicity, sexuality, class, and ability systems exert tremendous social pressures to shape, regulate, and normalize subjugated bodies. Such disciplining is enacted primarily through the two interrelated cultural discourses of medicine and appearance.

Feminist disability theory offers a particularly trenchant analysis of the ways that the female body has been medicalized in modernity. As I have already suggested, both women and the disabled have been imagined as medically abnormal—as the quintessential sick ones. Sickness is gendered feminine. This gendering of illness has entailed distinct consequences in everything from epidemiology and diagnosis to prophylaxis and therapeutics.

Perhaps feminist disability theory's most incisive critique is revealing the intersections between the politics of appearance and the medicalization of subjugated bodies. Appearance norms have a long history in Western culture. . . . The classical ideal was to be worshiped rather than imitated, but increasingly, in modernity the ideal has migrated to become the paradigm that is to be attained. As many feminist critics have pointed out, the beauty system's mandated standard of the female body has become a goal to be achieved through self-regulation and consumerism (Haiken 1997; Wolf 1991). Feminist disability theory suggests that appearance and health norms often have similar disciplinary goals. For example, the body braces developed in the 1930s to ostensibly correct scoliosis discipline the body to conform to dictates of both the gender and the ability systems by enforcing standardized female form similarly to the nineteenth-century corset, which, ironically, often disabled female bodies. Although both devices normalize bodies, the brace is part of medical discourse while the corset is cast as a fashion practice.

Similarly, a feminist disability theory calls into question the separation of reconstructive and cosmetic surgery, recognizing their essentially normalizing function as what Sander L. Gilman calls "aesthetic surgery" (1998). Cosmetic surgery, driven by gender ideology and market demand, now enforces feminine body ideals and standardizes female bodies toward what I have called the "normate"—the corporeal incarnation of culture's collective, unmarked, normative characteristics (Garland-Thomson 1997, 8). Cosmetic surgery's twin, reconstructive surgery, eliminates disability and enforces the ideals of what might be thought of as the normalcy system. Both cosmetic and reconstructive procedures commodify the body and parade mutilations as enhancements that correct flaws to improve the psychological well-being of the patient. The conception of the body as what Susan Bordo terms "cultural plastic" (1993, 246) through surgical and medical interventions increasingly pressures people with disabilities or appearance impairments to become what Michel Foucault calls "docile bodies" (1979, 135). The twin ideologies of normalcy and beauty posit female and disabled bodies, particularly, as not only spectacles to be looked at, but as pliable bodies to be shaped infinitely so as to conform to a set of standards called *normal* and *beautiful*.

Normal has inflected beautiful in modernity. What is imagined as excess body fat, the effects of aging, marks of ethnicity such as supposedly Jewish noses, bodily particularities thought of as blemishes or deformities, and marks of history such as scarring and impairments are now expected to be surgically erased to produce an unmarked body. This visually unobtrusive body may then pass unnoticed within the milieu of anonymity that is the hallmark of social relations beyond the personal in modernity. The purpose of aesthetic surgery, as well as the costuming of power, is not to appear unique—or to "be yourself," as the ads endlessly promise—but rather not to be conspicuous, not to look different. This flight from the nonconforming body translates into individual efforts to look normal, neutral, unmarked, to *not* look disabled, queer, ugly, fat, ethnic, or raced. Beauty, then, dictates corporeal standards that create not distinction but utter conformity to a bland look that is at the same time unachievable, so as to leash us to consumer practices that promise to deliver such sameness. In the language of contemporary cosmetic surgery, the unreconstructed female body is persistently cast as having abnormalities that can be corrected by surgical procedures which supposedly improve one's appearance by producing ostensibly natural-looking noses, thighs, breasts, chins, and so on. Thus, our unmodified bodies are presented as unnatural and abnormal while the surgically altered bodies are portrayed as normal and natural. The beautiful woman of the twenty-first century is sculpted surgically from top to bottom, generically neutral, all irregularities regularized, all particularities expunged. She is thus nondisabled, deracialized, and de-ethnicized.

In addition, the politics of prosthetics enters the purview of feminism when we consider the contested use of breast implants and prostheses for breast cancer survivors. The famous 1993 *New York Times Magazine* cover photo of the fashion model, Matushka, baring her mastectomy scar or Audre Lorde's account of breast cancer in *The Cancer Journals* challenge the sexist assumption that the amputated breast must always pass for the normative, sexualized one either through concealment or prosthetics (1980). . . .

Feminist disability theory can press far its critique of the pervasive will-to-normalize the nonstandard body. Take two related examples: first, the surgical separation of conjoined twins and, second, the surgical assignment of gender for the intersexed, people with ambiguous genitalia and gender characteristics. . . . So threatening to the order of things is the natural embodiment of conjoined twins and intersexed people that they are almost always surgically normalized through amputation and mutilation immediately after birth (Clark and Myser 1996; Dreger 1998; Fausto-Sterling 2000; Kessler 1990). . . . In truth, these procedures benefit not the affected individuals, but rather they expunge the kinds of corporeal human variations that contradict the ideologies the dominant order depends upon to anchor truths it insists are unequivocally encoded in bodies.

. . . The medical commitment to healing, when coupled with modernity's faith in technology and interventions that control outcomes, has increasingly shifted toward an aggressive intent to fix, regulate, or eradicate ostensibly deviant bodies. Such a program of elimination has often been at the expense of creating a more accessible environment or providing better support services for people with disabilities. The privileging of medical technology over less ambitious programs such as rehabilitation has encouraged the cultural conviction that disability can be extirpated; inviting the belief that life with a disability is intolerable. As charity campaigns and telethons repeatedly affirm, cure rather than adjustment or accommodation is the overdetermined cultural response to disability (Longmore 1997). For instance, a 1949 March of Dimes poster shows an appealing little girl stepping out of her wheelchair into the supposed redemption of walking: "Look, I Can Walk Again!" the text proclaims, while at once charging the viewers with the responsibility of assuring her future ambulation. Nowhere do we find posters suggesting that life as a wheelchair user might be full and satisfying, as many people who actually use them find their lives to be. . . .

The ideology of cure directed at disabled people focuses on changing bodies imagined as abnormal and dysfunctional rather than on changing exclusionary attitudinal, environmental, and economic barriers. The emphasis on cure reduces the cultural tolerance for human variation and vulnerability by locating disability in bodies imagined as flawed rather than social systems in need of fixing. A feminist disability studies would draw an important distinction between prevention and elimination. Preventing illness, suffering, and injury is a humane social objective. Eliminating the range of unacceptable and devalued bodily forms and functions the dominant order calls disability is, on the other hand, a eugenic undertaking. The ostensibly progressive socio-medical project of eradicating disability all too often is enacted as a program to eliminate people with disabilities through such practices as forced sterilization, so-called physician-assisted suicide and mercy killing, selective abortion, institutionization, and segregation policies.

A feminist disability theory extends its critique of the normalization of bodies and the medicalization of appearance to challenge some widely held assumptions about reproductive issues as well. The cultural mandate to eliminate the variations in form and function that we think of as disabilities has undergirded the reproductive practices of genetic testing and selective abortion (Parens and Asch 2000; Rapp 1999; Saxton 1998). Some disability activists argue that the "choice" to abort fetuses with disabilities is a coercive form of genocide against the disabled (Hubbard 1990). A more nuanced argument against selective abortion comes from Adrienne Asch and Gail Geller, who wish to preserve a woman's right to choose whether to bear a child, but who at the same time object to the ethics of selectively aborting a wanted fetus because it will become a person with a disability (1996). Asch and Geller counter the quality-of-life and prevention-of-suffering arguments so readily invoked to justify selective abortion, as well as physician-assisted suicide, by pointing out that we cannot predict or, more precisely, control in advance such equivocal human states as happiness, suffering, or success. Neither is any amount of prenatal engineering going to produce the life that any of us desires and values. Indeed, both hubris and a lack of imagination characterize the prejudicial and reductive assumption that having a disability ruins lives. A vague notion of suffering and its potential deterrence drives much of the logic of elimination that rationalizes selective abortion (Kittay 2000). Life chances and quality are simply far too contingent to justify prenatal prediction.

Similarly, genetic testing and applications of the Human Genome Project as the key to expunging disability are often critiqued as enactments of eugenic ideology, what the feminist biologist Evelyn Fox Keller calls a "eugenics of normalcy" (1992). The popular utopian belief that all forms of disability can be eliminated through prophylactic manipulation of genetics will only serve to intensify the prejudice against those who inevitably will acquire disabilities through aging and encounters with the environment. . . .

Identity

The third domain of feminist theory that a disability analysis complicates is identity. Feminist theory has productively and rigorously critiqued the identity category of woman, on which the entire feminist enterprise seemed to rest. Feminism increasingly recognizes that no woman is ever *only* a woman, that she occupies multiple subject positions and is claimed by several cultural identity categories (Spelman 1988). This complication of *woman* compelled feminist theory to turn from an exclusively male/female focus to look more fully at the exclusionary, essentialist, oppressive, and binary aspects of the category "woman" itself. Disability is one such identity vector that disrupts the unity of the classification woman and challenges the primacy of gender as a monolithic category.

Disabled women are, of course, a marked and excluded—albeit quite varied—group within the larger social class of women. The relative privileges of normative femininity are often denied to disabled women (Fine and Asch 1988). Cultural stereotypes imagine disabled women as asexual, unfit to reproduce, overly dependent, unattractive—as generally removed from the sphere of true womanhood and feminine beauty. Women with disabilities often must struggle to have their sexuality and rights to bear children recognized (Finger 1990). Disability thus both intensifies and attenuates the cultural scripts of femininity. Aging is a form of disablement that disqualifies older women from the limited power allotted females who are young and meet the criteria for attracting men. Depression, anorexia, and agoraphobia are female-dominant, psychophysical disabilities that exaggerate normative gender roles. Feminine cultural practices such as footbinding, clitorectomies, and corseting, as well as their less hyperbolic costuming rituals such as stiletto high heels, girdles, and chastity belts—impair women's bodies and restrict their physical agency, imposing disability on them.

Banishment from femininity can be both a liability and a benefit. Let me offer—with some irony—an instructive example from popular culture. Barbie, that cultural icon of femininity, offers a disability analysis that clarifies both how multiple identity and diversity are commodified and how the commercial realm might offer politically useful feminist counter images. Perhaps the measure of a group's arrival into the mainstream of multiculturalism is to be represented in the Barbie pantheon. While Barbie herself still identifies as able-bodied—despite her severely deformed body—we now have several incarnations of Barbie's "friend," Share-A-Smile Becky. One Becky uses a cool hot pink wheelchair; another is Paralympic Champion Becky, brought out for the 2000 Sydney Olympics in a chic red-white-and-blue warm-up suit with matching chair. . . .

. . . Becky challenges notions of normalcy in feminist ways. The disabled Becky, for example, wears comfortable clothes: pants with elastic waists, sensible shoes, and roomy shirts. Becky is also one of the few dolls with flat feet and legs that bend at the knee. The disabled Becky is dressed and poised for agency, action, and creative engagement with the world. In contrast, the prototypical Barbie performs excessive femininity in her restrictive sequined gowns, crowns, and push-up bras. So while Becky implies, on the one hand, that disabled girls are purged from the feminine economy, on the other hand, Becky also suggests that disabled girls might be liberated from those oppressive and debilitating scripts. . . .

The paradox of Barbie and Becky, of course, is that the ultra-feminized Barbie is a target for sexual appropriation both by men and by beauty practices while the disabled Becky escapes such sexual objectification at the potential cost of losing her sense of identity and power as a feminine sexual being. Some disabled women negotiate this possible identity crisis by developing alternate sexualities, such as lesbianism (Brownworth and Raffo 1999). However, what Harlan Hahn calls the "asexual objectification" of people with disabilities complicates the feminist critique of normative sexual objectification (1988). Consider the 1987 *Playboy* magazine photos of the paraplegic actress Ellen Stohl. After becoming disabled, Stohl wrote to editor Hugh Hefner that she wanted to pose nude for Playboy because "sexuality is the hardest thing for disabled persons to hold onto" ("Meet Ellen Stohl" 1987, 68). For Stohl, it would seem that the performance of excessive feminine sexuality was necessary to counter the social interpretation that disability cancels out sexuality. This confirmation of normative heterosexuality was then for Stohl no Butlerian parody, but rather the affirmation she needed as a disabled woman to be sexual at all.

Ellen Stohl's presentation by way of the sexist conventions of the porn magazine illuminates the relation between identity and the body, an aspect of subject formation that disability analysis can offer. Although binary identities are conferred from outside through social relations, these identities are nevertheless inscribed on the body as either manifest or incipient visual traces. Identity's social meaning turns on this play of visibility. The photos of Stohl in *Playboy* both refuse and insist on marking her impairment. The centerfold spread—so to speak—of Stohl nude and masturbating erases her impairment to conform to the sexualized conventions of the centerfold. This photo expunges her wheelchair and any other visual clues to her impairment. In other words, to avoid the cultural contradiction of a sexual, disabled woman, the pornographic photos must offer up Stohl as visually nondisabled. But to appeal to the cultural narrative of overcoming disability that sells so well, seems novel, and capitalizes on sentimental interest, Stohl must be visually dramatized as disabled at the same time. So Playboy includes several shots of Stohl that mark her as disabled by picturing her in her wheelchair, entirely without the typical porn conventions. In fact, the photos of her using her wheelchair invoke the asexual poster child. Thus, the affirmation of sexuality that Stohl sought by posing nude in the porn magazine came at the expense of denying, through the powerful visual register, her identity as a woman with a disability, even while she attempted to claim that identity textually.

Another aspect of subject formation that disability confirms is that identity is always in transition. Disability reminds us that the body is, as Denise Riley asserts, "an unsteady mark, scarred in its long decay" (1999, 224). . . . Disability is an identity category that anyone can enter at any time, and we will all join it if we live long enough. As such, disability reveals the essential dynamism of identity. . . .

Disability's clarification of the body's corporeal truths also suggests that the body/self materializes—in Judith Butler's sense—not so much through discourse, but through history (1993). The self materializes in response to an embodied engagement with its environment, both social and concrete.

The disabled body is a body whose variations or transformations have rendered it out of sync with its environment, both the physical and the attitudinal environments. In other words, the body becomes disabled when it is incongruent both in space and in the milieu of expectations. Furthermore, a feminist disability theory presses us to ask what kinds of knowledge might be produced through having a body radically marked by its own particularity, a body that materializes at the ends of the curve of human variation. For example, an alternative epistemology that emerges from the lived experience of disability is nicely summed up in Nancy Mairs's book title, *Waist High in the World* (1996), which she irreverently considered calling "Cock High in the World."[2] What perspectives or politics arise from encountering the world from such an atypical position? Perhaps Mairs's epistemology can offer us a critical positionality called *sitpoint theory*, a neologism I can offer that interrogates the ableist assumptions underlying the notion of standpoint theory (Harstock 1983). . . .

A feminist disability theory can also highlight intersections and convergences with other identity-based critical perspectives such as queer and ethnic studies. Disability coming-out stories, for example, borrow from gay and lesbian identity narratives to expose what previously was hidden, privatized, and medicalized in order to enter into a political community. The politicized sphere into which many scholars come out is feminist disability studies, which enables critique, claims disability identity, and creates affirming counternarratives. Disability coming-out narratives raise questions about the body's role in identity by asking how markers so conspicuous as crutches, wheelchairs, hearing aids, guide dogs, white canes, or empty sleeves be closeted.

Passing as nondisabled complicates ethnic and queer studies' analyses of how this seductive but psychically estranging access to privilege operates. Some of my friends, for example, have measured their regard for me by saying, "But I don't think of you as disabled." What they point to in such a compliment is the contradiction they find between their perception of me as a valuable, capable, lovable person and the cultural figure of the disabled person whom they take to be precisely my opposite: worthless, incapable, and unlovable. People with disabilities routinely announce that they do not consider themselves as disabled. Although they are often repudiating the literal meaning of the word *disabled*, their words nevertheless serve to disassociate them from the identity group of the disabled. Our culture offers profound disincentives and few rewards to identifying as disabled. The trouble with such statements is that they leave intact, without challenge, the oppressive stereotypes that permit, among other things, the unexamined use of disability terms such as *crippled, lame, dumb, idiot,* and *moron* as verbal gestures of derision. The refusal to claim disability identity is in part due to a lack of ways to understand or talk about disability that are not oppressive. People with disabilities and those who care about them flee from the language of *crippled* or *deformed* and have no other alternatives. Yet, the civil rights movement and the accompanying black-is-beautiful identity politics have generally shown white culture what is problematic with saying to black friends, "I don't think of you as black.". . .

Activism

The final domain of feminist theory that a disability analysis expands is activism. There are many arenas of what can be seen as feminist disability activism: marches; protests; action groups such as the Intersex Society of North America (ISNA) [closed in 2007, but its mission continues through the organization Accord Alliance]; and Not Dead Yet, which opposes physician-assisted suicide, or the American Disabled for Accessible Public Transit (ADAPT). What counts as activism cuts a wide swath through U.S. society and the academy. I want to suggest here two unlikely, even quirky, cultural practices that function in activist ways but are seldom considered as potentially transformative. One practice is disabled fashion modeling and the other is academic tolerance. Both are different genres of activism from the more traditional marching-on-Washington or chaining-yourself-to-a-bus modes. Both are less theatrical, but perhaps fresher and more interestingly controversial ways to change the social landscape and to promote equality, which I take to be the goal of activism. . . .

Images of disabled fashion models in the media can shake up established categories and expectations. Because commercial visual media are the most widespread and commanding sources of images in modern, image-saturated culture, they have great potential for shaping public consciousness—as feminist cultural critics are well aware. Fashion imagery is the visual distillation of the normative, gilded with the chic and the luxurious to render it desirable. The commercial sphere is completely amoral, driven as it is by the single logic of the bottom line. As we know, it sweeps through culture seizing with alarming neutrality anything it senses will sell. This value-free aspect of advertising produces a kind of pliable potency that sometimes can yield unexpected results.

Take, for example, a shot from the monthly fashion feature in *WE Magazine*, a *Cosmopolitan* knock-off targeted toward the disabled consumer market. In this conventional, stylized, high-fashion shot, a typical female model—slender, white, blonde, clad in a black evening gown—is accompanied by her service dog. My argument is that public images such as this are radical because they fuse two previously antithetical visual discourses, the chic high-fashion shot and the earnest charity campaign. Public representations of disability have traditionally been contained within the conventions of sentimental charity images, exotic freak show portraits, medical illustrations, or sensational and forbidden pictures. Indeed, people with disabilities have been excluded most fully from the dominant, public world of the marketplace. Before the civil rights initiatives of the mid-twentieth century began to transform the public architectural and institutional environment, disabled people were segregated to the private and the medical spheres. . . .

I am arguing that the emergence of disabled fashion models is inadvertent activism without any legitimate agent for positive social change. Their appearance is simply a result of market forces. This both troubling and empowering form of entry into democratic capitalism produces a kind of instrumental form of equality: the freedom to be appropriated by consumer culture. In a democracy, to reject this paradoxical liberty is one thing; not to be granted it is another. Ever straining for novelty and capitalizing on titillation, the fashion-advertising world promptly appropriated the power of disabled figures to provoke responses. Diversity appeals to an upscale liberal sensibility these days, making consumers feel good about buying from companies that are charitable toward the traditionally disadvantaged. More important, the disability market is burgeoning. At 54 million people and growing fast as the Baby Boomers age, their spending power was estimated to have reached the trillion-dollar mark in 2000 (Williams 1999).

For the most part, commercial advertising presents disabled models in the same way as nondisabled models, simply because all models look essentially the same. The physical markings of gender, race, ethnicity, and disability are muted to the level of gesture, subordinated to the overall normativity of the models' appearance. Thus, commercial visual media cast disabled consumers as simply one of many variations that compose the market to which they appeal. Such routinization of disability imagery—however stylized and unrealistic it may be—nevertheless brings disability as a human experience out of the closet and into the normative public sphere.

Images of disabled fashion models enable people with disabilities, especially those who acquire impairments as adults, to imagine themselves as a part of the ordinary, albeit consumerist, world rather than as a special class of excluded untouchables and unviewables. Images of impairment as a familiar, even mundane, experience in the lives of seemingly successful, happy, well-adjusted people can reduce the identifying against oneself that is the overwhelming effect of oppressive and discriminatory attitudes toward people with disabilities. Such images, then, are at once liberatory and oppressive. They do the cultural work of integrating a previously excluded group into the dominant order—for better or worse—much like the inclusion of women in the military. . . .

The concluding version of activism I offer is less controversial and subtler than glitzy fashion spreads. It is what I call academic activism, the activism of integrating education, in the very broadest sense of that term. The academy is no ivory tower but rather it is the grassroots of the educational enterprise. Scholars and teachers shape the communal knowledge and the pedagogical archive that is disseminated from kindergarten to the university. Academic activism is most self-consciously vibrant in the aggregate of interdisciplinary identity studies—of which women's studies is exemplary—that strive to expose the workings of oppression, examine subject formation, and offer counternarratives for subjugated groups. Their cultural work is building an archive through historical and textual retrieval, canon reformation, role modeling, mentoring, curricular reform, and course and program development.

A specific form of feminist academic activism can be deepened through the complication of a disability analysis. I call this academic activism the methodology of intellectual tolerance. By this I do not mean tolerance in the more usual sense of tolerating each other—although that would be useful as well. What I mean is the intellectual position of tolerating what has been thought of as incoherence. As feminism has embraced the paradoxes that have emerged from its challenge to the gender system, it has not collapsed into chaos, but rather it has developed a methodology that tolerates internal conflict and contradiction. This method asks difficult questions, but accepts provisional answers. This method recognizes the power of identity, at the same time that it reveals identity as a fiction. This method both seeks equality and claims difference. This method allows us to teach with authority at the same time that we reject notions of pedagogical mastery. This method establishes institutional presences even while it acknowledges the limitations of institutions. This method validates the personal but implements disinterested inquiry. This method both writes new stories and recovers traditional ones. Considering disability as a vector of identity that intersects gender is one more internal challenge that threatens the coherence of woman, of course. But feminism can accommodate such complication and the contradictions it cultivates. Indeed, the intellectual tolerance I am arguing for espouses the partial, the provisional, the particular. Such an intellectual habit can be informed by disability experience and acceptance. To embrace the supposedly flawed body of disability is to critique the normalizing phallic fantasies of wholeness, unity, coherence, and completeness. The disabled body is contradiction, ambiguity, and partiality incarnate.

. . . Disability, like gender and race, is everywhere, once we know how to look for it. Integrating disability analyses will enrich and deepen all our teaching and scholarship. Moreover, such critical intellectual work facilitates a fuller integration of the sociopolitical world—for the benefit of everyone. As with gender, race, sexuality, and class: To understand how disability operates is to understand what it is to be fully human.

Notes

1. Interestingly, in Fiske's study, feminists, businesswomen, Asians, Northerners, and black professionals were stereotyped as highly competent, thus envied. In addition to having very low competence, housewives, disabled people, blind people, so-called retarded people, and the elderly were rated as warm, thus pitied.
2. Personal conversation with Nancy Mairs, Columbus, Ohio, 17 April 1998.

References

Aristotle. 1944. *Generation of Animals,* trans. A. L. Peck. Cambridge, MA: Harvard University Press.

Asch, Adrienne, and Gail Geller. 1996. Feminism, bioethics and genetics. In *Feminism, Bioethics: Beyond Reproduction*, edited by S.M. Wolf. Oxford, UK: Oxford University Press.

Bordo, Susan. 1993. *Unbearable Weight: Feminism, Western Culture, and the Body.* Berkeley: University of California Press.

Braidotti, Rosi. 1994. *Nomadic Subjects: Embodiment and Sexual Difference in Contemporary Feminist Thought.* New York: Columbia University Press.

Brownworth, Victoria A., and Susan Raffo, eds. 1999. *Restricted Access: Lesbians on Disability.* Seattle, WA: Seal Press.

Butler, Judith. 1993. *Bodies that Matter.* New York: Routledge.

Clark, David L., and Catherine Myser. 1996. Being humaned: Medical documentaries and the hyperrealization of conjoined twins. In *Freakery: Cultural Spectacles of the Extraordinary Body*, edited by Rosemarie Garland-Thomson. New York: New York University Press.

de Beauvoir, Simone. (1952)1974. *The Second Sex*, trans. H. M. Parshley. New York: Vintage Press.

Dreger, Alice Domurat. 1998. *Hermaphrodites and the Medical Invention of Sex.* Cambridge, MA: Harvard University Press.

Fausto-Sterling, Anne. 2000. *Sexing the Body: Gender Politics and the Construction of Sexuality.* New York: Basic Books.

_____. 1995. Gender, race, and nation: The comparative anatomy of Hottentot women in Europe, 1815–1817. In *Deviant Bodies: Cultural Perspectives in Science and Popular Culture*, edited by Jennifer Terry and Jacqueline Urla. Bloomington: Indiana University Press.

Fine, Michelle, and Adrienne Asch, eds. 1988. *Women with Disabilities: Essays in Psychology, Culture, and Politics.* Philadelphia: Temple University Press.

Finger, Anne. 1990. *Past Due: A Story of Disability, Pregnancy, and Birth.* Seattle, WA: Seal Press.

Fiske, Susan T., Amy J. C. Cuddy, and Peter Glick. 2001. *A Model of (Often Mixed) Stereotype Content: Competence and Warmth Respectively Follow from Perceived Status and Competition.* Unpublished study.

Foucault, Michel. 1979. *Discipline and Punish: The Birth of the Prison*, trans. Alan M. Sheridan-Smith. New York: Vintage Books.

Garland-Thomson, Rosemarie. 1997. *Extraordinary Bodies: Figuring Physical Disability in American Culture and Literature.* New York: Columbia University Press.

_____. 1999. Narratives of Deviance and Delight: Staring at Julia Pastrana, "The Extraordinary Lady." In *Beyond the Binary*, edited by Timothy Powell. New Brunswick, NJ: Rutgers University Press.

Gilman, Sander L. 1985. *Difference and Pathology: Stereotypes of Sexuality, Race, and Madness.* Ithaca, NY: Cornell University Press.

_____. 1998. *Creating Beauty to Cure the Soul.* Durham, NC: Duke University Press.

Hahn, Harlan. 1988. Can disability be beautiful? *Social Policy* 18(Winter):26–31.

Haiken, Elizabeth. 1997. *Venus Envy: A History of Cosmetic Surgery.* Baltimore, MD: Johns Hopkins University Press.

Haraway, Donna. 1991. *Simians, Cyborgs, and Women.* New York: Routledge.

Harstock, Nancy. 1983. The feminist standpoint: Developing the ground for a specifically feminist historical materialism. In *Discovering Reality*, edited by Sandra Harding and Merrell Hintikka. Dortrecht, Holland: Reidel Publishing.

Hubbard, Ruth. 1990. Who should and who should not inhabit the world? In *The Politics of Women's Biology.* New Brunswick, NJ: Rutgers University Press.

Keller, Evelyn Fox. 1992. Nature, nurture and the human genome project. In *The Code of Codes: Scientific and Social Issues in the Human Genome Project*, edited by Daniel J. Kevles and Leroy Hood. Cambridge, MA: Harvard University Press.

Kessler, Suzanne J. 1990. *Lessons from the Intersexed.* New Brunswick, NJ: Rutgers University Press.

Kittay, Eva, with Leo Kittay. 2000. On the expressivity and ethics of selective abortion for disability: Conversations with my son. In *Prenatal Testing and Disability Rights*, edited by Erik Parens and Adrienne Asch. Georgetown, MD: Georgetown University Press.

Linton, Simi. 1998. *Claiming Disability: Knowledge and Identity.* New York: New York University Press.

Longmore, Paul K. 1997. Conspicuous contribution and American cultural dilemmas: Telethon rituals of cleansing and renewal. In *The Body and Physical Difference: Discourses of Disability*, edited by David Mitchell and Sharon Snyder. Ann Arbor: University of Michigan Press.

Lorde, Audre. 1980. *The Cancer Journals.* San Francisco, CA: Spinsters Ink.

Mairs, Nancy. 1996. *Waist High in the World: A Life among the Nondisabled.* Boston, MA: Beacon Press.

"Meet Ellen Stohl." 1987. *Playboy* July:68–74.

Morrison, Toni. 1992. *Playing in the Dark: Whiteness and the Literary Imagination.* Cambridge, MA: Harvard University Press.

Parens, Erik, and Adrienne Asch. 2000. *Prenatal Testing and Disability Rights.* Georgetown, MD: Georgetown University Press.

Piercy, Marge. 1969. Unlearning not to speak. In *Circles on Water.* New York: Doubleday.

Rapp, Rayna. 1999. *Testing Women, Testing the Fetus: The Social Impact of Amniocentesis in America.* New York: Routledge.

Riley, Denise. 1999. Bodies, identities, feminisms. In *Feminist Theory and the Body: A Reader*, edited by Janet Price and Margrit Shildrick. Edinburgh, Scotland: Edinburgh University Press.

Russo, Mary. 1994. *The Female Grotesque: Risk, Excess, and Modernity.* New York: Routledge.

Saxton, Marsha. 1998. Disability rights and selective abortion. In *Abortion Wars: A Half Century of Struggle (1950–2000)*, edited by Ricky Solinger. Berkeley: University of California Press.

Sedgwick, Eve Kosofsky. 1990. *Epistemology of the Closet.* Berkeley: University of California Press.

Spelman, Elizabeth, V. 1988. *Inessential Woman: Problems of Exclusion in Feminist Thought.* Boston, MA: Beacon Press.

Tuana, Nancy. 1993. *The Less Noble Sex: Scientific, Religious and Philosophical Conceptions of Woman's Nature.* Indianapolis: Indiana University Press.

Williams, John M. 1999. And here's the pitch: Madison Avenue discovers the "invisible consumer." *WE Magazine* July/August:28–31.

Wolf, Naomi. 1991. *The Beauty Myth: How Images of Beauty Are Used Against Women.* New York: William Morrow and Co.

Young, Iris Marion. 1990. Throwing Like a Girl. In *Throwing Like a Girl and Other Essays in Feminist Philosophy and Social Theory.* Bloomington: Indiana University Press.

II

THE POLITICS OF SEXUALITY

Sexuality is an integral part of everyone's life. Even those who are celibate generally retain sexual feelings, whether of longing or revulsion, and still define themselves in terms of their sexual history and sexual orientation. Moreover, sexual activity provides a broad canvas on which individuals express their personalities and values. For these reasons, both individuals and societies have found that controlling women's sexuality is an effective way to control women's lives.

The articles in this part address the link between women's bodies, women's sexuality, and the control of women's lives. In the first article, "Breasted Experience: The Look and the Feeling," Iris Marion Young explores women's embodied experiences of their breasts and how that experience is and is not affected by men's ideas about women's breasts. Following, Deborah L. Tolman's article, "Daring to Desire: Culture and the Bodies of Adolescent Girls," discusses young women's feelings about sexual desire and sexual danger, as well as how social privilege (based on race or social class) affects those feelings. Then, in "A Tale of Two Technologies: HPV Vaccination, Male Circumcision, and Sexual Health," Laura M. Carpenter and Monica J. Casper look at how new medical technologies can reinforce existing ideas about young women's sexuality.

The next two articles explore media representations of women's sexuality. In "'Get Your Freak On': Sex, Babies, and Images of Black Femininity," Patricia Hill Collins analyzes contemporary media messages about African American women's bodies and sexuality, while in "Brain, Brow, and Booty:

Latina Iconicity in U.S. Popular Culture," Isabel Molina Guzmán and Angharad N. Valdivia look at the portrayal of iconic Latinas in U.S. media.

Whereas African American and Latina women are often marginalized by other Americans and mainstream U.S. culture, other young women choose to place themselves outside the mainstream. The final article in this section, "'So Full of Myself as a Chick': Goth Women, Sexual Independence, and Gender Egalitarianism," by Amy C. Wilkins, looks at the "polyamorous" culture of Goths, in which both men and women are expected to have "open" sexual and romantic relationships.

7

Breasted Experience

The Look and the Feeling

Iris Marion Young

From Maxim *to films to religious iconography, we receive a constant stream of messages regarding men's view of the female breast. Only rarely, however, do we get a glimpse of women's relationships with their breasts. This is the topic Iris Marion Young explores in her article "Breasted Experience: The Look and the Feeling."*

A key distinction addressed by Young is the distinction between body as object and body as subject. Men may view women's bodies as objects, evaluating them as they might any other tool or toy, with little or no attention to the person who inhabits that body. Women, too, may internalize or merely accommodate this perspective, and view their bodies as tools to be used or judged by men or themselves. At the same time, as Young points out, women's lives and women's bodies are inseparable, and so women must also experience the body as subject (that is, as part of their essential self, not simply as an almost-external resource to be used). Thus, in this article she also focuses on how women experience physical sensations of pleasure and pain through their breasts.

A second key distinction Young explores is that between the "Madonna" and the "whore." An underlying thread in Western culture is the assumption that women are either sexually and morally pure or impure—Madonnas or whores. This dichotomy is threatened whenever (as is sometimes the case) women experience breastfeeding as a sensual and even sexual experience, rather than experiencing motherhood and breastfeeding as selfless sacrifice. This, Young argues, is why nipples are considered so much more scandalous than are the rest of women's breasts.

Young's article is based in part on a neo-Freudian perspective. According to Sigmund Freud (1856–1939), a Viennese doctor, to become a mentally healthy adult one had to respond successfully to a series of biological events and

Originally published as Iris Young (1992), "Breasted Experience," pp. 215–230 in Drew Leder (ed.) *The Body in Medical Thought and Practice*, Boston: Kluwer. Reprinted with kind permission from Springer Science+Business Media B.V.

experiences, each invested with sexual meaning. One of these was breastfeeding, which Freud claimed gave sexual pleasure to both girls and boys. Freud believed that to become psychologically healthy, girls needed to shift their sexual desires from their mothers' breasts to males, while boys needed to shift from their mothers' breasts to the bodies and breasts of other females. Although Freud's theories were highly conservative and unsupported by empirical evidence, many feminists have found useful ideas within them. Young uses this theory to help explain our cultural discomfort with viewing mothers in sexual terms. She also uses it to argue in favor of highlighting women's and mothers' sexuality, and against the tendency (seen in some feminists) to celebrate women as selfless nurturers.

. . . For many women, if not all, breasts are an important component of body self-image; a woman may love them or dislike them, but she is rarely neutral.

In this patriarchal culture, focused to the extreme on breasts, a woman, especially in those adolescent years but also through the rest of her life, often feels herself judged and evaluated according to the size and contours of her breasts, and indeed she often is. For her and for others, her breasts are the daily visible and tangible signifier of her womanliness, and her experience is as variable as the size and the shape of breasts themselves. A woman's chest, much more than a man's, is *in question* in this society, up for judgment, and whatever the verdict, she has not escaped the condition of being problematic.

In this essay I explore some aspects of the cultural construction of breasts in our male-dominated society and seek a positive women's voice for breasted experience. . . .

I. Breasts as Objects

I used to stand before the mirror with two Spalding balls under my shirt, longing to be a grown woman with the big tits of Marilyn Monroe and Elizabeth Taylor. They are called boobs, knockers, knobs; they are toys to be grabbed, squeezed, handled. In the total scheme of the objectification of women, breasts are the primary things.

A fetish is an object that stands in for the phallus—the phallus as the one and only measure and symbol of desire, the representation of sexuality. This culture fetishizes breasts. Breasts are the symbol of feminine sexuality, so the "best" breasts are like the phallus: high, hard, and pointy. Thirty years ago it was de rigueur to encase them in wire, rubber, and elastic armor that lifted them and pointed them straight out. Today fashion has loosened up a bit, but the foundational contours remain; some figures are better than others, and the ideal breasts look like a Barbie's.

We experience our objectification as a function of the look of the other, the male gaze that judges and dominates from afar (Bartky 1979; Kaplan

1983, 23–35). We experience our position as established and fixed by a subject who stands afar, who has looked and made his judgment before he ever makes me aware of his admiration or disgust. When a girl blossoms into adolescence and sallies forth, chest out boldly to the world, she experiences herself as being looked at in a different way than before. People, especially boys, notice her breasts or her lack of them; they may stare at her chest and remark on her. If her energy radiates from her chest, she too often finds the rays deflected by the gaze that positions her from outside, evaluating her according to standards that she had no part in establishing and that remain outside her control. She may enjoy the attention and learn to draw the gaze to her bosom with a sense of sexual power. She may loathe and fear the gaze that fixes her in shock or mockery, and she may take pains to hide her chest behind baggy clothes and bowed shoulders. She may for the most part ignore the objectifying gaze, retaining nevertheless edges of ambiguity and uncertainty about her body. The way women respond to the evaluating gaze on their chests is surely as variable as the size and character of the breasts themselves, but few women in our society escape having to take some attitude toward the potentially objectifying regard of the other on her breasts. . . .

Breasts are the most visible sign of a woman's femininity, the signal of her sexuality. In phallocentric culture sexuality is oriented to the man and modeled on male desire. Capitalist, patriarchal American media-dominated culture objectifies breasts before a distancing gaze that freezes and masters. The fetishized breasts are valued as objects, things; they must be solid, easy to handle. Subject to the logic of phallocentric domination of nature, their value, her value as a sexual being, appears in their measurement. Is she a B-cup or a C-cup? Even when sleek athletic fashions were current, breasts were often still prominent. And today the news is that the big bosom is back (Anderson 1988; *Wall Street Journal* 1988).

What matters is the look of them, how they measure up before the normalizing gaze. There is one perfect shape and proportion for breasts: round, sitting high on the chest, large but not bulbous, with the look of firmness. The norm is contradictory, of course. If breasts are large, their weight will tend to pull them down; if they are large and round, they will tend to be floppy rather than firm. In its image of the solid object this norm suppresses the fleshy materiality of breasts, this least muscular, softest body part.[1] Magazines construct and parade these perfect breasts. They present tricks for how to acquire and maintain our own—through rigorous exercise or $50 creams (neither of which generally produces the desired effect), or tricks of what to wear and how to stand so as to appear to have them.

Like most norms of femininity, the normalized breast hardly describes an "average" around which real women's breasts cluster. It is an ideal that only a very few women's bodies even approximate; given the power of the dominant media, however, the norm is ubiquitous, and most of us internalize it to some degree, making our self-abnegation almost inevitable (Bartky 1988). Even those women whose breasts do approximate the ideal can do so only for a short period in their lives. It is a pubescent norm from which most women deviate increasingly with each passing year. Whatever her age, if she has given birth her breasts sag away from the ideal; perhaps they have lost some of their prepartum fullness and roundness, and her nipples protrude. Whether a woman is a mother or not, gravity does its work, quickly defining a woman's body as old because it is no longer adolescent. The truly old woman's body thereby moves beyond the pale. Flat, wrinkled, greatly sagging, the old woman's breasts signify for the ageist dominant culture a woman no longer useful for sex or reproduction, a woman used up. Yet there is nothing natural about such a decline in value. Some other cultures venerate the woman with wrinkled, sagging breasts; they are signs of much mothering and the wisdom of experience. From their point of view an obsession with firm, high breasts would be considered to express a desire to be immature (Ayalah and Weinstock 1979, 136).

II. Woman-centered Meaning

However alienated male-dominated culture makes us from our bodies, however much it gives us instruments of self-hatred and oppression, still our bodies are ourselves. We move and act in this flesh and these sinews, and live our pleasures and pains in our bodies. If we love ourselves at all, we love our bodies. And many women identify their breasts as themselves, living their embodied experience at some distance from the hard norms of the magazine gaze. However much the patriarchy may wish us to, we do not live our breasts only as the objects of male desire, but as our own, the sproutings of a specifically female desire.

But phallocentric culture tends not to think of a woman's breasts as hers. Woman is a natural territory; her breasts belong to others—her husband, her lover, her baby. It's hard to imagine a woman's breasts as her own, from her own point of view, to imagine their *value* apart from measurement and exchange. I do not pretend to discover a woman-centered breast experience. My conceptualization of a woman-centered experience of breasts is a construction, an imagining. . . .

From the position of the female subject, what matters most about her breasts is their feeling and sensitivity rather than how they look. The size or age of her breasts does not matter for the sensitivity of her nipples, which often seem to have a will of their own, popping out at the smallest touch, change of temperature, or embarrassment. For many women breasts are a multiple and fluid zone of deep pleasure quite independent of intercourse, though sometimes not independent of orgasm. For a phallic sexuality this is a scandal. A woman does not always experience the feeling of her breasts positively; if they are large she often feels them pulling uncomfortably on her neck and back. Her breasts are also a feeling of bodily change. She often experiences literal growing pains as her body moves from girl to woman. When she becomes pregnant, she often knows this first through changes in the feeling of her breasts, and many women have breast sensitivity associated with menstruation. When she is lactating, she feels the pull of milk letting down, which may be activated by a touch, or a cry, or even a thought.

Breasts stand as a primary badge of sexual specificity, the irreducibility of sexual difference to a common measure. Yet phallocentric sexuality tries to orient the sexual around its one and only sexual object. Active sexuality is the erect penis, which rises in its potency and penetrates the passive female receptacle. Intercourse is the true sex act, and nonphallic pleasures are either deviant or preparatory. Touching and kissing the breasts is "foreplay," a pleasant prelude after which the couple goes on to "the real thing." But in her own experience of sexuality there is a scandal: she can derive the deepest pleasure from these dark points on her chest, a pleasure maybe greater than he can provide in intercourse. Phallocentric heterosexist norms try to construct female sexuality as simply a complement to male sexuality, its mirror, or the hole—lack that he fills. But her pleasure is different, a pleasure he can only imagine. To the degree that he can experience anything like it, it's only a faint copy of female potency. Imagine constructing the model of sexual power in breasts rather than penises. Men's nipples would have to be constructed as puny copies, just as men have constructed women's clitorides as puny copies of the penis. Of course this all presumes constructing sexuality by a common measure. Phallocentric construction of sexuality denies and represses the sensitivity of breasts.

> For what male "organ" will be set forth in derision like the clitoris?—that penis too tiny for comparison to entail anything but total devaluation, complete decathexization. Of course, there are the breasts. But they are to be classed among the secondary, or so-called secondary, characteristics. Which no doubt justifies the fact that there is so little questioning of the effects of breast atrophy in the male. Wrongly, of course. (Irigaray 1985, 22–23)

Both gay men and lesbians often defy this niggardly attitude toward nipple sexuality. Gay men often explore the erotic possibilities of one another's breasts, and lesbians often derive a particular pleasure from the mutual touching of breasts.

The breasts, for many women, are places of independent pleasure. Deconstructing the hierarchical privilege of heterosexual complementarity, giving equal value to feelings of the breast diffuses the identity of sex. Our sex is not one but, as Irigaray says, plural and heterogeneous; we have sex organs all over our bodies, in many places, and perhaps none is privileged. We experience eroticism as flowing, multiple, unlocatable, not identical or in the same place (Irigaray 1985, 23–33).

The brassiere functions partly as a barrier to touch. Without it, every movement can produce a stroking of cloth across her nipples, which she may find pleasurable or distracting, as the case may be. But if the chest is a center of a person's being-in-the-world, her mode of being surely differs depending on whether her chest is open to touch, moving in the world, or confined and bordered.

Without a bra, a woman's breasts are also deobjectified, desubstantialized. Without a bra, most women's breasts do not have the high, hard, pointy look that phallic culture posits as the norm. They droop and sag and gather their bulk at the bottom. Without a bra, the fluid being of breasts is more apparent. They are not objects with one definite shape, but radically change their shape with body position and movements. Hand over the head, lying on one's back or side, bending over in front—all produce very different breast shapes. Many women's breasts are much more like a fluid than a solid; in movement, they sway, jiggle, bounce, ripple even when the movement is small.

Women never gathered in a ritual bra burning, but the image stuck. We did, though, shed the bra—hundreds of thousands, millions of us. I was no feminist when, young and impetuous, I shoved the bras back in the drawer and dared to step outside with nothing on my chest but a shirt. It was an ambiguous time in 1969. I had a wondrous sense of freedom and a little bit of defiance. I never threw the bras away; they were there to be worn on occasions when propriety and delicacy required them. Why is burning the bra the ultimate image of the radical subversion of the male-dominated order?[2] Because unbound breasts show their fluid and changing shape; they do not remain the firm and stable objects that phallocentric fetishism desires. Because unbound breasts make a mockery of the ideal of a "perfect" breast. The bra normalizes the breasts, lifting and curving the breasts to approximate the one and only breast ideal.

But most scandalous of all, without a bra, the nipples show. Nipples are indecent. Cleavage is good—the more, the better—and we can wear bikinis that barely cover the breasts, but the nipples must be carefully obscured. Even go-go dancers wear pasties. Nipples are no-nos, for they show the breasts to be active and independent zones of sensitivity and eroticism.

What would a positive experience of ourselves as breasted be in the absence of the male gaze? There are times and places where women in American society can experience hints of such an experience. In lesbian-dominated women's spaces where women can be confident that the male gaze will not invade, I have found a unique experience of women's bodies. In such women's spaces women frequently walk around, do their chores, sit around and chat naked from the waist up. Such a context deobjectifies the breasts. A woman not used to such a womanspace might at first stare, treating the breasts as objects. But the everydayness, the constant engagement of this bare-breasted body in activity dereifies them. But they do not thereby recede, as they might when clothed. On the contrary, women's breasts are *interesting*. In a womanspace with many women walking around bare-breasted, the variability and individuality of breasts becomes salient. I would like to say that in a womanspace, without the male gaze, a woman's breasts become almost like part of her face. Like her nose or her mouth, a woman's breasts are distinctive, one sign by which one might recognize her. Like her mouth or her eyes, their aspect changes with her movement and her mood; the movement of her breasts is part of the expressiveness of her body.

III. Motherhood and Sexuality

The woman is young and timeless, clothed in blue, a scarf over her head, which is bowed over the child at her breast, discreetly exposed by her hand that draws aside her covering, and the baby's hand rests on the round flesh. This is the Christian image of peace and wholeness, the perfect circle of generation (Miles 1985). With hundreds of variations, from Florentine frescoes to the cover of dozens of books at B. Dalton's, this is a primary image of power, female power. To be purity and goodness itself, the origin of life, the source to which the living man owes his substance—this is an awesome power. For centuries identification with that power has bonded women to the patriarchal order, and while today its seductive hold on us is loosening, it still provides women a unique position with which to identify (Kristeva 1985; Suleiman 1985).

But it is bought at the cost of sexuality. The Madonna must be a virgin mother. The logic of identity that constructs beings as objects also constructs categories whose borders are clear and exclusive: essence/accident, mind/body, good/bad. The logic of such oppositions includes everything, and they exclude one another by defining the other as excluded by their oneness or essence. In Western logic woman is the seat of such oppositional categorization, for patriarchal logic defines an exclusive border between motherhood and sexuality. The virgin or the whore, the pure or the impure, the nurturer or the seducer is either asexual mother or sexualized beauty, but one precludes the other.

Thus psychoanalysis, for example, regards motherhood as a substitute for sexuality. The woman desires a child as her stand-in for the penis, as her way of appropriating the forbidden father. Happily, her desires are passive, and she devotes herself completely to giving. Helene Deutsch (1985), for example, identifies normal motherhood with feminine masochism; the true woman is one who gets pleasure from self-sacrifice, the abnegation of pleasure.

Barbara Sichtermann (1986, 57) discusses this separation of motherhood and sexuality:

> Basically, women were only admitted to the realm of sexuality as guests to be dispatched off towards their "true" vocation as agents of reproduction. And reproduction was something which happened outside the realm of pleasure, it was God's curse on Eve. Women have to cover the longest part of the road to reproduction with their bodies and yet in this way they became beings existing outside sexuality, outside the delights of orgiastic release,

> they became asexual mothers, the bearers of unborn children and the bearers of suffering. Breastfeeding too was of course part of this tamed, pleasureless, domesticated world of "maternal duties."

Patriarchy depends on this border between motherhood and sexuality. In our lives and desires it keeps women divided from ourselves, in having to identify with one or another image of womanly power—the nurturing, competent, selfless mother, always sacrificing, the soul of goodness; or the fiery, voluptuous vamp with the power of attraction, leading victims down the road of pleasure, sin, and danger. Why does patriarchy need this division between motherhood and sexuality? This is perhaps one of the most overdetermined dichotomies in our culture; accordingly, I have several answers to this question.

In the terms in which Kristeva (1980) puts it, for both sexes entrance into the symbolic requires repressing the original jouissance of attachment to the mother's body. A baby's body is saturated with feeling, which it experiences as undifferentiated from the caretaking body it touches; repeated pains break the connection, but its pleasure is global and multiple. Eroticism must be made compatible with civilization, submission to the law, and thus adult experience of sexuality must repress memory of this infantile jouissance. Adult meanings of eroticism thus must be divorced from mothers. Even though for both genders, sexual desire and pleasure are informed by presymbolic jouissance, this must be repressed in the particular cultural configuration that emphasizes rationality as unity, identity, thematic reference.

The dichotomy of motherhood and sexuality, I said, maps onto a dichotomy of good/bad, pure/impure. These dichotomies play in with the repression of the body itself. One kind of attachment, love, is "good" because it is entirely defleshed, spiritual. Mother love and the love of the child for the mother represent the perfection of love—eroticism entirely sublimated. Fleshy eroticism, on the other hand, goes on the other side of the border, where lies the despised body, bad, impure. The separation of motherhood and sexuality thus instantiates the culture's denial of the body and the consignment of fleshy desires to fearful temptation.

The incest taboo also accounts for the separation, as even classical Freudianism suggests. Such patriarchal propriety in women's bodies may be unconsciously motivated by a desire to gain control over himself by mastering the mother. But sexual desire for the mother must be repressed in order to prepare the man for separation from femininity and entrance into the male bond through which women are exchanged. As Dinnerstein (1977) suggests, repression of desire for the mother is also necessary to defend his masculinity against the vulnerability and mortality of the human condition.

Now to some explanations more directly related to the interests of patriarchy. By separating motherhood and sexuality men/husbands do not have to perceive themselves as sharing female sexuality with their children. The oedipal triangle has three nodes, and there are issues for the father as well as the child. The Law of the Father establishes ownership of female sexuality.

The satisfactions of masculinity are in having her to minister to his ego, the complement to his desire; he has private ownership of her affections (Pateman 1988). Her function either as the phallic object or the mirror to his desire cannot be maintained if her mother love is the same as her sex love. They need to be projected onto different people or thought of as different kinds of relationships.

The separation between motherhood and sexuality within a woman's own existence seems to ensure her dependence on the man for pleasure. If motherhood is sexual, the mother and child can be a circuit of pleasure for the mother, then the man may lose her allegiance and attachment. So she must repress her eroticism with her child, and with it her own particular return to her repressed experience of jouissance, and maintain a specific connection with the man. If she experiences motherhood as sexual, she may find him dispensable. This shows another reason for repressing a connection between motherhood and sexuality in women. A woman's infantile eroticism in relation to her mother must be broken in order to awaken her heterosexual desire. Lesbian mothering may be the ultimate affront to patriarchy, for it involves a double displacement of an erotic relation of a woman to a man.

Without the separation of motherhood and sexuality, finally, there can be no image of a love that is all give and no take. I take this as perhaps the most important point. The ideal mother defines herself as giver and feeder, takes her existence and sense of purpose entirely from giving. Such a mother-giver establishes a foundation for the self-absorbed ego, the subject of modern philosophy, which many feminists have uncovered as being happily male (Schemen 1983; Flax 1983). Thus motherhood must be separated from her sexuality, her desire. She cannot have sexual desire in her mothering because this is a need, a want, and she cannot be perfectly giving if she is wanting or selfish.

In all these ways, then, patriarchy is founded on the border between motherhood and sexuality. Woman is both, essentially—the repository of the body, the flesh that he desires, owns and masters, tames and controls; and the nurturing source of his life and ego. Both are necessary functions, bolstering male ego, which cannot be served if they are together, hence the border, their reification into the hierarchical opposition of good/bad, pure/impure. The separation often splits mothers; it is in our bodies that the sacrifice that creates and sustains patriarchy is reenacted repeatedly (Ferguson 1983). Freedom for women involves dissolving this separation.

The border between motherhood and sexuality is lived out in the way women experience their breasts and in the cultural marking of breasts. To be understood as sexual, the feeding function of the breasts must be suppressed, and when the breasts are nursing they are desexualized. A great many women in this culture that fetishizes breasts are reluctant to breastfeed because they perceive that they will lose their sexuality. They believe that nursing will alter their breasts and make them ugly and undesirable. They fear that their men will find their milky breasts unattractive or will be jealous of the babies who take their bodies. Some women who decide to breast-feed report that they themselves are uninterested in sex during that period or that they cease to think of their breasts as sexual and to take sexual pleasure in their breasts while they are nursing.[3]

Breasts are a scandal because they shatter the border between motherhood and sexuality. Nipples are taboo because they are quite literally, physically and functionally *undecidable* in the split between motherhood and sexuality. One of the most subversive things feminism can do is affirm this undecidability of motherhood and sexuality.

When I began nursing I sat stiff in a chair, holding the baby in the crook of my arm, discreetly lifting my shirt and draping it over my breast. This was mother work, and I was efficient and gentle, and watched the time. After some weeks, drowsy during the morning feeding, I went to bed with my baby. I felt that I had crossed a forbidden river as I moved toward the bed, stretched her legs out alongside my reclining torso, me lying on my side like a cat or a mare while my baby suckled. This was pleasure, not work. I lay there as she made love to me, snuggling her legs up to my stomach, her hand stroking my breast, my chest. She lay between me and my lover, and she and I were a couple. From then on I looked forward with happy pleasure to our early-morning intercourse, she sucking at my hard fullness, relieving and warming me, while her father slept.

I do not mean to romanticize motherhood, to suggest by means of a perverted feminist reversal that through motherhood, women achieve their access to the divine or the moral. Nor would I deny that there are dangers in the eroticization of mothering—dangers to children, in particular, that derive from the facts of power more than sexuality. Mothers must not abuse their power, but this has always been so. Certainly I do not wish to suggest that all women should be mothers; there is much that would be trying about mothering even under ideal circumstances, and certainly there is much about it in our society that is oppressive. But in the experience of many women we may find some means for challenging patriarchal divisions that seek to repress and silence those experiences.

Some feminist discourse criticizes the sexual objectification of women and proposes that feminists dissociate women from the fetishized female body and promote instead an image of women as representing caring, nurturing, soothing values. American cultural feminism exhibits this move: women will retreat from, reject patriarchal definitions of sexuality and project motherly images of strength, wisdom, and nurturance as feminist virtues, or even redefine the erotic as like mother love.[4] Much French feminism is also in danger of a mere revaluation that retains this dichotomy between motherhood and sexuality, rather than exploding patriarchal definitions of motherhood (Stanton 1989).

A more radical move would be to shatter the border between motherhood and sexuality. What can this mean? Most concretely, it means pointing to and celebrating breast-feeding as a sexual interaction for both the mother and the infant (Sichtermann 1986). It means letting women speak in public about the pleasure that many report they derive from their babies and about the fact that weaning is often a loss for them (Myers and Siegel 1985). But there is a more general meaning to shattering the border, which applies even to mothers. Crashing the border means affirming that women, all women can "have it all." It means creating and affirming a kind of love in which a woman does not have to choose between pursuing her own selfish, insatiable desire and giving pleasure and sustenance to another close to her, a nurturance that gives and also takes for itself. Whether they are mothers or not, women today are still too often cast in the nurturant role, whatever their occupation or location. This nurturant position is that of the self-sacrificing listener and stroker, the one who turns toward the wounded, needful ego that uses her as mirror and enclosing womb, giving nothing to her, and she of course is polite enough not to ask. As feminists we should affirm the value of nurturing; an ethic of caring does indeed hold promise for a more human justice, and political values guided by such an ethic would change the character of the public for the better. But we must also insist that nurturers need, that love is partly selfish, and that a woman deserves her own irreducible pleasures.

Notes

I am grateful to Sandra Bartky, Lucy Candib, Drew Leder, and Francine Rainone for helpful comments on an earlier version of this paper. Thanks to Nancy Irons for research help.

Considering the vast explosion of women's-studies literature in the past two decades, there is an amazing absence of writing about women's experience of breasts, and some of what little there is does not arise from feminist sensibility. One wants to explain why it is that feminists have not written about breasts, even when there is a great deal of writing about sexuality, mothering, the body, and medical interactions with women's bodies. Why this silence about breasts, especially when if you tell women you are writing about women's breasted experience, they begin to pour out stories of their feelings about their breasts? Women are interested in talking about their breasted bodies and interested in listening to one another. But we almost never do it conversation, let alone in writing.

In the darkness of my despair about women's own breast censorship, I uncovered a gold mine: Daphna Ayalah and Isaac Weinstock (1979), *Breasts: Women Speak About Their Breasts and Their Lives.* This is a collection of photographs of the breasts, with accompanying experiential accounts, of fifty women. Ayalah and Weinstock asked all the women the same set of questions about growing up, sexuality, aging, birthing and nursing, and so on. Thus while each woman's stories are her own and in her own words, they can be compared. The authors were careful to interview different kinds of women: old, young, and middle-aged; women of color as well as white women; women who have and have not had children; lesbians as well as straight women; models; call girls; etc. This is an extraordinary book, and many of the generalizations I make about women's experience in this paper are derived from my reading of it.

1. Susan Bordo (1989) suggests that achievement society takes Western culture's denial of the body and fleshiness to extremes, projecting norms of tightness and hardness for all bodies. This is the particular contemporary cultural meaning of

the demand for slenderness in both men and women, but especially women. Bordo does not mention breasts specifically in this discussion, but clearly this analysis helps us understand why media norms of breasts make this impossible demand for a "firm" breast.

2. Susan Brownmiller (1984, 45) suggests that women going braless evoke shock and anger because men implicitly think that they own breasts and that only they should remove bras.
3. Women's attitudes toward breast-feeding and its relation or lack of it to sexuality are, of course, extremely variable. Teenage mothers, for example, have a great deal more difficulty than do older mothers with the idea of breast-feeding, probably because they are more insecure about their sexuality (Yoos 1985). Ayalah and Weinstock (1979) interview many mothers specifically about their attitudes toward and experiences in breast-feeding. The reactions are quite variable, from women who report the experience of breast-feeding as being nearly religious to women who say they could not consider doing it because they thought it was too disgusting.
4. In the feminist sexuality debate, some sexual libertarians accuse those whom they debate of holding a kind of desexualized, spiritualized, or nurturant eroticism. [See Ann Ferguson (1989) for an important discussion of the way out of this debate.] I do not here wish to take sides in this debate, which I hope is more or less over. The debate certainly reveals, however, the strength of a good/bad opposition around eroticism as it plays out in our culture. Ferguson suggests that the debate sets up an opposition between pleasure and love, which is an unhelpful polarity.

References

Anderson, Jeremy Weir. 1988. Breast frenzy. *Self* December:83–89.

Ayalah, Daphna, and Isaac Weinstock. 1979. *Breasts: Women Speak About Their Breasts and Their Lives.* New York: Simon and Schuster.

Bartky, Sandra. 1979. On psychological oppression. In *Philosophy and Women*, edited by Sharon Bishop and Marjorie Weinzweig. Belmont, CA: Wadsworth.

———. 1988. Foucault, femininity and the modernization of patriarchal power. In *Feminism and Foucault: Reflections on Resistance*, edited by Irene Diamond and Lee Quimby. Boston: Northeastern University Press.

Bordo, Susan. 1989. Reading the slender body. In *Body/Politics: Women and the Discourses of Science*, edited by Mary Jacobus, Evelyn Fox Keller, and Sally Shuttleworth. New York: Routledge, Chapman and Hall.

Brownmiller, Susan. 1984. *Femininity.* New York: Simon and Schuster.

Deutsch, Helene. 1985. *The Psychology of Women: A Psychoanalytic Interpretation.* Vol. II. New York: Grune & Stratton.

Dinnerstein, Dorothy. 1977. *The Mermaid and the Minotaur.* New York: Harper and Row.

Ferguson, Ann. 1983. On conceiving motherhood and sexuality: A feminist materialist approach. In *Mothering: Essays in Feminist Theory*, edited by Joyce Trebilcot. Totowa, NJ: Rowman and Allenheld.

———. 1989. *Blood at the Root.* London: Pandora Press.

Flax, Jane. 1983. Political philosophy and the patriarchal unconscious: A psychoanalytic perspective on epistemology and metaphysics. In *Discovering Reality: Feminist Perspectives on Epistemology, Metaphysics, Methodology and Philosophy of Science*, edited by Sandra Harding and Merrill B. Hintikka. Dordrecht, the Netherlands: D. Reidel Publishing.

Irigaray, Luce. 1985. *Speculum of the Other Woman*. Ithaca, NY: Cornell University Press.

Kaplan, E. Ann. 1983. *Women and Film: Both Sides of the Camera*. New York: Methuen.

Kristeva, Julia. 1980. The father, love, and banishment. In *Desire in Language*, edited by Leon S. Roudiez. New York: Columbia University Press.

———. 1985. Sabat Mater. In *The Female Body in Western Culture*, edited by Susan Rubin Suleiman. Cambridge, MA: Harvard University Press.

Miles, Margaret R. 1985. The virgin's one bare breast: Female nudity and religious meaning in Tuscan early Renaissance culture. In *The Female Body in Western Culture*, edited by Susan Rubin Suleiman. Cambridge, MA: Harvard University Press.

Myers, Harriet H., and Paul S. Siegel. 1985. Motivation to breastfeed: A fit to the opponent-process theory? *Journal of Personality and Social Psychology* 49:188–93.

Pateman, Carole. 1988. *The Sexual Contract*. Stanford, CA: Stanford University Press.

Schemen, Naomi. 1983. Individualism and the objects of psychology. In *Discovering Reality: Feminist Perspectives on Epistemology, Metaphysics, Methodology and Philosophy of Science*, edited by Sandra Harding and Merrill B. Hintikka. Dordrecht, the Netherlands: D. Reidel Publishing.

Sichtermann, Barbara. 1986. The lost eroticism of the breasts. In *Femininity: The Politics of the Personal*. Minneapolis: University of Minnesota Press.

Stanton, Donna. 1989. Difference on trial: A critique of the maternal metaphor in Cixous, Irigaray, and Kristeva. In *The Thinking Muse: Feminism and Modern French Philosophy*, edited by Jeffner Allen and Iris Marion Young. Bloomington: Indiana University Press.

Suleiman, Susan Rubin. 1985. Writing and motherhood. In *The (M)other Tongue: Essays in Feminist Psychoanalytical Interpretation*, edited by Shirley Nelson Garner, Claire Kahane, and Madelon Sprengnether. Ithaca, NY: Cornell University Press.

Wall Street Journal. 1988. Forget hemlines: The bosomy look is big fashion news, 2 December, 1.

Yoos, Lorie. 1985. Developmental issues and the choice of feeding method of adolescent mothers. *Journal of Obstetrical and Gynecological Nursing* 28:68–72.

8

Daring to Desire

Culture and the Bodies of Adolescent Girls

DEBORAH L. TOLMAN

Deborah L. Tolman's article, "Daring to Desire: Culture and the Bodies of Adolescent Girls," offers a groundbreaking analysis of how teenage girls think about their own sexual desires. This research challenges the commonly held idea that teenage girls engage in sexual activity because they want intimate relationships rather than because they feel sexual desire. In contrast, among the small and nonrandom group of adolescents Tolman interviewed, more than half clearly articulated feelings of desire: intense bodily sensations that demanded a response of some sort.

In addition, through contrasting the experiences and voices of urban and suburban girls, Tolman shows how teens' feelings of sexual desire are shaped both by the promise of sexual pleasure and the threat of sexual dangers. The "urban girls" in her study live in an environment in which the dangers of sexuality—unwanted pregnancy, sexual violence, and the social stigma of having a "bad reputation"—are apparent. Consequently, most consciously work to silence their desires. In contrast, the "suburban girls," who live in a physically and emotionally safer environment, feel far freer to acknowledge and enjoy their sexual desires, although they struggle with the conflict between those desires and the desire to maintain their image as "good girls." Thus, Tolman's research both demonstrates that young girls experience sexual desire and shows how social context substantially limits girls' ability to acknowledge and enjoy those feelings.

Originally published as "Daring to Desire: Culture and the Bodies of Adolescent Girls," in Janice M. Irvine (ed.), *Sexual Cultures and the Construction of Adolescent Identities* (Philadelphia: Temple University Press, 1994), 250–284.

This culture's story about adolescent girls and sexuality goes like this: girls do not want sex; what girls really want is intimacy and a relationship. This concept of girls' sexuality, which permeates education and psychology, focuses on girls' emotional feelings and desire for intimacy and excludes their sexual feelings and their bodies. Statistics indicate that girls do in fact have sex (that is, sexual intercourse) and are beginning to have sex at younger and younger ages.[1] Keeping within the terms of the cultural story, the fact of girls' sexual activity is explained in terms of relationships: girls have sex in the service of relationships. However, the assumption that girls are having sex for the sake of relationships rather than in relation to their own desire has precluded empirical explorations of this aspect of girls' experiences of adolescence. The most striking feature of a review of the psychological research on adolescent girls' sexual desire is that there is virtually none. . . .

Recent research in the psychology of women's development reveals that at adolescence girls come into a different and more problematic relation with themselves, with others, and with the culture(s) in which they are growing.[2] In essence, many girls appear to face a relational impasse or crisis. Carol Gilligan has characterized this crisis as a division between what girls know through experience and what is socially constructed as "reality." It is also at adolescence that girls come into relationship with their social contexts as sexual beings. As the unmistakable contours of a female body emerge, a girl's body becomes defined in cultural terms as an object of men's fantasies and desires.[3] When breasts grow and hips form, girls' bodies are rendered sexual, and the relationship between internal and external, the subjective experience of desire and the objective experience of finding oneself objectified, is essentially confusing and problematic for girls.[4] This psychologically difficult yet very real psychological challenge, coupled with the fact that adolescent girls are sexually active, makes the question of how adolescent girls experience sexual desire especially pressing. . . .

The Missing Discourse of Desire in the Literature of Developmental Psychology

Why have psychologists maintained this silence on girls' sexual desire? Feminist analyses of patriarchal culture offer some insight. Feminist scholars have observed that the cultural context of women's lives denies female sexual desire or acknowledges it only to denigrate it, suppressing women's voices and bodies by making it socially, emotionally, and often physically dangerous for women to be in touch with or to speak openly about their own sexual feelings.[5] The absence of inquiry about girls' sexual desire occurs within this dominant culture that denigrates and suppresses female sexual desire. Yet even in feminist analyses of female sexual desire, a subject heavily theorized by feminist scholars outside of psychology, scant attention is paid to female adolescents. A handful of feminist researchers have studied female adolescent sexuality; since they did not inquire directly about girls' sexual desire, their occasional observations regarding girls' sexual desire, their occasional observations regarding girls' sexual desire are grounded in what girls do not say[6] or in sparse, vague quotes from girls that are difficult to interpret.[7] That few feminists have explicitly identified adolescent girls' sexual desire as a domain of theory or research suggests the extent to which girls' own sexual feelings are resisted in the culture at large.

At best, psychologists seem to be colluding with the culture in simply assuming that adolescent girls do not experience sexual desire; at worst, by not using the power and authority conferred upon them to say what is important in human experience and growth, psychologists participate in the larger cultural resistance to this feature of female adolescence and thus reify and perpetuate this resistance. If desire is not theorized as a potentially relevant aspect of female experience or development, then what adolescent girls may know and feel about their desire and about the place of their bodies in their experiences of desire can and will remain unknown. The very existence of this silence about girls' sexual desire within the culture in which girls develop may have psychological, physical, and material consequences for girls and also for women. The aim of my study was to ask girls directly, in no uncertain terms, about their experiences of sexual desire and about the place of their bodies in those experiences.

The Study

My study was framed by basic questions: Do adolescent girls speak of themselves as experiencing sexual desire? What do they say about it and about their bodies? In this study, I asked thirty girls—fourteen from an urban school, fourteen from a suburban school, and two from a gay and lesbian youth group—about their experiences of sexual desire. To "interrupt" the cultural story that denies girls their bodies, that says girls are interested solely in relationships and not in exploring or expressing their sexual feelings, I made a particular effort to include questions about if and how their bodies figure in these sexual experiences. The thirty young women who took part in my study brought many differences to my project—structural differences, such as class, culture, educational privilege, race, and religion, and individual differences in family situation, history of sexual abuse or violence, history of closeness and safety, physical appearance, and sexual experience. I interviewed each of these girls in a clinical interview between one and two hours long; in this explicitly relational approach to psychological inquiry the interviewer attends to the participant's experience as the guide for inquiring, using a flexible protocol. . . .

Three Voices of Desire

While many of the girls in this study found it odd, uncomfortable, or unusual for an adult woman to want to know about their experiences of sexual desire, all of the girls who participated knew that sexual desire was something that adolescent girls could and did experience, even if they themselves said they did not feel sexual desire. Of the thirty girls I interviewed, eighteen said they did feel sexual desire; four of these eighteen girls said they felt desire but also said they were confused about their sexual feelings. Three of the thirty said they did not feel desire, and four said, "I don't know," when I asked them if they experienced sexual desire. For seven of the thirty girls who answered my questions, I could not tell by what they told me whether they felt sexual desire. The distribution of these answers is remarkably similar across the race and class differences embedded in my study. Although I realize that this is a small sample, this pattern suggests the ways girls speak about their sexual desire may be distributed consistently across some structural differences.

When these girls spoke to me about their desire, they described their relationships with themselves—a relationship embedded in a web of other relationships, with other people, with the social world in which they lived. I discerned three distinct themes, or voices, in what they said: an erotic voice, a voice of the body, and a response voice.[8] For them, sexual desire is a feature of a relationship; the three voices of desire are relational voices. However, these girls make a key distinction between their sexual desire and their wish for a relationship. While their feelings of sexual desire most often arise in the context of relationships, they are not the same as or a substitute for wanting relationships. Rather, these girls say that sexual desire is a specific "feeling," a powerful feeling of wanting that the majority of these girls experience and describe as having to do with sex and with their bodies, a feeling to which they respond in the context of the many relationships that constitute their lives.

An Erotic Voice

In her essay, "Uses of the Erotic: The Erotic as Power," Audre Lorde has described what she calls the power of the erotic as "the *yes* within ourselves, our deepest cravings," and "how fully and acutely we can feel in the doing."[9] Lorde writes that in this culture, women have been systematically kept from this power in themselves because, she surmises, the power of the erotic makes women dangerous. She encourages women to reclaim and reconnect with this affirmative force that resides in them to enable them to glean pleasure in their work and in their existence. Lorde does not characterize the erotic as an explicitly sexual force but conceptualizes it more expansively; when she does speak of the connection between the sexual and the erotic, she observes how the erotic has often been reduced to the merely sexual in ways that have traditionally exploited and denigrated women, in ways, she says, that are in fact pornographic rather than sexual or erotic. In listening to the girls in my study, I was struck by the gap between how adolescent girls are portrayed, studied, and discussed and what they were saying. Out of sync with the cultural story about girls' sexuality, their words when speaking specifically about the sexual expressed the power, intensity, and urgency of their feelings and resonated with Lorde's description of the erotic. This resonance led me to call these ways that girls speak about their sexual desire an erotic voice.

What comes across powerfully in the narratives of the girls who say they feel sexual desire is that they experience it as having an unmistakable intensity. Inez knows she is feeling desire when "my body says yes yes yes yes." Lily calls feeling desire "amazing." Rochelle feels it "so, so bad . . . I wanna have sex so bad, you know"; she explains, "you just have this feeling, you just have to get rid of it." Liz explains, "I just wanted to have sex with him really badly and I just . . . and we just took off our bathing suits really fast [with laugh], and, um, it was almost like really rushed and really quick." For Barbara it is "very strong . . . an overwhelming longing" and "a wicked urge." Paulina's heart "would really beat fast"; she is "extremely aware of every, every touch and everything." Alexandra speaks of being "incredibly attracted" to her friend. Jane calls the power of her desire "demanding" and says "the feelings are so strong inside you that they're just like ready to burst." These direct acknowledgments of the power of sexual desire as these girls know it resonate across differences of class, race, and sexual orientation. These descriptions suggest a challenge to characterizations of "female" sexual desire as having an essence that is gentle, diffuse, and ephemeral.[10]

Some girls also convey the intensity of their desire by the strength of their voiced resistance to it; in response to her body's "yes yes yes yes," Inez explains that "my mind says no no no; you stop kissing him." Cassandra evidences the strength and the urgency of her feeling in narrating what she does not want to do, "stop": "He just like stopped all of a sudden, and I was like 'What are you doing?' Cause I didn't want to stop at all." She says that for her, desire is "powerful." Lily contrasts not being "in the mood to do anything . . . because I just have all my clothes on . . . because it's just too inconvenient," with the power of her desire when she feels it "once in a while": "Even though it's inconvenient for me, sometimes I just have this feeling, Well I just don't care if I have to put my pantyhose on or not," the power of her desire overriding the usual paramount concern she has for maintaining a proper appearance. These girls, who express the intensity of their sexual feelings without speaking about them directly, use a kind of code; by not saying explicitly and directly that they have strong sexual feelings, perhaps they retain the power to deny being girls who desire, should they need to exercise that power for their own protection.

A Voice of the Body

I identified a voice of the body when the girls described bodily sensations or parts of their bodies as aspects of their sexual desire. A voice of the body is central in these narratives and often interacts with the erotic voice. Across class differences and also across differences in sexual orientation, the girls who said they did not feel sexual desire also spoke of voiceless, silent bodies, of an absence of feeling in their bodies. The girls who said they did not know if they experienced sexual desire, and the girls who said they felt desire but also voiced confusion about their desire, said they were confused about their bodies; it was unclear to them and to me what their bodily feelings signaled, or they were not sure if they felt feelings in their bodies. That is, the voices of their bodies were muffled, at best. The girls whose experience of sexual desire remained uncertain voiced their bodies in ways that raised questions for me about the presence or absence of desire in their lives. For the girls in this group who said they did not feel desire, the voices of their bodies were audible, rendering their statements about the absence of their desire confusing to me. For those in this group who said they did feel desire, the silence or distress of their bodies made me wonder whether they did in fact feel sexual feelings.

Girls spoke about their bodies in two ways: they named the involvement of their bodies directly, or they signified their bodily feelings in veiled, subtle, and indirect ways. Megan spoke of knowing she was feeling sexual desire for boys because of what she felt in her body; as she said, "Kind of just this feeling, you know? Just this feeling inside my body." The voice of her body is explicitly sexual when she explains how she knows she is feeling desire for a boy: "Well, my vagina starts to kinda like act up, and it kinda like quivers and stuff, and, um, like I'll get like tingles, and you can just feel your hormones [laughing] doing something weird, and you just . . . you get happy, and you just get, you know, restimulated kind of, and it's just . . . and oh! Oh!" And "your nerves feel good." Although these girls spoke about feelings in their stomachs, shoulders, necks, and legs, as well as about all-over bodily sensations, Megan was one of the few girls who connected her desire to her "vagina," naming the sexual nature of her bodily feelings directly. Very few girls named the sexual parts of their bodies in these interviews. As Mary Calderone has observed, girls are not taught the names of the sexual parts of their bodies—"vagina," "labia," and "clitoris" are words that are not said to girls.[11]

Other girls spoke in less direct ways, revealing the embodied nature of their feelings through the logic of their stories rather than in explicit language. Trisha says of her feelings when she sees a boy to whom she is attracted, "And every time I see him, I just, like, just wanna go over and grab him and say, Let's go; I just . . . 'cause I just want him so bad; he just . . . I don't know . . . he just gives me a funny feeling; he's just, like . . . you just wanna go over and grab him" even though "I know it's just gonna be one of those one-night stand type of things." Trisha's "want" is not for a relationship, since she is talking about a potential "one-night stand type of thing"; it is to be sexual in a way that is explicitly physical, to "grab" him. Although Trisha avoids overtly placing the "funny feeling" he gives her in her body, the facts of the story lead to no other conclusion but that this "feeling" is embodied. Not surprisingly, voicing their bodies was not easy for these girls. While many of them did speak about their bodies, they also spoke sparingly and said little. When they voiced their bodies in response to my direct questions, their reticence suggested their knowledge, which I shared, that in speaking about desire itself, we were breaking with culture, resisting a cultural taboo that renders the body, particularly a girl's body and the sexual parts of her body, unspeakable.

Voices of Response

The girls who said they felt sexual desire also described how they responded to their own embodied feelings of sexual desire when they told me narratives about their experiences. All of these girls voiced conflict in speaking of their responses to their sexual desire, conflict between the voices of their bodies and the realities of their lives. Whether they spoke of the reality of physical risk and vulnerability or the reality of getting a bad reputation or of cultural messages that silence or are silent about girls' sexual desire, these girls knew and spoke about, in explicit or more indirect ways, the pressure that they felt to silence the voices of their bodies, to disconnect from the bodies in which they inescapably live. When I asked these girls to speak specifically about their own experiences, a lot of these girls spoke about controlling their own sexual feelings rather than about controlling the sexual feelings of boys, raising the question to what or whom girls are being encouraged to "just say no." When asked what they think and feel, they challenged the cultural story about their sexuality—which frames sexual feelings as male—by describing the conflict they experience between the feelings in their bodies and the cultural taboo on what they want. When they spoke of their responses to their sexual desire, they gave voice to an agency in which they are sexual objects of their own feelings rather than simply objects of the desire of others. This agency is informed by their own embodied erotic voice and the voices of the social world in which they live.

Although an erotic voice and a voice of the body sounded similar across the differences of social context embedded in the study, I began to hear in these girls' descriptions differences between urban girls' and the suburban girls', heterosexual girls' and lesbian/bisexual girls', responses to sexual desire. These differences seemed to be connected to the real differences in the social contexts of these girls' lives that the design of this study highlighted.[12] I noticed distinct tones and characters in their voices that I think are related to the fact that some of these girls were bisexual and lesbian and some straight, that some of them lived in overtly dangerous urban areas, while others lived in the relatively safe environment of the suburbs. One way to characterize these differences is that some girls described an agency in the service of protection, whereas others told of an agency in the service of pleasure. . . .

Urban Girls: Cautious Bodies

The urban girls share an environment in which violence as well as adolescent pregnancy and parenthood are highly visible and an unavoidable part of their daily routines. The urban girls in this study share a social experience in which girls' physical movements and sexual activities are a topic of conversation and gossip, subject to a not-so-subtle and entrenched system of social control.

When the urban girls describe their responses to their own sexual desire, themes of self-control, caution, and conflict predominate. Speaking primarily about a conflict between two real features of their experience, the voices of their bodies and what they know and say about the reality of their vulnerability—physical vulnerability to AIDS and pregnancy, as well as social vulnerability in the form of getting a "bad reputation"—they make explicit connections between their sexual desire and danger. In a social context in which danger and violence, the constant threat of violation, is palpable, visible, and unavoidable, most of these girls make conscious choices to sacrifice pleasure as an attempt to protect themselves from danger, a self-protective strategy that costs them a connection to themselves and to their own bodies and unfortunately provides little real safety.

Inez is a Puerto Rican girl with green eyes, light skin, and a shapely figure. She knows she is feeling desire when "my body gets into the pleasure mood." Connecting her desire to "pleasure," Inez speaks of her sexual desire in terms of her body—she knows she is feeling desire "when my body says yes." She lays out the relationship she experiences between her "mind" and her "body," narrating one resolution to the mind-body split permeating Western culture and alive in Inez: "My body does not control my mind. My mind controls my body, and if my body gets into the pleasure mood, my mind is gonna tell him no . . . tell, tell my body . . . my, my mind's gonna tell my body no. And it can happen, because I said so, because I control you, and my mind is lookin' towards my body." Inez describes what she frames as a general rule for how to resolve the differences between her body and her mind: her response to her sexual desire, to the "yes" she knows in her body, is to "control" her body with her mind, that is, to override the voice of her body with other knowledge. When Inez speaks of her experiences of sexual desire, she speaks of two ways she experiences her sexuality, of knowing and feeling pleasure and of knowing, fearing, and avoiding danger. While she knows that having her breasts touched by a former boyfriend to whom she is still attracted "feels so wonderful," Inez also thinks and speaks about the physical dangers that make her vulnerable: "Let's say you don't have no kind of contraceptives like a condom, and he has AIDS, and you don't know that; you can get AIDS just by having sex with him, because your body said yes, your mind said no, but your body said yes." Inez knows that her own sexual desire can bring both danger and pleasure, knowledge that poses a dilemma for her: whether to pursue pleasure and an embodied sense of self or to avoid the dangers she perceives, sacrificing a part of herself to keep herself safer in a larger sense. Inez speaks about how listening and responding to the "yes" of her body can lead to pregnancy and AIDS and how her "mind is lookin' towards my body," thereby acting as a shield to protect her body from vulnerabilities about which she is very aware. Inez resolves this dilemma by choosing to keep safe from danger, the "no" in her mind drowning out her body's "yes," to protect her from disease and death and from pregnancy or early motherhood at the expense of pleasure.[13] The erotic voice that she recognizes and knows can bring her pleasure and can also make her feel empowered and self-confident and that she feels she must silence is a voice that receives no nurturing or sustenance in her social context. This logic, which implements the disembodied discourses she hears in the school corridors, does not acknowledge or value her ability to know herself or what is happening in her relationship via the information conveyed in her own bodily feelings. At other times in this interview, Inez raises the danger stakes, speaking not only about the physical dangers that her own desire can invoke but also about social risks, about the danger of losing her reputation and of not being "respected," which can lead to physical abuse, and of revealing her true wishes and thereby risking humiliation and a loss of dignity. The erotic voice of her body sounds in a silence, the only response to her body's "yes" she has been offered and now describes is her mind's absolute "no," leaving her seemingly with no safe choice but to silence the voice of her body.

Throughout this interview, Inez voices her knowledge of her own sexual desire and her choice to keep herself out of danger by silencing the voice of her body. She tries to avoid situations in which she will feel desire, keeping herself out of situations in which her desire might be inflamed and lead to danger and minimizing the moments when she will have to cope with this mind-body conflict. Inez derives her knowledge not only from her own experience but also from her observations of other girls:

> Desire? Yes, because she's [a girl] probably in one of those; like let's say she's just drunk, and she doesn't know what she's doin', and she's dancing with this guy—you know how they dance reggae—ever seen somebody dance reggae? How they rubbin' on each other? Well that gets a guy real, I'll say, hard. And it gets a girl very horny. And they could just be dancin' together for like five minutes, and all the sudden [snaps fingers] they just . . . they . . . something just snaps in 'em and they say, "Oh, let's go to the bedroom." And, it'll just happen, just because they were dancing. That's why I don't dance reggae with guys.

Interrupting the cultural story about girls and sex, Inez does not frame the danger of dancing reggae as the lure of romance or the promise of a romantic relationship; this kind of dancing is sexually arousing for the girl as well as for the boy—the boy gets "hard"; the girl gets "very horny." In this interview Inez has told me that she enjoys dancing and describes herself as a very good dancer, something about herself that makes her feel proud. However, in order to avoid getting "very horny," Inez does not dance reggae. To keep her body safe, she keeps her body still, not "danc[ing] reggae with guys" so that she will not risk having "something just [snap]" in her.

Barbara is white and has blue eyes framed by long blonde hair that falls across the back of her track jacket, flung over her slight yet athletic frame. In the interview, she speaks of her own sexual desire often in the context of her current relationship. She tells a story about a time with her boyfriend "before [we] had sex, 'cause I wasn't sure how he looked at sex. . . . There was this time he was giving me a backrub, and all I could think about is what I wanted him to do besides have backrubs [with small laugh], and he has to rub my body, forget the back, just do the whole body. . . . It was a very strong desire just to have him rub all over, and that was the one time I can think of I've really had it bad [with laugh]. . . . I'm laying there thinking this, and I didn't want to tell him that, 'cause I didn't know him that well at the time, and its like, noooo, no, we'll just wait [laugh]." Barbara conveys the strength of her sexual feelings as consuming, embodied, and disruptive: "all I could think about," "he has to rub my body," "I . . . had it bad." Yet Barbara's response to "a very strong desire" is to "wait"; like Inez, she tells herself, "Noooo, no." Her caution is evident in her way of speaking by not speaking directly about her sexual feelings; she seems to rely on my ability to imagine what kinds of sexual things she "wanted him to do besides have backrubs" and what she means by "do the whole body," and thereby she does not have to risk the embarrassment, the indictment, or saying explicitly what she wanted. Her response is shaped by the fact that feeling desire is a risky proposition for a girl, as she makes clear in her explanation of how she comes to her decision not to express her desire at this moment in this relationship, not to say or act in conformity with what she is feeling and wanting: "I didn't know him well enough. I subtly like to initiate; I don't like to come outright and say, Oh let's go do this; I just like doing things very subtly, 'cause I'm not a very . . . when it comes to sex, the first few times with the person, I'm not very forthright about anything, until after I've gotten to know them, and I trust them a little bit more, and I know that they're not going to look at me funny when I say I want to do something like this."

Barbara is keenly aware that if she is "forthright," if she says what she wants to do—that is, if she reveals her desire—boys might "look at [her] funny," a precursor perhaps to humiliation and even to loss of the relationship. Because she does not know if she can "trust" this boy, because she "didn't know him well enough," Barbara's way of dealing with this identified risk is to be "subtle"—to "initiate" and "[do] things," to be an agent of her own feelings, but to be a kind of secret agent, to behave in a way that is veiled and not readily identifiable, similar to her cautious choice of words in telling her story to me. Yet in this particular situation, she chose not to act on her feelings but to stay still, to "[lie] there thinking," to "wait" to act on her feelings. The logic of her choice resonates with Gilligan's observation that, at adolescence, some girls seem to move into what she has called a female "underground." She suggests that some girls make a conscious psychic retreat within relationships, being aware of their true thoughts and feelings but choosing to protect themselves by keeping their authentic voices out of their relationships, essentially silencing themselves[14] by not acting on their own knowledge or by keeping what they know from view.[15] Girls make this choice because saying what they really think and feel can be dangerous; that is, their authentic thoughts and feelings could threaten relationships or make them vulnerable to physical or psychic attack. Barbara knows that she is feeling desire; she chooses not "to tell him," to keep her genuine feeling out of this relationship, as a way of protecting herself from the possibility that her boyfriend might "look at me funny when I say what I want." This response is a conscious choice not to be "very forthright," which she is fully capable of being and which she decided not to be in this moment. She will "wait" until she "[knows] him well enough." Why is she so cautious, and why might this caution be problematic?

Barbara goes on to explain her choice. Her sense that she needs to keep herself from "com[ing] outright and say[ing], Oh let's go do this," from being known as a young woman who "[wants] to do something," who knows and wants to act in response to her own desire, is a result of her own experience of making her desires known, of letting herself be known as a girl who has sexual wants:

> That was like with oral sex, I never thought I would meet a guy that didn't like oral sex, and I met a guy. 'Cause I hadn't had oral sex with this boyfriend, but the boyfriend before that I was wanting to attempt that, and he would have no part in that. And so I was kind of . . . you feel really embarrassed after you've asked to do something, and it's like . . . and then they're, "Oh no, no, no, get away." And so I came to this boyfriend I'm thinking; I was very [with laughter] subtle about doing this 'cause I wanted to make sure I wasn't going to make a fool of myself. It depends on the guy, if I'll be forthright or not.

Having been "embarrassed" and "[made] a fool of" when she expressed her curiosity and desire to have oral sex with a boy, Barbara has learned that voicing her sexual wishes can lead to humiliation. The relational context in which she feels and expresses her desires is paramount: how she will respond to her own sexual feelings "depends on the guy." By being "subtle," Barbara takes great care to try to balance expression of her desire and avoidance of making a fool of herself. This subtlety incurs the risk of not having her desire met.

Although both Inez and Barbara tell narratives about deciding not to voice their desires, there is an important difference in how they respond to their own sexual feelings. In contrast to Inez, Barbara does not silence the "yes" in her body, drowning out the erotic voice with the dangers of desire in the way that Inez describes. While she chooses not to express her desire, Barbara continues to feel it, keeping it alive in the underground world of her real thought and feelings. And this solution has a psychological cost for Barbara to which she gives voice: "It's kinda depressing in its own way afterwards, 'cause you're like sitting there, Well I, you know, I should have said something, or, you know, actually left and gone home. You're laying there, Well I should have said something [with small laugh], 'cause later on it's like, well, I didn't fulfill it [moan, laugh]." Barbara's voice is filled with regret and frustration at having silenced herself. Perhaps precisely because Barbara does not silence her body, she understands the costs of her choice, making it possible for her to know and bemoan the frustration she now feels in the wake of her choice not to respond to her own sexual feelings and curiosity. In telling this desire narrative, Barbara describes the doubt and sense of loss surrounding her choice to respond to her desire by silencing her body and sacrificing her pleasure and herself. What is key about Barbara's dilemma is how very real it is: How can she express her desire and protect herself from potential punishment through humiliation or desertion?

The urban girls in this study describe a self-silencing and portray a vigilant caution regarding their own sexual desire. Because they are in fact experiencing sexual desire, this response requires a substantial investment of energy in what they feel are efforts to ensure their physical and social safety. Missing from these narratives are positive descriptions of sexual curiosity or sexual exploration as responses to their desire; rather, I heard girls tempering or disconnecting from any curiosity they felt. I began to notice what was not said in what they did say. I wondered whether curiosity and the pleasure of feeling and learning about themselves and others in sexual interactions and relationships, whether staying in connection with the power of the erotic in their bodies, were luxuries for these girls, ones they could ill afford. The one exception among the urban girls was Paulina, a young woman who immigrated from Eastern Europe several years ago, who describes a response to her sexual desire in which caution and curiosity intermingle: "[That feeling] makes me like really aware of what somebody's doing. . . . You're like aware of every move he makes—you just know it. . . . I don't mind touching the other person; I mean, I don't feel like any part of the other person is dirty in any way. And like, I like guys' chests especially, especially if it's broad, and I like touching the chest, especially if it smells nice; I like it. And I like playing just like especially if it's like little hairs; I just like playing with it; I don't mind." Paulina speaks clearly about responding to her desire by doing what she wants and "likes." In knowing what she likes sexually, she develops her knowledge of herself. She knows and says exactly what she "likes," giving voice to how she comes to this knowledge about herself through her own senses of "touch" and "smell," through her willingness to "play."

But there is a distinct note of caution in how Paulina speaks about her enjoyment, a certain defensiveness woven into her description of pleasure. I am struck by Paulina's repeated caveat that, in exploring a man's body, she "[doesn't] mind" doing what she likes and that she "[doesn't] feel like any part of the other person is dirty in any way." The extremes of her parenthetical commentary suggest to me that she knows or feels that she should mind and that she should find "the other person" to be "dirty." When I tell her I am curious that she is telling me that she does not mind something that she has also said she likes, she explains that she knows—as do I—that girls are "aware" of how others view and judge them if they explore and express sexual desire: "Because there's a lot of girls that I know who just wouldn't do it; they're kind of like . . . they wouldn't have oral sex with somebody because the person might think something of them. And I don't really care what the person will think, because the person will know me well enough, so I just do it." Paulina seems to be engaged in another conversation with a voice she and I both know well, the social voice that says girls who have oral sex are thought about and spoken about in denigrating ways. Paulina's words suggest that she is aware that she is resisting a social imperative to curb her actions in order to keep other people from judging her to be a bad girl. Knowing the power of this voice, I ask her why she "just [does] it." Her answer provides the linchpin to the logic of Paulina's actions: her own desire. She says she defies conventions intended to keep her from exploring her sexual feelings "because I would want to"—because of her insistence on staying connected with and acting on her own desire. Paulina voices a resistance to "what other people will think," not "really car[ing]" if "something" is thought or said about her if she is exploring her desire by having oral sex, doing what she wants to do. Yet her editorial comments on her own statements of desire, that she "[doesn't] mind" and that a man's body is not "dirty," belies the fact that she is under pressure to modulate her desire and her response to it. In order to stay with the knowledge and pleasure of her senses, Paulina maintains an active program of not caring about the potentially painful social stigma of being talked about—or shunned—which constantly threatens her ability to stay connected with the power of the erotic. If she is to stay connected with the erotic voice, the voice of her body, she must engage in an active resistance to the social pressure she feels to silence herself. . . .

Suburban Girls: Curious Bodies

When the suburban girls told me about their responses to sexual desire, they spoke frequently of a sexual curiosity that was hardly audible among the urban girls and that sometimes challenged their wish to control themselves when they felt desire, a wish that echoed that of the urban girls. Like the urban girls, they too spoke of conflict when speaking of desire, of the power of the erotic and the voices of their bodies. Rather than speak directly about the problems of physical or social vulnerability, these suburban girls voiced a more internal conflict in relation to their sexual desire, a discrepancy between what they described feeling in their bodies and the cultural messages about female sexuality and appropriate female sexual behavior that they have internalized. Instead of silencing their bodies in respones to this conflict, these suburban girls described their often failed struggle to stay in connection with themselves and their bodies and at the same time to maintain a positive sense of themselves as good girls and daughters.

For some, confusion dominates their responses to my questions as they describe their experiences of desire to me.[16] Zoe is white, blond-haired, and blue-eyed, clad in a suit that gives her an air of maturity and also a prim bearing. She sounds very confused, though this confusion is punctuated by moments of intense clarity, when she tells me about her experience: "I guess [three second pause] . . . I can't, I mean, I can't think of what I . . . it feels like; I don't know; I think about it; it feels like to me that I want to do something I'm longing to do, but, I mean, I don't know that; I don't know; I don't know what it feels like really." Zoe is, frankly, tongue-tied when she tries to describe her feelings. The fact that she is capable of a clear description of what desire feels like for her—"it feels like to me I want to do something I'm longing to do"—suggests that her struggle to find her voice holds meaning. Perhaps she is embarrassed; perhaps finding the words to articulate her feelings is a challenge. Another way to think about her flustered response is that she is resisting her own knowledge or resisting bringing this knowledge about herself into relationship with me. That I may have met in Zoe or inspired in Zoe a moment of resistance is suggested as I listen to her undo her own knowledge: after telling me that her sexual desire is "that I want to do something I'm longing to do," she immediately undoes her knowledge by telling me, "I don't know what it feels like really." This knowing and then not knowing is typical of the way many girls of Zoe's age, race, and class speak about aspects of their own experience that they, as "good" or "perfect" girls coming of age in a patriarchal culture, are pressured not to know or speak about.[17]

As Zoe describes her response to her own sexual desire, she describes how her wish and effort to be a "good" young woman results in a tenuous connection to her sexual feelings. When Zoe speaks of herself, the voice of the culture that demands capitulation to feminine conventions of passivity is audible, as is the conflict within herself that this norm creates. She says she is someone who has "to wait for other people to do things," yet she has sexual feelings that make her "want to do it." Zoe's response to this "want" is that she "just . . . can't for some reason."

D: What do you do in a situation you've just described, when you're kissing and you feel like you want to do more; what do you do?

Z: What do I do? I don't know; I don't really; I'm not the person who is initiating things as much [laugh]. I don't know, I guess. I mean, I guess, I know it happens to both of us at the same time, because I don't know—well, I mean, do you mean—like, do I say something? I mean, he's usually the one who will like start more things. I mean, I don't take the initiative; like, I don't—I don't know—start something.

D: Because?

Z: I don't know; I've never been able to, like—I'm not an outgoing person—I've never been able to start things as much; I don't know what it is. I have to wait for other people to do things.

D: Would you like to be able to start things more in that kind of situation?

Z: Yeah.

D: What do you think might make that possible?

Z: I don't know. I have to be sure of myself in that way more. I mean, maybe sometimes I'm afraid that the other person doesn't want to do something, and so I wait until they want to, and then I'll say, Okay, I'm ready now.

D: What gets in the way of your doing that?

Z: Well, I have always worried about what other people think. I'll just wait or something. I mean, I want to do it, but I just . . . I can't for some reason; I don't like physically just do it, you know.

D: How does that make you feel?

Z: Frustrated.

D: What kinds of things are you wanting to do that you don't do?

Z: I don't know. I mean, at first, it's like little things like, I don't know, just like starting to kiss or something like that, instead of them, having them coming to you to, you know; I mean little things like that. I don't know.

Zoe describes a conflict between what she wants to do when she feels desire and what she does—"I'll just wait"—which leads to her feeling "frustrated." When she feels desire, other feelings as well are aroused in Zoe. She feels a moral imperative not to act on her desire. She experiences distress and fear—she feels "worried" and "afraid that the other person doesn't want to do something." To respond to her own sexual feelings passively, "to wait for other people to do things," is one way to lessen or avoid the uncomfortable feelings that her desire incites. She associates the way she responds to her desire with how she behaves in relationship with others in general: she is not "the person who is initiating things" because she is "not an outgoing person," she has "never been able to start things as much," and she has "to wait for other people to do things." When I ask her specifically about her own thoughts and feelings, she undercuts her analysis repeatedly, interrupting her lucid explanations of her behavior by telling me, "I don't know," over and over again, making us both spin. I wonder what it is that she does not know about. Is it an unsureness or a curiosity about this understanding of herself? Is it doubt about being a person who is "not outgoing," "never . . . able to start things much"? Zoe knows there is "some reason" she cannot do what she wants; she knows that she does not "take the initiative" and is "worried about what other people think," but she speaks of having no sense that her behavior or feelings are at odds with larger social forces that may be at play in her psyche. This description of herself echoes the ways that a "good" girl or woman should behave. By definition, to be an acceptable young woman within her social context, she must not know or exercise her own agency, a lesson in being appropriately feminine that Zoe has learned to apply to her sexuality. When I listen to Zoe's story, I hear that she may in part be engaged in a struggle that is shaped by social norms rendering problematic a girl's agency in general and her sexual agency in particular. Yet Zoe also knows that this way of behaving leaves out her desire; knowing that she should not act, yet also experiencing sexual feelings and frustration that contradict this ban on agency, seems to fuel her confusion.

Emily, who is white, has distinctly Jewish features. In our interview she seems to be trying to appear comfortable, and she is also obviously eager to talk to me. Emily tells of an experience of exploring her desire, when her boyfriend, "tan and great looking," came to her house for a family dinner upon his return from a vacation in Florida. Riveted by a renewed realization of how attractive she found him, she was "just staring at him across the table. It was almost fun, because I knew that we were going out later and I would be able to kiss him and stuff, but it was like, I mean, all through dinner I was just like looking at him and just . . . I was almost trying myself to increase it, so that the fulfillment would be better at the end, when we were alone."

Two things stand out about the way that Emily characterizes her experience of sexual desire. First, her desire seems to be an aspect of herself with which she experiments, interacts, even plays; through trying to manipulate her own desire, she is in fact finding out about herself, how her embodied feelings work, and ways in which she can and cannot control them. Second, the tentative quality in the way that Emily describes her experience—"almost fun" and "almost trying myself to increase it"—makes me wonder if Emily, while speaking about playing with her desire, is also holding herself back. Her reference to her desire as "it," more a way to speak about a foreign body than about a part of oneself, also suggests some distance between her sense of self and her desire. As she continues to describe how her desire "escalates," she seems to recede even further: "You're like very excited and revved up, and then, it's like it starts when you're fooling around at a higher level, like you don't have to work up to anything. It doesn't get you in the mood; you're already in the mood. And you start at a higher level, which means you probably escalate to an even higher level, and that's like cool; I mean, it's fun." When I ask Emily to speak specifically about "it," her words shift from the particulars of her own feelings and behavior to an abstract description of a mechanistic process that I can hardly follow. The "I" of Emily's story has been supplanted by a less direct and clear "you," which makes this description sound more distant from herself. I am puzzled by this shift, and so I ask her about it. Shifting back to "I," Emily begins to speak about her sexual desire in another way:

E: I hadn't thought about it, you know; maybe I feel self-conscious using "I," perhaps.

D: How come?

E: I don't know; I just thought about myself; *I* get to a higher level, and then I was saying, oh, that sounds a little . . .

D: Sounds a little what?

E: Well I guess, just going back, I don't like to think of myself as feeling really sexual. I guess that's probably the whole thing—I think I just hit it—that I don't like to think of myself as being like someone who needs to have their desires fulfilled; that's it. That's what it is.

D: Hm. What do you think about that?

E: I mean, I understand that it's wrong and that everybody has needs, but I just feel like self-conscious when I think about it, and I don't feel self-conscious when I say that we do these things, but I feel self-conscious about saying, I need this kind of a thing.

D: What do you think about that?

E: I don't know what to blame it on. Maybe my family. Maybe I see my father as the more sexual part of my family, and my mom as more just the fun member of my family. Maybe it's that all through growing up, he's gonna try to get this off you, and he's gonna try to do—you know, when you're little and he's gonna try to kiss you and you have to say no, you know—stuff like that, not that you have to say no, but be prepared for that, and stuff like that. I mean, it could be societal, it could be family, it could be, it could be me, I don't know.

When I ask Emily about her shift from "I" to "you," she tells me another story about her experience of sexual desire, how acknowledging her own desire makes her feel. She is self-conscious when she says that she "needs this," and she does not like to think of herself as "feeling really sexual," as "being like someone who needs to have their desires fulfilled." By speaking as a "you" rather than an "I," Emily is able to speak about her desire without explicitly having to acknowledge that the sexual feelings she is describing are her own, thus enabling her to protect herself from feeling self-conscious. She is aware that her feeling self-conscious contradicts what she "understands" about her sexual desire, that "everyone has needs," that she does in fact feel "really sexual." Emily knows and can speak about the source of this contradiction and offers a comprehensive description of how her socialization makes it difficult for her to be in connection with her body and her own desire. She explains that "all through growing up" she learned that "you [the girl] have to say no," that men are "sexual" and will "try to get this off you," and that girls "have to say no . . . [and] be prepared for that." Having taken in a story that does not acknowledge her sexual feelings, it is no wonder that Emily feels self-conscious when she speaks about and claims her "sexual needs." Emily remembers hearing that "he's gonna try to kiss you"; she does not speak of hearing that she might want to kiss him. The disjuncture between the sexual feelings that she does experience and the ways that male and female sexuality have and have not been spoken about makes it hard for

Emily to speak about and to know or respond to her "needs." While still unsure "what to blame it on," Emily demonstrates a sophisticated understanding of how she has been guided through "societal" means out of her body and into self-consciousness.

Sophie's blue eyes sparkle impishly, her lithe body clothed casually; yet also perhaps in a studied fashion, in T-shirt and jeans. She is white. In speaking about a time when she experienced sexual desire, Sophie describes an experience that evokes an episode from a romance novel or a soap opera:

> My friend [Eugenia] was on the phone, and he was like chasing me around, like we were totally joking. He was like chasing me with some like bat or something like that? And I like went to get away, and he like more like pinned me down. It sounds like cruel and like ferocious, but he was like holding me down, and I was like [calling to my friend], Eugenia! But I was literally like, I was like, Eugenia! But she knew that I liked him [laughing], so she was just staying on the phone. And he was just right above me and had both my arms down, and it was like I knew that I was acting like I just wanted to get away, but really I just would've wanted to just totally kiss him or something? And it is those great brown eyes again, he just looked right at me, and he's just so—it's that sexual desire thing, you just feel a certain way, and it was just like it's almost like a waiting feeling?

Sophie is narrating a story of how she disguised her true feelings but also of how she enjoyed the pleasure of "the waiting feeling" that her feigning resistance incited. She is direct about how she has acted her part—"I knew that I was acting like I just wanted to get away"—the role of the good girl who does not feel desire. This "act" is in fact just the opposite of what she is really feeling, "that sexual desire thing I said"; in fact, her desire is unequivocally clear to her and suggests a wish to take action—she "would've wanted to just totally kiss him or something?" Although Sophie played the prescribed role of ingenue, I am struck that what she pretended was "want[ing] to get away." This phrase evokes fear and distress, suggesting that Sophie has an awareness of a link between fear and desire that is not conscious but that may shape her actions and responses. In speaking about desire, Sophie outlines a complicated response to the link between pleasure and danger that she does not identify explicitly but that appears just beneath the surface of her words.

For Sophie, desire is connected to "waiting." In her explanation of why she waits rather than acts in this situation, she reveals that she is cognizant of, though somewhat confused about, a connection between her passivity and her gender: "Maybe that's because I'm a female, and usually guys make the first move. That isn't always the way, but a lot of times it's that way. . . . But, it's not so much because I would be intimidated to; it just tends to happen that way? Like, they tend to . . . maybe they tend to just get to it faster or . . . I don't know." Sophie associates with being "female" her feeling of "waiting" and her conscious decision to "act" as if she wanted to escape, when in fact she wants to "totally kiss him or something." She has taken in the cultural message that the prerogative of sexual action is male—"guys usually make the first move." Sophie says she does not know why this is so. While she senses that how she acts and waits has to do with being a girl, she has no logical explanation for why girls wait and boys "make the first move"; she does not seem satisfied by her own explanation that boys "just get to it faster." Yet Sophie seems also to hold subliminal knowledge that her actions reflect a vulnerability to being "intimidated."

The passive role that creates excitement and anticipation—"a waiting feeling" that Sophie likes—also creates vulnerability. In raising the question of intimidation, Sophie suggests that she is not entirely unaware of the potential violence that pervades her story. Sophie gives words to the violent undertones of her experience, saying that there is something "cruel" and "ferocious" about a young man chasing her with a bat, even though they are merely friends engaged in a charged flirtation. The fuzzy overlap between fear and excitement, desire and danger, is captured in Sophie's description of her own vulnerability. Because she is safe in this particular situation—her friend does not respond to Sophie's cries but is in fact in full view—Sophie can enjoy this play. However, Sophie voices the possibility that she is being intimidated only to discount that possibility, suggesting that she both does and does not know (or does not wish to know) or speak about the potential for danger that is braided into "that sexual desire thing."

Although I was struck by the struggle in the voices of these suburban girls to find ways to stay connected to their sexual desire within the contours of womanhood available to them, when I brought the voices of the urban girls into relation with the voices of the suburban girls, I began to notice what the suburban girls did not say: the suburban girls did not speak overtly about danger when they voiced their sexual desire, a striking contrast to how the urban girls spoke. Getting a reputation was not much of a concern among the suburban girls, and few of them spoke about fears of getting pregnant or getting AIDS. A few of these girls, like Sophie, spoke, yet did not directly acknowledge, an association between their sexual desire and the potential for physical violence or violation by men; their narratives were structured by the romance plot alive in the culture and in their lives that plays subtly with, but does not distinctly define, the connection between pleasure and danger.[18] These suburban girls seemed to know subconsciously about a real danger that they could encounter, in fact, that many of them *had* encountered. In this study, one-third of these thirty girls told me that they had experienced sexual abuse or sexual violence, in childhood or in adolescence; what was striking about the occurrence of violation is that it did not matter whether a girl lived in the city or in the suburbs—abuse and violence were distributed evenly, regardless of social context, in this sample. Beyond this small sample, statistics indicate that sexual violence is prevalent and real in the lives of all female adolescents. Sexual harassment is prevalent in high schools.[19] Research has shown that one out of ten female adolescents has experienced physical violence while dating in high school. FBI statistics reveal that 20 percent of female homicide victims are between fifteen and twenty-four and that many young women are murdered by their boyfriends; conflicts about sex often lead to such violence.[20] Although I found that the suburban girls seemed more able to know themselves through exploring their sexual desire, more able to be enlivened by the power of the erotic voice in their own bodies than the urban girls were, I also became concerned that these girls did not know—or at least did not speak to me in direct ways—about the real risks they faced in exploring their sexual curiosity, in staying connected to their own bodies in a social context in which sexual and physical violence against women is a real threat. . . .

Desire for the Future

When these girls spoke to me about their sexual desire, they talked about their bodies, the power of the erotic as it surged through their bodies, and how to respond to these embodied feelings. The differences in the ways these girls spoke about their responses to their sexual desire, embedded in the different social contexts in which they live, enabled me to know and articulate one of the most powerful findings of this inquiry: that their responses to these sexual feelings are deeply informed and shaped by the social contexts in which they live—inevitably, inescapably—in female bodies, bodies that hold the possibility of pleasure and also the potential for violation. Developing an ability to know and balance both pleasure and danger may be a way for girls and women to enhance their psychological well-being and to protect themselves from danger within the current social landscape of women's lives. However, this "solution" falls short on several counts. Such a balance was very rare among these girls; girls seemed to align with pleasure or with danger rather than strike a balance. Their voices suggest that when girls align with danger, acknowledgment of pleasure may be impossible or implausible, and that if girls align with pleasure, this move may necessitate that they obscure danger. Knowing only danger seems to deny girls access to important knowledge about themselves and their relationships. While "not knowing" danger may be a necessary psychic strategy in order for a girl or woman to pursue her desire, the cost of this denial of a frightening and enraging aspect of reality may also serve to perpetuate violence against women and to keep women's sexual desire unnecessarily dangerous. If women do not know they are in danger, they will not feel compelled to combat it.

Thus, what these girls say and do not say when they speak about their experiences of sexual desire raises a psychological question and gives shape to the dilemma that women's sexual desire, in the context of patriarchal culture, poses. It is a dilemma that raises unavoidable psychological implications: How can girls and women experience pleasure and know about and protect themselves from, as well as fight against, danger? What are the psychological ramifications and adaptations that girls and women make in light of the fact that they live in female bodies, through which the erotic has the potential to flow, in the context of a culture in which their bodies are subjected to the violence of objectification and physical violation as well as the possibility of pleasure? In the context of these bodies and this culture, what does it mean, then, for girls and women to know their sexual desire or, for that matter, any desire at all? The voices of these girls speaking about their sexual feelings suggest a complexity that sexual desire poses for girls in adolescence, as well as for adult women. Whether these girls say they feel desire, are confused about their desire, do not feel desire, or speak about desire in contradictory ways, sexual desire is a key feature of adolescence for them. Their voices are out of harmony with what is and is not said about them in the literature and in the dominant cultural story about girls and sexuality. By resisting and interrupting the accepted notion that girls do not want sex, that they just want relationships, and by asking girls direct questions—that is, engaging in an empirical endeavor—about their experiences of sexual desire, I discovered that sexual desire is something that girls know. . . .

Notes

This research was supported in part by the Henry A. Murray Dissertation Award through the Murray Center for Research at Radcliffe College.

1. The national average age at first intercourse is 16.2 years for girls. See Melvin Zelnik and John Kantner, "Sexual and Contraceptive Experience of Young Unmarried Women in the United States, 1976 and 1978," in *Teenage Sexuality, Pregnancy, and Childbearing*, ed. Frank Furstenburg, Richard Lincoln, and Jane Menken (Philadelphia: University of Pennsylvania Press, 1981), 68–92. In addition, Lillian Rubin observes that recent studies show that girls are having sex at younger and younger ages. See Lillian Rubin, *Erotic Wars* (New York: Harper Collins, 1990).
2. Carol Gilligan, "Joining the Resistance: Psychology, Politics, Girls, and Women," *Michigan Quarterly Review* 29, no. 4 (1990): 501–36; Lyn Mikel Brown, "Narratives of Relationship: Development of a Care Voice in Girls Ages Seven to Sixteen" (Ed.D. diss., Harvard University, 1989); idem, "Telling a Girl's Life: Self-Authorization as a Form of Resistance," in *Women, Girls, and Psychotherapy: Reframing Resistance*, ed. Carol Gilligan, Annie Rogers, and Deborah L. Tolman (New York: Haworth Press, 1992), 71–86.
3. Susan Bordo, "The Body and the Reproduction of Femininity: A Feminist Appropriation of Foucault," in *Gender/Body/Knowledge*, ed. Alison Jaggar and Susan Bordo (New Brunswick, N.J.: Rutgers University Press, 1989), 13–33.
4. Carol Gilligan, "Joining the Resistance"; Elizabeth Debold and Lyn Brown, "Losing the Body of Knowledge: Conflicts Between Passion and Reason in the Intellectual Development of Adolescent Girls" (Paper presented at the annual meeting of the Association for Women in Psychology, March 1991); Deborah L. Tolman and Elizabeth Debold, "Conflicts of Body and Image: Female Adolescents, Desire, and the No-Body Body," in *Feminist Treatment and Therapy of Eating Disorders*, ed. Melanie Katzman, Pat Fallon, and Susan Wooley (New York: Guilford Press, 1994).

5. See, for example, *Powers of Desire: The Politics of Sexuality*, ed. Ann Snitow, Christine Stansell, and Sharon Thompson (New York: Monthly Review Press, 1983); *Pleasure and Danger: Exploring Female Sexuality*, ed. Carole S. Vance (Boston: Routledge and Kegan Paul, 1984); and Janice Irvine, *Disorders of Desire: Sex and Gender in Modern American Sexology* (Philadelphia: Temple University Press, 1990).
6. Mica Nava, "'Everybody's Views Were Just Broadened': A Girls' Project and Some Responses to Lesbianism," *Feminist Review* 10 (1982): 37–59; Michelle Fine, "Sexuality, Schooling, and Adolescent Females: The Missing Discourse of Desire," *Harvard Educational Review* 58, no. 1 (1988): 29–53; Pat Macpherson and Michelle Fine, "Hungry for an Us: Adolescent Women Narrating Sex and Politics" (Unpublished manuscript, Philadelphia, 1991); Michelle Fine and Pat Macpherson, "Over Dinner: Feminism and Adolescent Female Bodies" (Unpublished manuscript, Philadelphia, 1991); Sharon Thompson, "Search for Tomorrow: On Feminism and the Reconstruction of Teen Romance," in *Pleasure and Danger: Exploring Female Sexuality*, 250–84; idem, "'Drastic Entertainments': Teenage Mothers' Signifying Narratives," in *Uncertain Terms*, ed. Faye Ginsberg and A. Tsing (Boston: Beacon Press, 1991); Celia Cowie and Susan Lees, "Slags or Drags," in *Sexuality: A Reader*, ed. Feminist Review (London: Virago, 1987); Susan Lees, *Losing Out: Sexuality and Adolescent Girls* (London: Hutchinson, 1986); idem, "Sexuality, Reputation, Morality, and the Social Control of Girls: A British Study," in *Aspects of School Culture and the Social Control of Girls* (European University Institute, no. 87/301), 1–20; Jane Ussher, *The Psychology of the Female Body* (London: Routledge and Kegan Paul, 1989).
7. Fine, "Sexuality, Schooling, and Adolescent Females," 1988.
8. For descriptions of these voices and how I articulated them, see Tolman, "Voicing the Body: A Psychological Study of Adolescent Girls' Sexual Desires" (Ph.D. diss., Harvard University, 1992).
9. Audre Lorde, "Uses of the Erotic: The Erotic as Power," in *Sister Outsider* (Freedom, Calif.: Crossing Press, 1984), 54.
10. Susan Griffin, *Pornography and Silence: Culture's Revenge Against Nature* (New York: Harper Colophon Press, 1981); Jana Sawicki, "Identity Politics and Sexual Freedom: Foucault and Feminism," in *Feminism and Foucault: Reflections on Resistance*, ed. Irene Diamond and Lee Quinby (Boston: Northeastern University Press, 1988), 177–92.
11. Mary Calderone, "One the Possible Prevention of Sexual Problems in Adolescence," *Hospital and Community Psychiatry* 34, no. 6 (1983): 528–30.
12. I do not think that these are the only, or even necessarily the most important, differences among this group of girls regarding their experiences of sexual desire. My initial readings of these data suggest that other, more psychological differences, such as the presence or absence of a history of sexual abuse, or whether or not a girl has a critical perspective on messages about girls' sexuality, may also differentiate how these girls experience sexual desire.
13. A question that emerges from Inez's fears is why contraception to protect her from pregnancy and why the use of condoms to protect against AIDS do not appear to salve her fears or make it possible to avoid these dangers in a way that might include her desire. The issue of access to contraception for poor girls, norms regarding female sexuality, and the use of contraception in the Hispanic community and how effective a girl's wish or demand for the use of condoms by boys really may explain her feelings.

14. Lori Stern, "Disavowing the Self in Female Adolescence," in *Women, Girls, and Psychotherapy*, 105–18.
15. Carol Gilligan, "Teaching Shakespeare's Sister," in *Making Connections: The Relational World of Adolescent Girls at the Emma Willard School*, ed. Carol Gilligan, Nona Lyons, and Trudy Hanmer (Cambridge: Harvard University Press, 1989), 6–29.
16. Two urban girls voiced confusion as well; see Tolman, "Voicing the Body," for in-depth analyses.
17. See, for example, Gilligan, "Joining the Resistance," and Lyn Mikel Brown, "Telling a Girl's Life," in *Women, Girls, and Psychotherapy*, 71–86.
18. Linda K. Christian-Smith, *Becoming a Woman Through Romance* (New York: Routledge and Kegan Paul, 1990).
19. Eleanor Linn, Nan Stein, and J. Young, "Bitter Lessons for All: Sexual Harassment in Schools," in *Sexuality and the Curriculum*, ed. Sears.
20. Liz Kelly, *Surviving Sexual Violence* (Minneapolis: University of Minnesota Press, 1991).

9

A Tale of Two Technologies

HPV Vaccination, Male Circumcision, and Sexual Health

LAURA M. CARPENTER AND MONICA J. CASPER

Both historically and recently, medical advances have been double-edged swords for women. For example, oral contraceptives, mammography, and assisted reproductive technologies (ARTs) have increased women's sexual freedom, advanced women's health, and expanded women's reproductive possibilities. On the other hand, as Sarah Jane Brubaker and Heather E. Dillaway highlighted in chapter 4 of this volume, new medical technologies can sometimes diminish women's agency. From the "twilight sleep" used in the early twentieth century to "knock out" pregnant women, to the epidurals used today, medical advances can decrease women's control over their bodies.

Similarly, in "A Tale of Two Technologies: HPV Vaccination, Male Circumcision, and Sexual Health," Laura M. Carpenter and Monica J. Casper illustrate how the deployment of the new human papillomavirus (HPV) vaccine, which was developed to reduce rates of various cancers in women, simultaneously reproduced conservative understandings of gender and revealed much about the control of young women's sexuality.

Carpenter and Casper ask why two medical technologies—the HPV vaccine and male circumcision—elicited very different public reactions even though both offered apparently safe means of reducing infectious diseases. Whereas efforts to promote circumcision as an HIV preventive for boys and men have gone largely uncontested, efforts to promote the HPV vaccine, which prevents common forms of cervical cancer, have been met with outcry from parents, politicians, and policy makers. Carpenter and Casper explain these different reactions by exploring how these two technologies are understood by the medical world

Laura M. Carpenter and Monica J. Casper, "A Tale of Two Technologies: HPV Vaccination, Male Circumcision, and Sexual Health," *Gender & Society* 23(6): 790–816.

and the public as "pharmacologies of containment" designed to prevent infection by cordoning off populations considered dangerously unhealthy from the rest of the population. The differing reactions to these two technologies reflect social ideas about who needs protection and who is dangerous. Not surprisingly, views regarding whose bodies, fluids, and sexual practices need disciplining and containment reflect social cleavages of gender, age, race, sexuality, and nationality. In addition, the authors argue, reactions to the HPV vaccination and male circumcision reproduce the familiar "double standard" that grants men greater sexual freedom than women.

In 2006, two technologies designed to protect sexual health—one very old and one very new—sparked headlines globally: male circumcision and the human papillomavirus (HPV) vaccine. Arguably more efficacious if administered to young children, both show considerable promise in reducing the risk of potentially fatal diseases—AIDS and cervical cancer (CC), respectively—by reducing sexually transmitted infections (STIs). Yet while proposals to promote circumcision as HIV preventive among boys and men in the United States have gone largely uncontested outside "intactivist" activist circles, efforts to implement the HPV vaccine raised an outcry among parents, politicians, and policy makers (Casper and Carpenter 2008). Much contention focused on the possibility that intervention—that is, use of the vaccine—would lead to promiscuity among preteen and teenage girls.

Why did reactions to two technologies with ostensibly similar goals—and similarly low reported complication rates—differ so dramatically? To answer this question, we draw on feminist science and technology studies (STS), the biographical approach to pharmaceuticals, and the literature on vaccines and other technologies of containment, specifically those related to sexual health. . . .

Feminist STS scholarship reveals that gender and sexuality can infuse every stage of a technology's life course, including design, development, marketing, and use (Haraway 1997; Oudshoorn 2003). In turn, new (and old) technologies can profoundly reshape gender relations and sexual lives by remaking human bodies, practices, and relationships. This is especially true of reproductive and sexual health technologies, which mark and refashion the body's capacity to reproduce not only "life itself" (Rose 2006) but also (in many cases) deadly diseases. Such technologies may also remake—and are remade by—notions of race and/or nationality, as shown by Briggs (2003) with respect to the birth control pill's origination in Puerto Rico and by Roberts (1997) regarding "population control" technologies' impact on black women. . . .

. . . Here and in our broader project, we reveal how sexual and reproductive health practices unfold in the shifting context of contemporary U.S. biopolitics (Rose 2006). We ask, how have cultural understandings of sexuality, gender, age, race, and nationality—and their interrelations—shaped responses to the two technologies? Why have attempts to mandate HPV vaccination activated concerns about female promiscuity, whereas talk of promoting circumcision as HIV preventive for boys has not (at least regarding U.S. boys)? How, in turn, might uptake of the HPV vaccine and the reframing of circumcision against HIV alter social constructions not only of gender and sexuality but also of age and race? Our focus is on the United States, but these deeply stratified processes have transnational implications (Carpenter and Casper 2009), insofar as American responses to the technologies also influence practices in the developing world.

Technologies such as the HPV vaccine are not therapeutic; rather, they are designed to *prevent* the onset of disease through containment of causal infection. The phenomena we have called "pharmacologies of containment" (Casper and Carpenter 2008) are implicated in the broader politics of contagion, which inevitably invoke intimacies shared among people. The threat of contagion—the transmissibility of disease—motivates "the establishment of *cordons sanitaire* in one form or another, the drawing of lines and zones of hygiene" (Bashford and Hooker 2001, 9). In our view, the HPV vaccine is a highly politicized pharmaceutical cordon sanitaire, formed within particular social, economic, and geographic contexts. It embodies the "dream of hygienic containment" (Bashford and Hooker 2001) and as such has activated social cleavages related to gender, sex, race, age, and especially sexuality. As Brandt (1987, 5) notes, "Since the late nineteenth century, venereal disease has been used as a symbol for a society characterized by a corrupt sexuality . . . as a symbol of pollution and contamination."

If we read circumcision as a kind of symbolic vaccine, as do its public health proponents, and analyze it using conceptual tools of intersectionality, what can we learn about the ways technologies are embedded in social relations? . . . Seeking conceptual innovation, we ask, how do social relations shape containment efforts as technologies are (re)invented? Whose bodies, fluids, and sexual practices need to be contained, when, by whom, and for what purposes? How do pharmaceutical and surgical containment strategies discipline some bodies and not others?

Our comparative examination of two different contexts of sexual containment holds particular promise for advancing the sociology of containment. Sexual beliefs and conduct have long been interpreted and assessed differently depending on the gender, race or ethnicity, social class, age, and nationality of the sexual actors in question (Brandt 1987). Men, people of color (especially people of African descent), the economically disadvantaged, and individuals who experience or express same-sex desire have been stereotyped as sexually uncontrollable and in need of containment (Nathanson 1991; Roberts 1997; Seidman 2002; Tolman 1996)—though considerable license is granted to white, heterosexual, middle-class men—while children and younger teenagers are typically viewed (depending on their race or ethnicity) as innocent and inherently asexual (Levine 2002). Exactly who and what are contained by technologies such as circumcision and HPV vaccination may best be understood through an analysis sensitive to intersectionality

(Collins 1990); conversely, interrogating the dynamics of containment technologies can illuminate the workings of intersecting social statuses. We are especially keen to include men's bodies and experiences in intersectional analysis (which all too often considers only women) and to explore emergent sites of containment where the "double standard" is both a strategically deployed cultural resource and an ongoing social accomplishment.

(Re)Introducing the Technologies

In 2006, with much fanfare, Merck & Co. announced U.S. Food and Drug Administration (FDA) approval of Gardasil, the first vaccine for HPV. Another similar HPV vaccine, Cervarix by GlaxoSmithKline, is currently undergoing FDA review. [The FDA granted approval in October 2009.] Composed of over one hundred strains, including thirty transmissible by sex, HPV is the most common STI in the world. It is also the key agent of infection in CC, now viewed as an STI rather than a typical cancer; however, not all HPV leads to CC (Koushik and Franco 2006). Globally, approximately 493,000 new cases of CC are diagnosed each year, representing 10 percent of all cancers in women (Koushik and Franco 2006). Over 80 percent of new cases occur in developing countries (Dailard 2006). In the United States, where screening is routine for most women, CC is relatively rare, yet morbidity and mortality from CC are higher among women of color and women from lower socioeconomic strata (Singh, Miller, Hankey, and Edwards 2004).

Gardasil prevents infections from HPV-16 and HPV-18, two strains that cause about 70 percent of CCs, as well as HPV-6 and HPV-11, which produce 90 percent of genital warts (Harper 2004; Harper et al. 2006). Although publicly framed by their manufacturers as vaccines against CC, Gardasil and Cervarix can also protect women *and men* against anal, penile, and throat cancers caused by HPV (and transmitted through sex with male or female partners; Kubba 2008; Nack 2008). Complication rates are low, under 2 percent in most studies, and side effects are generally minor, although more than seven thousand "adverse events" have been reported, and safety remains a concern of many who oppose mandating widespread vaccination (CNN 2008; Wheeler 2007).[1] . . .

The HPV vaccine is a profitable pharmaceutical commodity with a distinctive biography and life course. Where Van der Geest, Whyte, and Hardon (1996) see pharmaceutical biographies as unfolding in the context of politics, in our view politics is not merely context. Rather, at *every* stage of their life courses—production, marketing, distribution, prescription, use, and efficacy—pharmaceuticals may influence politics and social relations, which in turn may (re)shape the technology itself. Drugs can instigate political struggles, and potentially social change, over time. . . .

Male circumcision is not a pharmaceutical vaccine but a surgical procedure for removing part or all of the foreskin of the penis. Yet circumcision has served as a technology of containment in the United States since its medicalization in the late nineteenth century (Carpenter 2010).[2] By the 1940s, about 60 percent of U.S. males were circumcised in infancy (Laumann, Masi, and Zuckerman 1997). Supported by medical professionals and the for-profit insurance system, infant circumcision grew in popularity until about 1970, when rates exceeded 90 percent, largely because of its purported ability to prevent STIs and "unhygienic" germs (it was widely, if erroneously, believed that intact penises are difficult to clean); circumcision also became a typical therapy for phimosis (unretractable foreskin). However, evidence that circumcision actually prevents STIs was, and is, mixed (Gollaher 2000).

In the 1970s, following a cost–benefit analysis, the American Academy of Pediatrics (AAP) declared circumcision to be medically unnecessary. This move, representing a general decline in medical support—along with grass-roots anticircumcision activism (on grounds including painfulness, human rights, and informed consent), the natural childbirth movement, cost-cutting measures by health insurers, and immigration from locales where circumcision is rare—resulted in much lower rates of circumcision, about 65 percent by 1999 (Darby 2005; Gollaher 2000). Since 1989, largely prompted by a vocal coterie of procircumcision physician–researchers, the AAP has recognized "potential medical benefits" (chiefly the containment of urinary tract infections and penile cancer, which is exceedingly rare) but declined to recommend *routine* circumcision. Complication rates of infant circumcision in the United States are generally thought to be low, about one in one thousand. In short, use of circumcision for disease containment is contested, both within and outside the U.S. medical community; each "new" use of circumcision comes into already existing contexts of dissent.

Circumcision has recently been positioned as a potentially effective intervention against HIV/AIDS following clinical trials conducted in sub-Saharan Africa, where HIV is contracted primarily via heterosexual vaginal intercourse. Trials there found that circumcision of adult men reduces female-to-male HIV transmission rates by 30 percent to 50 percent (Auvert et al. 2005; Talbott 2007). Male circumcision has not proven effective in protecting women from heterosexually transmitted HIV infection, however (Altman 2008). About 62 percent of adult men in Africa are circumcised, with rates varying widely by region and ethnic group (e.g., nearly universal among African Muslims but an anathema among ethnic groups that view intact foreskins as a sign of cultural distinction). In southern Africa, where rates of HIV are highest, fewer than 20 percent of men are circumcised (see http://www3.niaid.nih.gov/news/QA/AMC12_QA.htm). Across Africa, complication rates of circumcision are high—ranging from 18 percent in public clinics to 35 percent among traditional practitioners—because of poor training and inadequate and/or unsanitary equipment (MacInnis 2008).

The HIV/AIDS epidemic is less severe in the United States but still of great concern, given an infection rate of 13.7 per 100,000 population, with the highest rates among blacks and Hispanics (54.1 and 18.0, respectively; Centers for Disease Control and Prevention [CDC] 2007). Of U.S. men diagnosed with AIDS in 2006, 72 percent contracted the disease through male-to-male sexual contact, and 9 percent through injection drug use; of women diagnosed in the same period, 20 percent contracted AIDS through injection drug use, and 80 percent through heterosexual contact (CDC 2009). Just over nine thousand of the nearly one million U.S. citizens with AIDS as of 2007 were younger than 13 at diagnosis, suggesting that preventive intervention in or before early adolescence could be effective (CDC 2009). Since 2007, prompted by the African clinical trials, the AAP has been reevaluating its position on infant circumcision (Konrad 2007), while the CDC is considering policies for infants and adults (Rabin 2009). Insofar as the vast majority of U.S. adult males are circumcised, "For now, the focus of public officials in this country appears to be on making recommendations for newborns" (Rabin 2009).

Although not a pharmaceutical, circumcision works like a relatively inefficient vaccine with respect to HIV. Virtually every vaccine fails to protect some of the people who receive it. However, vaccines recommended by the U.S. Advisory Committee on Immunization Practices (ACIP; e.g., for polio, chicken pox) produce immune responses in 90 percent to 98 percent of individuals who receive them. If circumcision were a vaccine, the comparable figure based on the African trials would be 30 percent to 50 percent. Both HPV vaccination and circumcision, then, are preventive technologies inscribed in the body, with delayed benefits presumed to accrue long after the procedures themselves. Both operate according to principles of herd immunity; that is, performing the procedure on a certain proportion of people—typically about 70 percent—greatly reduces a disease's chances of spreading (Colgrove 2006). The HPV vaccine and male circumcision are also similar in that they require individuals to assume embodied risks for later, perhaps invisible personal and collective benefits, something people in general dislike doing—although parents are more apt to consent to risks on behalf of their children for the sake of prevention (Colgrove 2006) and may even choose procedures for their children that they would not choose for themselves.[3] To the extent that both technologies are supported, recommended, and even mandated by governments (and allied institutions), they represent biopolitical solutions to contemporary public health quandaries.

Methods and Data

. . . Our data sources, listed in Table 9.1, include primary and secondary literatures in science, medicine, and public health; print and Internet materials produced by major medical associations (e.g., Web sites, press releases, policy statements), grassroots groups, and health advocacy organizations; formal and informal interviews with key biomedical, public health, and activist figures; participant observation at scientific, clinical, and activist conferences;

TABLE 9.1 Data Sources

Science and public health research	*Journal of the American Medical Association*, *New England Journal of Medicine*, *American Journal of Public Health*, *Pediatrics*, *Lancet*, *British Medical Journal*
Medical associations	American Academy of Pediatrics, American College of Obstetrics and Gynecology, American Medical Association, American Medical Women's Association, American Public Health Association
Grassroots and health advocacy organizations	National Organization of Circumcision Information Resource Centers, Circumcision Information and Research Pages, Attorneys for the Rights of the Child, Alliance for Cervical Cancer Prevention, National Cervical Cancer Coalition, Alan Guttmacher Institute, PATH, Planned Parenthood
Public health organizations and figures	Centers for Disease Control, World Health Organization, UNAIDS
Government documents and Web sites	National Cancer Institute, U.S. Food and Drug Administration, U.S. Department of Health and Human Services
Conferences	Gardasil in Our Schools: Should States Mandate the HPV Vaccine for Their Students? symposium, February 2008, Vanderbilt University, USA; International Symposium on Genital Integrity, September 2008, Keele University, UK
News media	*New York Times* and *Washington Post* (all items addressing HIV and male circumcision, 2005–2008), selected other newspapers and magazines (2005–2008)
Pharmaceutical actors	GlaxoSmithKline, Merck & Co.

news media coverage; materials produced by pharmaceutical actors; and government documents and Web sites.

We analyzed these data using modified grounded theory (Charmaz 2006), which builds original theoretical arguments from data, as Glaser and Strauss (1967) recommended, but acknowledges that all data *and analysts* are already situated within social and cultural contexts. Critical to grounded theory methodology is the constant comparative technique through which data are coded, conceptualized, and categorized based on meanings. . . .

In addition, we also undertook content analysis of key texts and documents, including a detailed analysis of every item (news report, letter to the editor, and editorial) published from 2005 to 2008 in the *New York Times* and *Washington Post* that addressed both HIV and circumcision. . . .

Responses to the HPV Vaccine

The HPV vaccine emerged into a dynamic set of cultural conflicts, embodied health movements, and sexual politics. Clinical trials indicate that Merck's Gardasil may prevent up to 70 percent of CCs and that GlaxoSmithKline's Cervarix may also protect against HPV-45 and HPV-31, the third and fourth most common strains (Harper et al. 2006). Although these strains of HPV also cause anal, penile, and throat cancers—in men as well as women—Merck focused on CC, thereby deflecting attention away from the *sexual* nature of HPV and from same-sex transmission vectors and reinforcing the widespread tendency to treat sexual health as a women's issue (Berer 2008; Kubba 2008; Nack 2008). Despite the herd immunity rationale behind vaccination, clinical trials in boys (approximately half the population) did not occur at first. By September 2009, when the FDA Advisory Panel approved Gardasil for use in boys and men ages 9 to 26 (see http://www.webmd.com/sexual-conditions/hpv-genital-warts/news/20090909/fda-panel-oks-gardasil-for-boys), the HPV vaccine had already been "feminized" in the scientific literature and news media.

Shortly after FDA approved Gardasil in 2006, ACIP provisionally recommended the vaccine for all girls 11 to 12, and the CDC added it to the Child and Adolescent Vaccination Schedule (http://www.cdc.gov/vaccines/acip/index.html). Leading medical associations such as the American College of Obstetricians and Gynecologists endorsed the recommendations—although some practitioners oppose widespread vaccination until long-term safety and efficacy are more definitively demonstrated. Sawaya and Smith-McCune (2007) assert, "While the trials are ongoing, mandatory vaccination is premature" (p. 1991).

Merck accompanied Gardasil's 2006 release with a massive public relations campaign including highly visible television and print ads. Campaign materials variously proclaimed, "Roll up your sleeves. It's your turn to help guard against cervical cancer" and "The power to prevent cervical cancer is in your hands. And on your daughter's arm." Even if this costly campaign failed to educate about HPV vaccination (including its risks), it likely ensured that people heard about the new technology simultaneous to it becoming available in clinics. News of the vaccine spread like wildfire, its arrival announced with exultant headlines such as, "First-ever cancer vaccine approved."

Yet almost immediately, and in contrast to the circumcision stories analyzed later in this article, media coverage of the HPV vaccine began to focus on the putative dangers to (and from) young women's sexuality. The vaccine is aimed at preadolescent and adolescent girls, with a recommended target age of 10 to 12, because Merck's trials found a stronger immunological response in girls 10 to 15 than in women 16 to 23 and because few girls begin sexual activity, and thus exposure to HPV, before those ages (Ault and Future II Study Group 2007). Numerous media sources, extrapolating from comments issued by the conservative organization Focus on the Family in 2005, began labeling the new technology the "promiscuity vaccine," in reference to its imagined capacity to encourage young women to engage in sexual activity. To those who fear that the HPV vaccine will contaminate "innocent" young people by exposing them to sexual knowledge, the technology backfires, containing HPV and CC only at the price of activating the more frightening scourge of adolescent sexual activity.

Cultural assumptions about youth and gender suggest that (some) young women (white, middle-class, heterosexual, without disabilities) are to be protected, while young men are largely expected, if not outright encouraged, to exercise their sexuality. As feminist scholars have long argued, prophylactic interventions related to sex—and sexual health—disproportionately target young women, in part because women's potential for pregnancy makes their role in reproduction more obvious and more salient (Berer 2008; Nack 2008). Although U.S. moral conservatives decry adolescent sexual activity in general, their efforts more frequently target girls. Calls to extend HPV vaccination efforts to boys have been rare in the United States (though they have been common in Canada and, to a lesser extent, Great Britain; Kubba 2008). . . .

Variation in state-level vaccination laws complicates matters further. School-based vaccination has historically been an effective means of ensuring rapid and widespread use of childhood or adolescent vaccines (Colgrove 2006). Laws requiring vaccination are especially beneficial to low-income children, who are covered by government programs that pay for vaccines. By late 2007, twenty-four states and Washington, D.C., had introduced legislation to mandate HPV vaccination for girls entering public schools. These efforts were forcefully resisted by conservatives, who argued, just as they did regarding the Plan B contraceptive, that vaccination "sends the wrong message" and that requiring it violates parental rights. In May 2007, just months after Texas became the first state to mandate HPV vaccination for all sixth-grade girls (with some exceptions), via a gubernatorial executive order, Texas legislators—largely prompted by vocal opposition from moral conservatives and parents who oppose vaccination in general—passed a bill overriding the mandate (Associated Press 2007). Legislators in California and Maryland withdrew their bills (only D.C.'s was enacted), and Virginia lawmakers, despite passing a school vaccine requirement in 2007, were by late 2008 considering a bill to delay that requirement (National Conference of State Legislatures [NCSL] 2009). [A bill to repeal mandatory HPV vaccination passed the Virginia House, but failed to receive Senate approval in 2012.]

These developments outraged many progressives. The National Organization for Women's Kim Gandy stated, "I have no doubt that right-wing organizations will lobby. . . . They've clearly shown that they are more concerned with women's chastity than their health" (Richert 2005). Lawmakers in many states have regrouped, finding success with nonmandatory measures. Since 2006, New Hampshire has provided over 14,000 doses of the vaccine at no cost to girls younger than 18, as has South Dakota since 2007; and

Washington State's legislature approved $10 million to voluntarily vaccinate 94,000 girls by 2009 (NCSL 2009).

Responses to Circumcision as an HIV Preventive

. . . Early in the HIV/AIDS epidemic in Africa, researchers observed lower rates of HIV infection among men who were circumcised compared with men who were not (Marx 1989). Although circumcision is associated with social factors, such as Islamic beliefs, that encourage relatively conservative sexual behavior, thereby reducing the likelihood of HIV transmission, the density of HIV-receptive Langerhans cells on the foreskin's inner surface provided a biologically plausible explanation for the proposed HIV-circumcision link (*New York Times*, July 11, 2000). Randomized clinical trials of circumcision began in Uganda, South Africa, and Kenya in the early 2000s and, by 2005, were finding HIV rates 50 percent to 60 percent lower among men in the circumcision groups than men in the control groups (Auvert et al. 2005). Some later analyses found smaller reductions in HIV transmission (Talbott 2007) as well as significant levels of nonsexual transmission (i.e., from contaminated instruments; Brewer, Potterat, Roberts, and Brody 2007).

With no AIDS cure in sight and progress stalled on an HIV vaccine, the international public health community greeted the circumcision studies with cautious optimism. At the 2006 International Conference on AIDS, advocates argued that "new HIV infections in men could be substantially reduced and millions of lives saved if [circumcision] were to be introduced" (*British Medical Journal* [*BMJ*] 2006, vol. 333, 409). Yet skeptics cautioned that men who believed themselves fully protected by circumcision might engage in riskier behavior (the disinhibition thesis), stressed the difficulties of generalizing outside African contexts, given regional variations in HIV strains and transmission patterns (primarily via vaginal intercourse in Africa), and emphasized the need to place circumcision in a comprehensive anti-HIV strategy.

Despite initially "refus[ing] to endorse [circumcision] as a prevention tool until more evidence is produced" (*BMJ* 2006, vol. 333), by March 2007, the World Health Organization (WHO) and the Joint United Nations Programme on HIV/AIDS (UNAIDS) were urging countries with high heterosexually transmitted HIV rates and low circumcision rates to recognize adult male circumcision as "an additional important intervention [in a comprehensive package] to reduce the risk of heterosexually acquired HIV infection in men," provided adequate medical safeguards were available (e.g., availability of sterilized instruments; WHO/UNAIDS 2007). Some experts welcomed circumcision as a sexual health intervention that, by targeting men, shifts some of the burden of sexual health from women, even as they continued to worry that, because circumcision is not 100 percent protective, women remain exposed to risk (Berer 2007; Sawires et al. 2007).

When considering how the African findings might translate to the United States, many in the public health and medical communities expressed a similar mixture of optimism and caution. National Institute of Allergy and Infectious Diseases director Anthony Fauci declared that circumcising adult men "could be an important addition to . . . HIV prevention" while noting that "it is not completely protective and must be seen as a powerful addition to . . . other HIV prevention methods" (*BMJ* 2007, vol. 334, 11). Other medical professionals contended that recommending circumcision in the United States was premature, given "the many differences between the underlying HIV epidemics in Africa and the U.S." and lacking evidence that circumcision can prevent HIV transmission between men (a major vector in the United States; Sullivan et al. 2007, e223). Some U.S. experts were more enthusiastic about circumcision. In 2005, King Holmes, a University of Washington-based STI scholar, said, "It's essentially ***an anatomic vaccine*** for life" (*Science* 2005, vol. 309, 860, emphasis added). In April 2007, New York City Health Commissioner Thomas Frieden (who became CDC director in May 2009) was reported as having "suggested circumcision could hold preventative promise here, despite differences between the two at-risk populations [U.S. and African]" (*USA Today,* April 7, 2007). Many news reports gave the impression that Frieden was actively promoting circumcision, but he averred that "the New York City Health Department has not planned, developed or announced a campaign to encourage at-risk men to get circumcised. . . . [W]e are encouraging people to discuss and study this issue" (*New York Times,* April 12, 2007). Frieden further noted, "A campaign to promote circumcision in this country would be premature without stronger evidence." His recommendation for dialogue met with a lukewarm reception. Despite "express[ing] support for seeking new ways to combat the disease," New York City Mayor Michael Bloomberg "was unconvinced that government should be involved in promoting or providing circumcisions" (*New York Times,* April 6, 2007).

Some HIV/AIDS activists "doubted that encouraging circumcisions would significantly decrease infection rates" (*USA Today,* April 7, 2007). The Community HIV/AIDS Mobilization Project's Julie Davids noted, "The U.S. has a healthy [i.e., high] HIV epidemic and high rates of circumcision" (*BMJ* 2007, vol. 334, 11). Others, like Peter Staley, cofounder of ACT-UP New York, expressed concern about local or regional variation even as they longed for reduced infection rates: "Should we proceed when we don't have hard data yet on the population here? . . . On the other hand, if we wait the three years it would take to answer that question, how many will be infected in the meantime?" (*USA Today,* April 7, 2007). Mark McLaurin, executive director of New York State Black Gay Network, reported hearing from men who "wanted to make sure that [circumcision] wasn't going to be mandatory" and speculated (based on low uptake for HIV vaccination trials) that it would be difficult to recruit black and Latino men for circumcision "because of everything from Tuskegee on up" (*New York Times,* April 15, 2007). Sawires et al. (2007, 711) emphasize "avoiding branding men as perpetrators of infection," especially African men, who are often painted with negative sexual stereotypes.

In June 2007, pursuant to the African trials and lobbying by longtime proponents of circumcision within the medical community, the AAP quietly began reviewing its 1999 policy that circumcision has "potential medical benefits" that "are not sufficient to recommend routine neonatal circumcision" (Konrad 2007). Notably, this policy would apply only to infants, not adult men. [In 2012, the AAP announced in a policy statement that the decision of newborn male circumcision should be left to parents.] . . .

Also in spring 2007, the CDC began "consult[ing] with external experts to receive input on the potential value, risks, and feasibility of circumcision as an HIV prevention intervention in the United States and to discuss considerations for the possible development of guidelines" (CDC 2008). By August 2009, the CDC had not taken an official position but was (newly under Frieden's direction) "considering promoting routine circumcision for all baby boys born in the United States" as well as "whether the surgery should be offered to adult heterosexual men whose sexual practices put them at high risk of infection" (Rabin 2009). Although the CDC's Web site contains numerous links to references and material on circumcision as a possible HIV-preventive, its fact sheet on circumcision stresses that

> individual men [who] wish to consider circumcision as an additional HIV prevention measure . . . must recognize that circumcision (1) does carry risks and costs . . . in addition to potential benefits; (2) has only proven effective in reducing the risk of infection through insertive vaginal sex; and (3) confers only partial protection and should be considered only in conjunction with other proven prevention measures [e.g., monogamy, condom use].

Anticircumcision activists responded to these developments by emphasizing that circumcision offers limited protection, causes complications, and is not cost-effective. For example, a 2005 brochure from the National Organization of Circumcision Information and Resource Centers (NOCIRC) noted that "both circumcised and intact males contracted HIV during the course of the [African] studies" and described circumcision as "less effective, more risky, and more expensive than . . . aggressive educational approaches that discuss . . . the importance of safe sex and condom use." Activists have also stressed disinhibition—"Promoting circumcision to protect against HIV could provide a false sense of safety, putting sexually active males and their partners at increased risk"—and human rights grounds for opposing circumcision: "There is a very real risk that . . . encouraging adults into circumcision will . . . lead to forcible circumcision of infants and children, who are unable to consent to surgery" (NOCIRC 2005). J. Steven Svoboda of Attorneys for the Rights of the Child has specifically critiqued "powerful international agencies" for "promoting circumcision as a vaccine" against HIV and argued that vaccines for diseases that are largely sexually transmitted (e.g., Hepatitis B vaccine) should not be given in infancy but when children are older (and risks are more immanent; author's field notes from the International Symposium on Genital Integrity 2008). Circumcision foes have also critiqued the African trials on scientific grounds (e.g., "all three studies were halted early [because HIV infection rates were so much lower among men in the circumcision groups than in the control groups] so there is no way to assess whether the preliminary reduced-transmission rate would persist if the study had continued to run the designed length"; NOCIRC 2005). Implications of targeting African bodies have not eluded activists: "Are poorer African men more expendable to such research and easier to coerce into needless surgery? This can easily be viewed as a colonial undercurrent" (Ferris n.d.).

For the most part, U.S. news media have reported findings of the African clinical trials with more enthusiasm than critique. Many reports framed circumcision as a near magic bullet in the fight against HIV in Africa:

> A series of studies have shown that circumcised men are at least 60 percent less likely to contract HIV. Far less clear is how meager public health systems already overwhelmed by the AIDS epidemic can offer the procedure widely enough to slow the epidemic's ruinous spread. (*Washington Post*, October 21, 2007)

Few (three of forty-eight) of the news items addressing both circumcision and HIV mentioned the possibility that different HIV transmission patterns might limit the applicability of African study findings to the United States or took note of decades-long opposition to routine circumcision on grounds such as human rights and informed consent ethics (five of forty-eight). Of the nine news items (18.8 percent of sample) mentioning concerns that African men might engage in "risky" behavior believing themselves to be protected by circumcision, none extended such arguments to circumcised boys (or men) in the United States.

Most major papers published editorials and letters to the editor calling for the expansion of circumcision to combat HIV. Some of these items specified the African context, but many were vague about location—and age of the targeted males—leaving readers to interpret. One *New York Times* editorial implied the widest possible scope of intervention:

> For years, the holy grail of AIDS prevention has been a vaccine, even one that is only 50 to 60 percent effective. A real vaccine is years away. But as of yesterday, we know its near equivalent exists. International donors and governments should join together to spread the good news about circumcision and *make the procedure available everywhere.* (December 14, 2006, emphasis added)

This item reflects the tendency of U.S. news coverage of circumcision: using HIV links to compare circumcision favorably to vaccination. Of forty-eight news items, six (four articles, one editorial, one letter) included language analogizing circumcision to a vaccine (e.g., "If an AIDS vaccine were suddenly discovered that could prevent 7 out of 10 new infections, the world would be rejoicing"; *New York Times*, October 15, 2005), and two letters were published under the headline, "A Real-World AIDS Vaccine?" (*New York Times*, January 28, 2007). One article and two letters instead argued, "Circumcision shouldn't be confused with an honest vaccine" (*New York Times*, December 16, 2006).[4]

Juxtapositions of Circumcision as HIV Preventive and the HPV Vaccine

Despite similarities between circumcision as HIV preventive and HPV vaccination as containment technologies and links made in clinical studies, they are seldom *explicitly* juxtaposed in public discourse. Several sites of coappearance are therefore worth exploring: international public health discourse, medical research, news coverage, and the anticircumcision activist community.[5] . . .

Juxtaposition of the technologies in international public health discourse is exemplified by UNAIDS executive director Peter Piot's 2007 speech to the 17th annual meeting of the International Society for Sexually Transmitted Diseases Research. Piot described "the feminization of the HIV epidemic and . . . burden of STIs on women," including HPV and cervical cancer, as the "most important" epidemiologic trend in STIs; called the HPV vaccine "an exciting development from which we will be able to learn a lot . . . if and when we have an HIV vaccine"; and noted that "HIV changes the natural history and pattern of STIs," including HPV, by affecting immune suppression (on HIV-HPV links unrelated to circumcision, see Carpenter and Casper 2009). Where Piot did invoke male circumcision, it was to express concern that increasing focus on circumcision is crowding out proven behavioral prevention efforts:

> When I was in South Africa . . . at the national AIDS conference . . . all the discussions were on male circumcision and on microbicides. . . . There was hardly any discussion about how we can make sure that people today have access to what we know is working [male and female condoms, behavioral interventions]. I think that is a very, very dangerous trend.

The Bill and Melinda Gates Foundation's support for global health initiatives likewise encompasses circumcision against HIV and HPV vaccination without explicitly citing linkages. . . .

. . . Medical researchers made a more direct connection in March 2009, when *New England Journal of Medicine* (*NEJM*) published a study finding lower rates of HPV infection among circumcised men. Based on clinical trial data from Uganda, authors Tobian et al. (2009, 1308) estimated that circumcision reduces transmission of cancer-causing HPV strains by 35 percent (and herpes [HSV-2] transmission by 25 percent). Despite noting that reduced HPV rates could result, in part, from the virus naturally clearing over the study period, the authors proposed that "these benefits should guide public health policies for neonatal, adolescent, and adult male circumcision programs" without specifying where. According to the *New York Times*, coauthor Ron Gray said, "There is no reason to believe that this is in any way unique to Africa" (Bakalar 2009).

Few overt comparisons of the two technologies appeared in print news media, before or after the *NEJM* article. The only example in our sample (through 2008) of thirty articles, seven editorials, and eleven letters to the editor is a letter published on December 30, 2006, in the *Washington Post*. Wrote Lynne Leonard,

> When a vaccine is introduced that can prevent the most common types of [HPV] . . . a hoopla ensues because of fear that this vaccine will promote promiscuity in girls [Health, November 7]. But when circumcision is promoted in boys because the risk of HIV infection is shown to be cut by half [front page, December 14], nary a word is said about promoting promiscuity in boys. The double standard is alive and well.

Letters to the editor are one means that the public uses to correct and protest depiction of issues in the news media (Wahl-Jorgensen 2007). Strikingly, only one of the forty-eight items addressing circumcision-HIV links before March 2009 mentions the HPV vaccine, much less posits any similarity between these technologies. The *New York Times* and *Washington Post* each published one story about the *NEJM* study; neither prompted letters to the editor or further news coverage.

The anticircumcision activist community has also juxtaposed circumcision as HIV preventive and the HPV vaccine. Many participants at the 2008 International Symposium on Genital Integrity, cosponsored by NOCIRC and NORM-UK, argued that circumcision for HIV prevention should be chosen only voluntarily by adult men and can wait until just before men become sexually active, a position consistent with that of activists who propose delaying the HPV vaccine until girls are "older" (i.e., legally capable of consent) and/or sexually active. In informal conversations with author Carpenter, several conference participants explicitly juxtaposed the two technologies, proposing that both could wait until sexual initiation was imminent (albeit arguing that circumcision was never advisable, whereas the HPV vaccine might be). Historically, anticircumcision activists have forcefully countered claims that circumcision protects against HPV/CC. According to one Circumcision Information and Resource Pages fact sheet, "Male circumcision has never been proved to offer any real protection against HPV infection in the female partner, but even if it did, it still would not be necessary because the vaccine will offer protection." . . .

Discussion and Conclusion

By juxtaposing HPV vaccination and circumcision as HIV preventive, our analysis makes several contributions to research on gender, sexuality, disease, and public health. We broaden and deepen arguments about containment by examining the public health principles and meanings surrounding the HPV vaccine and circumcision. The "dream of hygienic containment" (Bashford and Hooker 2001) is alive and well in these overlapping public health worlds, but ultimately it does not reflect the reality of what circumcision—or even HPV vaccination—can do. Beyond actual public health successes (and failures), provaccination and containment practices work to intensify extant structural relations, extending hierarchies and inequalities. Members of some groups—"fallen" women, racial or ethnic minorities, poor people, people in developing nations—are typically culturally positioned as unhygienic, with toxic bodies and transmissible "conditions," and thus in need of containment. Pharmacological and surgical containment related to sexual health promises to discipline the bodies of some to ensure immunity for all. With no end to cancer or HIV/AIDS in sight, this kind of biopolitical symbolism is powerful and may encourage discriminatory action.

The sexually transmitted nature of HPV/CC and HIV/AIDS affects responses to the vaccine and circumcision in two ways. First, although HIV can be contracted through injection drug use and other nonsexual means (although chief infection vectors in the United States are sexual), strains of HPV that cause CC are contracted *only* sexually (unlike strains that cause nongenital warts). The possibility of nonsexual transmission may deflect concerns about disinhibition among circumcised men, as when the (rare) possibility of nonsexual transmission of Hepatitis B helped to forestall serious opposition to efforts to mandate that vaccine (J. Colgrove, pers. comm., June 1, 2007). Thus, the effectiveness of containment metaphors and actual containment strategies may depend on how deeply they are shaped by gender, race, sexual politics, and notions of bodily transmission. What kinds of fluids and organisms matter as much as which bodies are engaged in "risky" practices. Comparing the "feminized" HPV vaccine to male circumcision brings men's bodies and health into the intersectional mix.

Of course, sexual transmission of disease raises the specter of sexual activity, especially among teenagers and/or outside of marriage, which is generally interpreted quite differently for men and women in most cultural contexts. Our comparative analysis demonstrates how responses to these two technologies have been powerfully shaped by intersections among gender, sexuality, age, race, and nationality. Attempts to market and mandate the HPV vaccine activated concerns about female promiscuity, whereas talk of promoting circumcision as HIV preventive has not spurred similar concerns about males in the United States (while men in Africa are treated as suspect). Cultural constructions of gendered sexuality—casting girls and women as either innocent or fallen and boys and men as sexually driven (Nathanson 1991)—helped proposals to promote circumcision as HIV preventive to escape the association with promiscuity that has dogged HPV vaccine mandates. Proposals that boys should receive the HPV vaccine to prevent CC in their (ostensibly) female partners—a claim far more common in public discourse than claims about preventing penile and anal cancers in men—invoke (implicitly) feminist notions of "equal opportunity" (for risk *and* protection) as well as traditional understandings of men as women's protectors. Conversely, risks and responsibility for circumcision are borne by men alone, and hoped-for benefits to women have not materialized (at least regarding HIV). In fact, men who believe themselves protected by circumcision may be less amenable to partners' requests for safer sex practices. These phenomena reveal and sustain obdurate gender hierarchies.

Understandings of gender and sexuality also intersect with notions about age, race, and nationality. Although U.S. boys have historically been circumcised as infants, well before sexual maturity and activity, girls would be vaccinated as preteens on the verge of sexual maturity—a situation that many parents appear to deem far more threatening. Pervasive stereotypes of women and men of color—especially of African descent—as promiscuous not only may inhibit stakeholders' ability to see them as deserving of, or able to benefit from, containment but also may prompt calls for containing them, as in proposals to target circumcision campaigns at "high-risk" men. Both HPV/CC and HIV/AIDS are more widespread and have considerably worse prognoses in the developing world than in the West. Ironically, circumcision is a routine U.S. practice that is now being exported to the developing world, whereas the HPV vaccine is desperately needed in the developing world but (potentially) being stalled by conservative opposition in the United States. By heeding feminist theorists' call for attention to intersectionality, we offer a nuanced analysis of gendered technologies—for women *and* men—in transnational context.

Finally, our analysis reveals that the introduction and/or reframing of these containment technologies is changing cultural understandings of gender, sexuality, race, age, and nationality. Most obviously, the HPV vaccine retrenches gender politics that position young girls simultaneously as sexually innocent (yet likely to fall) and sexually available. The vaccine's use is, in fact, predicated on the eventual fact of girls' sexual activity; conservative resistance to the vaccine rests on fears of adolescent female sexuality unleashed. Conversations about circumcision in the United States show no similar dynamics; indeed, in many instances boys and men are represented as somewhat inert but with the capability of infecting girls and women via heterosexual activity. On the other hand, African men, like gay men and men of African descent in the United States, are routinely framed as dangerously subject to disinhibition. Our analysis highlights the importance of considering how technologies like HPV vaccination and circumcision contribute to the ongoing construction of gender (including "good" and "bad" men and women), race, and sexuality. It is precisely at these intersections of bodies with technologies that the "double standard" is reproduced. . . .

Notes

1. About 2.5 million girls were vaccinated in Gardasil's first year of availability in the United States (Paddock 2008).

2. Prior to being adopted by U.S. physicians, around 1870, as a measure for curing and preventing masturbation, cancer, and venereal disease, circumcision was almost exclusively a Jewish ritual practice in the United States (Glick 2006; Gollaher 2000).
3. Bioethicist and pediatrician Ellen Clayton (pers. comm., numerous dates).
4. However, even the highest estimates of circumcision's effectiveness against HIV are far lower than typical vaccine failure rates of about 5 percent to 10 percent. By comparison, the HPV vaccine failure rate is nearly 0 percent among women never exposed to the virus (see http://www.merck.com/product/usa/pi_circulars/g/gardasil/gardasil_pi.pdf).
5. Two historical links between HPV/cervical cancer (CC) and circumcision are worth noting. In the 1950s, some researchers believed that women contracted CC by having vaginal sex with uncircumcised men who let smegma build up under their foreskins (McNeil 2006), a theory subsequently "disproved by high cancer rates among Muslim women, who had circumcised husbands, and by relatively low rates among Soviet Jewish women, who often did not." In the 1980s, when low levels of virus in human warts stymied efforts to develop an HPV vaccine, U.S. researchers discovered that "grafting bits of foreskin collected from hospital circumcisions and infected with genital wart extract into mice" produced "cysts [containing] enough human virus to work with" (McNeil 2006).

References

Altman, Lawrence K. 2008. Male circumcision no aid to women in study. *New York Times,* February 4, 12.

Associated Press. 2007. *Texas governor backs down on HPV vaccine bill.* May 9.

Ault, K. A., and Future II Study Group. 2007. Effect of prophylactic human papillomavirus L1 virus-like-particle vaccine on risk of cervical intraepithelial neoplasia grade 2, grade 3, and adenocarcinoma in situ: A combined analysis of four randomised clinical trials. *Lancet* 369:1861–68.

Auvert, Bertran, Dirk Taljaard, Emmanuel Lagarde, Joëlle Sobngwi-Tambekou, Rémi Sitta, and Adrian Puren. 2005. Randomized, controlled intervention trial of male circumcision for reduction of HIV infection risk: The ANRS 1265 trial. *PLoS Medicine* 2(11):e298.

Bakalar, Nicholas. 2009. Circumcision reduces rates of two STDs. *New York Times,* March 27. http://www.nytimes.com/2009/03/27/health/27std.html.

Bashford, A., and C. Hooker. 2001. *Contagion: Historical and Cultural Studies.* London: Routledge.

Berer, Marge. 2007. Male circumcision for HIV prevention: Perspectives on gender and sexuality. *Reproductive Health Matters* 15(29):45–48.

———. 2008. Reproductive cancers: High burden of disease, low level of priority. *Reproductive Health Matters* 16(32):4–8.

Brandt, Allan M. 1987. *No Magic bullet: A Social History of Venereal Disease in the United States Since 1880.* New York: Oxford University Press.

Brewer, D., J. Potterat, Jr., J. Roberts, and S. Brody. 2007. Male and female circumcision associated with prevalent HIV infection in virgins and adolescents in Kenya, Lesotho, and Tanzania. *Annals of Epidemiology* 17(3):217.e1–217.e12.

Briggs, Laura. 2003. *Reproducing Empire: Race, Sex, Science, and U.S. Imperialism in Puerto Rico.* Berkeley: University of California Press.

Carpenter, Laura M. 2010. On remedicalisation: Male circumcision in the United States and Great Britain. *Sociology of Health and Illness* 32(4):613–630.

Carpenter, Laura M., and Monica J. Casper. 2009. Global intimacies: The HPV vaccine and transnational women's health. *Women's Studies Quarterly* 37(1–2):80–100.

Casper, Monica J., and Laura M. Carpenter. 2008. Sex, drugs, and politics: The HPV vaccine for cervical cancer. *Sociology of Health and Illness* 30(6):886–99.

Centers for Disease Control and Prevention. 2007. *Table 3. HIV/AIDS Surveillance Report 17.* Atlanta, GA: Centers for Disease Control and Prevention.

———. 2008. Male circumcision and risk for HIV transmission and other health conditions: Implications for the United States. http://www.cdc.gov/hiv/resources/factsheets/index.htm (accessed July 1, 2013).

———. 2009. *HIV/AIDS Surveillance Report 19.* Atlanta, GA: Centers for Disease Control and Prevention.

Charmaz, Kathy. 2006. *Constructing Grounded Theory.* Thousand Oaks, CA: Sage.

CNN. 2008. *Should parents worry about HPV vaccine?* July 7. http://www.cnn.com/2008/HEALTH/conditions/07/07/cervical.cancer.vaccine/index.html (accessed July 1, 2013).

Colgrove, James. 2006. *State of Immunity: The Politics of Vaccination in Twentieth-Century America.* Berkeley: University of California Press.

Collins, Patricia Hill. 1990. *Black Feminist Thought.* New York: Routledge.

Dailard, C. 2006. The public health promise and potential pitfalls of the world's first cervical cancer vaccine. *Guttmacher Policy Review* 9(1):6–9.

Darby, Robert. 2005. The sorcerer's apprentice: Why can't we stop circumcising boys? *Contexts* 4(2):34–39.

Ferris, Dean. n.d. *Male circumcision and HIV: Playing Russian roulette with African lives. http://www.researchgate.net/publication/228496321_MALE_CIRCUMCISION_AND_HIV_PLAYING_RUSSIAN_ROULETTE_WITH_AFRICAN_LIVES* (accessed July 1, 2013).

Glaser, Barney G., and Anselm L. Strauss. 1967. *The Discovery of Grounded Theory.* Chicago: Aldine.

Glick, Leonard B. 2006. *Marked in Your Flesh: Circumcision from Ancient Judea to Modern America.* New York: Oxford University Press.

Gollaher, David L. 2000. *Circumcision: A History of the World's Most Controversial Surgery.* New York: Basic Books.

Haraway, Donna J. 1997. *Modest_Witness@Second_Millenium.FemaleMan_Meets OncoMouse: Feminism and Technoscience.* New York: Routledge.

Harper, Diane M. 2004. Efficacy of a bivalent L1 virus-like particle vaccine in prevention of infection with human papillomavirus types 16 and 18 in young women: A randomised controlled trial. *Lancet* 364:1757–65.

Harper, Diane M., Eduardo L. Franco, Cosette M. Wheeler, Anna-Barbara Moscicki, Barbara Romanowski, Cecilia M. Roteli-Martins, David Jenkins, Anne Schuind, Sue Ann Costa Clemens, and Gary Dubin. 2006. Sustained efficacy up to 4·5 years of a bivalent L1 virus-like particle vaccine against human papillomavirus types 16 and 18: Follow-up from a randomised control trial. *Lancet* 367:1247–55.

Konrad, Rachel. 2007. U.S. circumcision rate drops. *Washington Post*, June 18.

Koushik, A., and E. L. F. Franco. 2006. Epidemiology and the role of human papillomaviruses. In *The Cervix,* edited by J. A. Jordan and A. Singer. Oxford, UK: Blackwell.

Kubba, Tamara. 2008. Human papillomavirus vaccination in the United Kingdom: What about boys? *Reproductive Health Matters* 16(32):97–103.

Laumann, E. O., C. M. Masi, and E. W. Zuckerman. 1997. Circumcision in the United States: Prevalence, prophylactic effects, and sexual practice. *Journal of the American Medical Association* 277(13):1052–57.

Levine, Judith. 2002. *Harmful to Minors: The Perils of Protecting Children from Sex.* Minneapolis: University of Minnesota Press.

MacInnis, Laura. 2008. Circumcision problems impair HIV prevention. *Reuters Online,* September 1. http://www.foreskin-restoration.net/forum/showthread.php?t=1337 (accessed May 31, 2013).

Marx, J. L. 1989. Circumcision may protect against the AIDS virus. *Science* 245 (4917):470–71.

McNeil, Donald G., Jr. 2006. How a vaccine search ended in triumph. *NewYorkTimes.com,* August 29. http://www.nytimes.com/2006/08/29/health/29hpv.html

Nack, Adina. 2008. *Damaged Goods: Women Living with Incurable Sexually Transmitted Diseases.* Philadelphia: Temple University Press.

Nathanson, Constance A. 1991. *Dangerous Passage: The Social Control of Sexuality in Women's Adolescence.* Philadelphia: Temple University Press.

National Conference of State Legislatures. 2009. HPV vaccine. http://ncsl.org/default.aspx?tabid=14381.

National Organization of Circumcision Information and Resource Centers. 2005. Answers to Your Questions about Circumcision and HIV/AIDS [Brochure]. San Anselmo, CA: National Organization of Circumcision Information and Resource Centers.

Oudshoorn, Nelly. 2003. *The Male Pill: A Biography of a Technology in the Making.* Durham, NC: Duke University Press.

Paddock, Catharine. 2008. HPV vaccine has reached quarter of teenage girls in U.S. *Medical News Today,* October 10.

Piot, Peter. 2007. STIs and HIV: Learning from each other for the long-term response? Speech at the 17th annual meeting of the International Society for Sexually Transmitted Diseases Research, Seattle, WA.

Rabin, Roni. 2009. Officials weigh circumcision to fight HIV risk. *New York Times,* August 24. http://www.nytimes.com/2009/08/24/health/policy/24circumcision.html.

Richert, C. 2005. Another medical culture war: How right-wing politics could keep a cancer vaccine off the market. *CampusProgress.org,* December 13.

Roberts, Dorothy. 1997. *Killing the Black Body: Race, Reproduction, and the Meaning of Liberty.* New York: Pantheon.

Rose, Nikolas. 2006. *The Politics of Life Itself: Biomedicine, Power, and Subjectivity in the Twenty-first Century.* Princeton, NJ: Princeton University Press.

Sawaya, George F., and Karen Smith-McCune. 2007. HPV vaccination—More answers, more questions. *New England Journal of Medicine* 356(19):1991.

Sawires, Sharif R., Shari L. Dworkin, Agnes Fiamma, Dean Peacock, Greg Szekeres, and Thomas J. Coates. 2007. Male circumcision and HIV/AIDS: Challenges and opportunities. *Lancet* 369:708–13.

Seidman, Steven. 2002. *Beyond the Closet: The Transformation of Gay and Lesbian Life.* New York: Routledge.

Singh, G. K., B. A. Miller, B. F. Hankey, and B. K. Edwards. 2004. Persistent area socioeconomic disparities in U.S. incidence of cervical cancer, mortality, stage, and survival, 1975–2000. *Cancer* 101(5):1051–57.

Sullivan, P. S., Peter H. Kilmarx, Thomas A. Peterman, Allan W. Taylor, Allyn K. Nakashima, Mary L. Kamb, Lee Warner, and Timothy D. Mastro. 2007. Male circumcision for prevention of HIV transmission: What the new data mean for HIV prevention in the United States. *PLoS Medicine* 4(7):e223.

Talbott, John R. 2007. Size matters: The number of prostitutes and the global HIV/AIDS pandemic. *PLoS ONE* 2(6):e543.

Tobian, Aaron A. R., David Serwadda, Thomas C. Quinn, Godfrey Kigozi, Patti E. Gravitt, Oliver Laeyendecker, Blake Charvat, Victor Ssempijja, Melissa Riedesel, Amy E. Oliver, Rebecca G. Nowak, Lawrence H. Moulton, Michael Z. Chen, Steven J. Reynolds, Maria J. Wawer, and Ronald H. Gray. 2009. Male circumcision for the prevention of HSV-2 and HPV infections and syphilis. *New England Journal of Medicine* 360(13):1298–1309.

Tolman, Deborah L. 1996. Adolescent girls' sexuality: Debunking the myth of the urban girl. In *Urban Girls: Resisting Stereotypes, Creating Identities,* edited by B. J. R. Leadbeater and N. Way. New York: New York University Press.

Van der Geest, S., S. R. Whyte, and A. Hardon. 1996. The anthropology of pharmaceuticals: A biographical approach. *Annual Review of Anthropology* 25:153–78.

Wahl-Jorgensen, Karin. 2007. *Journalists and the Public: Newsroom Culture, Letters to the Editor, and Democracy.* Cresskill, NJ: Hampton Press.

Wheeler, Cosette M. 2007. Advances in primary and secondary interventions for cervical cancer: Prophylactic human papillomavirus vaccines and testing. *Nature Clinical Practice Oncology* 4(4):224–35.

WHO/UNAIDS. 2007. *WHO and UNAIDS Announce Recommendations from Expert Consultation on Male Circumcision for HIV Prevention.* Geneva: UNAIDS.

10

"Get Your Freak On"

Sex, Babies, and Images of Black Femininity

PATRICIA HILL COLLINS

For most of American history, racist prejudice and discrimination were overt. African Americans were restricted to segregated housing, kept from higher education and professional jobs, described by politicians and ministers as morally and physically inferior, and so on. These days, such explicit racism is rarely voiced publicly. At the same time, many scholars argue, a new kind of racism has emerged. Under this new racism, *many white Americans now declare both that all races are created equal* and *that racial equality has been achieved. Thus, they conclude, there is no longer any need for policies that combat racism, and any African Americans who do not succeed have only themselves to blame.*

In "'Get Your Freak On': Sex, Babies, and Images of Black Femininity," Patricia Hill Collins explores the popular images of African American women that have emerged under this new racism, and discusses both how these images reinforce racism and how African American women use these images to assert control over their bodies and lives. So, for example, male rappers (both white and black) may stereotype African American women as hypersexual, manipulative bitches, thus simultaneously reinforcing both sexism and racism. At the same time, some female rappers have adopted the bitch *label as a way to declare their sexual independence.*

Hill Collins also examines how the popular image of the "Bad Black Mother" (which appears in Hollywood films about female drug addicts, news stories about "welfare queens," and elsewhere) reinforces gendered social class stereotypes. Taken together, these various stereotypes help white Americans to conclude that the troubles experienced by poor African American women stem from these women's inherent moral failings, rather than from racist, classist, and sexist prejudice and discrimination.

2001: Established songwriter, producer, rapper, and singer Missy Elliott's smash hit "Get Your Freak On" catapults her third album to the top of the charts. Claiming that she can last 20 rounds with the "Niggahs," Missy declares that she's the "best around" because she has a "crazy style." In tribute to and in dialogue with Elliott, singer Nelly Furtado also records her version of "Get Your Freak On." Describing Elliott, Furtado sings "she's a freak and I'm a chief head banger." In case listeners might think Furtado is not as down as Elliott, Furtado sings "Who's that bitch? Me!" Elliott's song becomes so popular that a series of websites offer its mesmerizing sitar tones as ringers for cell phones. They ring in Burger King. "Get your freak on" . . . "Hello?"

. . . [Singer] Missy Elliott's "Get Your Freak On" may have appeared to come from nowhere, but the differing meanings associated with the term *freak* are situated at the crossroads of colonialism, science, and entertainment. Under colonialism, West African people's proximity to wild animals, especially apes, raised in Western imaginations the specter of "wild" sexual practices in an uncivilized, inherently violent wilderness.[1] Through colonial eyes, the stigma of biological Blackness and the seeming primitiveness of African cultures marked the borders of extreme abnormality. For Western sciences that were mesmerized with body politics, White Western normality became constructed on the backs of Black deviance, with an imagined Black hyper-heterosexual deviance at the heart of the enterprise. . . .[2] Entertainment contributed another strand to the fabric enfolding contemporary meanings of freak. In the nineteenth century, the term *freak* appeared in descriptions of human oddities exhibited by circuses and sideshows. Individuals who fell outside the boundaries of normality, from hairy women to giants and midgets, all were exhibited as freaks of nature for the fun and amusement of live audiences. . . .

"Freaky" sex consists of sex outside the boundaries of normality. . . . As boundaries of race, gender, and sexuality soften and shift, so do the meanings of *freaky* as well as the practices and people thought to engage in them. The term initially invoked a sexual promiscuity associated with Blackness, but being freaky is no longer restricted to Black people. As Whodini raps, "freaks come in all shapes, sizes and colors, but what I like about 'em most is that they're real good lovers." . . . African American artists may have led the way, but the usages of *freak* have traveled far beyond the African American experience. The term has shown a stunning resiliency, migrating onto the dance floor as a particular dance (*Le Freak*) and as a style of dancing that signaled individuality, sexual abandon, craziness, wildness, and new uses of the body. "Get your freak on" can mean many things to many people. To be labeled a freak, to be a freak, and to freak constitute different sites of race, gender, and sexuality within popular culture. . . .

In modern America where community institutions of all sorts have eroded, popular culture has increased in importance as a source of information and ideas. African American youth, in particular, can no longer depend on a deeply textured web of families, churches, fraternal organizations, school clubs, sports teams, and other community organizations to help them negotiate the challenges of social inequality. Mass media fills this void, especially movies, television, and music that market Black popular culture aimed at African American consumers. With new technologies that greatly expand possibilities for information creation and dissemination, mass media needs a continuing supply of new cultural material for its growing entertainment, advertising, and news divisions. Because of its authority to shape perceptions of the world, global mass media circulates images of Black femininity and Black masculinity and, in doing so, ideologies of race, gender, sexuality, and class.

In the 1990s, Black popular culture became a hot commodity. Within mass media influenced social relations, African American culture is now photographed, recorded, and/or digitalized, and it travels to all parts of the globe. This new commodified Black culture is highly marketable and has spurred a Black culture industry, one that draws heavily from the cultural production and styles of urban Black youth. In this context, representations of African American women and African American men became increasingly important sites of struggle. The new racism [which replaces overt racism with covert racism, assumes that racial equality already exists, and therefore rejects policies designed to increase racial equality] requires new ideological justifications, and the controlling images of Black femininity and Black masculinity participate in creating them. At the same time, African American women and men use these same sites within Black popular culture to resist racism, class exploitation, sexism, and/or heterosexism.

Because racial desegregation in the post–civil rights era needed new images of racial difference for a color-blind ideology, class-differentiated images of African American culture have become more prominent. In the 1980s and 1990s, historical images of Black people as poor and working-class Black became supplemented by and often contrasted with representations of Black respectability used to portray a growing Black middle class. Poor and working-class Black culture was routinely depicted as being "authentically" Black whereas middle- and upper-middle class Black culture was seen as less so. Poor and working-class Black characters were portrayed as the ones who walked, talked, and acted "Black," and their lack of assimilation of American values justified their incarceration in urban ghettos. In contrast, because middle- and upper-middle-class African American characters lacked this authentic "Black" culture and were virtually indistinguishable from their White middle-class counterparts, assimilated, propertied Black people were shown as being ready for racial integration. This convergence of race and class also sparked changes in the treatment of gender and sexuality. Representations of poor and working-class authenticity and middle-class respectability increasingly came in gender-specific form. As Black femininity and Black masculinity became reworked through this prism of social class, a changing constellation of images of Black femininity appeared that reconfigured Black women's sexuality and helped explain the new racism.

"Bitches" and Bad (Black) Mothers: Images of Working-Class Black Women

Images of working-class Black women can be assembled around two main focal points. The controlling image of the "bitch" constitutes one representation that depicts Black women as aggressive, loud, rude, and pushy. Increasingly applied to poor and/or working-class Black women, the representation of the "bitch" constitutes a reworking of the image of the mule of chattel slavery. Whereas the mule was simply stubborn (passive aggressive) and needed prodding and supervision, the bitch is confrontational and actively aggressive. The term *bitch* is designed to put women in their place. Using *bitch* by itself is offensive, but in combination with other slurs, it can be deadly. Randall Kennedy reports on the actions of a 1999 New Jersey state court that removed a judge, in part, for his actions in one case. The judge had attempted to persuade the prosecutor to accept a plea bargain from four men indicted for robbing and murdering a sixty-seven-year-old African American woman. The judge told the prosecutor not to worry about the case since the victim had been just "some old nigger bitch."[3]

Representations of Black women as bitches abound in contemporary popular culture, and presenting Black women as bitches is designed to defeminize and demonize them. But just as young Black men within hip-hop culture have reclaimed the term *nigger* and used it for different ends, the term *bitch* and the image of Black women that it carries signals a similar contestation process. Within this representation, however, not all bitches are the same. Among African American Studies undergraduate students at the University of Cincinnati, the consensus was that "bitch" and "Bitch" referenced two distinctive types of Black female representations. All women potentially can be "bitches" with a small "b." This was the negative evaluation of "bitch." But the students also identified a positive valuation of "bitch" and argued (some, vociferously so) that only African American women can be "Bitches" with a capital "B." Bitches with a capital "B" or, in their language, "Black Bitches," are super-tough, super-strong women who are often celebrated. . . .

Ironically, Black male comedians have often led the pack in reproducing derisive images of Black women as being ugly, loud "bitches." Resembling Marlon Riggs' protestations about the "sissy" and "punk" jokes targeted toward Black gay men, "bitches" are routinely mocked within contemporary Black popular culture. For example, ridiculing African American women as being like men (also, a common representation of Black lesbians) has long been a prominent subtext in the routines of Redd Foxx, Eddie Murphy, Martin Lawrence, and other African American comedians. In other cases,

Black male comedians dress up as African American women in order to make fun of them. Virtually all of the African American comics on the popular show *Saturday Night Live* have on occasion dressed as women to caricature Black women. Through this act of cross-dressing, Black women can be depicted as ugly women who too closely resemble men (big, Black, and short hair) and because they are aggressive like men, become stigmatized as "bitches." . . .

In the universe of Black popular culture, the combination of sexuality and bitchiness can be deadly. Invoking historical understandings of Black women's assumed promiscuity, some representations of the "bitch" draw upon American sexual scripts of Black women's wildness. Here, the question of who controls Black women's sexuality is paramount. One sign of a "Bitch's" power is her manipulation of her own sexuality for her own gain. Bitches control men, or at least try to, using their bodies as weapons. . . .

This theme of the materialistic, sexualized Black woman has become an icon within hip-hop culture. The difficulty lies in telling the difference between representations of Black women who are sexually liberated and those who are sexual objects, their bodies on sale for male enjoyment. On the one hand, the public persona of rap star Lil' Kim has been compared to that of a female hustler. Resembling representations of her male counterpart who uses women for financial and sexual gain, the public performance of Lil' Kim brings life to the fictional Winter Santiago. An exposé in *Vibe* magazine describes Kim's public face: "Lil' Kim's mythology is about pussy, really: the power, pleasure, and politics of it, the murky mixture of emotions and commerce that sex has become in popular culture. . . . She is, perhaps, the greatest public purveyor of the female hustle this side of Madonna, parlaying ghetto pain, pomp, and circumstances into main stream fame and fortune."[4] But should we think that Lil' Kim is shallow, the article goes on to describe her "soft center": "Kim's reality, on the other hand, is about love. It is her true currency. . . . Her appeal has much to do with the fact that love—carnal, familial, self-destructive, or spiritual—is the root of who Kim is. Pussy is just the most marketable aspect of it."[5] What do we make of Lil' Kim? Is she the female version of misogynistic rappers? If so, her performance is what matters. To be real, she must sell sexuality as part of working-class Black female authenticity.

On the other hand, many African American women rappers identify female sexuality as part of women's freedom and independence. Being sexually open does not make a woman a tramp or a "ho." When Salt 'n Pepa engage in role reversal in their video "Most Men Are Tramps," they contest dominant notions that see as dangerous female sexuality that is not under the control of men. Lack of male domination creates immoral women. Salt 'n Pepa ask, "Have you ever seen a man who's stupid and rude . . . who thinks he's God's gift to women?" The rap shows a group of male dancers wearing black trench coats. As Salt 'n Pepa repeat "tramp," the men flash open their coats to reveal outfits of tiny little red G-strings. The video does not exploit the men—they are shown for just a second. Rather, the point is to use role reversal to criticize existing gender ideology.[6] In their raps "Let's Talk about Sex," and "It's None of Your Business," the group repeats its anthem of sexual freedom.

This issue of control becomes highly important within the universe of Black popular culture that is marketed by mass media. Some women are bitches who control their own sexuality—they "get a freak on," which remains within their control and on their own terms. Whether she "fucks men" for pleasure, drugs, revenge, or money, the sexualized bitch constitutes a modern version of the jezebel [stereotype of African American women as sexually wanton], repackaged for contemporary mass media. In discussing this updated jezebel image, cultural critic Lisa Jones distinguishes between gold diggers/skeezers (women who screw for status) and crack hos (women who screw for a fix).[7] Some women are the "hos" who trade sexual favors for jobs, money, drugs, and other material items. The female hustler, a materialistic woman who is willing to sell, rent, or use her sexuality to get whatever she wants constitutes this sexualized variation of the "bitch." This image appears with increasing frequency, especially in conjunction with trying to "catch" an African American man with money. Athletes are targets, and having a baby with an athlete is a way to garner income. Black women who are sex workers, namely, those who engage in phone sex, lap dancing, and prostitution for compensation, also populate this universe of sexualized bitches. The prostitute who hustles without a pimp and who keeps the compensation is a bitch who works for herself.

Not only do these images of sexualized Black bitches appear in global mass media, Black male artists, producers, and marketing executives participate in reproducing these images. As cultural critic Lisa Jones points out, "what might make the skeezer an even more painful thorn in your side is that, unlike its forerunners, this type is manufactured primarily by black men."[8] If the cultural production of some African American male artists is any indication, Jones may be on to something.

In the early 1990s, and in conjunction with the emergence of gangsta rap, a fairly dramatic shift occurred within Black popular culture and mass media concerning how some African American artists depicted African American women. In a sense, the *celebration* of Black women's bodies and how they handled them that had long appeared in earlier Black cultural production (for example, a song such as "Brick House" within the rhythm and blues tradition) became increasingly replaced by the *objectification* of Black women's bodies as part of a commodified Black culture. Contemporary music videos of Black male artists in particular became increasingly populated with legions of young Black women who dance, strut, and serve as visually appealing props for the rapper in question. The women in these videos typically share two attributes—they are rarely acknowledged as individuals and they are scantily clad. One Black female body can easily replace another and all are reduced to their bodies. Ironically, displaying nameless, naked Black female bodies has a long history in Western societies, from the display of enslaved African women on the auction block under chattel slavery to representations of Black female bodies in contemporary film and music videos. Describing the placement and use of primitive art in Western exhibits, one scholar points out, " 'namelessness' resembles 'nakedness': it is a category always brought to bear by the Westerner on the 'primitive' and yet a phony category insofar as the namelessness and nakedness exist only from the Euro-American point of view."[9]

Not only can the entire body become objectified but also parts of the body can suffer the same fate. For example, music videos for Sir Mix A Lot's "Baby Got Back," the film clip for "Doing Da Butt" from Spike Lee's film *School Daze*, and the music video for 2LiveCrew's "Pop That Coochie" all focused attention on women's behinds generally, and Black women's behinds in particular. All three songs seemingly celebrated Black women's buttocks, but they also objectified them, albeit differently. "Baby Got Back" is more clearly rooted in the "Brick House" tradition of celebrating Black women's sexuality via admiring their bodies—in his video, Sir Mix A Lot happily wanders among several booty swinging sisters, all of whom are proud to show their stuff. "Doing Da Butt" creates a different interpretive context for this fascination with the booty. In Lee's party sequence, being able to shake the booty is a sign of authentic Blackness, with the Black woman who is shaking the biggest butt being the most authentic Black woman. In contrast, "Pop That Coochie" contains a bevy of women who simply shake their rumps for the enjoyment of the members of 2LiveCrew. Their butts are toys for the boys in the band. Ironically, whereas European men expressed fascination with the buttocks of the Hottentot Venus as a site of Black female sexuality that became central to the construction of White racism itself, contemporary Black popular culture seemingly celebrates these same signs uncritically.

Objectifying Black women's bodies turns them into canvases that can be interchanged for a variety of purposes. Historically, this objectification had a clear racial motive. In the post-civil rights era, however, this use of Black women's bodies also has a distinctive gender subtext in that African American men and women participate differently in this process of objectification. African American men who star in music videos construct a certain version of manhood against the backdrop of objectified, nameless, quasi-naked Black women who populate their stage. At the same time, African American women in these same videos often objectify their own bodies in order to be accepted within this Black male-controlled universe. Black women now can get hair weaves, insert blue contact lenses, dye their hair blond, get silicone implants to have bigger breasts, and have ribs removed to achieve small waists (Janet Jackson) all for the purpose of appearing more "beautiful."

Whether Black women rappers who use the term *bitch* are participating in their own subordination or whether they are resisting these gender relations remains a subject of debate. Rap and hip-hop serve as sites to contest these same gender meanings. The language in rap has attracted considerable controversy, especially the misogyny associated with calling women "bitches" and "hos."[10] First popularized within rap, these terms are now so pervasive that they have entered the realm of colloquial, everyday speech. Even White singer Nelly Furtado proudly proclaims, "Who's that bitch? Me!" Yet because rap is a sphere of cultural production, it has space for contestation. For example, in 1994 Queen Latifah's "U.N.I.T.Y." won a Grammy, an NAACP Image Award, and a Soul Train Music Award. Latifah claims that she did not write the song to win awards, but in response to the verbal and physical assaults on women that she saw around her, especially in rap music. As one line from her award-winning song states, "Every time I hear a brother call a girl a bitch or a ho, trying to make a sister feel low, you know all of that's got to go."[11]

Black bitches are one thing. Black bitches that are fertile and become mothers are something else. In this regard, the term *bitch* references yet another meaning. Reminiscent of the association of Africans with animals, the term *bitch* also refers to female dogs. Via this association, the term thus invokes a web of meaning that links unregulated sexuality with uncontrolled fertility. Female dogs or bitches "fuck" and produce litters of puppies. In a context of a racial discourse that long associated people of African descent with animalistic practices, the use of the term bitch is noteworthy. Moreover, new technologies that place a greater emphasis on machines provide another variation on the updated bitch. In contrast to Black female bodies as animalistic, Black female bodies become machines built for endurance. The Black superwoman becomes a "sex machine" that in turn becomes a "baby machine." The thinking behind these images is that unregulated sexuality results in unplanned for, unwanted, and poorly raised children.

The representation of the sexualized bitch leads to another cluster of representations of working-class Black femininity, namely, controlling images of poor and working-class Black women as bad mothers. Bad Black Mothers (BBM) are those who are abusive (extremely bitchy) and/or who neglect their children either in utero or afterward. Ironically, these Bad Black Mothers are stigmatized as being inappropriately feminine because they reject the gender ideology associated with the American family ideal. They are often single mothers, they live in poverty, they are often young, and they rely on the state to support their children. Moreover, they allegedly pass on their bad values to their children who in turn are more likely to become criminals and unwed teenaged mothers.

Reserved for poor and/or working-class Black women, or for women who have fallen into poverty and shame as a result of their bad behavior, a constellation of new images describes variations of the Bad Black Mother. The image of the crack mother illustrates how controlling images of workingclass Black femininity can dovetail with punitive social policies. When crack cocaine appeared in the early 1980s, two features made it the perfect target for the Reagan administration's War on Drugs. Crack cocaine was primarily confined to Black inner-city neighborhoods, and women constituted approximately half of its users. In the late 1980s, news stories began to cover the huge increase in the number of newborns testing positive for drugs. But coverage was far from sympathetic. Addicted pregnant women became demonized as "crack mothers" whose selfishness and criminality punished their children in the womb. Fictional treatments followed soon after. For example, in the feature film *Losing Isaiah*, Academy Award–winning actress Halle Berry plays a woman on crack cocaine who is so high that she abandons her baby. A kindly White family takes Isaiah in, and they patiently deal with the host of problems he has due to his biological mother's failures.

Representations such as these contributed to a punitive climate in which the criminal justice system increasingly penalizes pregnancy by prosecuting women for exposing their babies to drugs in the womb and by imposing birth control as a condition of probation. Between 1985 and 1995, thirty states charged approximately 200 women with maternal drug use. Charges included distributing drugs to a minor, child abuse and neglect, reckless endangerment, manslaughter, and assault with a deadly weapon.[12] In virtually all of these cases, the women prosecuted were poor and African American. As legal scholar Dorothy Roberts points out, "prosecutors and judges see poor Black women as suitable subjects for these reproductive penalties because society does not view these women as suitable mothers in the first place."[13]

Drug use is one sure-fire indicator used to create the BBM representation, but simply being poor and accepting public assistance is sufficient. In the 1960s, when African American women successfully challenged the racially discriminatory policies that characterized social welfare programs, the generic image of the "Bad Black Mother" became crystallized into the racialized image of the "welfare mother." These controlling images under went another transformation in the 1980s as part of Reagan/Bush's efforts to reduce social welfare funding for families. Resembling the practice of invoking the controlling image of the Black rapist via the Bush campaign's use of Willie Horton in 1988, the Reagan/Bush administrations also realized that racializing welfare by painting it as a program that unfairly benefited Blacks was a sure-fire way to win White votes. This context created the controlling image of the "welfare queen" primarily to garner support for refusing state support for poor and working-class Black mothers and children. Poor Black women's welfare eligibility meant that many chose to stay home and care for their children, thus emulating White middle-class mothers. But because these stay-at-home moms were African American and did not work for pay, they were deemed to be "lazy." Ironically, gaining rights introduced a new set of controlling images. In a political economy in which the children of poor and working-class African Americans are unwanted because such children are expensive and have citizenship rights, reducing the fertility [of African Americans] becomes critical. . . .

Beyond the efforts to criminalize the pregnancies of crack-addicted women, a series of public policies have been introduced that aim to shrink state and federal social welfare budgets, in part by reducing Black women's fertility. Despite its health risks and unpleasant side effects, Norplant was marketed to poor inner-city Black teenagers. As a coercive method of birth control, users found that they had little difficulty getting their physicians to insert the contraceptive rods into their bodies but, since only physicians were qualified to remove the rods, getting them out was far more difficult. Depo Provera as a birth control shot was also heavily marketed to women who seemingly could not control their fertility and needed medical intervention to avoid motherhood. Finally, welfare legislation that threatens to deny benefits to additional children is designed to discourage childbearing. In a context in which safe, legal abortion is difficult for poor women to obtain, the "choice" of permanent sterilization makes sense. Representations of Bad Black Mothers help create an interpretive climate that normalizes these punitive policies.

Controlling images of working-class Black women pervade television and film, but rap and hip-hop culture constitute one site where misogyny is freely expressed and resisted. Given this context, African American women's participation in rap and hip-hop as writers, producers, and as performers illustrates how African American women negotiate these representations. In a sense, Black female rappers who reject these representations of working-class Black women follow in the footsteps of earlier generations of Black blues women who chose to sing the "devil's music." The 1990s witnessed the emergence of Black women who made music videos that were sites of promotion, creativity, and self-expression. For example, hip-hop artists Salt 'n Pepa, Erykah Badu, Lauryn Hill, and Missy Elliott depict themselves as independent, strong, and self-reliant agents of their own desire. Because rap revolves around selfpromotion, female rappers are able to avoid accusations of being self-centered or narcissistic when they use the form to promote Black female power. Rap thus can provide an important forum for women.

Black women's self-representation in rap results in complex, often contradictory and multifaceted depictions of Black womanhood. One study of representations of Black women in popular music videos found that controlling images of Black womanhood occurred simultaneously with resistant images. On the one hand, when music videos focused on Black women's bodies, presented one-dimensional womanhood by rarely depicting motherhood, and showcased women under the aegis of a male sponsor, they did re-create controlling images of Black womanhood. On the other hand, the music videos also contained distinctive patterns of Black women's agency. First, in many videos, Blackness did not carry a negative connotation, but instead served as a basis for strength, power, and a positive self-identity. Second, despite a predominance of traditional gender roles, Black women performers were frequently depicted as active, vocal, and independent. But instead of exhibiting the physical violence and aggression found in men's videos, the music videos sampled in the study demonstrate the significance of verbal assertiveness where "speaking out and speaking one's mind are a constant theme." Another theme concerns achieving independence—Black women may assert independence, but they look to one another for support, partnership, and sisterhood. Black women's music videos may be situated within hip-hop culture, but they reflect the tensions of negotiating representations of Black femininity: "what emerges from this combination of agency, voice, partnership, and Black context is a sense of the construction of Black woman-centered video narratives. Within these narratives, the interests, desires, and goals of women are predominant. . . . Black women are quite firmly the subjects of these narratives and are able to clearly and unequivocally express their points of view." . . .

[In sum,] images of working-class Black femininity all articulate with the social class system of the post–civil rights era. Depicting African American women as bitches; the sexual use of African American women's bodies by circulating images of Black women's promiscuity; [and] derogating the reproductive capacities of African American women's bodies . . . all work to obscure the closing door of racial opportunity in the post–civil rights era. On the surface, these interconnected representations offer a plausible explanation for poor and/or working-class African American women's class status: (1) too-strong, bitchy women are less attractive to men because they are not feminine; (2) to compensate, these less-attractive women use their sexuality to "catch" men and hopefully become pregnant so that the men will marry them; and (3) men see through this game and leave these women as single mothers who often have little recourse but to either try and "catch" another man or "hustle" the government. But on another level, when it comes to poor and working-class African American women, this constellation of representations functions as ideology to justify the new social relations of hyper-ghettoization, unfinished racial desegregation, and efforts to shrink the social welfare state. Collectively these representations construct a "natural" Black femininity that in turn is central to an "authentic" Black culture.

Notes

1. Jordan 1968, 3–43.
2. Fausto-Sterling 1995; Giddings 1992.
3. Kennedy 2002, 63.
4. Marriott 2000, 126.
5. Marriott 2000, 126.
6. Roberts 1995.
7. Roberts 1995, 79.
8. Jones 1994, 80.
9. Torgovnick 1990, 90.
10. Cole and Guy-Sheftall 2003, 182–215.
11. Latifah 1999, 3.
12. Roberts 1997, 153.
13. Roberts 1997, 152. Even worse are those who remain on drugs, sell their bodies, and decide to keep their children. Those Black women who engage in sex work in order to support their children are especially chastised. The hoochie mama popularized in Black popular culture constitutes a bad mother who sells sex and neglects her children. The derogated Black mother who is on drugs also fits within this nexus of representations of bad Black mothers.

References

Cole, Johnetta Betsh, and Beverly Guy-Sheftall. 2003. *Gender Talk: The Struggle for Women's Equality in African American Communities.* New York: Ballantine.

Fausto-Sterling, Anne. 1995. Gender, race, and nation: The comparative anatomy of "Hottentot" women in Europe, 1815–1817. *Deviant Bodies: Critical Perspectives on Differences in Science and Popular Culture*, edited by Jennifer Terry and Jacqueline Urla, pp. 19–48. Bloomington, Indiana University Press.

Giddings, Paula. 1992. "The Last Taboo." *Race-ing Justice, En Gendering Power*, edited by Toni Morrison, pp. 441–465. New York: Pantheon.

Jones, Lisa. 1994. *Bullet Diva: Tales of Race, Sex, and Hair.* New York: Doubleday.

Jordan, Winthrop D. 1968. *White Over Black: American Attitudes towards the Negro, 1550–1812.* New York: W. W. Norton.

Kennedy, Randell. 2002. *Nigger: The Stranger Career of a Troublesome Word.* New York: Pantheon.

Latifah, Queen. 1999. *Ladies First: Revelations of a Strong Woman.* New York: Quill.

Marriott, Robert. 2000. "'Blowin' Up." *Vibe* 8:5 (June–July 2000):124–30.

Roberts, Dorothy E. 1997. *Killing the Black Body: Race, Reproduction, and the Meaning of Liberty.* New York: Pantheon Books.

Roberts, Robin. 1995. "Sisters in the Name of Rap: Rapping for Women's Lives." *Black Women in America*, edited by Kim Marie Vaz, pp. 323–333. Thousand Oaks, CA: Sage.

Torgovnick, Marianna. 1990. *Gone Primitive: Savage Intellects, Modern Lives.* Chicago: University of Chicago Press.

11

Brain, Brow, and Booty

Latina Iconicity in U.S. Popular Culture

Isabel Molina Guzmán and Angharad N. Valdivia

Latinos and Latinas now comprise over 16 percent of the U.S. population, more than any other U.S. minority group. Not surprisingly, media images of Latinos and Latinas have become considerably more common, as media producers have recognized that they can commodify *them (i.e., turn them into images that can be sold for profit). In "Brain, Brow, and Booty: Latina Iconicity in U.S. Popular Culture," Isabel Molina Guzmán and Angharad N. Valdivia describe how Jennifer Lopez, Salma Hayek, and Frida Kahlo have become icons of female* Latinidad—*that is, how their media representations have become symbols of what it means to be Latina.*

The authors illustrate how the women's differing images reflect and reinforce various tropes of Latinidad, *such as the trope of* tropicalism *which reduces Hispanic culture and identity to bright colors, rhythmic music, and eroticism.* Trope, *in film and cultural studies, means a recognizable and recurrent media theme, storyline, or image. For example, both the "Cinderella trope" and the trope of heterosexual romance appear in many films, including* Pretty Woman *and* Maid in Manhattan.

In addition, Molina Guzmán and Valdivia observe that the images of Lopez, Hayek, and Kahlo are both gendered *and* racialized—*that is, each woman's media image highlights her racial identity and how she fits gender norms. Although their images vary substantially, in each case they emphasize the women's status as* others *who differ in important ways from dominant American society.*

Finally, Molina Guzmán and Valdivia note that the images of these Latina icons emphasize their hybridity (i.e., their status as hybrids). Hybridity *refers to any new and distinct culture or identity that emerges from the mixing of cul-*

Isabel Molina Guzmán and Angharad N. Valdivia. 2004. "Brain, Brow, and Booty," *Communication Review* 7: 205–221. Reprinted by permission of the publisher, Taylor & Francis Ltd. (http://www.informaworld.com).

tures or identities. The authors suggest that because these women do not fit neatly into the long-standing U.S. racial categories of black or white, they have the potential to threaten U.S. cultural assumptions about race.

We were shooting on the steps of the Metropolitan Museum one night. It was lit romantically, and Jennifer was wearing an evening gown, looking incredibly stunning. Suddenly there must have been a thousand people screaming her name. *It was like witnessing this icon.*

Ralph Fiennes in the *New York Times*, 2002, p. 16 (emphasis added)

This stamp, honoring a Mexican artist who has transcended "la frontera" and *has become an icon to Hispanics, feminists, and art lovers*, will be a further reminder of the continuous cultural contributions of Latinos to the United States.

Cecilia Alvear, President of National Association of Hispanic Journalists (NAHJ) on the occasion of the introduction of the Frida Kahlo U.S. postage stamp; 2001 (emphasis added)

"Nothing Like the Icon on the Fridge"

Column about Salma Hayek's *Frida* by Stephanie Zacharek in the *New York Times*, 2002

The iconic location of Latinas and their articulation into commodity culture is an inescapable affirmation of the increasing centrality of Latinidad and Latinas to U.S. popular culture. We live in an age when Latinidad, the state and process of being, becoming, and/or appearing Latina/o, is the "It" ethnicity and style in contemporary U.S. mainstream culture. This construction of Latinidad is transmitted primarily, though not exclusively, through the mainstream media and popular culture. We also continue to live in an age when women function as a sign [or icon], a stand-in for objects and concepts ranging from nation to beauty to sexuality (Rakow and Kranich 1991). This article examines the representational politics surrounding three hypercommodified Latinas in contemporary U.S. culture, Salma Hayek, Frida Kahlo, and Jennifer Lopez. . . . We focus on the contemporary representations of Hayek, Kahlo, and Lopez in order to explore the gendered and racialized signifiers surrounding Latinidad and Latina iconicity and investigate the related processes of producing and policing Latina bodies and identities in mainstream texts such as films and magazines.[1] . . .

The iconic position of Latinas within U.S. popular culture presents a critical space from which to study the racialized and gendered construction of meaning surrounding transnational identities and hybrid bodies. Iconicity, as a form of representation, involves the transformation of meaning that arises through the interactive relationship between an image, the practices surrounding the production of that image, and the social context within which the image is produced and received by audiences. As Giles and Middleton (2000) propose it is not so much that iconic images communicate a specific meaning or message, but that they "resignify" the meanings surrounding a particular image, event, or issue through their circulation in popular culture. Within contemporary U.S. popular culture, three women—Salma Hayek, Frida Kahlo, and Jennifer Lopez—have gained iconic status as representatives of feminine Latinidad. In other words, popular representations of each woman communicate more than the visuals, instead the images are invited to sign-in for mainstream narratives about Latina identity and sexuality. . . .

Jennifer Lopez

At $13 million dollars per movie, Lopez is the highest paid Latina identified actress in Hollywood history. . . . Unlike Cameron Diaz whose Latinidad remains relatively invisible by virtue of her proximity to and performance of Whiteness, Lopez has explicitly highlighted and in some instances subverted her malleable ethnic and racial identity. In unprecedented fashion Lopez has catapulted her on-screen image to multiple domains most notably the music, clothing, lingerie, perfume, and television industries. . . . New perfume and fashion lines as well as forthcoming films and albums are part of a carefully orchestrated effort to remain at the forefront of the mainstream. . . .

Salma Hayek

The fall 2002 release of *Frida* by Miramax catapulted its producer and star Salma Hayek onto the cover of U.S. magazines, ranging from *Parade* to *Elle*. Her success in Mexican soap operas inspired Hayek to cross the entertainment border, where her first Hollywood role was a 30-second stint as a sultry and angry Chicana ex-girlfriend in Alison Ender's 1993 film *Mi Vida Loca*. As Hayek's hair has gotten progressively straighter and thus more "Anglo"-looking, her on-screen image also has become less stereotypically ethnic, consequently yielding more complex supporting and leading roles. While not achieving the multimedia profile of Lopez, Hayek is one of the most prolific contemporary Latinas in Hollywood, recently earning an Oscar nomination for her role in *Frida*, a rare achievement perceived as recognition of an actress's skill and talent. . . .

Frida Kahlo

Decades after her death, [Mexican painter Frida] Kahlo is one of the most popular and commodified mainstream images of Latinidad globally, and in the United States particularly. One can find Frida Kahlo stationery, posters, jewelry, hair clips, autobiographies, cookbooks, biographical books, chronological art books, refrigerator magnets, painting kits, wall hangings, and wrapping paper, to mention a few of the items in bookstores and novelty stores throughout the U.S., Mexico, Puerto Rico, and Spain. . . . Her paintings received the highest ever bid for a Latin American artwork auctioned at the prestigious House of Sotheby. Highlighting Kahlo's representational significance Hayek and Lopez raced to release biopics of the artist. Thus, it is not so much the art works themselves, including her own self-representational images, in which we are interested, but rather how Kahlo the symbol transcends the high and low culture divide by signing in for Latina identity and authenticity.

Racializing Latina Bodies and Sexuality in U.S. Popular Culture

One of the most enduring tropes surrounding the signification of Latinas in U.S. popular culture is that of tropicalism (Aparicio and Chavez-Silverman 1997; Perez-Firmat 1994). Tropicalism erases specificity and homogenizes all that is identified as Latin and Latina/o. Under the trope of tropicalism, attributes such as bright colors, rhythmic music, and brown or olive skin comprise some of the most enduring stereotypes about Latina/os, a stereotype best embodied by the excesses of Carmen Miranda and the hypersexualization of Ricky Martin. Gendered aspects of the trope of tropicalism include the male Latin lover, macho, dark-haired, mustachioed, and the spitfire female Latina characterized by red-colored lips, bright seductive clothing, curvaceous hips and breasts, long brunette hair, and extravagant jewelry. The tropes of tropicalism extend beyond those people with Caribbean roots to people from Latin America, and recently to those in the United States with Caribbean and/or Latin American roots.

Sexuality plays a central role in the tropicalization of Latinas through the widely circulated narratives of sexual availability, proficiency, and desirability (Valdivia 2000). For centuries the bodies of women of color, specifically their genitals and buttocks, have been excessively sexualized and exoticized by U.S. and European cultures (Gilman 1985). Not surprisingly popular images of Latinas and the Latina body focus primarily on the area below the navel, an urbane corporeal site with sexualized overdetermination (Desmond 1997). Within the Eurocentric mind/body binary, culture is signified by the higher intellectual functions of the mind while nature is signified by the lower biological functions of the body. That is, Whiteness is associated with a disembodied intellectual tradition free from the everyday desires of the body, and non-Whiteness is associated with nature and the everyday needs of the body to consume food, excrete waste, and reproduce sexually. Dominant representations of Latinas and African American women are predominantly characterized by an emphasis on the breasts, hips, and buttocks. These body parts function as mixed signifiers of sexual desire and fertility as well as bodily waste and racial contamination.

Contemporary Latina iconicity inherits traces of this dichotomous representational terrain. Despite Jennifer Lopez's multimedia successes, it is her buttocks insured by Lopez for $1 billion that most journalists and Lopez herself foregrounds. Like other popular Latinas, Lopez is simultaneously celebrated and denigrated for her physical, bodily, and financial excess. Whenever she appears in the popular press, whether it is a newspaper, a news magazine, or *People*, Lopez's gorgeous stereotypical Latina butt is glamorized and sexually fetishized. Indeed, she is often photographed in profile or from the back looking over her shoulders—her buttocks becoming the focus of the image, the part of her body that marks Lopez as sexy but different from Anglo female bodies. . . .

Likewise, while news media images of Lopez foreground her buttocks, photographs of Hayek emphasize her bountiful breasts, small waist, and round hips. Hayek's petite yet hyper-curvaceous frame embodies the romanticized stereotypical Latina hourglass shape, a petite ethnic shape that stands in opposition to the resonances of Blackness surrounding Lopez's hyperbuttocks and music video representations. Profile shots of Hayek in movies and magazine covers show both her breasts and her perfectly shaped booty. Frontal shots of Hayek's body highlight her deep cleavage as well as her long dark hair, worn straightened when performing a more glamorous image, and by implication Anglo identity, or curly when performing a more exotic ethnic identity.

Accompanying images of her body are journalistic texts that ultimately frame Hayek's body and identity within narratives of Latinidad, in particular references to her personality, voracious appetite, and loud, talkative nature. Thus, unlike Lopez whose sexualized image primarily foregrounds her racialized booty, sexualized representations of Hayek center on her body as the stereotyped performance of Latina femininity. . . .

The marginalization of Latina bodies is defined by an ideological contradiction—that is, Latina beauty and sexuality is marked as other, yet it is that otherness that also marks Latinas as desirable. In other words, Latina desirability is determined by their signification as racialized, exotic Others. For example, in the movies *Blood and Wine* and *U-Turn* Lopez's body is framed as animalistic, primitive, and irresistibly dangerous to the Anglo American male characters. In both movies, Lopez's body is fetishized through extreme close-ups of her eyes, lips, breasts, legs, and buttocks, visuals that often link her highly sexualized body to the physical environment around her. Similarly, Hayek's characters in *From Dusk Till Dawn* (1996), *54* (1998), and *Timecode* (2000) construct the ethnic feminine other as a temptress, a source of sexual and racial contamination, whose sexuality ultimately destroys her.

Consequently, representations of Hayek's body provide a symbolic bridge between the racialized and sexualized narrative of Lopez's buttocks and the ethnic and desexualized narrative of Kahlo's self-representations of her physically injured body. Whereas Lopez's body, especially her butt, signifies a racialized exotic sexuality, Kahlo's body asserts her ethnicity and foregrounds her identity beyond or outside of her sexuality. Portraits and images of Kahlo emphasize her face, in particular her hyper-eyebrow as a signifier of ethnic-difference, feminine-strength, and intellectual rather than bodily work. Nevertheless, intellectual efforts by Kahlo to complicate both her identity and Latina body do not necessarily transfer into twenty-first century commodifying practices. Instead we get the reification of difference through the everyday commodification of her face in the form of earrings, shirts, and other mainstream products, and her intellectual labor is resignified as aberrant and exotic. Within these popular products, the emphasis on her colorful-ethnic dress and facial hair, both physical markers of ethnic bodies, work to mediate her ethnic identity for capitalist consumption. In the end, the physical representations of all three women are informed by the racializing discourses of ethnic female bodies as simultaneously physically aberrant, sexually desirable, and consumable by the mainstream. These discourses cannot be examined outside of a framework of analysis that allows for fluidity and mixture.

Hybridity, Authenticity and the Latina Body

. . . Due to their mixed cultural and ethnic heritage, Hayek, Kahlo, and Lopez as hybrid women often problematize and work against the discursive field of popular ethnic and racial categories. While remaining at the margins of representations of Whiteness, they also exist outside the marginalizing borders of Blackness. Instead, they occupy a racialized space in between the dominant U.S. binary of Black or White identities. Given their dark, full-bodied hair, brown eyes, somatically olive skin, and a range of more or less European facial features, they are physically "any-woman"—with the perception of their identity determined both by the context of reception and the relationally encoded setting of production. . . .

Not coincidentally, . . . Hayek and Lopez have portrayed characters whose ethnic identity is ambiguous and peripheral to the role, text, and narrative action of particular movies. In at least five movies, *Dogma, Enough, Out of Sight, Timecode*, and *Gigli*, Hayek and Lopez perform characters whose ethnic and/or racial identity are "absent" from the text. This narrative absence has proven historically difficult if not impossible for actresses who explicitly identify as African American and are always already marked by the relatively fixed discourse of Blackness in the United States. . . .

Conclusion

Whether we examine women's magazines, television programs, cinematic texts, girl's toys, clothing, pulp fiction, road signs, medical videos, or popular music and dance, it is difficult to avoid the unmistakable presence of Latinidad and its gendered components in mainstream U.S. culture. While these contemporary representations may provide the opportunity for individual Latinas to open spaces for vocality and action, they nevertheless build on a tradition of exoticization, racialization, and sexualization, a tradition that serves to position Latinas as continual foreigners and a cultural threat. As such Latinas occupy a liminal space in U.S. popular culture, that is, we can be both marginal and desired. Recently popular representations of Latina booties as large, aberrant yet sexy, desirable, and consumable contribute to the reification of racial dichotomies where Latinas occupy that in-between space between the White booty (or the pre-adolescent invisible androgynous White booty) and the Black booty whose excess falls beyond the boundary of acceptability and desirability within U.S. popular culture. . . .

Nevertheless, the representational tensions surrounding the three iconic Latinas highlighted in this article present a potentially emancipatory challenge or at least an unsettling intervention to Eurocentric discourses of racial and ethnic purity. Kahlo, Lopez, and Hayek are iconic presences that engage the stereotyped representation of Latinas to sell products and open a space from which Latina bodies can vex notions of racial and national purity and therefore authentic ethnicity. Although historically Latina actresses have been relegated to exist within the racialized binary narrative of virgin and whore, popular discourses surrounding Salma Hayek, Frida Kahlo, and Jennifer Lopez disrupt some of Hollywood's symbolic boundaries surrounding ethnicity, race, gender, and sexuality. The commodification of Latinidad has signaled a homogenization of Latinidad and simultaneously provided access to roles previously unavailable to Latinas. Despite the exoticized nature of the representations surrounding the bodies of Lopez and Hayek, they successfully have marketed themselves in order to sell mainstream movie tickets, music, clothing, and perfume.

Furthermore, as transnational figures these three icons exist within the representational conflict between the hybrid and the authentic that many diasporic cultures occupy. Kahlo, a German-Hungarian-Jewish-Mexican, recuperates female sexuality and indigenous Mexican culture as a way of challenging the imperialistic Western gaze. Mainstream circulation of her image reinscribes difference, especially in terms of the ubiquitous unibrow, but also inescapably represent her head, her face, and, through her intellectual efforts, her brain. As such, given binary tendencies in our culture, one would expect Kahlo to exist outside the realm of the sensual. However Hayek's further representation of Kahlo takes Kahlo into the sensual and sexual thus fully completing her signification as a contemporary iconic Latina. Lopez, a U.S. born Puerto Rican, a Nuyorican, privileges both her U.S. Americanness and her Puerto Ricanness as way of challenging dichotomous discourses and the erasure of Latina bodies in Hollywood films. Repeated affirmations of love and marriage also firmly place her within that Roman Catholic component so predominant in popular constructions of Latinidad. Finally, Hayek, a Lebanese-Mexican, foregrounds the bodies of Latinas themselves as a way of challenging mainstream narratives about women and Latinidad and uses Eurocentric discourses of authenticity to position her self in relation to other iconic Latinas.

Hayek, Kahlo, and Lopez are not simply passive subjects manipulated by the media and popular culture, but transnational women caught in the dialectic between agency and the objectification of identity that operates within many mediated products. Although the stereotypic representation of Latina sexuality continues, the popular representations of Hayek, Kahlo, and Lopez also problematize emerging constructions of Latinas within dominant discourses about gender, ethnicity, and race. As independent, racially and ethnically undetermined, and transnational women, their Latina iconicity ruptures and affirms the borders that surround contemporary popular significations of Latinas. Latinidad and iconic Latinas render Eurocentric discourses of racial and national purity untenable. All three women point to the uneasy harnessing of transnational, hybrid, and gendered bodies that meet the media's demand for the production and consumption of ethnic identity.

Note

The authors would like to thank Cameron McCarthy, Lori Reed, and Kumarini Silva for their comments and suggestions to drafts of this article.

1. We recognize that the category "Latina" is fluid and porous. As such, Penélope Cruz, who is Spanish, is often categorized by both the popular press and websites as "Latina." As well, although Cameron Diaz is currently (February 2004) Hollywood's highest paid actress, only *Latina* magazine claims her as Latina. Neither she nor most coverage of her ever mentions her Latinidad.

References

Aparicio, F. R., and S. Chavez-Silverman eds. 1997. *Tropicalizations: Transcultural Representations of Latinidad.* Hanover, CT: University Press of New England.

Barthes, R. 1973. *Mythologies.* London: Granada.

Desmond, J. C. 1997. *Meaning in Motion: New Cultural Studies of Dance.* Durham, NC: Duke University Press.

Giles, J., and T. Middleton. 2000. *Studying Culture: A Practical Introduction.* London: Blackwell.

Gilman, S. 1985. *Difference and Pathology: Stereotypes of Sexuality, Race, and Madness.* Ithaca, NY: Cornell University Press.

Perez-Firmat, G. 1994. *Life on the Hyphen: The Cuban American Way.* Austin: University of Texas Press.

Rakow, L., and K. Kranich. 1991. Woman as sign in television news. *Journal of Communication* 41, 8–23.

Valdivia, A. 2000. *A Latina in the Land of Hollywood.* Tucson: University of Arizona Press.

12

"So Full of Myself as a Chick"

Goth Women, Sexual Independence, and Gender Egalitarianism

Amy C. Wilkins

The 1960s saw the rise of second-wave feminism *(as opposed to the first wave of feminism, which had focused on getting the right to vote). Within this second wave, liberal feminists emphasized the importance of obtaining equal treatment for women within existing social structures such as the job market and the legal system. Radical feminists, on the other hand, believed that gender inequality and patriarchal oppression lay at the root of all other forms of inequality, and believed that society needed to be radically restructured before it could truly meet women's needs. Among other things, the radical feminist movement was the first to stress the need to combat rape, incest, and other sexual dangers—issues that had received almost no public discussion previously.*

By the 1980s, however, "sex-positive" or "pro-sex" feminists had begun to challenge this position, and to argue that the battle for gender equality should shift to celebrating women's sexual freedom and sexual pleasure and away from highlighting sexual dangers. This call was picked up beginning in the 1990s by younger feminists (sometimes referred to as third-wave feminists*) who wanted to emphasize how women's position had improved since the 1960s.*

A related philosophical shift, sometimes referred to as postfeminism, *has occurred among many young women who do not necessarily think of themselves as feminists. The term* postfeminism *is often used to refer to a somewhat vague belief in gender equality, coupled with a belief that women already have won equality and so should now focus on enjoying their freedoms—especially*

Amy C. Wilkins, "'So Full of Myself as a Chick': Goth Women, Sexual Independence, and Gender Egalitarianism," *Gender & Society* 18(3): 328–349.

sexual freedom. The young Goth women described in Amy C. Wilkins' "'So Full of Myself as a Chick': Goth Women, Sexual Independence, and Gender Egalitarianism" exemplify this philosophy, its strengths, and its weaknesses. As Wilkins shows, Goth culture allows these women to resist many of the social pressures placed on other women, and to celebrate their resistance. At the same time, the particular structure of Goth sexual norms, coupled with Goth women's belief that the battles of feminism have been won within Goth culture, makes it difficult for these women to recognize the ways in which Goth culture reinforces gender and sexual inequality or to recognize the need for broader social change.

At the Haven, a Goth dance club, Goths adorned in black fetish wear, leather and PVC, and dog collars and leashes gather weekly. While some men "gender blend," wearing makeup and skirts, the women are dressed in sexy feminine outfits. The sidelines of the dance floor are populated by pairs and groups of people kissing, caressing, sucking on each other's necks. This environment, Siobhan tells me, is "liberating."

Drawing on interviews, participant observation, and Internet postings, this article analyzes gender in a local Goth scene. These Goths use the confines of the subcultural scene, where they are relatively safe from outsider views, and the scene's celebration of active sexuality as resources to resist mainstream notions of passive femininity. Sexually active femininity is not, of course, unique to the Goth scene: Contemporary young women in a variety of arenas use active sexuality to stake out gender independence. This emphasis on women's emancipated sexuality reflects the substantive turn of postfeminism—what Anna Quindlen has labeled "babe feminism" (1996, 4)—a focus on women's right to active sexuality rather than on broader issues of gender equality. In this article, I probe this Goth scene's (sub)cultural contradictions to critically examine the possibilities and the limitations of strategies of active feminine sexuality in gaining gender egalitarianism. . . .

Young Women's Sexuality: "Walk[ing] a Narrow Line"

The erosion of the old gender bargain, in which women exchanged sex and emotion work for financial support, has propelled young women to experiment with new rules about gender and sexuality (Sidel 1990; Thompson 1995). But while the rules of the sex game are changing, women are still held to a sexual double standard predicated on deep-rooted cultural understandings about differences between men and women. This double standard continues to impede women's sexual agency, but without the economic payoff promised (for many women) by the old gender bargain. Within this disadvantageous framework, young women struggle to exercise sexual agency on their own terms.

Young women's attempts to stretch their sexual wings are greeted with alarm by adults. The media frequently portray young women's sexual behavior to be converging with young men's, as more and more girls and young women engage in sexual relations outside of the context of marriage, engagement, or love. Moreover, changes in expectations for young women (i.e., college, career, and the consequent later marriage) have created a longer period of nonmarital sexuality for women. This alarm is crystallized in outcries about the "epidemic" of teen pregnancy. As Luker (1996) pointed out, the "epidemic" is actually an increase in nonmarital births, indicating that many young women are opting out of the marital prerogative that has been traditionally imposed on pregnant, unmarried, white, middle-class women.

While some feminists applaud women's increasing sexual agency, others argue that changes in sexual expectations have only increased the pressure for young women to engage in sexual behaviors they might not otherwise choose (Jacobs Brumberg 1997; Pipher 1994). A discourse of victimization thus pervades discussions of adolescent girls' sexuality. This discourse, which positions young women as passive recipients of unwanted sexual attention or as pressured into early or more frequent sexual behavior acknowledges girls' relative disempowerment in heterosexual interactions but precludes any discussion of sexual desire on the part of young women. In an article aptly subtitled "The Missing Discourse of Desire," Michelle Fine (1988) noted that girls' voices of desire, submerged under this discourse of victimization, are glimpsed only fleetingly.

By positioning girls as victimized rather than desiring subjects, this argument reproduces the cultural construction of girls as naturally less interested in sex than in emotions and less interested in sex than are men. Girls who violate this construction of proper femininity are heavily stigmatized. As Lees (1993) argued, fear of being labeled a "slag" (slut, ho, or hootchie in the United States) constrains young women's behavior in a number of ways—by keeping them from going to a variety of public places, from walking alone, from dressing too provocatively, from talking to too many boys. The power of the label is that it can be applied at any time for reasons that seldom have anything to do with sexual behavior. To avoid the potentially ruinous label, young women must constantly manage their self-presentations, shelving their own freedom and desires. The label thus results in very real gender differences in behavior, strengthening young men's power over and distinction from young women. Moreover, the label divides young women, pitting good girls against sluts, categories that are often overlaid with race and class codings (see Tolman 1996).

Caught in the cultural trap of increasing expectations for sexual competency, the mandate to appear heterosexually attractive (see Wolf 1991), and the powerful persistence of the "slut" stigma, "girls walk a narrow line: they must not be seen as too tight, nor as too loose" (Lees 1993, 29). The sexual balancing act in which most girls and young women engage has a number of consequences. First, the desire to appear as "good girls" impedes the use of sexual protection, since carrying condoms suggests that the girl anticipated having sex (rather than being "swept away" by the moment) (Thompson 1995). Second, the pressure to fulfill men's sexual needs combined with the absence of a "discourse of [female] desire" reduces young women's ability to make sexual decisions that are rooted in their own desires, putting them in a passive position in sexual negotiations. The result, too frequently, is heterosexual experiences that do not meet the criteria for rape but are also not actively chosen by young women, reinforcing the normativity of female passivity in heterosexual relations (Phillips 2000). . . .

In her study of adolescent girls' sexuality, Sharon Thompson concluded, "the greatest danger girls narrated was love. Once in love or set on trying to get in love, even cautious girls said they closed their eyes to sexual and psychological danger" (1995, 285). It is the ideology of romance, rather than sexuality, that encourages girls and women to sacrifice for the sake of the relationship or in desperate attempts to hang onto a relationship. Indoctrinated in the intertwined ideologies that "love conquers all" and that "hetero-relationships are the key to women's happiness," girls and women read romantic relationships as signs of their self-worth and of their identities, and thus risk losing both when they lose a relationship. The idea, moreover, that women are responsible for the maintenance of relationships adds to the pressure women feel to make their romantic alliances endure (Phillips 2000). Thus, because romance continues to be ideologically privileged for women, the emancipatory potential of their sexual agency is limited. Furthermore, women's sexual liberation itself is often hard to unpin from romance, as Radway (1984, 16) argued in her study of romance novels, in which she found that the radical validation of women's sexual passion was based on "the natural and inevitable expression of a prior *emotional* attachment, itself dependent on a natural, biologically based sexual difference."

In this article, I explore young women's use of active sexuality as a strategy for gaining gender egalitarianism in one Goth subculture. This Goth scene is a space in which women are actively struggling to reject conventional standards of feminine sexual comportment. They do this both by embracing their sexual agency and by rejecting the restrictions of monogamy and heterosexuality. In many ways, these women are ideally situated to enact this struggle: Race/class and generational privilege enable these women's experiments. They are moderately secure economically, do not have to contend with "welfare queen" demonization, and have clearly benefited from second-wave feminism. Furthermore, the Goth scene allows them to draw boundaries around themselves that mitigate the consequences of their sexual experiments. The "freak" label provides insularity, and the club that is the scene hub is repeatedly described as safe from outside judgment. Moreover, their scene is centered in a Northeastern college town that prides itself on its progressive gender politics and tolerance of sexual diversity. But while these women conduct their sexual negotiations in an unusually advantageous context, some women outside the Goth scene employ similar strategies. The Goth women's efforts provide an exceptional vantage on the limits and the potentialities of young women's struggles both to gain sexual freedom and to use sexuality to enact gender equality. . . .

The Local Goth Scene

Most accounts of Goth locate its roots in an early 1980s melding of the punk scene with glam rock. Goth is thus considered a music-based scene. But to be Goth implies much more than shared musical tastes; it is, as I was repeatedly informed, an "aesthetic," a particular way of seeing and of being seen.

My study is concerned with the local Goth scene rather than the Goth subculture writ large. The participants in my study consider the local scene to be atypical, mostly, I think, because of its location in a less urban area than, say, Boston or New York (the immediate geographic comparisons). The local scene seems to be less rigidly bounded than the scene in other localities and hosts a large number of "Tuesday Goths" (people who dress Goth only for the club on Tuesday nights). While internal debates about authenticity proliferate, tolerance for people who downplay their "freakiness" for work seems to be the norm.

The scene prides itself on its inclusivity. Many in the scene claim overlapping memberships in the queer, polyamorous, bondagediscipline/sadomasochism, and pagan communities. Yet it is demographically homogeneous: With a few exceptions, local Goths are youth or young adults, white, middle-class, college educated, liberal but not radical, unmarried, and childless. They are technologically adept; if they are not employed in tech support, they spend an enormous amount of time online. They are known for their brooding solitude, yet they call each other to task for perceived apathy toward the Goth community. Indeed, they are surprisingly social, coming together regularly at their local club night (called the Haven), at parties, for coffee, and on PVGoth, their online community.

The data for this article combine formal interviews, participant observation, and Web listserver data. I conducted in-depth, open-ended interviews with 17 self-identified Goths (10 women and 7 men). This scene is small enough that groups of friends are highly interconnected. Every person I interviewed knows, to a greater or lesser degree, everyone else in my sample. In addition, I engaged in numerous casual conversations with the interviewees as well as with other Goths. . . .

Goth Women's Sexual Agency: "So Full of Myself as a Chick"

The Goth women in this study present themselves as agentic, independent women in control of their personal lives and their social spaces. PVGoth is replete with such assertions: "I'm so full of myself as a chick in general that I don't want people talking to me whose sole purpose is to stick their dick in my cooter"; "I'm not interested in making someone's life more exciting when they haven't done anything on their own. I'm not a novelty item"; and "Treat me like a person first, and then I might start flirting with you."

Interviews with women root their interpersonal independence in the sexual norms of the local Goth scene. Siobhan describes the "open sexuality" of the Goth scene as "liberating," while for Rory, the scene is a space in which she can be "predatory and female." And for Lily, it engenders the "ability to insist on safer sex." Consistent across these accounts is a notion both of Goth women as strong and independent and of the Goth scene as supportive of women's sexual power. Honeyblossom, one of the most consciously political women in my sample, claims, "From what I've seen, most Goth women are feminists—tends to strongly inform their relationships." In her generalized attribution of feminism to Goth women, she, like those quoted on PVGoth and my other interviewees, locates feminism clearly within the realm of the interpersonal.

These claims are further developed in discussions of two aspects of the Goth scene: The rule to respect spatial boundaries and the freedom "for women to dress sexy." These discussions, elaborated below, elucidate the contradictions in these women's claims to independence and thus point to some of the possibilities and limits of sexual agency as a platform for women's emancipation.

Spatial Boundaries: "I Really, Really Liked It that Nobody Grabbed My Butt"

In a formulation that appears contradictory, Goths present rules as the basis for women's sexual freedom. Rules, in these explanations, serve to rein in predatory men and thus create conditions of greater sexual freedom for women. Perhaps the preeminent Goth social rule is the mandate to respect individual spatial boundaries. People who violate this rule are, by all accounts, shunned: "The rules are that strong that if you break them, you're ostracized" (Honeyblossom). While this phenomenon is in many ways gender neutral, the Goth women and men I interviewed frequently invoked it as a particular benefit to women. Goths presented the rule about spatial boundaries as a fundamental departure from outside norms about heterosexual interactions, one that provides women with the freedom to dress more provocatively and to exercise more control over their sexuality. Alyssa connects these ideas: "If a guy dances closely to you, people will come down on him with a vengeance. They don't say, 'Oh, you wore a corset, what did you expect?' "

The spatial rules at the Haven are a big attraction to women. Many of the women I spoke with told me that the absence of unsolicited physical contact pulled them back to the Haven even if they did not immediately feel at home. For example, Honeyblossom comments, "I really, really liked it that nobody tried to grab my butt." Similarly, a woman on PVGoth writes, "At a regular club, it's fairly common for a guy to come up and grind with random girls. . . . In fact that's one of the reasons I prefer goth clubs to regular clubs."

Goths repeatedly use "regular" clubs as a foil against which they articulate the cultural and moral superiority of the Haven's social norms. Importantly, they portray their club behavior as superior not because it protects women's sexual purity but because it allows women more control over heterosexual interactions. A woman on PVGoth posts, "I'm perfectly capable of letting people know I'm interested in them, and I don't need to be pursued persistently. If I like you, I'll let you know. I wonder if most women in our scene are like that?" Honeyblossom, who responded affirmatively to the previous woman's query, later told me that "[Goth] women are more comfortable initiating relationships. . . . I think there is a definite idea within Gothic culture that to be a powerful woman who is able to say yes and no to things is sexy."

Although some Goth men comment that the spatial rules add to their sense of personal comfort, they also construct them as a particular benefit to women. This suggestion, while not necessarily invalid, glosses over the specific benefits Goth men accrue from the combination of spatial boundaries and women's sexual agency. The norms of heterosexual interaction in the Haven do not desex the club but rather change the game rules, distributing the labor of the chase between men and women and reducing the risk of sexual rejection for men. Goth men can count on getting sex, but without the pressures (often lamented by mainstream men) of a unilateral chase.

Dressing Sexy: "An Empowering Statement of Female Choice"

The clubbing outfits worn by most Goth women in this scene are highly sexualized. The typical Goth woman's club ensemble fetishizes the whore, combining corsets with short skirts and fishnet stockings. Goth women use the heterosexual etiquette of the Goth scene to frame their clothing choices in ways that sidestep conventional interpretations of such dress. For example, Beth insists that the rules in the Goth scene allow her "to dress in a way that's sexy without people assuming that [she is] there to get laid." A Goth man echoes this sentiment on PVGoth: "I think people unfamiliar with this scene assume that just because some woman is wearing a short vinyl dress and fish nets that she wants to get some from you."

Goth women, then, use the Haven rule about spatial boundaries to look and feel sexy without the risks that come with overtly sexualized self-presentations in other arenas. Most obviously, the Goth community spatial norms reduce the incidences of unsolicited physical contact, making sexy self-presentations a physically safer option for women than in mainstream clubs or other contexts.[1] But in a questionable conceptual move, Goth women interpret the absence (or invisibility) of sexual assault as the absence of sexual objectification. This interpretation allows them to position themselves as the ones in control of their own sexuality. In Dallas's words, the Goth woman is not "objectified unless that's what [she] wants." At the same time, however, this construction plays off of the culturally hegemonic Madonna-whore dichotomy by allowing Goth women to see themselves as sexually appealing but not easy.

The Goth women's strategy negotiates the feminist dilemma of pleasure and oppression. The ability to participate in sexy self-presentations is pleasurable. For many Goth women, the Haven is an unusual arena in that it validates their particular expressions of sexiness. Many of these women may not be able to access sexual attractiveness in conventional contexts where sexy femininity is defined according to narrow beauty standards that emphasize thin, disciplined bodies. At the Haven, even women with larger bodies wear revealing ensembles involving, for example, the aforementioned corsets and short skirts. This freedom was pointed out to me repeatedly and was quickly confirmed by a cursory appraisal of the Haven crowd. Zoe says, "It's also true that anyone can go and feel sexy," presenting the Haven as a space in which women of all shapes and sizes are sexually validated. . . .

Goths value the Haven because it allows them to play with self-presentations, validates sexual experimentation, and provides an arena for sexual interactions. Goths, especially Goth women, present these possibilities as liberating and enjoyable. But underlying these freedoms and choices is the unspoken (and perhaps unseen) absence of choice. While Goth women may enjoy sexual dress and sexual play, their claim to Goth membership depends on their participation. In Zoe's words, "as long as you dress sexy [you'll fit in]." And in Rory's, "if there is such a thing as a Goth is supposed to be, a Goth is supposed to be sexually open."

Moreover, sporadic evidence that the Goth gaze is not always so friendly peeks through. For example, during my visits to the Haven, I was occasionally advised by women to avoid certain guys with "sketchy" reputations. Likewise, when Beth arranged an interview with a Goth man for me, she warned me not to "hook up with him." The man apparently was willing to participate in the interview only if I were "cute and available." The "loser dance" (described to me independently by Beth, Zoe, and Chad), in which women use a series of gestures to signal their discomfort with an overly aggressive male dance partner to their friends, who then intervene, also indicates an awareness among Goth women that Goth men may not always respect their sexual space.

In addition, the Goth gaze may not always be supportive of the appropriation of sexy self-presentations by all women. One woman self-disparagingly confesses on PVGoth,

> I've been known to be sitting on a cozy little chair at haven and think to myself (or even whisper to a nearby friend) about a passerby "omigod even if I were half her size I would NEVER try to squeeze my ass into something like that, how embarrassing!"

And Zoe admits, "Some women wear very little—large women. I feel two ways. I think it's good that they can feel sexy but think they'd look so much more attractive if they wore something else." Moreover, a number of women (and one man, Hunter) mentioned a few women who made a habit of traversing the Haven naked. While Hunter suggested that this behavior was not appropriate outside of a strip club, the women told me that many of the men complained because the naked women were not attractive. Thus, despite contentions that women are not objectified or limited by mainstream beauty standards, Goth women are objects of the critical gazes of both men and women. . . .

Sexuality and Romance: "It's Not about Sex, It's about Love"

This Goth community's construction of itself as proactively sexual is complicated by the continued reliance on, and even the reproduction of, an ideology of romance. These Goths present free sexuality as an avenue to achieving emotional sophistication. In their attempts to legitimize their sexual experimentation, they reinvest romance with moral and emotional importance without questioning women's special responsibility for emotional intimacy. By positioning romantic relations as a preeminent personal goal, this strategy undermines the benefits of women's sexual agency.

For many Goth women, gender discrepancies increase when they enter romantic relationships. The predominantly heterosexual relationships within the Goth community [typically reflect a commitment to polyamory and] often restrict women's sexual freedoms but not men's. . . .

"Polyamory," which means more than one love, embraces romantic intimacy but rejects sexual exclusivity. According to the polyamory Web site (alt.poly) that many Goths visit regularly, polyamorous relationships can take on a number of forms. For example, each member of a couple may engage in subsidiary sexual and/or emotional relationships with other people or with the same person. Or a polyamorous person may engage in several equally privileged sexual/emotional relationships. Or three or more people may be simultaneously involved.

While the permutations seem endless, they are held together by central relationship ideals of emotional and physical responsibility, honesty, communication, and trustworthiness, which in turn structure a moral differentiation between polyamory and sleeping around. These Goths, polyamorous or not, emphasize the moral dimensions of "real" polyamory, describing it as a lifestyle based in love. "In its purest form, it's not about sex, it's about love," Jeff explains. And Lily says, "I don't think it's impossible to be in love with more than one person at a time romantically." These descriptions routinely level contempt at people who, in Beth's words, "use [the label] as an excuse to sleep around." She adds, drawing a boundary around her own practice of polyamory, "I don't want to be associated with people who I think are irresponsible—whether it be emotionally irresponsible or not using protection." In these claims, Goths suggest that sexuality is a tool they use to rebuild genuine emotional commitment.

Polyamorous discourse thus reinvigorates the importance of emotional intimacy to relationships. For the Goth woman, these relationship values and their assumed moral superiority mitigate her presentation of herself as sexually free, allowing her to play both sides of the Madonna-whore card. At once, she is sexually experimental and emotionally responsible. She is thus able to expand her sexual options without jeopardizing her position as a good woman. Rory raises these issues in her self-described (un)"popular" critique of the use of the "poly" label:

> My experience is it [the poly label] is used to imply that everyone you sleep with you're having a relationship with. People use it who can't handle the label of promiscuity. No matter how open minded or free people say they are, there still needs to be an emotional justification behind the sex.

The values attributed to polyamory may be desirable to many Goth women for other reasons as well. By emphasizing trust and communication, proponents of polyamory privilege relationship styles commonly seen as more important to women. "There truly needs to be openness and respect between all people," Crow comments. Similarly, both Lily and Greg attribute the success of their (separate) polyamorous relationships to "honest[y]" and "communication." Especially in the context of polyamorous relationships, honesty and trust necessitate ongoing negotiations between partners as well as "self-knowledge" (alt. poly) and "emotional literacy" (Beth's phrase). Thus, even if individual relationships do not actually live up to these ideals, the predominance of this discourse may be useful to some women who are seeking to make men more emotionally accountable in relationships. In addition, as Goths themselves claim, the ideal of honesty about other sexual partners combined with strong pressure within the Goth community to practice safe sex may protect women physically from some of the risks associated with sexual behavior (e.g., HIV). . . .

But while they may benefit women in some ways, these values are not inherently gender egalitarian. . . . When Goths talk about the dynamics of specific intimate relationships, the contention that relationship negotiations are gender neutral breaks apart. For example, both Beth and Zoe describe a polyamorous couple (Siobhan and Bill) in which (in Zoe's words) "he's dated lots of women but she's only dated one guy. She says it's never worked out but I think he's always protested it." Siobhan, no longer in the relationship, bitterly recalls, "[Bill] was jealous and insecure and didn't want me to date any other men. Women were fine as long as he got a piece of ass too."

While Siobhan condemns Bill as an individual, her situation adheres to a common pattern in the Goth community in which straight men are involved with bisexual women. In these relationships, as Zoe complains, "there seems to be a double standard—girls in heterosexual relationships can date other women but not other men." . . .

Goth women's relationships with other women are frequently subsidiary to heterosexual relationships. While some Goth women do get involved in enduring relationships with other women, short-lived relationships are normative. Zoe comments,

> I know a lot of bisexual girls who just date other girls for a week at a time. . . . Even for my own self, I tend to be in these really long relationships with men and barely ever date women.

And Beth notes that "permanent relationships are more likely to be heterosexual—bi girls with boyfriends go looking for girls."

The predominance of this arrangement has both benefits and drawbacks for women. The prevalence of women's bisexuality creates an atmosphere in which women who might otherwise practice strict heterosexuality are able to experiment sexually with other women. Moreover, some women (both in and out of the Goth scene) are able to use bisexuality to traverse the boundaries of monogamy, as Zoe points out:

> I've been in relationships with men who didn't care if I saw other women but I felt like he didn't perceive women as a threat. . . . I can still fall in love with a woman . . . felt like he didn't take it seriously but I took advantage of it.

Women like Zoe are able to maintain the advantages of a central heterosexual relationship while also engaging in sexual play outside the relationship. . . .

But, as Zoe's earlier quote makes clear, while individual women may be able to use bisexuality to push against the constraints of feminine sexuality, this strategy is fragile precisely because it uses the terms of gender hierarchy to garner some sexual space. The predominant construction of bisexuality "that doesn't perceive other women as a threat" is predicated on a sexual double standard that defines sex between women as less real. This construction is then turned into reality by the structures that support heterosexual relationships. Furthermore, the eroticization of women's bisexuality (at least between "properly" feminine women) heterosexualizes it by turning it into a performance or a fantasy for men and thereby devaluing the women's own sexual pleasure. Not unique to the Goth scene, this dual use of bisexuality demonstrates the ways in which seeming gender progress can be harnessed to serve traditional sex/gender hierarchies.

Moreover, in polyamorous relationships, women's bisexuality may be used to circumscribe women's sexuality, as in Lily and Sean's case. While Sean's participation in a central committed relationship does not require him to delimit his chosen field of sexual eligibles, Lily's participation requires her to cut hers in half. Her bisexuality is used as the justification for this imbalance. Her ability to sexually engage other women makes it seem like she is gaining something and thus obfuscates the inequity of the arrangement by suggesting that her sexual freedom is equivalent to Sean's.

But it is not sexuality that underpins Lily's relative disempowerment; it is her romantic commitment to Sean. Because of her belief in the enduring love of that relationship, Lily does the emotion work necessary to allow her to stay in it. The pervasiveness of conventional relationship ideals is further evidenced by their on-again/off-again discussions of marriage and by Lily's confession that she engages in fewer and fewer outside relationships at all. Further indicating that monogamous sexuality and love have not been so successfully unpinned after all, Rory, Zoe, and Siobhan, all previously polyamorous, told me that they were currently monogamous because they did not want to hurt their boyfriends. And the woman and man with whom Beth once had a triangular relationship (all three participants were romantically and sexually involved with each other) have recently sealed their monogamy with marriage. In all of these examples, the promise of love triumphs over the freedom and choice of Goth sexual experimentation. . . .

Conclusion

The local Goth subculture at the heart of this study, and its members' sexual negotiations, provide a case study of the relationships between sexual attitudes, sexual behavior, and gender egalitarianism. The victories and limitations of the Goth women's struggle provide insight into the role of sexuality in the quest to create gender egalitarian spaces. The active negotiation of sexual roles by the Goths in this study show that it is possible for women to create a space in which they are able to access sexuality on more gender-egalitarian terms even while they encounter stumbling blocks to full sexual autonomy. Goth women's attempts to balance gender equality on a platform of sexual agency are not successful, however. Intervention in the arena of sexuality does not propel a reconfiguration of other gendered negotiations.

Perceived as freaks by outsiders, Goths create an insulated space for their community in which they can experiment with behaviors that are stigmatized in the mainstream culture. The sexual haven created by the Goths in my study allows Goth women to engage in proactive sexual behavior without the "slut" label. Goth women experience their sexuality as personally empowering: It provides them with a sense of control over their bodies, with the right to feel and act on desire and with external validation of their expressions of sexiness. For women struggling to walk the narrow sexual line mandated by the mainstream culture, these gains should not be understated. They are mitigated, however, by the persistence of sociocultural ideas that position men as sexual consumers/owners. As feminists have argued about the sexual revolution, simply increasing women's right to enjoy sex does not undo the basic heterosexual relationship that confers men with sociocultural power. Indeed, in the absence of other changes, women's sexual freedom benefits men more than it does women by providing men with greater sexual access to women without altering heterosexual power arrangements.

Goth women hope that by transforming the terms of sexuality, they can also transform sexism. But even though they do enact significant transformations in the internal sexual culture of their scene, they do not significantly alter gendered power. First, centering gender change on sexuality only partially challenges interpersonal inequalities between men and women. The relative escape from sexual double standards does not necessitate an accompanying escape from heterosexual, monogamous romance. Even when sexuality and romance are sometimes uncoupled, the meanings attached to relationships within this Goth scene privilege successful romantic ties as symbols of moral and emotional development, maintaining women's sociocultural reliance (for personal meaning, for self-esteem, and even for justification of their sexual behaviors) on the sexual relationships they establish. This reliance, in turn, reproduces their disempowerment within those relationships by undercutting their ability to demand men's accountability for sexism in intimate relationships. As Stombler and Padavic (1997) found in their study of women in fraternity little sister organizations, a central focus on "getting a man" impedes women's ability to enact forms of resistance. Thus, when sexuality is the central emancipatory tool, its continued entanglement with heterosexual romance may even be counterproductive—centering, rather than decentering, sexuality and romance in women's lives.

Second, the focus on sexuality leaves systemic inequality unchallenged. Focusing on sexuality as the arena of change deflects conversations from other areas where gendered power is being enacted. But even more than simply leaving other aspects of sexism undiscussed, the focus on sexuality may also undermine the possibility of enacting systemic change. The psychological investment in the equation of sexual emancipation with feminism too easily allows for the idea that substantial change is already occurring. Interpreting transformed sexuality as inherently feminist allows participants to feel morally and politically superior to people who have not transformed their sexuality and allows participants to justify their own lifestyles on political and moral grounds. The psychological benefit of identifying individually and collectively as gender progressive is often as seductive as the sexual gains themselves and can thus be used to stifle internal or external challenges to sexism. In effect, participants can use their involvement in transformed sexual relations as evidence of their de facto feminism, shielding themselves and their community from further challenges to the configuration of gendered power.

Note

AUTHOR'S NOTE: I would like to thank Robert Zussman, Naomi Gerstel, Janice Irvine, Jill McCorkel, and the anonymous reviewers at *Gender & Society* for their insightful comments and thoughtful reading of multiple drafts of this article. I would also like to thank Shawn McGuffey, Alice Julier, and Meg Yardley for enduring endless conversations about these issues, for plying me with coffee, and especially for dropping their own work to nourish this project.

1. This discussion is not meant to imply that women's dress is responsible for sexual assault in other arenas.

References

Fine, Michelle. 1988. Sexuality, schooling and adolescent females: The missing discourse of desire. *Harvard Educational Review* 58:29–53.

Jacobs Brumberg, Joan. 1997. *The Body Project: An Intimate History of American Girls*. New York: Random House.

Lees, Sue. 1993. *Sugar and Spice: Sexuality and Adolescent Girls*. London: Penguin.

Luker, Kristin. 1996. *Dubious Conceptions: The Politics of Teenage Pregnancy*. Cambridge, MA: Harvard University Press.

Phillips, Lynn M. 2000. *Flirting with Danger: Young Women's Reflections on Sexuality and Domination*. New York: New York University Press.

Pipher, Mary B. 1994. *Reviving Ophelia: Saving the Selves of Adolescent Girls*. New York: Putnam.

Quindlen, Anna. 1996. And now, babe feminism. In *Bad Girls/Good Girls: Women, Sex, and Power in the Nineties*, edited by Nan Bauer Maglin and Donna Perry. New Brunswick, NJ: Rutgers University Press.

Radway, Janice A. 1984. *Reading the Romance: Women, Patriarchy, and Popular Literature*. Chapel Hill: University of North Carolina Press.

Sidel, Ruth. 1990. *On Her Own: Growing Up in the Shadow of the American Dream*. New York: Penguin.

Stombler, Mindy, and Irene Padavic. 1997. Sister acts: Resisting men's domination in black and white fraternity little sister programs. *Social Problems* 44(2):257–75.

Thompson, Sharon. 1995. *Going All the Way: Teenage Girls' Tales of Sex, Romance, and Pregnancy*. New York: Hill and Wang.

Tolman, Deborah. 1996. Adolescent girls' sexuality: Debunking the myth of the urban girl. In *Urban Girls: Resisting Stereotypes, Creating Identities*, edited by Bonnie J. Ross Leadbeater and Niobe Way. New York: New York University Press.

Wolf, Naomi. 1991. *The Beauty Myth: How Images of Beauty Are Used against Women*. New York: W. Morrow.

III

THE POLITICS OF APPEARANCE

In a society still largely controlled by men, women's appearance dramatically affects women's lives. Attractiveness serves as an indirect form of power by increasing women's odds of obtaining resources from powerful men, whether jobs, promotions, marriage proposals, social approval, or simple courtesies. The articles in this part explore the social norms (i.e., unwritten rules regarding how members of a society should behave) for women's appearance, the impact of these norms on women's lives, and the ways women respond to these norms.

The first three articles in this part describe how women grapple with social expectations regarding their breasts, hair, and body size. In "Designing Women: Cultural Hegemony and the Exercise of Power among Women Who Have Undergone Elective Mammoplasty," Patricia Gagné and Deanna McGaughey examine women's embodied experience of their breasts, focusing on women who have breast implants as a means of increasing their power. Similarly, in "Women and Their Hair: Seeking Power through Resistance and Accommodation," Rose Weitz uses women's narratives about their hair to analyze the advantages, as well as the limitations, of using hair as a source of power. Samantha Kwan then explores how women are affected by and manage the stigma of being "overweight" in "Navigating Public Spaces: Gender, Race, and Body Privilege in Everyday Life."

The final two articles shift our focus away from the ways in which women discipline their own bodies to look at the *context* of those disciplines and at the ways in which women can *challenge* those disciplines. In "The Moral

Underpinning of Beauty: A Meaning-Based Explanation for Light and Dark Complexions in Advertising," Shyon Baumann develops a theory to explain women's lighter skin tone ideals in popular culture. And in "Reclaiming the Female Body: Women Body Modifiers and Feminist Debates," Victoria Pitts explores the decisions of women who *choose* to place themselves outside of mainstream appearance norms through tattoos and other forms of body modification.

13

Designing Women

Cultural Hegemony and the Exercise of Power among Women Who Have Undergone Elective Mammoplasty

PATRICIA GAGNÉ AND DEANNA MCGAUGHEY

Earlier in this volume we discussed the shift among both feminists and the general public toward emphasizing women's sexual pleasure and deemphasizing the sexual dangers women face. This shift was part of a broader shift toward emphasizing women's agency (that is, their ability to freely choose their actions), rather than emphasizing how women's lives are controlled by others and by powerful social forces.

Beginning in the 1960s, second-wave feminists typically had focused on the overlapping issues of constraint (how women's lives are restricted by men's power and by cultural norms that reflect men's desires), subordination (how women are kept under men's control and below men in the social hierarchy), and "false consciousness" (how women internalize men's desires as their own, often seeing themselves through men's eyes, a process sometimes referred to as the "male gaze" or the "internalized male connoisseur"). Each of these forces lead to the "docile bodies" described by Sandra Lee Bartky.

This emphasis made great sense for those writing in the 1960s and 1970s. At the time, the legal, social, cultural, and economic constraints faced by women were far greater than they are today. Moreover, the extreme pressures placed on women by violence (whether rape, incest, battering, or some other form) were typically either blamed on the women or ignored altogether, and so many feminists considered it especially crucial to highlight these pressures.

As women's position in society improved, however, a "third wave" of feminists arose. Compared to second-wave feminists, third-wave feminists (and other writers who might not necessarily accept that label) often downplayed constraint and false consciousness and instead emphasized women's agency.

In "Designing Women: Cultural Hegemony and the Exercise of Power among Women Who Have Undergone Elective Mammoplasty," Patricia Gagné and Deanna McGaughey argue that we can best understand women's bodily experiences by synthesizing these two approaches. Their argument is based on interviews with women who have undergone elective breast surgery, primarily breast augmentation—the most common cosmetic surgical procedure in the United States. According to the American Society for Aesthetic Plastic Surgery, over 330,000 U.S. women underwent this procedure in 2012. Using the example of cosmetic breast surgery, they show how women actively choose to have surgery to improve their lives (exercising free will), but do so in the context of hegemonic (i.e., dominant and dominating) cultural norms that make it difficult for them to even consider other choices (suggesting false consciousness). As Gagné and McGaughey suggest, for women to feel comfortable with their "embodied self"—the part of their self-identity that reflects their sense of their physical body—they must find ways to change their physical self to better match their internalized sense of what an appropriate female body should look like.

Elective cosmetic surgery, like other practices designed to help women achieve hegemonic standards of feminine beauty, is problematic for feminist scholars because it involves agency as well as subordination. On one hand, women choose what procedures to have done. On the other, the choices women make are determined by hegemonic cultural norms.

The academic debate regarding women and beauty has included examinations and theoretical discussions of fashion, makeup, diet and exercise, eating disorders, and elective cosmetic surgery (Bartky 1997; Bordo 1993, 1997; Morgan 1991; Wolf 1991). A salient debate within this literature is based on assumptions about whether women are socially coerced into striving to achieve cultural standards of beauty or whether they freely choose to do so. As Padmore (1998) argued, a dualistic approach to social issues is overly simplified and wrong. What is needed is a theoretical model that incorporates social pressures and agency.

In this article, we draw on in-depth interviews with a nonrandom sample of women who have undergone elective cosmetic mammoplasty [breast surgery] to expand our understandings of women's experiences and motives for trying to achieve hegemonic ideals of beauty, as well as the social forces that compel them to do so. Our goal is to move beyond dualistic conceptualizations of agency and power by demonstrating how power is exercised on women's bodies even as they exercise it themselves.

Unlike most current literature on women and beauty, we do not assume that women are either victims of false consciousness or free agents in their quest to achieve cultural standards of beauty. Rather, our analysis reveals some of the ways that women are caught up in a hegemonic culture of beauty in which they often experience cosmetic surgery as liberating and empowering. In this article, we argue that dualistic conceptualizations of agency and power are inappropriate and inadequate. Our work contributes to the feminist literature by offering a theoretical model that synthesizes the strengths of both perspectives on women and beauty.

Feminist Perspectives on Cosmetic Surgery

In general, there have been two feminist approaches to understanding why women elect to undergo cosmetic surgery and the relationship between plastic surgery and women's subordination in society (Padmore 1998; Wijsbek 2000). The first can be characterized as the false consciousness perspective in which women are assumed to be objectified by men's standards of beauty. The second can be thought of as the free will perspective in which women are assumed to freely exercise agency in electing to undergo cosmetic surgery.

False Consciousness and the Male Gaze

The false consciousness perspective posits that although women freely choose cosmetic surgery, the standards they seek to achieve have been constructed by men and serve men's interests (Morgan 1991). Therefore, women are culturally coerced into seeking cosmetic surgery to meet the standards of beauty constructed by and for men. As Morgan (1991) explained, these are both actual men and abstract, symbolic male figures who may even exercise power over women through women's interactions with one another. Women perceive these hypothetical men as judging them and encouraging them to meet men's standards of beauty. The notion that men exercise power over women through socially constructed standards is known as the "male gaze," a concept developed by Mulvey (1989) to explain how feminine subjectivity is constructed as women judge and create themselves on the basis of their perceptions of men's desires. Mulvey argued that feminine subjectivity is constructed through spectatorship as the viewer identifies with the male and objectifies the female. While women may appear to be active in the social construction of self, they are actually the passive recipients of men's desires and standards (Culbertson 1999).

The male gaze has been criticized for suggesting that women are devoid of agency (Chandler 2000; Saco 1994) and for its lack of specificity (Pratt 1992). The theory presumes that all men have the same control over all women. But relations of power tend to intersect with one another. Therefore, not all men are equally powerful (Bhaba 1995). Men of color, for example, do not have as much social power as do white men (Pratt 1992), and working-class and poor men have less power than more affluent men. Finally, there are no empirical data to support the assumption that women's perceptions of men's desires are accurate reflections of what men want in women (Chandler 2000). Without supporting empirical data, the theory of the male gaze comes into question because it is based on the premise that what men desire in women must change before women can be empowered.

One of the strengths of the male gaze is how the concept highlights the centrality of looking and being seen in the social construction of gender and maintenance of social relations (Chandler 2000). In this way, looking and being looked at are fundamental steps in the process of establishing, perpetuating, or challenging social order. Looking is central to the social construction of the self and has been demonstrated to play an important role in culture by regulating social interaction (Argyle 1983). Specifically, it is through looking that we are constituted as subjects and objects. The problem with the male gaze is not the notion that looking is important but the patriarchal and heterosexist premise that actual and hypothetical men are the sole agents and beneficiaries of the gaze. The extent to which actual and hypothetical women are agents and beneficiaries of a hegemonic cultural gaze has received little academic attention (but see Chapkis 1986). Furthermore, outside of film, few if any scholars have focused on the processes through which women exercise agency by gazing and presenting themselves as objects of the looks of others.

Free Choice

In contrast to the notion of false consciousness is the view that women are rational decision makers and that they seek cosmetic surgery through free choice. Davis (1995) argued for such a perspective in her research on decision-making processes among women who have undergone elective cosmetic surgery. Davis acknowledged that the decision to undergo elective cosmetic surgery can be problematic but concluded that it can be an instrument used by women to control their bodies and lives. In this formulation, the benefits of exercising free choice—feeling and being perceived as normal—outweigh the consequences of embodying hegemonic gender norms.

One of the problems with Davis's (1995) approach is her uncritical adoption of hegemonic ideas of what is normal or natural. The discourse of free choice is predicated on the idea that it is natural for women to want to look better. In addition, looking better or being satisfied with the results of cosmetic surgery is based on judgments of how natural one looks (Adams 1997). This premise is problematic because it presumes that "natural" is outside of culture and hence outside of power relations (Brush 1998). By arguing that the goal of elective cosmetic surgery is to look normal or natural, the relations among cosmetic surgery, the objectification of women, and social relations of power, including race and class, are foreclosed from critique.

In sum, the false consciousness and free will perspectives differ in their understanding of the motivations for, and consequences of, seeking cosmetic surgery. The false consciousness approach assumes that women are duped by a beauty system that is defined by men. Therefore, women are objects of men's desires and standards. The free will perspective argues that although the practices of femininity may be problematic, women are nevertheless active in choosing cosmetic surgery. Therefore, cosmetic surgery is an expression of women's agency.

Although these two perspectives appear to be diametrically opposed, there are two theoretical threads running through them that are more similar than different. First, both draw on a conventional understanding of power that is conceived as a zero-sum phenomenon, which Foucault (1978) argued is incomplete. For the false consciousness approach, power is held by men and exercised over women. For the free will perspective, the power to choose is held by women and is outside existing gendered power relations. The only difference between these two explanations is with respect to who is holding power over whom. Both overlook the sites at which power is exercised, such as through self-perception, social interaction, the fashion industry, the media, and medicine, making both perspectives incomplete.

Second, both approaches perpetuate the idea that an individual is composed of two discrete and opposed qualities: a mind and a body (Cheng 1996; Ender 1999; Grosz 1994; Weiss 1999). The false consciousness and free will perspectives both treat the body as a passive object that is either inscribed by hegemonic norms constructed by men or used by women as a tool in their social construction of a gendered self. In treating the body as an object, both approaches perpetuate dualistic thinking by ignoring the constitutive role the body plays in forming thoughts, feelings, and actions, as well as the interaction between body and mind in the formation and experience of self (Grosz 1994; Weiss 1999).

A Synthesized Approach: Cosmetic Surgery as a Technology of the Embodied Self

We propose a synthesized theoretical perspective that simultaneously accounts for women's agency and subordination within the practice of cosmetic surgery (Padmore 1998). Our approach incorporates aspects from both the false consciousness and the free will perspectives by embracing women's agency in the construction of self while acknowledging and criticizing hegemonic gender norms through which the apparent possibilities of self are created (Padmore 1998). Specifically, we draw on Gramsci's (1971) concept of hegemony to examine the ways in which the dominant culture and major institutions coerce women into having their bodies surgically altered. And we examine women's internalization of a narrow range of acceptable embodiments, which serves as the foundation of their consent to be governed and their desire to have their bodies surgically altered. With this perspective, we transcend the dualism inherent in both perspectives by drawing on the concepts of disciplinary power and the embodied self.

Disciplinary Power and the Embodied Self

The conceptualization of power in the false consciousness and free will perspectives is not so much wrong as it is incomplete (Foucault 1979). Although power may be unequally distributed, it cannot be divided neatly into haves and have nots. Identifying who has power simply masks how it is dispersed throughout social networks. For example, concentrating on the male gaze blinds us to how the gaze emerges through other sites, including women's gazes at one another (Winkler 1994); the clinical gaze (Foucault 1973), in which women's bodies are constructed through the lens of medicine; selfgazing, in which women look at themselves (Brush 1998); and racialized and sexualized gazes, through which white supremacy and heterosexism are constituted. A more comprehensive approach to understanding power seeks to identify not who has power but how it operates and the consequences of those operations (Dreyfus and Rabinow 1982; Foucault 1980; Ransom 1997; Sawicki 1991). The benefit of such an approach is that it allows for critical intervention into multiple sites of power.

Cosmetic surgery does not simply repress or hold women down; it is a tool among many used literally to create the female body and feminine subjectivity. As such, cosmetic surgery can both contest and reify hegemonic culture,[1] although it is more often a tool for creating and maintaining cultural hegemony. Most plastic surgery is completed to meet cultural standards that are informed implicitly by race and class (Gilman 1999). For example, white women tend to have their breasts augmented, African American women tend to have their noses made narrower, and Asian American women tend to have their eyes Westernized (Kaw 1998; Padmore 1998). Class polarization is also reified through cosmetic surgery practices. For example, thinness is currently the norm and is more easily accomplished by affluent women who have access to better foods and a certain amount of expendable income they can use for lyposuction (Fallon 1990). Although women willingly elect to create their embodied selves through plastic surgery and other means, one of the unintended consequences of their actions is the perpetuation and proliferation of sexism, heterosexism, racism, and classism. Hence, it is not the surgery itself that is oppressive but the ends it serves, particularly when those ends reify cultural hegemony.

Understanding self-formation from a disciplinary perspective of power requires examining how people are pressured to become "normal." From a Foucauldian perspective, society constructs a norm and then encourages people literally to embody that standard (Foucault 1979). Individuals are not coerced to do so but instead are guided in their willing obedience (Ransom 1997). Specifically, women are not forced to undergo cosmetic surgery or most of the other practices in their beauty regimens. Rather, they internalize as natural and normal the standards of beauty that are pervasive in the hegemonic culture. As Gramsci (1971) argued, hegemony is insidious because it is internalized. Cosmetic surgery is a technique of feminization located at the intersection between agency and subordination, in which women actively and passively create themselves—through a literal construction of the body—as desirable women.

For the purpose of this article, we assume cosmetic surgery to be a technology drawn on by women in their construction of an embodied self. Therefore, we highlight women's agency in constructing an embodied self, along with the role of hegemonic gender norms that guide women to meet, and literally embody, those norms. We assume women are both subjects and objects of the designing process. "Designing women" refers to women's agency in the process of body/self formation, as well as the ways in which society designs women through hegemonic discourse.

Method

Between 1997 and 1998, we recruited a volunteer sample of women who had undergone elective mammoplasty that was not related to cancer or other medical conditions. We specifically sought women who had undergone breast augmentation, but because of difficulties in recruiting an adequate sample, we included everyone who volunteered whose surgery was elective. We offered a $20 honorarium to encourage participation. Our sample includes 15 women, of whom 12 had breast augmentation, 2 breast reductions, and 1 corrective surgery (augmentation on one breast and reduction of the other). Our sample consisted of 14 white women and 1 African American woman who had breast surgery. The approximate annual family incomes of these women ranged from $10,000 to $105,000 with a mean of $61,181. All but 2 women had some college education, and 2 were pursuing master's degrees. Because our recruitment included posting flyers on the campus of a midsized, Midwestern commuter university, 10 of the women we interviewed were students, 9 of whom held part-time jobs. Three nonstudents worked full-time, 1 worked part-time, and 1 was a homemaker. Their occupations included postal worker, bartender, salesperson, dietician, cosmetologist, secretary, waitress, health care administrator, and teaching assistant. . . .

To enhance the reliability of the data, the first author conducted all of the interviews. They were in-depth and semistructured and lasted approximately two hours. With the written consent of the women in our sample, we tape-recorded all the interviews and then had them transcribed verbatim. We analyzed the data using established principles of analytic induction for the discovery of grounded theory (Charmaz 1983; Miles and Huberman 1984; Strauss and Corbin 1994). . . .

Findings

In the following sections, we first explain the motives the women in our sample expressed for seeking and undergoing elective cosmetic breast surgery.

In those sections, women discuss cosmetic surgery as a solution to a problem, one that opens new opportunities and has a liberating effect on them. Later, we examine the impact that hegemony had on the decisions these women made, as well as some of the sites through which power was exercised over their bodies, even as they believed they were exercising free will. We conclude with a discussion of the ramifications of approaching this issue with the synthetic perspective we advance.

Agents of Beauty: The Motives of Designing Women

The women in our sample all wanted to achieve a level of normalcy, based on their perceptions of who they were as well as what others expected from women in general. Their perceptions came from a variety of sources, including ideals generated by the media and fashion, their own observations of other women, and their own perceptions of men's observations of themselves and other women.

REPRESENTING ONE'S SELF ACCURATELY. In social interactions, individuals are often judged by their appearance, and one's body is an integral component of such assessments. In every social interaction, individuals are looked on, judged, and interacted with on the basis of whether their bodies are young or old; overweight or thin; tall or short; brown, tan, or beige; female or male. The reactions that one receives from others, which are inherently affected by one's embodiment, are crucial factors in the formation of the self. Yet we found that the women in our sample frequently thought of themselves in different terms than those their bodies conveyed to the world. The body and mind are intertwined. When the body does not accurately convey who one believes oneself to be, one option is to readjust one's self-concept to reflect physical reality, giving in to the judgments of others. Another is to exercise power by altering one's body.

As might be expected, each of the women in our sample identified something about her breasts with which she was dissatisfied. But the perception that their breasts belied the self within the body was a primary motive for women's desire to undergo cosmetic surgery. This motive affected women who perceived their breasts as too large, too small, or not appropriately firm and youthful.

Our sample included women who had been pregnant and had breastfed their babies. Pregnancy and breast-feeding gave temporary satisfaction to women who thought their breasts were too small. This satisfaction was later followed by a realization that the biological changes caused by these aspects of motherhood had taken what women perceived to be a negative toll on their breasts. Even those women who were happy with their breasts and their bodies before childbirth found that after giving birth or breast-feeding their children, they were unhappy with the shape, size, or firmness of their breasts. For example, Ann, a 32-year-old white married woman with three children, who had breast augmentation surgery, explained,

> After I had my third son . . . my body was destroyed. I had three C-sections, and I breast-fed all my children. So prior to any of my pregnancies, I was a full 34C. I really loved my body, had no problems with my body ever. After the children, I was very saggy.

Like this woman, most of the women we interviewed talked about their breasts (before surgery) in terms of their being too small, too large, or too saggy. Some were very distressed about their appearance. For example, Beth, a 44-year-old white married mother of four, said, "I was always a flat-chested, redheaded, freckle-faced kid and was teased a lot about being flat. . . . After my children were born and I nursed them, my breasts were saggy nothings and very unappealing to me." Perceptions of physical deformity, combined with a self-concept that did not include physical abnormalities, motivated the women in our sample to seek elective mammoplasty. The reasons they gave for having their bodies surgically altered reflect both agency and an internalization of hegemonic cultural ideals of beauty. Although one's body might not be all one might desire, the post-childbirth body was inevitably described as worse.

The incongruence between body and self-concept was not limited to women who had given birth or breast-fed their children. Age was also a factor. Every woman in our sample had a self-concept or an idealized self that was not represented by her body. Some women thought that because their breasts were too small, they were not treated with the respect normatively accorded adult women. Instead, they were treated like children. For example, Jane, a 21-year-old white woman, explained, "I hated it because I felt like I was getting older mentally and everything else, but I still looked like I was 12 years old." And indeed, that is how she perceived that people treated her. She turned to breast augmentation surgery as a tool that helped her correct the incongruence she felt between who she was and how people treated her. Similarly, women with larger breasts said that people perceived them as older or overweight. For example, Sue, a white mother of three, said that before her surgery, "I had several people say to me, 'Well you're not fat. You just have big boobs. They make you look matronly.'" At 32 years of age, matronly was not the way she thought of herself.

Cosmetic breast surgery was a means of establishing congruency between the body and mind, or developing an embodied self that was comfortable to the women we interviewed. Moreover, by making such bodily changes, the women in our sample perceived that people interacted with them the way they wanted to be treated. Sue, for example, explained that before her surgery, people would stare at or "talk to" her breasts. She said that since her surgery,

> People are paying attention to [me] and not a part of [my] body. They see me for who I am now. I've always been very outgoing. I've always been bubbly. But now, I can relax and be myself and not worry that people don't see that anymore. They see me for who I am, and people do react differently to me.

Women explained that undergoing mammoplasty was important because it prompted people to treat them in the way they perceived themselves. Moreover, they explained that this change alone brought with it greater social opportunities. With more positive reactions from others, their self-confidence was increased, and many said they felt liberated.

INCREASING SOCIAL OPPORTUNITIES. The women we interviewed identified several ways that they thought surgically altering their bodies enhanced their social interactions with others and increased their social opportunities. Because the self is formed in interaction with others (Blumer 1986; Cooley 1902; Mead 1934) and because one's body affects the reactions one receives from others (Grosz 1994; Weiss 1999), it seems logical that changing one's body to fit hegemonic ideals of attractiveness would improve one's social opportunities.

Some women recognized early in their lives that they were ignored by men while their friends received more attention. Interestingly, the women we talked with did not have mammoplasty because they wanted to date or become romantically or sexually involved with more men. Instead, they wanted their bodies to represent them as attractive women. . . .

Taking control of the way one is seen is a way of exercising power in a heterosexist and ageist society. Mammoplasty made it possible for women to project a desired image, achieve greater comfort in sexual situations, command greater respect, and compete in a job market that favors youth. Having others interact with them as the people they believed themselves to be was a motivator for most of the women we interviewed. Jane emphasized, "I feel more confident in my job so I'm able to present what I'm selling better."

By accepting the hegemonic culture, the women we interviewed believed they had learned the rules of the game and thus how to compete and achieve the social opportunities and rewards they desired. Moreover, they looked on cosmetic surgery as a logical technology implemented to achieve rewards that every woman wants. All of the women we interviewed talked about cosmetic surgery as a normal procedure that nearly all women would choose if they had the means to do so. Every one of them explained that all women are dissatisfied with their bodies and that given the opportunity, almost all would change something. For example, Tara, a 27-year-old, white mother of one, said,

> No woman is totally happy with her body. You know, they'll say, oh, "I'm in great shape," but then you'll see them and they're, you know, "Look at this," or "Look at this." Nobody is happy with their body. Or if they are, they're a jerk. . . . So it's just, I think if a guy was like, "Here, I'll give you the money, go get your boobs done," you know, no strings or anything like that, just, "If I give it to you, would you do it?" I think most women would do it.

For the women we interviewed, cosmetic surgery was just another part of the technologies of beauty available to women, on a continuum with makeup, hair color, diet, exercise, or the use of special bras. The main difference between mammoplasty and using clothing or bras to disguise or enhance breasts was that breast surgery was a more permanent choice in the exercise of power. This relative permanence gave women more fashion options and greater control over their choices of clothing. In short, cosmetic surgery was a way of exercising power, controlling their bodies, and normalizing the embodied self within a disciplining beauty regime that is based on compulsory heterosexuality. Although their beauty regimens were more extreme than those of women who have the means yet do not opt for cosmetic surgery, the point here is that the women in our sample experienced breast surgery as liberating rather than oppressive. We believe that this is likely due to a greater level of internalization of standards of hegemonic beauty, which permitted them to overlook the potential risks.

I'M WORTH IT. Despite the distress that many women expressed about their breasts, all of them emphasized that they did not feel coerced or as if they had to have surgery. Instead, most talked about how having mammoplasty was something nice they could do for themselves. For example, Ann said,

> I find that these [types of surgery] are things that suburban mothers are having done after their children. Kind of a treat to themselves. I figure I went through all that to have these kids, I could put myself back together.

Her view reflected that of the other women—that cosmetic surgery is a beauty secret employed by women with the means to pay for it. Like a day at the spa or the beauty parlor, women seek cosmetic surgery not because someone pressures them to do so but because they are worth it.

In all but one interview, participants repeatedly emphasized that no one coerced, cajoled, or otherwise forced them to have cosmetic surgery. Indeed, in most cases, women's family members and partners tried to convince them not to have surgery. In this way, women asserted that they owned and controlled their bodies. They often expressed their desire to have surgery in terms of self-improvement. For example, Sue said, "I did it for me, because I wanted to feel better about myself." And Jane explained, "I wanted to do it because I wanted the self-confidence. I wanted to be able to walk into a room and feel like I didn't have to hide myself."

The women we interviewed framed cosmetic surgery in the feminist discourse of choice. They expressed strong beliefs that no one had the right to judge them for having altered their bodies, just as no one had the right to pressure them into having surgery. For example, Kelly, a 22-year-old, white, single, childless woman who had augmentation surgery said, "[This is] my body, and wanting to get it done has nothing to do with anyone else. . . . This is for me, to feel better about myself."

The women we interviewed thought of cosmetic surgery as a normal part of the culture and technology of beauty in the United States. All but one woman were pleased with the results of their mammoplasties, and all of them said they felt more confident and better about themselves as a result. All but one said they made their decision to have surgery without pressure from any other person or source. The primary motivation for seeking breast augmentation was their prior sense of disembodying femininity. That is, they perceived that before having surgery, they did not present a desirable feminine self, nor did they experience themselves as desirable women. Cosmetic surgery, then, was a tool for creating the self by altering the body in an effort to enhance existing social opportunities or create new ones. What the women in our sample failed to recognize, however, was the way that their personal exercise of power reified the hegemonic culture, including compulsory heterosexuality as well as inequalities based on race, social class, and age.

Within a hegemonic culture in which heterosexuality is compulsory, women's breasts are interpreted as signifiers of who they are as people. Accordingly, pregnancy, childbirth, and breast-feeding are cultural indicators of the achievement of womanhood. Yet, as women pass these mileposts in life, or as they simply age, their bodies may lose the ability to convey youthful femininity, as signified by firm breasts. Thus, as women achieve adulthood, they lose an important aspect of self within a heterosexist society. In this way, society puts reproductive women in a no-win situation in which they can be perceived as perpetually youthful and sexual or in which they can achieve womanhood but risk no longer being perceived as young, sexual, or vital. For many of the women we interviewed, mammoplasty allowed them to regain a sexually vital image after achieving motherhood and mature womanhood or after reaching middle age. For women who thought their breasts were too small, breast augmentation surgery was used as a tool to help them achieve adulthood, just as women who thought their breasts were too large used breast reduction surgery so that their breasts would convey a more youthful image.

Clearly, women exercised agency in deciding to undergo surgery, particularly in the face of opposition from others. The decision, however, to undergo the surgery reified existing hegemonic norms regarding beauty and femininity and has unintended consequences for all women. First, the embodied self these women chose to construct was based on a norm that is inherently ageist. Although some women chose reduction and some chose augmentation, all were seeking a look that signified youthful sexual vitality. The women in our sample sought to distance themselves from a postreproductive look as is suggested by having saggy breasts or an overall matronly look. Second, by literally constructing the feminine self through the body, they contributed to the process of judging women on the basis of their bodies and appearance rather than on performance. And finally, in claiming that they were worth it, they abstracted themselves from the cultural context in which femininity is constructed. In doing so, they reified existing inequalities among women.

The practice of consmetic surgery perpetuates racism and classism because only a minority—generally white, economically privileged women—have the means to have surgery and because the hegemonic heterosexist ideal of feminine beauty is essentially a white standard. That surgery is a treat for suburban mothers unintentionally implies that all women should look like (or want to look like) white suburbanites and that their urban and rural counterparts are not worth it. Still, several questions remain: Where did these women get their ideas of what their breasts should look like? What factors influenced them in their desire for cosmetic surgery? Where did they get the idea to have mammoplasty to achieve the bodies they desired? And what factors influenced them as they made their decisions to have the surgery done?

Beauty Objects: The Hegemony of Beauty and the Decision to Undergo Elective Mammoplasty

Listening to the motives women gave for undergoing elective mammoplasty, it appears that surgery had the potential to ease distress they felt about their bodies, to help them overcome insecurities, make them feel more attractive and confident, and give them greater social opportunities. Yet it is important to recall that anyone who makes any bodily alteration—whether wearing makeup, coloring hair, dieting, exercising, getting pierced, getting a tattoo, or having cosmetic surgery—is invariably influenced by the wider society in which one lives. In this section, we identify the social factors that the women we interviewed discussed as having had an influence on their ideas about beauty and their decision to have surgery.

THE MEDIA. Women in the United States are bombarded by images of what it means to be beautiful and desirable. Perhaps the most egregious of the messages women receive about the inadequacy of their own bodies are those portrayed in women's magazines, which are filled with waifishly thin models and buxom babes who know exactly what "your man" wants. Capitalism and the modern media are predicated on the idea that sex sells, but the underlying current is an effort to create anxiety and insecurity among women who otherwise might not realize they have something to worry about (Wolf 1991). The influence of the media was apparent in the narratives of the women we interviewed. For example, Abbey, a 32-year-old, white woman who had breast augmentation surgery, explained how women's magazines had affected her consciousness about her body. She said,

> I do remember when I had made the decision to have the implants, I didn't want them real big and I wanted them to look like they were mine. Like this is what I grew. I remember seeing a model in *Cosmopolitan*, and her breasts weren't very big, but she had some. And I thought, "That's what I want mine to look like."

Referring back to *Cosmopolitan* magazine, she later added, "I'm sure even subconsciously, even if I didn't realize it, yea, it had a big influence on my decision to have bigger breasts."

By appealing to media-induced anxieties, magazines sell themselves while vendors hawk their products through advertisements and articles geared toward teaching women how to improve their looks, their skills as lovers, and ultimately how to save their sexual desirability. Without toning, shaping, working out, dieting, making up, and ultimately going under the knife, women are led to believe that they will end up ugly, undesirable, asexual, and alone. It is for this reason that designing women use all the resources they can summon to fashion and embody what they perceive to be the ultimate expression of feminine beauty.

The print media are only one source of women's anxieties. Perhaps more encompassing is the impact that movies and television programs have on women's ideas of the social adequacy of their bodies and ultimately of their selves. Although the print media often say quite directly that women must do something (e.g., exercise) or purchase a certain product (e.g., perfume or diet aids) to avoid something terrible happening to them (e.g., ending up alone and unloved), the messages of movies and television are more subtle. Those messages take their effect when women consciously or unconsciously compare their own bodies to those of movie and television stars and then seek ways to approximate those bodies (see Mulvey 1989).

As part of our interview, we asked women to describe what they thought to be the body of the ideal woman. Interestingly, almost all began with an abstract physical description, such as "tall, thin, not big chested" or, invoking a reproductive norm, "curvy, vivacious, [the] fertile look." But before they finished the abstract description, almost every woman gave a specific example from the media of the ideal woman's body. Lisa said, "She [the ideal woman] has big breasts, tiny waist, and fairly thin hips. A Barbie Doll or a Pam Anderson." And Abbey began with a concrete example and moved to an abstract description based on that ideal. She said, "What I tend to think of is what everyone else does: Christie Brinkley. You know, the blonde, the tanned skin, the perfect white teeth." Ideals included Helen Hunt, Meryl Streep, and Tyra Banks, who are tall and thin with smaller breasts, and Sophia Loren, Ann Margaret, and Marilyn Monroe, who have larger breasts and portray a curvy and vivacious image. Among our sample, heavier women tended to think the curvy, voluptuous Marilyn Monroe look approximated the ideal, while thinner women preferred the Helen Hunt look. Each idealized an image she thought she could approximate by drawing on medical technology. . . .

FASHION. With apparel, humans cover their bodies, protect themselves from the environment, and communicate important information about status and self. But the fashion industry, like the media, is geared toward making profits. To do so, it is oriented toward what it perceives as normal-sized humans so that the mass production of clothing will result in the maximum number of sales. For women, the norm of fashion is thin and proportionate. Rather than the industry increasing the availability of larger sizes or clothing where the top is smaller or larger than the bottom, women struggle to meet the ideal to enhance the choices available to them even when they recognize the tyranny of fashion. Chris expressed the issue succinctly when she said, "The average size of a model is like a 2 or a 4. The average size of a regular woman is like a 14. What's up with that?"

Fashions are used to create a certain look or image. Some fashions are oriented toward emphasizing the abdomen, breasts, and buttocks for a sensual feminine look. Others streamline the body into an hourglass shape, for a professional, businesslike appearance. Whatever the look women seek, clothing is mass-produced to fit the idealized thin and proportionate body. Women who are overweight, tall, big boned, or whose hips are wider or narrower than their bust sizes often find it difficult to dress fashionably or even to find clothing that fits properly. It is impossible for certain women to conform to the fashion industry's standards of feminine beauty unless they have the resources to have their clothing personally tailored for them. And in not being able to fit, many women blame themselves for not being able to discipline their bodies. The fashion industry dictates available clothing, and when women fail to meet the ideal, it exercises the power to (re)create women's bodies.

Most of the women we interviewed talked about how their too small or too large breasts made it impossible to wear certain styles. For example, Kelly said,

> I was a B before, and a lot of dresses didn't fit. Tank tops were always too low, and I had to get real small sizes, and they didn't fit the proportions of my body. So I wanted more [breast size] for dressing. . . . [Before surgery] it was just finding a bra that was padded. Always trying not to get low low cut shirts because, you know, when you bend over you could see my belly button.

Sue, whose skirts and slacks were size 7 and who had breast reduction surgery said, "[Before surgery] I couldn't buy dresses. I would have to get a [size] 12 dress just to get it to button." Chris recognized the power of the fashion industry when she said, "They select that few 5 percent of the population that are anorexic [whom] they're going to attend to." Still, she said she felt better being able to buy clothing off the rack since having her breast reduction surgery. . . .

OTHER WOMEN: THE FEMALE GAZE AND REGIME OF BEAUTY. Our respondents believed that women in general have a shared beauty culture, or a sense of a generalized gaze. Speaking about themselves, they said that they constantly compared their own bodies and appearance to that of other women. This comparison was evident in the influence the media had on them and carried over into their everyday lives. For example, Tara said,

> When you think about when you go to the grocery store, if you see a woman walking down the aisle, a voluptuous figure, you notice it. And it's just, you know, there was always a kind of envy. It was like, gosh, I mean, to have a build like that. . . . Of course, you envy, I mean every time you see somebody that you think is prettier than you or having a better body or anything, of course you're envious. . . . I always look at other women.

In addition to constant comparison to other women, the participants in our study explained that an important part of feminine culture is the sharing of beauty tips, including information about makeup, diet, exercise, weight loss products, undergarments, and—more recently—cosmetic surgery. For them, part of being a woman and belonging to feminine culture was knowing and being willing to share the techniques of beauty.

For the women we interviewed, beauty was an element of feminine power. By sharing beauty tips, women believed they empowered one another. Although this practice may empower individual women, it also standardizes ideals of beauty while constantly raising the bar of beauty. In this way, the practice of beauty power is similar to that exercised by the media and fashion industry. Women must become ever thinner; become more muscular; have longer, fuller lashes; permanently avoid becoming gray; have less and less body hair; and now have breasts that meet an increasingly unrealistic ideal. The power regime (Foucault 1979) through which beauty is constructed and deployed is internalized by women. Those who achieve it feel more confident—more powerful. At the same time, they are the women most subjugated by the regime of beauty, which is, ironically, enforced by the totalizing, disciplining gaze of other women less than that of the men in their lives.

With one exception, all of the women we interviewed insisted that they were not influenced by husbands or boyfriends to have surgery on their breasts. In most instances, boyfriends and husbands opposed their partners' decisions. . . .

Men's attitudes stood in stark comparison to the interactions the participants in our study had with other women in their lives. Although many had thought about having breast surgery before actually seeking it, knowing someone who actually had surgery, or was about to do so, made mammoplasty seem less radical and more like a reasonable solution to a problem over which they had only temporary control (e.g., with padded bras and Wonderbras). For example, Kelly said,

> Probably about a year [ago], we all went out . . . and we had started talking about it [getting implants] then. And she [a friend who had surgery before I did] was more serious on actually doing it than I was. I had been interested in it but just felt it was more out of my reach, I guess. . . . I really didn't know anything about it. So then a couple of months later . . . she had a consultation . . . and started to proceed with what she was going to do. So that's when I started getting books at the library . . . checking out doctors . . . I saw her the day that she had it done and . . . when she came back to work, and I was like, you know, "Oh, how did it go?" . . . So I knew every detail from her and that really influenced me. . . . Because she did it, that made me realize that, hey . . . it's in reach.

Every one of the women in our sample knew at least one other woman who had undergone some form of elective cosmetic surgery, most often mammoplasty. Although they had thought about doing something to correct their breasts, all of them identified their immersion in a culture of beauty and involvement in a network of women whose beauty practices included cosmetic surgery as the most significant influence on their decision to go forward with surgery. Once their minds were made up, the next step was to find a surgeon and decide what their breasts would look like.

MEDICINE AS RESOURCE AND OPPRESSOR. Most of the women we talked with made their decisions to have surgery and found their surgeons over time periods ranging from a few days to more than a year. Those who took longer to decide on a doctor tended to consult with more surgeons and to do more research, including library work and checking on the medical backgrounds, certifications, and work of the physicians they were considering. Those who took the least time acted almost impulsively, choosing a doctor who offered a good deal or credit or whom a friend had used.

Just as there were differences in the amount of information women sought before selecting a surgeon, there were differences in the agency women exercised in their choice of breasts. Some women, such as those previously described, cut out photographs and gave specific instructions to their doctors about how they wanted to look after surgery. Others depended on their surgeons to instruct them on the type and size breasts that would suit them best. Most often, breasts were decided on in consultation between physician and patient. Doctors employed a variety of techniques to help their patients choose breasts, including computer simulation and having women bring in larger size bras and clothing to be worn with prostheses. Although the women we interviewed knew of doctors who would do whatever women wanted, they said that their own doctors placed limits on what they were willing to do. Kelly summarized the use of technology and the exercise of power between patient and doctor. She said,

> You went in and the nurse took a picture of you and then put it in the computer and said that for your weight and the width of your shoulders . . . this is what I would recommend. And he draws it up on the computer . . . and says, "What do you think about that? What are your expectations?" . . . So I said, "I want to be a C . . . no possibility of being a D . . . I didn't want to be that big. I wanted to look right." He said, "OK," went into details medically, and that was . . . basically it with the size. . . . He will do bigger . . . [but] he won't do anything that looks outrageous, just because of his name.

As this woman's narrative indicates, medicine can be a resource in constructing the body and self, at the same time that its practitioners dictate the limits of possibility. Therefore, in the commodification of women's bodies, postsurgical breasts are a marketing tool for surgeons.

THE MALE GAZE AND THE GENERALIZED GAZE. The women in our sample appeared to have an internalized idea of what men want or expect in terms of beauty. Even when their ideas were not reflected in the desires of the actual men in their own lives—that is, their own boyfriends or husbands thought they looked fine without surgery or opposed the surgery altogether—they still sought mammoplasty so that they could meet a generalized, perceived male gaze.

Just as women look at and compare themselves to one another, the women we interviewed were aware of men watching other women. They perceived this male gaze as what men desire in women. Perhaps because of the subject matter of our interview, none of the women in our sample talked about what men wanted in women in terms of personality traits or other attributes. Instead, they observed men gazing on other women, noted that men were not looking at them, and deduced—based on media portrayals and common cultural knowledge—what men want. For example, Abbey talked about how men ignored her before she had breast augmentation surgery. She said,

> I think down at the beach, the men . . . spent most of their day . . . looking at the girls . . . looking at the actual breasts. . . . [I remember] being at the beach and . . . talking to a guy one time and he was talking about his ex-girlfriend. . . . [He said,] "She thought she looked so good. She didn't have any tits." And I thought, "I didn't either."

Rather than seeking to please a particular man, however, the women we talked with generalized from specific interactions, such as those described here, to perceptions of what all men want. Based on a sense of a generalized other (Mead 1934), women attempted to meet a generalized gaze that may be established by men but that is internalized by all women and exercised by women on themselves and other women. Thus, the hegemony of beauty is exercised less in one-on-one interactions wherein a significant other expresses dissatisfaction with a specific woman's beauty than with women's internalization of the generalized other, communicated through the hegemonic gaze.

The hegemonic gaze is an accepted standard of beauty—a sense that individual women have that everyone is looking at them—and the discomfort women feel if they fail to meet this standard of beauty. Having an unruly body is similar to breaking a social norm, with the social sanctions that normally apply to other forms of deviance. Among the women we interviewed, there was a sense that a beautiful body was a proportionate body and that successful breast surgery would look natural or normal. In choosing to have surgery, the women in our sample exercised power over their own bodies. In meeting the ideals of the hegemonic gaze, they could finally relax about their unruly breasts and feel good about themselves. In short, they were liberated from the gaze because they conformed to it, just as deviants are liberated from the sanctions of deviance when they conform to societal expectations. In this way, cosmetic surgery is an expression of the totalization of power rather than a means of liberation. Yet ironically, it is at this point that women feel liberated.

Conclusion

This study has contributed to existing research that examines how women are both objectified by and complicitous in the construction and proliferation of hegemonic gender. Our findings suggest that neither the false consciousness nor free will approach is wrong but that both are incomplete (Foucault 1979). Specifically, our research suggests that it is essential for gender scholars to consider both the agency of those being studied and the ways the larger society compels individuals to meet a social standard and then rewards them for doing so.

Women electing cosmetic mammoplasty exercise agency, but they do so within the confines of hegemonic gender norms. Heterosexual standards of feminine beauty may be created by men, and within a heterosexist, ageist, and racist society, it is primarily socially privileged men who exercise the power to mete out interpersonal and institutional rewards for conformity, including social and economic benefits. Nonetheless, women are complicitous in disciplining themselves and one another. It appears that men exercise power interpersonally, by virtue of the visual attentions they devote to women deemed physically attractive. Interpersonal interactions are one site among many where the power of the male gaze is exercised. Furthermore, men exercise power institutionally, through medicine, the fashion industry, the media, and the workplace. And because the standards of the male gaze are recognized and internalized by many women, men are capable of exercising an insidious form of power over heterosexual women, whether they seek to conform to or resist hegemonic standards of beauty.

Despite the pervasiveness of men's power, women also exercise power. Individual women may choose to resist or rebel against hegemonic standards of feminine beauty, but they are likely to risk discrimination in institutional settings, in large part because they do not fit with the dominant culture. We believe that this is because women's power is primarily limited to personal agency and interpersonal interactions. Specifically, in our study, women exercised considerable power in disciplining one another's embodiment. We find it significant, despite the limitations of our sample, that every one of the women we interviewed knew at least one other woman who had undergone cosmetic breast surgery. It appears that among middle-class, heterosexual women, cosmetic surgery has become an increasingly accepted and expected beauty technique. In this way, women are "token torturers" (Daly 1978) who play a pivotal, though often unrecognized, role in disciplining one another. To the extent that these women seek one another's approval, as well as the attentions of men, they internalize the standard and are led to willing compliance. And it is at the point of this compliance that the torture stops and rewards are achieved, leaving women feeling liberated and empowered at the same time that they embody and thus reify the hegemonic standards.

Ultimately, what our research shows is that the subject-object dualism that characterizes the free will (subject) and false consciousness (object) approaches is limited in conceptualizing the multifarious nature of the beauty regime. This is an issue of language. We know that the language we currently have is limited—women are neither simply subjects nor simply objects in the beauty regime but are both/neither. Nevertheless, the language still does not exist to allow us to transcend the dualism. But by investigating the exercise of power, rather than assuming it to be a zero-sum game, and by investigating the interpersonal, cultural, and institutional sites where it is exercised, researchers and theorists are likely to come to a more complete and dynamic understanding of the social world.

Notes

AUTHORS' NOTE: We are equal coauthors. An earlier version of this article was presented at the annual meetings of the Women's Studies Network (UK) Association International Conference, hosted by the Leisure and Sport Research Unit, Cheltenham and Gloucester College of Higher Education, Cheltenham, England, 12–14 July 2001. Research for this article was funded, in part, by a Research Initiative Grant and a Research on Women Grant from the Office of the Vice President for Research and Development at the University of Louisville. The authors wish to thank Dr. James K. Beggan, Department of Psychology, University of Louisville, for his assistance with this project and are grateful for the insightful comments of three anonymous reviewers.

1. For example, French feminist performance artist Orlan contests hegemonic constructions of femininity by going through a series of cosmetic surgeries in which she literally inscribes her body with European icons of beauty. Through this performance, Orlan demonstrates the ugliness of gender hegemony.

References

Adams, A. 1997. Molding women's bodies: The surgeon as sculptor. In *Bodily Discursions: Genders, Representations, and Technologies*, edited by D. Wilson and C. Laennec. Albany: State University of New York Press.

Argyle, M. 1983. *The Psychology of Interpersonal Behavior*. 4th ed. Harmondsworth, London: Penguin.

Bartky, S. 1997. Foucault, femininity, and the modernization of patriarchal power. In *Writing on the Body: Female Embodiment and Feminist Theory*, edited by K. Conboy, N. Medina, and S. Stanbury. New York: Columbia University Press.

Bhaba, H. 1995. Are you a man or a mouse? In *Constructing Masculinity*, edited by M. Berger, B. Wells, and S. Watson. New York: Routledge.

Blumer, H. 1986. *Symbolic Interactionism: Perspective and Method*. Berkeley, CA: University of California Press.

Bordo, S. 1993. *Unbearable Weight: Feminism, Western Culture, and the Body*. Los Angeles: University of California Press.

———. 1997. The body and the reproduction of femininity. In *Writing on the Body: Female Embodiment and Feminist Theory*, edited by K. Conboy, N. Medina, and S. Stanbury. New York: Columbia University Press.

Brush, P. 1998. Metaphors of inscription: Discipline, plasticity, and the rhetoric of choice. *Feminist Review* 58:22–44.

Chandler, D. 2000. Notes on "the gaze." Retrieved from http://www.aber.ac.uk/media/Documents/gaze/gaze09.html.

Chapkis, W. 1986. *Beauty Secrets: Women and the Politics of Appearance.* Boston: South End.

Charmaz, K. 1983. The grounded theory method: An explication and interpretation. In *Contemporary Field Research: A Collection of Readings*, edited by R. Emerson. Prospect Heights, IL: Waveland.

Cheng, P. 1996. Mattering. *Diacritics* 26(1):108–39.

Cooley, C. 1902. *Human Nature and Social Order.* New York: Scribner.

Culbertson, P. 1999. Designing men: Reading the male body as text. *Textual Reasoning.* Retrieved from http://www.bu/mzank/Textual_Reasoning/tr-arthive/tr7.html/Culbertson1.html.

Daly, M. 1978. *Gyn/ecology: The Metaethics of Radical Feminism.* Boston: Beacon.

Davis, K. 1995. *Reshaping the Female Body: The Dilemma of Cosmetic Surgery.* New York: Routledge.

Dreyfus, H., and P. Rabinow. 1982. *Michel Foucault: Beyond Structuralism and Hermeneutics.* Chicago: Chicago University Press.

Ender, E. 1999. Speculating carnally or, some reflections on the modernist body. *Yale Journal of Criticism* 12(1):113–30.

Fallon, A. 1990. Culture in the mirror: Sociocultural determinants of body image. In *Body Images: Development, Deviance, and Change*, edited by T. Cash and T. Pruzinsky. New York: Guilford.

Foucault, M. 1973. *The Birth of the Clinic.* New York: Pantheon.

———. 1978. *History of Sexuality: An Introduction.* Vol. 1. New York: Pantheon.

———. 1979. *Discipline and Punish: The Birth of the Prison.* New York: Vintage.

———. 1980. Body/power. In *Power/knowledge*, edited by C. Gordon. New York: Pantheon.

Gilman, S. 1999. *Making the Body Beautiful: A Cultural History of Aesthetic Surgery.* Princeton, NJ: Princeton University Press.

Gramsci, A. 1971. *Prison Notebooks.* New York: International.

Grosz, E. 1994. *Volatile Bodies: Toward a Corporeal Feminism.* Bloomington: Indiana University Press.

Kaw, E. 1998. Medicalization of racial features: Asian-American women and cosmetic surgery. In *The Politics of Women's Bodies: Sexuality, Appearance, and Behavior*, edited by R. Weitz. New York: Oxford University Press.

Mead, G. H. 1934. *Mind, Self, and Society*, Vol. 1, edited by C. W. Morris. Chicago: University of Chicago Press.

Miles, M., and M. Huberman. 1984. *Qualitative Data Analysis: A Sourcebook of New Methods.* Beverly Hills, CA: Sage.

Morgan, K. 1991. Women and the knife: Cosmetic surgery and the colonization of women's bodies. *Hypatia* 6(3):25–33.

Mulvey, L. 1989. *Visual Pleasures and Narrative Cinema.* Bloomington: Indianapolis University Press.

Padmore, C. 1998. Significant flesh: Cosmetic surgery, physiognomy, and the erasure of visual difference(s). *Lateral: A Journal of Textual and Cultural Studies.* Retrieved from http://www.latrobe.edu.au/www/english/lateral/simple_cp1.htm:1–22.

Pratt, M. 1992. *Imperial Eyes: Travel Writing and Transculturation.* New York: Routledge.

Ransom, J. 1997. *Foucault's Discipline: The Politics of Subjectivity*. Durham, NC: Duke University Press.

Saco, D. 1994. Feminist film criticism: "The piano" and the female gaze. Retrieved from http://www.gate.net/'dsaco/Female_Gaze.htm.

Sawicki, J. 1991. *Disciplining Foucault: Feminism, Power, and the Body*. New York: Routledge.

Strauss, A., and J. Corbin. 1994. Grounded theory methodology: An overview. In *Handbook of Qualitative Research*, edited by N. Denzin and Y. Lincoln. Thousand Oaks, CA: Sage.

Weiss, G. 1999. *Body Images: Embodiment as Intercorporeality*. New York: Routledge.

Wijsbek, H. 2000. The pursuit of beauty: The enforcement of aesthetics or a freely adopted lifestyle? *Journal of Medical Ethics* 26(6):454–58.

Winkler, M. 1994. Model women. In *The Good Body: Ascentism in Contemporary Culture*, edited by M. Winkler and L. Cole. New Haven, CT: Yale University Press.

Wolf, N. 1991. *The Beauty Myth: How Images of Beauty Are Used Against Women*. New York: Anchor Books Doubleday.

14

Women and Their Hair

Seeking Power through Resistance and Accommodation

ROSE WEITZ

Like the articles by Iris Marion Young and by Patricia Gagné and Deanna McGaughey, "Women and Their Hair: Seeking Power through Resistance and Accommodation" addresses the interplay between constraint and agency in women's decisions about and experiences with their bodies. As with breasts, hair plays an especially important role in contemporary Americans' assessments of women's attractiveness. In this article, Rose Weitz shows how women can consciously seek power (exercising agency) through conforming *to social norms regarding women's hair (an example of constraint). For example, women who work as waitresses will often dye their hair blonde to get bigger tips. Conversely, Weitz shows how women can also seek power by* resisting *those same norms, as, for example, when women trial lawyers cut their hair shorter to be taken more seriously by jurors.*

Weitz uses her research not only to explore women's relationship to their hair but also to explore larger issues of resistance and accommodation. Building on the work of previous scholars, Weitz offers a more explicit (and stringent) definition of resistance. At the core of this definition are challenges to cultural ideologies that support structures of subordination. She also explores how resistance and accommodation are interwoven in women's everyday bodily experiences. Finally, she analyzes the price women pay for conforming to, as well as resisting, the different kinds of power women gain through these two different strategies, and the limits embedded in the types of power these strategies offer.

Hairstyles serve as important cultural artifacts, because they are simultaneously public (visible to everyone), personal (biologically linked to the body), and highly malleable to suit cultural and personal preferences (Firth 1973; Synott 1987). In this article, I argue that women's hair is central to their social position.[1] I explore how women use their hair to try to gain some power and analyze the benefits and limitations of their strategies. More broadly, I use these data to explore how accommodation and resistance lie buried in everyday activities, how they are often interwoven, and why resistance strategies based on the body have limited utility (Dellinger and Williams 1997; Elowe MacLeod 1991). Finally, I use these data to suggest the importance of defining resistance as actions that reject subordination by challenging the ideologies that support subordination.

Introduction

Power refers to the ability to obtain desired goals through controlling or influencing others. . . . The body is [an important] site for struggles over power. . . . As Michel Foucault (1979, 1980) describes, to carry out the tasks of modern economic and social life, societies require "docile bodies," such as regimented soldiers, factory workers who perform their tasks mechanically, and students who sit quietly. To create such bodies, "disciplinary practices" have evolved through which individuals both internalize and act on the ideologies that underlie their own subordination. In turn, these disciplinary practices have made the body a site for power struggles and, potentially, for resistance, as individual choices about the body become laden with political meanings. . . . [In this article, I] study hair as a means of exploring the ordinary ways in which women struggle daily with cultural ideas about the female body. . . . By describing the strategies women develop to seek power using their hair, I will show that women are neither "docile bodies" nor free agents, but rather combine accommodation and resistance as they actively grapple with cultural expectations and social structures. . . .

Defining Resistance and Accommodation

To date, the term *resistance* remains loosely defined, allowing some scholars to see it almost everywhere and others, almost nowhere. One way that the latter group limits their vision of resistance is by defining actions as resistance only if they are effective. Such a definition seems far too narrow, however, for even failed revolutions would not qualify. Moreover, as Stombler and Padavic (1997) suggest, even small acts with no obvious effects on the broader system may affect individuals and pave the way for later social change. . . .

Another possibility is to define an action as resistance if its intent is to reject subordination, regardless of either its effectiveness or the extent to which it also supports subordination (Stombler and Padavic 1997). . . . Yet individuals' stated intentions often bear little relationship to the nature of their actions, because individuals often either cannot or will not articulate their motives; Black slaves, for example, routinely denied (for obvious reasons) that their spirituals asking God for freedom reflected anything other than religious longings. . . . At any rate, intent alone seems a weak measure of resistance: By this measure, for example, women who wear "sexy" clothing to gain power in relationships with men are engaging in resistance against male domination, even though their actions reinforce sexist ideologies and foment competition between women.

The problems with using either effectiveness or intent as definitions of resistance leave us no choice but to try to assess the nature of the act itself. Scott (1990) suggests defining resistance simply as actions that "reject subordination" (with subordination defined as any ideas, practices, and systems that devalue one social group relative to another and place the first group under the domination of the second). For example, low-paid workers who pilfer goods from their factories to sell on the black market fit this definition of resistance because they reject a system that considers their work worthy of only minimal financial compensation and that denies them control over the products of their labor.

When factory workers pilfer, however, their actions and motives remain largely invisible both to their fellow workers and to factory management. As a result, while pilfering benefits individual workers, it neither challenges the ideological basis of the system of subordination nor offers the potential to unite workers as a group in a movement for social change. Moreover, because factory owners recognize that pilfering goes on, interpret it as an indication of workers' low moral values, and use it as an argument for keeping wages low (to counterbalance financial losses caused by employee theft), pilfering unintentionally bolsters the system that keeps workers undervalued and underpaid.

This example suggests the dangers of defining resistance too broadly. In this article, I use examples from women's hair management strategies to suggest that we need to more narrowly define resistance as actions that not only reject subordination but do so *by challenging the ideologies that support that subordination.* For example, factory workers' collective efforts to raise wages through union activity challenge the ideological basis of class subordination by arguing that factory workers have as much right as factory managers and owners to a decent wage. Similarly, and as I will show, some women consciously adopt hairstyles (such as short "butch" cuts or dreadlocks) in part to challenge the ideology that women's worth depends on their attractiveness to men and that women's attractiveness depends on looking as Euro-American as possible. Like slaves' rebellious songs, women's rebellious hairstyles can allow them to distance themselves from the system that would subordinate them, to express their dissatisfaction, to identify like-minded others, and to challenge others to think about their own actions and beliefs. Thus these everyday, apparently trivial, individual acts of resistance offer the potential to spark social change and, in the long run, to shift the balance of power between social groups. . . . By extension, *accommodation* refers to actions that accept subordination, by either adopting or simply not challenging the ideologies that support subordination. . . .

Methods

This paper is based on interviews collected between 1998 and 2001 with 44 women, all but five of whom live in Arizona. Respondents were obtained primarily through word of mouth. To avoid biasing the sample toward women who were unusually invested in their hair, I asked for referrals to women who "like to talk in general and are willing to talk about their hair." In addition, in three cases, I obtained respondents by approaching women in public places who had specific, unusual characteristics: a store clerk whose hair had the same simple style but a different color each time I saw her, a middle aged woman with a wild mass of shoulder-length graying curls, and a woman with an American accent wearing full Moslem garb including face veil. Because the sample is nonrandom, it is appropriate for exploring the range of attitudes among American women but not for calculating the proportion who hold such attitudes.

Although nonrandom, the sample is highly diverse. Respondents ranged in age from 22 to 83. Twenty-nine were Anglo, eight Mexican-American, four African-American, two Asian, and one half-Chicana and half-Anglo. Twenty-two were raised Protestant, 17 Catholic, one Jewish, and one Moslem; the remaining three were not raised in a religion. Twenty-one of the women are single, 14 are married, 7 are divorced, and 2 are widowed. Four of the 37 describe themselves as lesbian, the rest as heterosexual. As is true nationally (U.S. Department of Commerce 1998), the employed women in the sample are almost equally divided between those who hold professional/ managerial jobs (n = 10) and those who do not (n = 11). Five women are retired, four are housewives, and fourteen are students (almost all of whom work part-time). The women in the sample disproportionately are middle class: 46 percent of those over age 25 hold college degrees, compared to 21 percent of similar-age U.S. women (Costello et al. 1998). However, 57 percent of the women come from working-class backgrounds (i.e., their mothers did not attend college and their fathers held nonprofessional jobs). . . .

Findings

In this section, I will describe the ways women use their hair to seek power in both their personal and professional lives. Analysis of the data revealed two strategies women used to accomplish this task: traditional strategies that emphasize accommodation to mainstream norms for female attractiveness and nontraditional strategies that emphasize resistance to those norms. I begin this discussion with traditional strategies (since they create the context that gives meaning to nontraditional strategies), and end the section with a brief discussion of why some women do not link their hair to power.

Seeking Power through Traditional Strategies

The most common way women use their hair to seek power is through strategies that de-emphasize resistance and instead emphasize accommodation to mainstream ideas about attractiveness. . . . For purposes of convenience, I will refer to those who meet these norms as "conventionally attractive."

There is widespread agreement that conventionally attractive hair gives women power, or at least makes them feel powerful—a point made by many women in this study.[2] . . . Results from numerous research studies (summarized in Jackson 1992 and Sullivan 2001) suggest that conventional attractiveness is in fact a realistic route to power for women, in both intimate relationships and careers. Attractive women are less lonely, more popular, and more sexually experienced, both more likely to marry and more likely to marry men of higher socioeconomic status. Compared to similarly qualified unattractive women, conventionally attractive women are more often hired, more often promoted, and paid higher salaries.

The following story, told by Cecilia, a twenty-something student, demonstrates the conscious and rational decision-making process women may use to get power through conventional attractiveness:

> I can think of an occasion where I changed my hair while I was dating this guy. I had this feeling that he was losing attraction for me and I'd just been feeling the need to do something to my appearance. And my hair is always the easiest way to go. It's too expensive to buy a new wardrobe. There's nothing you can do about your face. So your hair, you can go and have something radically done to it and you'll look like a different person. At least that's the way I see it.
>
> So I remember I was dating this guy, and I was away at school when I was dating him, and I went home for the weekend, and he was going to come down that weekend. . . . So I went home and I got my hair cut off. I cut off about seven or eight inches, and it was kind of a radical haircut, you know shaved, kind of asymmetrical again, and I put a red tint on it. . . . And when he saw me, when he walked into my house, it was like, "Whoa!" You know? And he said, "Oh, my God, look at it!" And he just couldn't stop talking about it. He made a comment saying that he felt differently about me. He said, "I don't know, there's just something about you. I don't know. I really want to be with you." (Cecilia)

When I asked Cecilia how she felt about his rekindled interest in her, she replied: "I was pretty pleased with myself."

Although this may seem like a limited form of power compared to, say, winning election to a government office, this power embedded in doing femininity well (Bordo 1989) is power nonetheless: With a minimum investment of money and time, this woman obtained a desired goal and influenced the behavior and emotions of another person.

Once a woman adopts this strategy, she can use her understanding of cultural ideologies surrounding women's hair to increase its effectiveness. Certainly women who dye their hair blonde are well aware of American cultural ideas that link blondeness to sexuality and beauty. For example, Roxanne, a divorced woman in her 40s with dyed blonde hair vowed she would "dye until she dies." When asked why, she responded singing the 1960s advertising ditty "Is it true blondes have more fun?" Other respondents similarly mentioned that they dye their hair blonde because they believe men find blondes more attractive. (Interestingly, none mentioned any concerns that, as blondes, they might be subject to the common stereotype of blondes as unintelligent [Kyle and Mahler 1996].) I did not ask why these women were unconcerned, but would hypothesize that they believed that these stereotypes were not widely held, that their intelligence would be obvious regardless of their hair color, or that looking attractive would benefit them more than would looking intelligent.)

Even women who are uninterested in male attention may find that meeting norms for conventional attractiveness works to their benefit: For example, Erica, a young lesbian, explained that her long hair allows her to pass as heterosexual and thus has helped her get and keep jobs (in the same way that using makeup benefited the lesbians interviewed by Dellinger and Williams [1997]). Similarly, and regardless of sexual orientation, female athletes often wear their hair long, curled, and dyed blonde as part of a "feminine apologetic" that enhances their attractiveness to men and protects them from being stigmatized as lesbian (Hilliard 1984; Lowe 1998).

Dyeing hair red can be an equally effective, if somewhat different, strategy, drawing on traditional stereotypes of redheads as wild and passionate. This was explained to me by Brenda, a quiet, petite young woman who began dyeing her hair red in her early twenties:

> I thought the red hair will let people know I'm a competent person, independent, maybe a little hotheaded—or maybe a lot hotheaded. So it was just conveying, fiery always comes to mind, although that's kind of romance novelish. (Brenda)

When asked if dyeing her hair succeeded in making people see her differently, Brenda replied:

> Yeah. Actually it *made* people see me. . . . Before I dyed my hair, my sister [who has blonde hair] and I, we would go out and all these guys would ask her to dance and talk to her and ask for her number and I would just be standing there. And after I started dyeing my hair, I started getting noticed a little bit more, but I also stopped waiting to be asked. . . . And around the time I started dyeing my hair I decided I was going to quit being what

> I thought other people wanted me to be, and I was going to just be who I was. And it gave me power because, I don't know, I guess just being myself made me feel more powerful. (Brenda)

Brenda, then, used traditional ideas about women, hair, and attractiveness to change not only how others saw her but also how she saw herself. This in turn opened up possibilities for action and affected the responses she received from others, giving her greater control over her life. Again, like the women who dyed their hair blonde, none of those who dyed their hair red expressed concern that they might be handicapped by stereotypes of redheads as oversexed, easily angered, or clownish (Clayson and Maughan 1986; Heckert and Best 1997; Kyle and Mahler 1996).

In sum, the women described in this section are neither blindly seeking male approval nor unconsciously making decisions based on an internalized ideology of femininity. Instead, like women who use cosmetic surgery (Davis 1995) or makeup (Dellinger and Williams 1997), they are actively and rationally making choices based on a realistic assessment of how they can best obtain their goals, given both their personal resources and the cultural and social constraints they face. Yet can these strategies be considered resistance? On the one hand, each of these strategies is an intentional course of action designed to resist subordination by helping members of a subordinate group increase their power—or at least sense of power—relative to the dominant group. On the other hand, most of these strategies pose little if any challenge to cultural ideas about women or to the broader distribution of power by gender, for they implicitly support the ideology that defines a woman's body as her most important attribute and that therefore conflates changes in a woman's appearance with changes to her identity. Because these strategies do not challenge the cultural ideologies supporting subordination, at best they can improve the position of an individual woman, but not of women as a group. If anything, these strategies both reflect and sustain competition between women for men's attention, thus diminishing the potential for alliances among women.

The only traditional strategy that challenged cultural ideas about women was that described by Brenda, the woman who dyed her hair red. Although that strategy supported the ideology that appearance defines a woman, it rejected the assumption that Brenda herself either was or should be meek, submissive, or the passive object of a man's desires. Thus only this strategy fits the definition of resistance proposed earlier. At the same time, however, this strategy does nothing to improve the situation of other women. Rather, by using her hair color to denote her personality and views, Brenda implies that women with other hair colors lack her independence. As a result, she simultaneously resists and accommodates, resembling those Arlene Elowe MacLeod (1991) describes as "accommodating protest" because they simultaneously express dissatisfaction with and acquiescence to current power relations.

The Limits of Power Obtained through Traditional Strategies

Not surprisingly, given the accommodations embedded in traditional strategies, women often find that power obtained through these strategies is circumscribed, fragile, bittersweet, and limiting. The power to attract a man, after all, is not the same as the power to earn a living independently—although a man can provide economic support, at least for a while. Similarly, women who attract men and increase their power through appearance can at best experience only a modest sense of accomplishment, since they receive attention only for physical characteristics at least partly outside their control. Moreover, women may find that attracting men through appearance is a hollow achievement if the men they attract have little interest in them as persons and, consequently, lose interest in the relationship over the long run.

Power based on conventional attractiveness is also fragile, achieved one day at a time through concentrated effort and expenditures of time and money. Linda, a 40 year old Asian-American woman, pays to have her hair permed every few months because she thinks otherwise it looks "too Asian." Because her hair straightens out when it gets wet, she always carries an umbrella, never swims with friends, and dries her hair after showering before letting anyone see her. Her concern proved justified the one time a lover (of four years) saw her with wet straight hair, and told her never to wear her hair straight.

Even those who look attractive on most days still face the occasional "bad hair day"—a true catastrophe for those who consider their hair a significant source of power. Felicia, a Chicana in her twenties, remarked, "If I'm having a bad hair day, I'm having a bad day in general. . . . My day is just shot." Moreover, conventional attractiveness must decline with age (although it can be fought with face lifts, hair dyeing, and the like).

This power is bittersweet, too, for it is only partly under the individual's control: A woman who seeks attention and power through her appearance cannot control who will respond, when, or how. As explained to me by LaDonna, a young African-American woman whose long and wavy hair attracts considerable male attention: "It's kind of funny because I know [my hair] will get me attention, and I do things to make it look nice that I know will get me attention, but sometimes I don't wear my hair down because I *don't* want the attention." Nor can she control which men will be attracted to her (will it be her handsome neighbor or her married boss?) or for what reasons (will he think she is pretty because he simply likes long hair or because he thinks anything that looks "white" is superior?).

Transforming oneself into someone considered conventionally attractive is also bittersweet if it requires a woman to abandon what she considers her true self, which by definition is alienating. The bittersweet nature of this process comes through clearly in Cecilia's story:

> [My friends] would talk about my hair because there wasn't much else they could do with me. I wore glasses, and I had braces, [and] there wasn't much

> else you could do about that. But they were trying to turn me into a sexy thing, like, you know, they aspired to be. And you want to make all your friends [sexy] like that because you want to go out together to the skating rink or to the mall. I was willing to go along with it, so I let them fix me up. (Cecilia)

When asked if she liked the process, she replied:

> Not especially. Because I felt like I was being transformed into something I just wasn't. [But I still did it] because I felt that perhaps there was a need to be transformed, because obviously what I was was not getting me where I wanted to be. I had no boyfriend, and I didn't have that many friends. I wanted to be who I was and have what I wanted. But I didn't feel I could have what I wanted unless I changed. (Cecilia)

Finally, power obtained through traditional strategies is not only circumscribed, fragile, and bittersweet, but also limiting, since increasing one's power in these ways may *reduce* one's power in traditionally male realms. Most basically, the same hairstyles that identify a woman as conventionally attractive and increase her power in intimate relationships highlight femininity. Yet our culture links femininity with incompetence (Valian 1998; Wiley and Crittenden 1992). Thus, although men can only benefit from attractiveness, women can also be harmed by attractiveness if it leads others to regard them as less competent. For example, Laura, now in her thirties, described how from a very young age she hated it when her mother would curl her hair or put barrettes or bows in it because she realized that, in her

> very male-dominated family, if I looked like a girl, I lost power. . . . I recall feeling that I had a different experience as a person depending on how I was dressed. . . . It was hard to be perceived, I felt, as competent [if I looked girlish]. . . . If you wanted to have power, you needed to be like a boy, because when you acted like a girl, you didn't get—, well, I didn't get what I wanted, I'll say that. (Laura)

Seeking Power through Nontraditional Strategies

The problems inherent in traditional strategies lead some women, either additionally or instead, to seek power through nontraditional strategies in which elements of resistance to mainstream ideas of attractiveness outweigh any elements of accommodation.

The meanings and implications of the strategies described in this section vary considerably depending on women's ethnicity. Reflecting the broader tendency for individuals to change hairstyles as a way of marking status transitions (McAlexander and Schouten 1989), white women often choose new hairstyles that highlight professionalism and downplay femininity as a first step toward entering professional training or work. For example, Tina, a young graduate student described how, after college, she cut her hair as

> sort of like the completion of transition to adulthood. . . . I felt like I needed to make some sort of definitive statement about if I was going to get through life . . . this was the way I was going to do it. . . . I'm not going to get through life by being girly. I don't want to live that way . . . relying on the attention, specifically of men, but also relying on people's responses to your appearance. And, particularly, [on] an appearance that is feminine by stereotypical social convention. (Tina)

She now has a short, spiky haircut which, she said, "makes me feel more powerful because it's like I've beat the system, you know? . . . The system's trying to take [my power] away and I've succeeded in not letting them."

Somewhat similarly, Darla, who had married at age 15 and had four children in quick succession, talked about the first time she cut her hair short, when she was in her 30s:

> That change in my hairstyle was indicative of that resolve [to change] from . . . sort of dependent and actually thinking there was no way out of that. And . . . I did not know how I was going to do it, [to change] from someone who had been raising children all her life, and still had a little girl [at home], someone who really felt kind of trapped, and used physical attractiveness as a sense of security, to a person who was going to become different. . . . And I think the hair was a symbol of that. I never did let my hair grow long again. (Darla)

Once in the world of work, other haircuts often follow, as white women learn to believe—or learn that others believe—that femininity and professional competence are antithetical. In such situations, women may consciously use their hair to defeminize themselves. Stacy, a bi-cultural (Anglo/Chicana) graduate assistant who typically pulls her long hair back into a ponytail when she teaches explained:

> If you have really long hair people tend to see you as more womanly. . . . Particularly when I teach, I don't want people to look at me as more womanly. That's why I wear my hair back: to be taken more seriously, to look more professional, to just be seen as a person as opposed to like a woman. (Stacy)

Even more than my white respondents, the college-educated Chicanas I interviewed underscored the necessity of "professional" haircuts for success in the work world. Coming from communities that valued long hair styled into large curls and heavily sprayed to meet distinctively Chicana images of femininity, they realized that, as Paloma explained, "Having lots of long hair intensifies the fact that you are a woman and that you are Chicana too, [both of which] make it more difficult to get jobs." As a result, she adopted a shorter hairstyle to meet mainstream ideas of professionalism. Others found themselves unable to take what seemed to them a drastic step, although some of these did take the intermediate step of binding their hair back or eliminating large curls while still leaving their hair long.

African-American women, on the other hand, are far less likely to adopt any strategy that might downplay their femininity. Faced with a dominant culture that already defines them as less attractive and feminine than other women (Hill Collins 1991, 67–90; Weitz and Gordon 1993), they are more likely to seek out a style that looks "professional" but still meets mainstream norms of femininity. They thus typically rely on wigs or on expensive formulations for changing the natural texture of their hair, and avoid both hairstyles that others might associate with radical political stances (such as dreadlocks or Afros) and the elaborate hairstyles often favored by working class African-American women (Fernandez Kelly 1995).

In addition to emphasizing professionalism, women can attempt to increase their power in nontraditional ways by avoiding or rejecting male attention. For example, Wendy, a traditionally pretty white woman described how she had worn her hair long, straight, and dyed blonde throughout high school but cut it drastically short in college when she came out as a lesbian. In her words, "Definitely, my hair cut was a way of protecting myself. It was shielding me, I felt, from men looking at me, from men being interested in me. It made me feel stronger to not be viewed in a traditional feminine way."

Most dramatically, Susan, a conventionally attractive, outgoing, young Anglo-American woman who had married an Arab immigrant and converted to Islam described how she began covering her hair in traditional Arabic fashion while visiting her husband's relatives in the Mideast. Even though her husband regarded hair-coverings as ugly and "backward" and none of his relatives wore them, Susan nevertheless chose to cover her hair to convince others that she was a chaste Moslem (cf. Elowe MacLeod 1991) and thus to protect herself from dangerous sexual harassment when her husband was absent. In this way, she both limited others' power over her (they no longer felt free to harass or touch her) and added to her own power by convincing others to take her more seriously. Against her husband's strenuously expressed wishes, Susan continued wearing the head-covering after returning from the Middle East not only as protection against unwanted male attention but also because it made her "feel empowered" by reminding her of her religion and the presence of God. Tellingly, she noted that in the United States, women "use their body and their beauty as their power. Now my power comes from within and I don't have to use my body."

Other women remain interested in attracting men, but not based on the traditional norms of submissive femininity that underlie mainstream attractiveness norms. Stacy provided a dramatic example:

> My boyfriend . . . used to say that . . . what made me attractive was my hair was so pretty. So I deliberately kind of cut it off, a little bit spitefully, but kind of just to say I'm more than my hair. I felt powerful when I cut my hair

> off. Like maybe in the sense that I feel that [men] prefer long hair, that I wasn't ruled by that and I could like set my own standards. And sort of like, it's being in control of your hair gives you somewhat of a power. (Stacy)

Still other women find a sense of power not through rejecting attractiveness *per se* but through broadening the definition of attractiveness to include appearances that occur more naturally within their own ethnic group (Banks 1997; Craig 1995). These new definitions explicitly challenge the ideology that defines minority women's appearances as inferior and that encourages minority women to engage in time-consuming and painful disciplines to conform to dominant appearance norms. Thus three of the four African-American women I interviewed described their past decisions to wear an Afro, braids, or dreadlocks as explicitly political statements about their identities. (The fourth woman, LaDonna, came of age after the Afro went out of the style and had relatively straight hair naturally.) Jenny, an African-American professional, who now wears dreadlocks, explained that her hairstyle

> expresses my individuality as well as my value of my heritage and my pride in what is distinctly me, distinctly mine. . . . I consider myself in a constant state of protest about the realities of cultural alienation, cultural marginalization, cultural invisibility, discrimination, injustice, all of that. And I feel that my hairstyle has always allowed me, since I started wearing it in a natural, to voice that nonverbally. And that has been a desire of mine, to do that. (Jenny)

In sum, like the traditional strategies described previously, the strategies described in this section are intentional actions designed to resist subordination and increase the power of members of a subordinate group. Unlike most of the traditional strategies, however, each of these strategies challenges the ideology that underlies subordination, even though only some of the women frame their actions in ideological terms. Thus all these strategies contain elements of resistance.

At the same time, however, these strategies contain elements of accommodation. Because it is difficult to analyze everyday actions taken for granted within one's own culture, most Americans can probably most easily identify the elements of accommodation embedded in the actions of the Muslim convert, who had to cover herself in a physically constraining, hot, and uncomfortable garment to ward off unwanted male attention and convince others to take her seriously. Although more difficult for most Americans to recognize, there are also elements of accommodation embedded in the other strategies described in this section. Most importantly, using the body as a political tool continues to place women's bodies at the center of women's identities. Moreover, like the woman who dyed her hair red, the women who cut their hair short to declare their competence or independence imply by extension that women who do not do so lack those qualities. Thus only those strategies that promote a hairstyle as a group aesthetic or political statement (such as Afros and hairstyles that are meant to be recognized as "dyke" haircuts) have at least the potential to unite rather than divide women and to help women as a group rather than simply helping some individuals.

The Limits of Obtaining Power through Nontraditional Strategies

Given these problems, it is not surprising that, like traditional strategies, nontraditional strategies also offer only limited effectiveness. Whereas those who emphasize conventional attractiveness and femininity risk unwanted male sexual attention, those who defeminize their appearance and/or adopt more professional hairstyles risk desexualization (Bartky 1988) and the loss of desired male attention. After all, just because a woman wants a professional job doesn't mean she doesn't want a boyfriend or husband. Although some women enjoy no longer being seen by men in sexual terms, others find this a steep price to pay. This issue seemed especially salient for Chicanas: The eight Chicanas I interviewed all believed they had to have long, waved hair both to attract Chicano men and to maintain their identity as Chicanas, but the six who had attended college also believed they needed shorter, more subdued hair to succeed as professionals. None had fully resolved this dilemma. (Although these numbers are small, this sentiment was shared by numerous other college-educated Chicanas who have commented on versions of this article.)

Moreover, if a woman adopts a look that others consider not only less feminine but frankly unattractive, she may find that professional success also eludes her, for, as described earlier, conventionally attractive women receive more job offers, higher salaries, and more promotions than unattractive women. And regardless of a woman's sexual orientation, she risks discrimination if her hairstyle leads others to label her a lesbian—experiences shared by several short-haired respondents.

The stories told by African-American women, meanwhile, emphasize the very real consequences paid by those who reject mainstream ideas about attractiveness—even if they still strive to look attractive by their own definitions (Banks 1997). As Norma described:

> I remember I went to interview for a job and the guy wouldn't hire me because I had an Afro. A white guy. He said, "It's your hair. I don't like your hair style. You've got to do something about your hair." I didn't change my hair style of course, I just walked out. I figured I didn't need that job that much. (Norma)

She went on to explain:

> I think that both white and Black employers, especially men, expect African American women to have straight hairstyles as opposed to their own natural

> hairstyles. That one guy rejected me right off the bat. But I see people treated differently depending on their hair style. Especially women who wear dreads, I see they have to fight for respect, demand it. It's almost a constant struggle. As opposed to women who wear their hair straight [and] are perceived to be more intelligent and professional. (Norma)

These comments were seconded by the other African-American women I interviewed. Similar remarks were made by a woman with wildly curling "Jewish" hair and by an immigrant who viewed long braided hair as a valued sign of her Pakistani identity but incompatible with American professional norms. For all these women, any aspect of their appearance that called attention to their minority status reduced their perceived competence and their social acceptability in the workplace. . . .

Conclusions

Findings from this study suggest that, far from being "docile bodies," women are often acutely aware of cultural expectations regarding their hair. Yet rather than simply acquiescing to those expectations, women can consciously seek power by accommodating to those expectations, resisting them, or combining these two strategies. Nevertheless, we must not overstate women's agency in this matter, for their options are significantly constrained by both cultural expectations and social structure. Consequently, the hair management strategies women adopt to increase their power in some realms often decrease it in others. As a result, women do not so much choose between the available strategies as balance and alternate them, using whichever seems most useful at a given time.

The inherent limitations on the power available to women through their hairstyles raise the question of why women continue to seek power in this way (or, more generally, through their appearance). As we have seen, women consciously use culturally-mandated appearance norms to achieve their personal ends. To say that women consciously use these norms, however, does not mean that they are free to ignore them. No matter what a woman does or doesn't do with her hair—dyeing or not dyeing, curling or not curling, covering with a bandana or leaving uncovered—her hair will affect how others respond to her, and her power will increase or decrease accordingly. Consequently, women use their hair to improve their position because they recognize that not doing so can imperil their position. Of course, the power and any other gains achieved through hair or other aspects of appearance are circumscribed, fragile, bittersweet, and limiting. Yet the power achieved in this way is no less real. Moreover, for many women, appearance remains a more accessible route to power than does career success, financial independence, political achievement, and so on.

The same constraints on women's options and agency that make seeking power through appearance a reasonable choice also explain why, although

some of the strategies women use to gain power through their hair contain elements of resistance, *all* contain elements of accommodation (cf. Elowe MacLeod 1991). Compared to resistance, accommodation offers women (and any other subordinate group) a far more reliable and safer route to power, even if that power is limited. As a result, the strategies women typically use can help individual women gain power, or at least a sense of power, in some arenas, but do little to improve the situation of women as a group. Rather, these strategies unintentionally lend support to those who equate women's bodies with their identities, consider women's bodies more important than their minds, assume that women use their bodies to manipulate men, or assume that femininity and competence are antithetical (thus handicapping visibly "feminine" women professionally and visibly "professional" women socially). Moreover, all these strategies inescapably foment competition between women. Finally, even the most explicitly radical actions described in this article—the adoption of Afros, dreadlocks, or visibly "lesbian" haircuts—have only temporary utility as tools for social change because of the inherent instability of fashions. Such styles can certainly help to spread a new and radical idea, help members of an incipient social movement identify each other, and spark social change. In the long run, though, even if a style is initially intended to challenge existing power relationships, the more people adopt it, the more likely it will lose its original meaning and become simply another fashion (Craig 1995). As the style goes out of fashion—as all styles do—those who continue to wear it look merely dated and unfashionable, as their hairstyles lose their political meanings. Thus both Afros and the spiky, asymmetrical haircuts once found only on radical lesbians and punks are now merely styles that occasionally appear on fashion runways. (By extension, it is even less likely that the transgressive gender performances of lesbian femmes, male drag queens, and transgendered persons can lead to meaningful social change, as Butler [1990], Bornstein [1994] and others have claimed, for most observers undoubtedly view these actions as personal aberrations devoid of any political meaning.)

As this discussion suggests, it is difficult to identify factors that facilitate resistance because the possibilities for resistance are so constrained and because resistance and accommodation are so intertwined, both in any given action and in each individual's life. Certainly resistance is easier if supported by others, such as husbands or friends who place little emphasis on meeting appearance norms. Resistance to appearance norms is also easier when an alternative ideology exists that can provide a basis for challenging dominant ideologies, especially if that alternative ideology is supported by a broad social movement (as was the Afro during the late 1960s). Finally, resistance is most feasible when individuals can count on other sources of power and status unrelated to appearance (such as a career, education, or inherited wealth) and thus need not worry as much about any loss in power or status that might come from a non-normative appearance. Similarly, resistance against norms for women's hair may be easiest for those who are naturally tall, thin, and blonde and thus otherwise meet appearance norms.

In sum, this research helps us understand both the meaning of resistance and the pitfalls of defining the term over-broadly. It also sheds light on how resistance can be embedded in women's daily lives, and highlights the limitations of resistance strategies based on the body. Despite these limitations, however, these strategies are not useless. For example, whenever women abandon time-intensive, difficult to maintain hairstyles, they gain both time and physical freedom and thereby contribute to changing ideas about and opportunities for women, regardless of their intentions and of how their intentions are interpreted by others. Future research should pay close attention to the interwoven dangers and benefits, opportunities and limitations, of resistance centered on the body.

Notes

Acknowledgments: I would especially like to thank Myra Dinnerstein for her help and support throughout this project. Also thanks to Kathy Davis, Kirsten Dellinger, Dan Hilliard, Judith Lorber, PJ McGann, Cecilia Menjívar, Karen Miller-Loessi, Irene Padavic, Mindy Stombler, George Thomas, and Christine Williams for their comments on this research project. In addition, I would like to thank Jennifer Mata, Sophia Hinojosa, Dana Gray, and Jami Wilenchik for assistance in data collection. Finally, I would like to express my appreciation to Arizona State University for granting me a sabbatical leave to pursue this project and to the Western Alliance to Expand Minority Opportunities and the ASU Women's Studies Program, both of which provided needed research funding.

1. Hair and appearance also affect men's social position, but to a much lesser extent (Jackson 1992; Sullivan 2001). In addition, because the parameters for acceptable male appearance are both narrower (allowing less experimentation and less pressure to adapt to fashion) and broader (allowing much more natural variation), most men can obtain a socially acceptable haircut with little time, energy, or cost. The exceptions are, truly, exceptional: actors and models, gay men whose communities emphasize appearance, middle-aged middle managers whose companies are downsizing, the recently divorced, and so on.
2. I do not distinguish in this paper between actual power and a sense of power because all the data are based on women's perceptions, and the distinction between a woman feeling that she has power or feeling a sense of power is slight at best.

References

Banks, Ingrid. 1997. *Social and Personal Constructions of Hair: Cultural Practices and Belief Systems among African American Women*. Ph.D. diss., University of California, Berkeley.

Bartky, Sandra Lee. 1988. Foucault, femininity, and the modernization of patriarchal power. In *Feminism and Foucault: Reflections on Resistance*, edited by Irene Diamond and Lee Quinby. Boston: Northeastern University Press.

Bordo, Susan R. 1989. The body and the reproduction of femininity: A feminist appropriation of Foucault. In *Gender/Body/Knowledge*, edited by Alison M. Jaggar and Susan R. Bordo. New Brunswick, NJ: Rutgers University Press.

Bornstein, Kate. 1994. *Gender Outlaws: On Men, Women, and the Rest of Us.* New York: Routledge.

Butler, Judith. 1990. *Gender Trouble: Feminism and the Subversion of Identity.* New York: Routledge.

Clayson, Dennis E., and Micol R. C. Maughan. 1986. Redheads and blonds: Stereotypic images. *Psychological Reports* 59:811–16.

Costello, Cynthia B., Shari E. Miles, and Anne J. Stone. 1998. *The American Woman 1999–2000: A Century of Change—What's Next?* New York: Norton.

Craig, Maxine. 1995. *Black Is Beautiful: Personal Transformation and Political Change.* Ph.D. diss., University of California, Berkeley.

Davis, Kathy. 1991. Remaking the she-devil: A critical look at feminist approaches to beauty. *Hypatia* 6(2):21–42.

———. 1995. *Reshaping the Female Body: The Dilemma of Cosmetic Surgery.* New York: Routledge.

Dellinger, Kirsten, and Christine L. Williams. 1997. Makeup at work: Negotiating appearance rules in the workplace. *Gender & Society* 11:151–77.

Elowe MacLeod, Arlene. 1991. *Accommodating Protest: Working Women, the New Veiling, and Change in Cairo.* New York: Columbia University Press.

Fernandez Kelly, M. Patricia. 1995. Social and cultural capital in the urban ghetto. In *The Economic Sociology of Immigration: Essays on Networks, Ethnicity, and Entrepreneurship*, edited by Alejandro Portes. New York: Russell Sage.

Firth, Raymond. 1973. *Symbols: Public and Private.* Ithaca, NY: Cornell University Press.

Foucault, Michel. 1979. *Discipline and Punish: The Birth of the Prison.* New York: Vintage.

———. 1980. *History of Sexuality.* New York: Pantheon.

Heckert, Druann Maria, and Amy Best. 1997. Ugly duckling to swan: Labeling theory and the stigmatization of red hair. *Symbolic Interaction* 20:365–84.

Hill Collins, Patricia. 1991. *Black Feminist Thought: Knowledge, Consciousness, and the Politics of Empowerment.* London: Routledge.

Hilliard, Dan C. 1984. Media images of male and female professional athletes: An interpretive analysis of magazine articles. *Sociology of Sport Journal* 1:251–62.

Jackson, Linda. 1992. *Physical Appearance and Gender: Sociobiological and Sociocultural Perspectives.* Albany: State University of New York Press.

Kyle, Diana J., and Heike I.M. Mahler. 1996. The effects of hair color and cosmetic use on perceptions of a female's ability. *Psychology of Women Quarterly* 20: 447–55.

Lowe, Maria R. 1998. *Women of Steel: Female Body Builders and the Struggle for Self-definition.* New Brunswick, NJ: Rutgers University Press.

McAlexander, James H., and John W. Schouten. 1989. Hair style changes as transition markers. *Sociology and Social Research* 74:58–62.

Scott, James C. 1990. *Domination and the Arts of Resistance: Hidden Transcripts.* New Haven, CT: Yale University Press.

Stombler, Mindy, and Irene Padavic. 1997. Sister acts: Resisting men's domination in black and white fraternity little sister programs. *Social Problems* 44:257–75.

Sullivan, Deborah A. 2001. *Cosmetic Surgery: The Cutting Edge of Commercial Medicine in America.* New Brunswick, NJ: Rutgers University Press.

Synott, Anthony. 1987. Shame and glory: A sociology of hair. *British Journal of Sociology* 38:381–413.

U.S. Department of Commerce. 1998. *Statistical Abstract of the United States 1997.* Washington, DC: U.S. Government Printing Office.

Valian, Virginia. 1998. *Why So Slow?: The Advancement of Women.* Cambridge, MA: MIT Press.

Weitz, Rose, and Leonard Gordon. 1993. Images of black women among Anglo college students. *Sex Roles* 28:19–45.

Wiley, Mary Glenn, and Kathleen S. Crittenden. 1992. By your attributions you shall be known: Consequences of attributional accounts for professional and gender identities. *Sex Roles* 27:259–76.

15

Navigating Public Spaces

Gender, Race, and Body Privilege in Everyday Life

SAMANTHA KWAN

In Part I, Sandra Lee Bartky discussed how women internalize social expectations about appearance and attempt to meet those expectations through various "disciplinary practices." These social expectations include body size norms that girls and women strive to embody through practices such as surgery, restrictive dieting, and the use of weight-loss drugs and supplements. Many third-wave feminists have written about the numerous deleterious effects these practices have on girls' and women's physical and psychological health—from low self-esteem to eating disorders.

In "Navigating Public Spaces: Gender, Race, and Body Privilege in Everyday Life," Samantha Kwan explores how the omnipresent thin ideal affects the everyday lives of "overweight" women. Extending earlier work by Peggy McIntosh on privilege—the invisible, taken for granted, and unearned advantages enjoyed by members of a dominant group—Kwan introduces the concept of "body privilege": the invisible package of unearned assets that individuals who conform to body norms can take for granted on a daily basis.

Like previous research showing that commitment to, as well as the effects of, body ideals varies by social group, Kwan's interviews suggest that body privilege can be conceptualized along a continuum. On the one end, overweight men and African American women report more body privilege than do other overweight people; on the other, overweight Hispanic and white women report less body privilege. Moreover, members of the latter group report a heightened level of "body consciousness," an awareness that their bodies do not conform to hegemonic body ideals. This body consciousness can lead to "physical body management,"

Kwan, Samantha. "Navigating Public Spaces: Gender, Race, and Body Privilege in Everyday Life." *Feminist Formations* 22:2 (2010), 144–166.

the physical manipulation of the body or props to manage this awareness, as well as "psychological body management," techniques to cope emotionally with the anxiety of body consciousness. In her article, Kwan explores both types of body management and illustrates how they serve as subtle yet invasive and powerful forms of bodily discipline.

Western cultural norms emphasize a thin and firm body ideal for women and a muscular ideal for men (Bordo 2003; Pope, Phillips, and Olivardia 2000). Feminist scholars have examined these norms (often described as "Eurocentric white ideals"), their effects, and the various demands of the "fashion beauty complex" (Bartky 1990; Chapkis 1991; Collins 2000). Today, many women continue to live under a "tyranny of slenderness" (Chernin 1994), engaging in widespread body-modification practices or "body work" (Gimlin 2002). These practices range from dieting to cosmetic surgery, and their negative physical, psychological, and social consequences indicate that hegemonic ideals remain a key site of women's oppression (Sprague-Zones 1997; Wolf 1991).

While scholars have studied these overt manifestations of body norms, in 1988, Peggy McIntosh (2000) changed our language and understanding of oppression by introducing the concept of "white privilege." Unlike overt forms of oppression—whether manifested in hate groups, anti-miscegenation laws, or racial slurs—white privilege is a package of unearned assets that whites cash in on a daily basis. In this article, I borrow and refine McIntosh's idea of white privilege to understand a parallel concept of "body privilege" to further the understanding of embodied oppressions. Drawing on in-depth interviews with forty-two "overweight" women and men, . . . I highlight how body privilege is patterned by gender and race/ethnicity . . . and illustrate how [it] sheds new light on crucial debates regarding cultural ideals, women's beauty work, and agency.

Body Privilege

McIntosh's concept of white privilege centers around a form of power that racially privileged people take for granted on a daily basis. According to McIntosh, as whites go about their everyday lives, they experience advantages that racial minorities do not. McIntosh notes that whites are often oblivious to their privilege, taking it for granted and operating as if their lives and experiences are normative and morally neutral. Instances of white privilege that help to clarify this concept abound. For example, McIntosh admits that, as a white woman, she can reasonably assume that her neighbors will be neutral or pleasant to her; she can turn on the television and see people of her race widely and positively represented; and she can easily buy dolls, toys, and magazines featuring people of her race. These so-called privileges come with various benefits. She says that "[s]ome privileges make me feel at home in the world. Others allow me to escape penalties or dangers that others suffer. Through some, I escape fear, anxiety, insult, injury, or a sense of not being welcome, not being real. Some keep me from having to hide, to be in disguise, to feel sick or crazy, to negotiate each transaction from the position of being an outsider. . . . Most keep me from having to be angry" (2000, 35). . . .

Like structures that privilege whiteness, cultural and social structures privilege the thin, or at least what has been deemed a "normal"-sized body. Classical social-psychological research indicates that beauty functions as a visible status cue that operates in a similar manner as race or gender and shapes expectations about an individual's personality and behavior (Webster and Driskell 1983). Individuals often assume that beautiful people are good and/or talented and expect them to be smarter, lead better lives, hold more prestigious jobs, and have happier marriages (Dion, Berscheid, and Walster 1972; Landy and Sigall 1974). Many of these expectations do, in fact, hold. For example, a meta-analysis of experimental studies finds that for both men and women, physical attractiveness is an asset in hiring, evaluation, and promotion (Hosoda, Stone-Romero, and Coats 2003). From cradle to grave, attractiveness correlates with desirable social outcomes. (For a review of both classic and contemporary studies, see Kwan and Trautner [2009].)

Moreover, not only do beautiful individuals have social "privileges," their bodies avert stigma. "Obese" individuals experience bias, discrimination, stigma, and stereotyping in many arenas of social life (Puhl and Brownell 2001; Sobal 2004; Solovay 2000). Poor treatment of "overweight" women is especially apparent; for example, large women face a significant wage penalty for their weight (Conley and Glauber 2005; Pagan and Dávila 1997; Rothblum, Miller, and Garbutt 1988), and for overweight women, size correlates with downward social and economic mobility (Rothblum 1992).

A Western cultural body hierarchy thus creates body privilege, an invisible package of unearned assets that thin or "normal"-sized individuals can take for granted on a daily basis. These "normal" bodies, because of size, shape, or appearance, unwittingly avert various forms of social stigma, while simultaneously eliciting social benefits. Their privilege is protected by structures that venerate a narrow conception of beauty, particularly for women (Bordo 2003; Wolf 1991). Applying McIntosh's (2000) original examples, we see: ubiquitous media images that reinforce and perpetuate the normalcy of thinness; that thinness is rarely challenged or questioned as a state of being; and that thin individuals are made to feel welcome and normal in the usual walks of public life. The thin body is such a coveted cultural standard that it is an unchallenged norm. Meanwhile, those without privilege must negotiate daily interactions, sometimes feeling shame, guilt, and anger because of their bodies. In short, body privilege allows its possessor to avoid physical and emotional injury. . . .

Methods

To understand how a lack of body privilege plays out in mundane life, I interviewed forty-two individuals who identify as "overweight" [and would be classified as "overweight" according to the Body Mass Index (BMI), a proxy for estimating body fat based on an individual's weight and height].[1] I conducted semi-structured interviews so as to explore in-depth the participants' perspectives. I recruited participants . . . at a community college in a mid-sized southwestern city. . . . While the methods I employed generated neither a representative nor a random sample, this exploratory study nevertheless illuminates important social processes concerning Western culture's body hierarchy. Additionally, because I intentionally turned to a community college, I recruited a lower social-class sample. . . .

The sample consists of twenty-three women and nineteen men, twenty of whom (47.6 percent) identified as white, ten (23.8 percent) as Hispanic, seven (16.7 percent) as African American, three (7.1 percent) as mixed race, one (2.4 percent) as South Asian, and one (2.4 percent) as Native American. According to medical-community standards, twenty (47.6 percent) would be labeled as overweight, and twenty-two (52.4 percent) as obese. . . . The mean BMI was 32.5, ranging from 25.1 to 46.3, and the average age was 34.4, ranging from 24 to 49. . . .Thirty-nine participants identified as heterosexual.

Navigating Public Spaces

As overweight participants perform mundane tasks, others remind them that they cannot take certain comforts for granted. Daily, they confront the reality that thin is the privileged norm. While body privilege enables thin individuals to perform simple tasks comfortably, for overweight individuals at times these tasks elicit hurtful and insulting comments and stares. The majority of participants, but particularly women in higher weight categories, reported that they experienced negative stereotyping, stigma, and/or social isolation because of their bodies. These experiences often began in childhood and carried on through adulthood and, as a whole, confirm the literature that the stigma of fat is widespread. For example, female participants reported that strangers accosted them by telling them that they were fat, should not be wearing certain types of clothing, or should have greater self-control. Alena (age 33, white) recalls walking with friends in a beach town when several young men rolled down their car windows and yelled, "You're too fat and ugly! Go home!" Sometimes this public harassment was framed altruistically; for example, at a hair salon, a woman approached Estella (age 27, Hispanic) to inform her, "You know, you need to love yourself." This woman then proceeded to provide Estella with various strategies. These annoyances can be frustrating, as Estella articulated: "When I go get my hair cut, I want to get my hair cut, right? You know, when I take the bus somewhere, I just want to take the bus somewhere!"

Alongside these overt acts, body privilege also surfaces in subtle ways. As McIntosh (2000) discusses, some privileges allow her to escape penalties or dangers like verbal harassment, while others allow her to escape the sense of not being welcome or real. For example, shopping was sometimes a difficult experience for female participants . . . not only did it induce anxiety about finding clothing, but . . . [they felt] invisible in these spaces. Melanie's (age 27, white) description of an incident at one international clothing franchise is exemplary. She spoke about how, as she carried out this simple task, she felt an awful stigma:

> I went into Banana Republic and I was a size 16. I walk in and I was like "Hi, could you help me?" And they didn't even look at me. So I went over and I found something. I found a sweater and I was like "Hi do you have this in my size?" Didn't look at me. . . . So it's been difficult. But because I've started to lose weight, my self-image is improving. I'm starting to fit into my old clothes again. I'm feeling better about myself. . . . I'm starting to feel like I'm a human being again. . . . I think that there's this awful, awful stigma. . . . I don't know if it's against men because I've never been a fat guy. But I have been a very fat girl and there's definitely this awful, awful stigma. And it's so hurtful, because it's like "Why are you judging me based on that?"

Similar experiences were described at, among other stores, Abercrombie & Fitch and Victoria's Secret. These experiences confirm McIntosh's (2000) claim that privilege enables its holder to "escape fear, anxiety, insult, injury, or a sense of not being welcome, not being real" (p. 35). As Melanie's quote indicates, it is only when she started to lose weight that she felt like a "human being again." Weight loss accompanies body privilege, which permits greater comfort in everyday interactions.

Body Consciousness and Body Management

Body nonprivilege [the absence of "body privilege"] is patterned insofar as women report greater instances of this type of body oppression in public spaces. Conforming to racial patterns that other researchers have observed (see, for example, Grabe and Hyde 2006; Lovejoy 2001), body privilege is also patterned by race. On the one hand, overweight men and African American women generally report fewer experiences of body oppression. On the other, a number of Hispanic and white women [report] a heightened awareness of their bodies and a need to somehow respond to this awareness. I label this awareness "body consciousness,"[2] which I define as a heightened awareness that one's body does not conform to hegemonic cultural ideals. In this way, it is an extension and magnified form of everyday body consciousness—namely, a general awareness that many participants expressed about their bodies being overweight. However, the body consciousness I describe here is greater in intensity and is often triggered by a stimulus that signifies to a participant that her [or his] body diverges from aesthetic norms. It also elicits a desire to perform some sort of physical or emotional adjustment, what I call "body management."

As scholars have pointed out, in Western cultures, [the] fat [body] can be understood as a form of "deviance," or a "deviant master status," which, like other undesirable labels, requires "impression management" or "neutralization" (Goffman 1959, 1963; Sykes and Matza 1957). . . . Strategies may even involve "passing" (Goffman 1963)—that is, trying to appear thin, since successfully passing may mean reaping the benefits of the body hierarchy and averting social sanction, however fleeting.

While impression management centers on one's attempts to influence public perceptions of the self, body management is a way of handling a difficult situation so that one does not feel psychologically scarred, particularly from the deviant label. In this way, similar to impression management, body management is sometimes a way of presenting a different and more socially desirable body—a conforming body that is privy to social benefits and eschews social stigma. This management can be physical and/or emotional. Physical management involves physically manipulating one's body or available props (such as clothing) to manage a situation, or changing one's actual behavior to avert a potentially anxious situation (such as a public setting). Psychological management can be a self-directed pep talk that reassures oneself of self-worth. In either form, body management is an attempt to cope with body consciousness—an awareness that elicits anxiety.

Examples from conversations with participants help to ground these new concepts and to illustrate them at work. As overweight women go about their daily tasks, they come across various objects, situations, and persons that make them aware of their body nonconformity. It is expected that women experience multiple triggers: Body image is not a static concept, and it fluctuates as women encounter new experiences and reinterpret old ones (Paquette and Raine 2004). For example, whereas thin or "normal"-sized individuals take things such as chairs, desks, and public bathrooms for granted, women like Jeanette (age 35, white) experience these objects as triggers to body consciousness and as a form of patrolling:

> The first day of class was awful because they had these evil little chairs that I couldn't fit into. And desks that are connected, I hate that. So I had [to use] the handicapped tables and chair which was kind of embarrassing. . . . Bathroom stalls are made for smaller people. It's all very subtle. It's all telling you in a way, you shouldn't be that big. . . . If you can't get into the bathroom stall, you should do something about it. I'm afraid of first being looked at. I mean, I'll use the handicapped stall. . . . But in a way, being overweight, big, is a handicap. You can't fit into things. You go to a restaurant, I hate booths. They're made for smaller people. You know, even though they're trying to feed you.

Physical structures built for thinner individuals become stressors that must be managed, emotionally and physically. Jeanette must choose a different desk and she must also neutralize her embarrassment. She likens being fat to being disabled, and this allows her to manage emotionally these stressful situations.

Rhonda (age 40, white) describes a similar level of body consciousness. In her case, triggers are both physical objects and a "generalized other"—an abstract concept representing the collective expectations of society (Mead

1934). Heavier female participants like Rhonda report that they sometimes feel they are the object of a constant and watchful eye:

> When you're on a bus or you're in an airplane, I'm self-conscious about making sure I'm in my own space. . . . In a movie theater, I go to the ballet and stuff. I get self-conscious about where my arm is and stuff, make sure I'm not in the other person's space. Because I don't want them to say, "You're heavy, you're taking up my space." . . . So it just makes me aware that I'm not the skinniest thing, so I don't want people glaring at me like that.

To ensure that she is not encroaching on other people's spaces, Rhonda tries to take up as little room as possible. She feels compelled to make adjustments, to perform body management. The gaze of this generalized other is present for her in many public spaces, as she says, whether on an airplane, riding a bus, or in a movie theater.

Heightened body consciousness because of this watchful eye meant continuous preoccupation with appearance management, despite reassurances from friends or significant others that one looks fine. The possibility that this generalized other is observing and judging prompts extensive body management for this audience, however imagined. This, of course, is the self-discipline of which Michel Foucault (1977) writes. Notably, Susan Bordo (2003) draws on a Foucauldian interpretation of hegemonic body norms, observing a shift from repressive strategies of physical restraint and coercion to more subtle disciplining techniques of self-correction. Central to this new form of postmodern power is "self-regulation."

Body consciousness and body management are forms of self-surveillance. Moreover, it is extreme self-regulation that demarcates various groups. Specifically, a handful of Hispanic and white women exhibit a heightened form of body consciousness and perform body management that can, at times, be very disruptive and invasive. It is sometimes so severe that it impedes their everyday routines. In many ways, this consciousness and management are hallmarks of body privilege: Individuals who possess body privilege can navigate public spaces comfortably and safely; those without it suffer emotionally and, sometimes, quite severely. For example, Brittany (age 24, Hispanic) shares how she is so aware of the fat under her chin that, in public spaces, she physically postures herself in a way that manages her profile: "In public situations, I'm really uncomfortable. I went [to a restaurant] with my boyfriend's family and I was just—Oh my God—you know, I'm sitting there and I had a little skirt on and a shirt. I sat up straight and I'd try and keep my head up so you can't see my chin. You know what I mean? So it's always there. It's always, always there!"

To appear thinner, female participants tugged, pulled at, twisted, and straightened clothing (a body-management prop), while physically holding in body parts. Alena (age 33, white) does something similar to Brittany in a restaurant, all the while questioning her own behavior: "I'm constantly kind of pushing, pulling my shirt down and trying to sit up straight and suck in my gut. And I'm going, 'You know, I'm here to eat. Who's looking at me, and who cares?' But I still do it. I'm very uncomfortable in those kinds of situations." Throughout dinner, both Brittany and Alena focus less on enjoying their meals than on ensuring that their fat does not show—or is, at the very least, minimized in appearance. Women's fidgeting and manipulation of clothing to strategically hide body parts may be partly due to the clothes available to women because, in general, women's clothing is designed to show off the body and is often neither functional nor comfortable. Overweight female participants, particularly in upper-weight categories, expressed difficulty finding clothes they thought were attractive, comfortable, and/or affordable.

Body consciousness in public settings may be so strong that some women do not even want to leave their homes. Only after some psychological management in the form of a self-reaffirming talk does Melanie find the courage to continue with her day. She describes the psychological processes that take place on these days: "I'll take a step back and go, 'You know what? No, it's okay. It's okay. It's okay. You're fine. Just go about your day.'" Similarly, Brittany experiences such pronounced body consciousness in public spaces that she prefers to stay within the safe confines of her home. Staying home allows her to avoid the gaze of the generalized other that might judge her. As she says: "Oh, I don't go out. Like at all. Really. I don't really go out and do anything. . . . I don't have to worry about what other people are thinking about me or how I look in other people's eyes. . . . Sometimes I don't even want to go out to eat at a restaurant or like go out. Even just coming to school is like really hard. . . . Go to a bar or go to the movies or go to the mall. Go to the pool for God's sake."

At the same time that these select Hispanic and white female participants were highly body conscious and performed body management, they conceded that often there was, in fact, no one watching them. For example, Jeanette admits a certain level of "paranoia," believing that "everybody's watching me. . . . And I had to talk myself out of that, that they're not watching me. And actually I learned to look around and I noticed that they're not looking at me." Similarly, Brittany admits that "I kind of look around and see who's looking . . . and nobody is, but still I just feel really uncomfortable." Yet even after admitting that nobody was watching them in these public spaces, they nevertheless felt compelled to manage their bodies.

Gender, Race, and Body Privilege

How women, and especially a number of Hispanic and white women, experience body consciousness and body management starkly contrasts with men's daily experiences with their bodies. When I asked male participants to discuss their experiences in public spaces like clothing stores and restaurants, they often responded nonchalantly. While they desired to look good, they expressed very little body consciousness, and rarely did they speak of extreme appearance management. For example, male participants believed that dining out is primarily about enjoyment—having a good meal and good time. They spoke about their favorite restaurants and foods, expressing minimal concern about others or the need to manage their bodies. As Matthew (age 31, white) put it: "I go to a restaurant, it's on. That's all there is to it. I eat whatever I want. I drink whatever I want. Because if you're going out to enjoy yourself, you're going out to enjoy yourself . . . when I go out to dinner, I go out to dinner."

On the rare occasions when men experienced heightened body consciousness, their reactions were quite different from women's. Kirk (age 26, white), for example, recounted a time when clothing elicited body consciousness: In a clothing store and unable to fit into a pair of size 44 pants, he threw them down and stormed out. However, upon exiting, he changed his mind and scolded himself: "Wow, you put way too much thought into what you've been doing with yourself physically. . . . When have you ever gotten this mad about being the way you are? And why in the world are you upset about it? Well, oh God, you're an idiot." While Kirk's behavior illustrates a certain level of body consciousness and emotional management, it was clearly a very different kind of management. Kirk was angry that he had become concerned about his weight in the first place; he vowed to be unapologetic about his size. He reframed the situation and prevented himself from feeling the need to do further body management, refusing to be *that* body conscious.

In the same way, none of the female participants who expressed an intense level of body consciousness or performed extensive body management was African American. Alesha's (age 34, African American) perspective was typical, making a special point to indicate that she was not body conscious. While she wished to be thinner and ideally would lose weight, body issues played a very minor role in her life. Throughout her narrative, she told me that "she is fine," emphasizing that she was able to do her job, take care of her family, and that she was generally content with her body. On a daily basis, then, body issues did not run her life. She experienced little body consciousness and consequently had little need for body management. Regarding being in public spaces, such as while shopping or dining out, Alesha and other African American women did not discuss in-depth a heightened awareness of their bodies being "deviant." For example, when I asked Shawntea (age 36, African American) whether she encountered differential treatment or stigma as she went about her daily routines, she responded: "Not that I've ever noticed. I remember one of my friends, like a couple of them, told me that they felt like that they were treated differently because they were overweight. I don't think I've ever experienced it that I can think [of] right offhand. I don't think so. But I'm just one of those people, I'm just, I'm me, and I'm outgoing so that's what you first see. . . . I'm just too outgoing, too bubbly."

Shawntea refocused the conversation on her personality and downplayed external responses to her body. This does not mean, however, that men or African American women do not want to lose weight or that they do not experience body stigma. They are not entirely immune from Western body norms; indeed, the majority of participants, regardless of gender and race, coveted weight loss. What their contrasting statements indicate is that as these men and African American women went about their daily lives, size was a less salient part of their cognitive repertoire. Consequently, they generally experienced a greater sense of entitlement and level of comfort when navigating public spaces, and did not experience a heightened awareness that their bodies deviated from cultural norms. Therefore they felt less compulsion to manage their bodies' nonconformity.

Discussion

. . . How might these experiences be theorized? What accounts for these differences?

Overweight men's experiences of body privilege can be theorized in part as a subset of "male privilege" (McIntosh 2000). Avoiding greater social sanction in public for their bodies and experiencing a higher level of comfort in daily interactions may be part of the invisible package of unearned assets that men—simply as men—can cash in on each day; overweight men can generally take for granted that they will be treated with respect and dignity as they go about their daily routines. This translates into a higher degree of comfort that is then internalized; their bodies rarely become an issue in public situations that affects or impedes action. The overall entitlement men experience in public spaces is thus a privilege that transfers to overweight men.

Men's reported experiences of greater body privilege must be situated in Western culture's construction of normative masculinity. Cultural scripts of hegemonic masculinity dictate certain acceptable behaviors (and even appearances) for men (Connell 1995). The behaviors and characteristics associated with so-called "real men" include, among other things, independence, physical strength, and emotional toughness (Kivel 2003). Conforming to this prevailing construction of masculinity may mean that men avoid a concern for weight loss, dieting, and other related issues, or at the very least avoid discussing these matters, as they are often viewed as a feminine preoccupation.[3] In other words, men may be "doing gender" by downplaying experiences of body oppression (West and Zimmerman 1987). In this context, Matthew's focus on food and fun may be interpreted in part as gender performance. . . .

Women's more extensive and intensive experiences of body oppression can be interpreted as part of a disadvantaged status caused by the intersection of multiple systems of oppressions. Patricia Hill Collins (1998) maintains that oppressions are not linear and can be understood as interlocking configurations that combine to influence important social outcomes, along with self-identity (see also West and Fenstermaker 1995). When theorizing the type of embodied oppressions observed here, this intersection potentially involves (at the very least) experiences based on body size, gender, and race/ethnicity. . . .

Overweight women are uniquely situated in a culture that not only exhibits a strong body hierarchy mandating thinness, but also a gendered body hierarchy mandating female thinness. Indeed, the overweight female participants I spoke with knew they did not comply with both aesthetic body norms and norms of femininity, acknowledging in part that "ideologies of weight closely parallel ideologies of womanhood" (McKinley 1999, 97). Most female participants, such as Kelly (age 37, white), are aware of this double standard. She highlighted how body norms are gendered: "I think society treats women worse. Because it goes back to the whole 36-24-36. You're supposed to have this hourglass figure. . . . I think that it's the whole generation thing, bred into society that if you don't look a certain way, if you're a female, then you're just . . . you're ousted from society." Failing to achieve both body norms and the interconnected norms of womanhood, female participants are thus doubly stigmatized: They are double failures.

Mass media reinforce these ideologies and objectify women's bodies, thereby exacerbating women's body consciousness. Objectification theory points to how media produce an objectifying gaze of women's bodies and their body parts (Frederickson and Roberts 1997). In a patriarchal heteronormative culture, a "male gaze" constructs women as objects for viewing by a male spectator (Berger 1972; Mulvey 1989). These images of objectification can then lead to women's heightened sensitivity to body norms, contributing to the self-correction and the performance of management observed.

A Foucauldian interpretation of hegemonic body norms that shifts our attention from repressive strategies of physical restraint and coercion to subtle disciplining techniques of self-correction is thus appropriate (Bordo 2003). Body consciousness and body management are, in fact, direct manifestations of this self-surveillance. We can understand Estella's (age 27, Hispanic) comments within this context:

> Just that you always have that feeling in the back of your mind like somebody's looking at you and judging you because you're fat, because you're overweight. But then you begin to look at the other people and you realize they're not even looking at you. You're like, they're not even looking! You yourself, I guess, are your own demon.

On an ongoing basis, society—as represented by individuals acting on behalf of their own or an institution's interests—reminds overweight women that they do not conform. Someone is watching, patrolling, and judging—a message that is then internalized. This patrolling heightens body consciousness and reminds women that body management is necessary for survival. So while it may appear that these women are acting in ways that are paranoid, their behavior and attitudes are actually far from extreme. As McIntosh (2000) puts it, it is privilege that enables one not "to feel sick or crazy" (p. 35).

Yet, experiences of the body are not only mediated by gender, they are complicated by another intersecting axis: race/ethnicity. At the same time that beauty ideals work in ways that distinctly disadvantage women as a group, certain racial/ethnic identifiers can buffer or intensify experiences of body oppression. . . . For example, researchers theorize that as Hispanic and Asian women are increasingly assimilated into American culture, their patterns of body satisfaction may eventually resemble those of whites (Altabe and O'Garo 2002; Kawamura 2002). Studies with young Latinas confirm this: Their ideal body image correlates with exposure to time spent in the United States (Lopez, Blix, and Blix 1995). Research also indicates that eating disorders are no longer just a white middle- to upper-class phenomenon; Mexican American adolescents from a lower socioeconomic status are just as susceptible (Joiner and Kashubeck 1996). Thus, heightened sensitivity leading to high levels of body consciousness and body management among certain Hispanic female participants may be attributed in part to their embracing the white ideal. In fact, several Latina participants explicitly stated that they rejected a more voluptuous Hispanic ideal, openly admitting that they subscribed to what they believed was the thin, white American ideal found in fashion magazines.

Moreover, studies of African American girls and women point to more flexible conceptions of beauty by blacks as compared to their white counterparts and higher levels of body satisfaction, although there is some dispute over the extent of racial differences (Collins 2000; Grabe and Hyde 2006; Parker et al. 1995). . . . Melissa Milkie's (1999) interviews indicate that minority girls' lack of identification with white media images serves as a buffer to their harmful effects on self-concepts. Meg Lovejoy (2001) captures the key dynamic at work when she claims that black women subscribe to an alternative aesthetic that comprises a form of cultural resistance. A more flexible and egalitarian aesthetic found in black communities celebrates uniqueness and harmony in diversity (Collins 2000). This black aesthetic encourages self-acceptance among African American girls and women, leading to higher levels of body satisfaction.

Laura Hensley Choate (2005) concisely summarizes several key correlates that insulate African American women from negative body images. These include a broader view of an ideal body type; family support that contributes to the development of independence, strength, and self-esteem; and supportive peer and community relationships that value distinctive, individual styles. . . .

While there are parallels between white privilege and body privilege, there are also several notable ways by which these concepts differ. First, McIntosh (2000) claims that individuals with privilege are often oblivious to its conferred benefits. However, because body size can fluctuate, individuals who lose weight may actually become aware of possessing a newfound body privilege. This heightened awareness may result in increased monitoring when weight gain occurs or when one's body does not conform to the ideal. For this reason, Foucauldian self-surveillance may manifest itself in the especially powerful and intrusive ways that were observed among this select group of women participants.

Second, unlike a lack of white privilege, the experiences of body oppression may actually be exacerbated by the belief that weight, unlike, say, race, is controllable. There is a widespread belief that bodies are malleable and thinness is attainable with the right combination of self-discipline, will, and determination (Brownell 1991); indeed, the body is often considered a reflection of one's emotional, moral, and/or spiritual state (Bordo 2003). Where an ideology of individualism is present, a blame-the-victim mentality is even more salient, and individuals are more likely to say that [the] fat [body] is due to a lack of willpower (Crandall and Martinez 1996). This individualist ideology may translate into intensified experiences of body oppression and self-surveillance. . . .

. . . The concept of body privilege sheds new light on key debates concerning culture, structure, and agency. On the one hand, scholars like Bordo (2003) have framed women's body-modification practices as part of a homogenizing and normalizing process that contributes to the creation of "docile bodies." In this vein, women who participate in, say, cosmetic surgery can be considered complicit in their own oppression because they are in need of consciousness raising and/or body acceptance (Chapkis 1991; Davis 1995). On the other hand, the concept of body privilege permits an understanding of body-conformity practices without abandoning individual agency. These practices can be interpreted as the actions of savvy cultural negotiators who understand cultural and social structures; conformity occurs partly because they know all too well that straying from body norms potentially leads to stigma and the denial of privilege (Gimlin 2000). As Kathy Davis (1995) observes, contrary to common feminist rhetoric that cosmetic surgery is a form of co-optation or false consciousness, beauty work [i.e., body modification practices that often result in conformity to hegemonic body norms] is a way of regaining control of one's life, feeling normal, and/or righting the wrong of ongoing suffering (see also Gimlin 2000; Kaw 1993; for an integrated perspective, see Gagné and McGaughey 2002). Similarly, overweight women's attempts at body conformity are not necessarily simplistic acts of complicity, but rather can be interpreted as active and conscious ways to pursue body privilege.

Conclusion

. . . Nearly two decades after Naomi Wolf (1991) exposed the cultural beauty ideal as myth, body ideals still continue to bind, both emotionally and physically, women's bodies and minds. This article's research with forty-two participants highlights the gendered and racial dimensions of body privilege, body consciousness, and body management. However, whether it is experienced by women or men, body privilege, like white or male privilege, is an unearned advantage that confers dominance (McIntosh 2000). In an egalitarian society, body privilege should not be a privilege, but "simply part of the normal civic and social fabric" (p. 36). Achieving this state requires questioning and restructuring the body hierarchy and its supporting institutions, along with individual responsibility in everyday interactions, where individuals take "responsibility for their actions, habits, feelings, attitudes, images, and associations" (Young 1990, 151). Such changes potentially contribute to a society wherein women of all body sizes can perhaps navigate their daily lives comfortably.

Notes

1. According to the medical community, an individual with a BMI between 19.5 and 24.9 is considered "normal" [weight], while an "overweight" individual has a BMI of between 25.0 and 29.9. A BMI above 30.0 indicates "obesity" (USDHHS 2001). Throughout this article, I generally use the term *overweight*, as this was preferred by interview participants. "Obese" has derogatory meanings and, as such, I generally avoid using it.
2. In contrast, Becky Thompson (1992) uses this term to describe "the ability to reside comfortably in one's body (to see oneself as embodied) and to consider one's body as connected to oneself" (p. 556). Her use of this term focuses primarily on the split between body and mind—that is, feeling unable to control one's body, hiding in one part of one's body, or not seeing oneself as having a body.
3. Hegemonic masculinity may have affected men's interview responses. That is, the men I spoke with may have been more reluctant than women to talk about body issues and to disclose incidents of body oppression. However, that male participants were actually quite candid and expressive during the interviews strengthens the validity of my findings; they were generally frank and forthright, even thanking me for the opportunity to discuss body issues behind closed doors.

References

Altabe, Madeline, and Keisha-Gaye N. O'Garo. 2002. Hispanic body images. In *Body Image: A Handbook of Theory, Research, and Clinical Practice*, edited by Thomas F. Cash and Thomas Pruzinsky. New York: Guilford Press.

Bartky, Sandra. 1990. *Femininity and Domination: Studies in the Phenomenology of Oppression*. New York: Routledge.

Berger, John. 1972. *Ways of Seeing*. London: Penguin.

Bordo, Susan. 2003. *Unbearable Weight: Feminism, Western Culture, and the Body*, 2nd ed. Berkeley: University of California Press.

Brownell, Kelly D. 1991. Dieting and the search for the perfect body: Where physiology and culture collide. *Behavior Therapy* 22:1–12.

Chapkis, Wendy. 1991. Remaking the she-devil: A critical look at feminist approaches to beauty. *Hypatia* 6(2):21–40.

Chernin, Kim. 1994. *The Obsession: Reflections on the Tyranny of Slenderness*. New York: Harper Perennial.

Collins, Patricia Hill. 1998. *Fighting Words: Black Women and the Search for Justice*. Minneapolis: University of Minnesota Press.

______. 2000. *Black Feminist Thought: Knowledge, Consciousness, and the Politics of Empowerment*, 2nd ed. New York: Routledge.

Conley, Dalton, and Rebecca Glauber. 2005. Gender, body mass and economic status. *National Bureau of Economic Research Working Paper Series*. National Bureau of Economic Research, Cambridge, MA.

Connell, R. W. 1995. *Masculinities*. Berkeley: University of California Press.

Crandall, Christian S., and Rebecca Martinez. 1996. Culture, ideology, and anti-fat attitudes. *Personality and Social Psychology Bulletin* 22:1165–76.

Davis, Kathy. 1995. *Reshaping the Female Body: The Dilemma of Cosmetic Surgery*. New York: Routledge.

Dion, Karen, Ellen Berscheid, and Elaine Walster. 1972. What is beautiful is good. *Journal of Personality and Social Psychology* 24(3):285–90.

Foucault, Michel. 1977. *Discipline and Punish: The Birth of the Prison*. Trans. Alan Sheridan. New York: Vintage Books.

Frederickson, Barbara L., and Tomi-Ann Roberts. 1997. Objectification theory: Towards understanding women's lived experiences and mental health risks. *Psychology of Women Quarterly* 21:173–206.

Gagné, Patricia, and Deanna McGaughey. 2002. Designing women: Cultural hegemony and the exercise of power among women who have undergone elective mammoplasty. *Gender & Society* 16(6):814–38.

Gimlin, Debra L. 2000. Cosmetic surgery: Beauty as commodity. *Qualitative Sociology* 23(1):77–98.

______. 2002. *Body Work: Beauty and Self-Image in American Culture*. Berkeley: University of California Press.

Goffman, Erving. 1959. *The Presentation of Self in Everyday Life*. New York: Doubleday.

______. 1963. *Stigma: Notes on the Management of Spoiled Identity*. Englewood Cliffs, NJ: Prentice-Hall.

Grabe, Shelly, and Janet Shibley Hyde. 2006. Ethnicity and body dissatisfaction among women in the United States: A meta-analysis. *Psychological Bulletin* 132(4):622–40.

Hensley Choate, Laura. 2005. Toward a theoretical model of women's body image resilience. *Journal of Counseling & Development* 83:320–30.

Hosoda, Megumi, Eugene F. Stone-Romero, and Gwen Coats. 2003. The effects of physical attractiveness on job-related outcomes: A meta-analysis of experimental studies. *Personnel Psychology* 56:431–62.

Joiner, Greg W., and Susan Kashubeck. 1996. Acculturation, body image, self-esteem, and eating-disorder symptomatology in adolescent Mexican American women. *Psychology of Women Quarterly* 20(3):419–35.

Kaw, Eugenia. 1993. Medicalization of racial features: Asian American women and cosmetic surgery. *Medical Anthropology Quarterly* 7:74–89.

Kawamura, Kathleen Y. 2002. Asian American body images. In *Body Image: A Handbook of Theory, Research, and Clinical Practice*, edited by Thomas F. Cash and Thomas Pruzinsky. New York: Guilford Press.

Kivel, Paul. 2003. The "act like a man" box. In *Masculinities: Interdisciplinary Readings*, edited by Mark Hussey. Upper Saddle River, NJ: Prentice Hall.

Kwan, Samantha, and Mary Nell Trautner. 2009. Beauty work: Individual and institutional rewards, the reproduction of gender, and questions of agency. *Sociology Compass* 3(1):49–71.

Landy, David, and Harold Sigall. 1974. Beauty is talent: Task evaluation as a function of the performer's physical attractiveness. *Journal of Personality and Social Psychology* 39(3):299–304.

Lopez, Esther, Glen Garry Blix, and Arlene Gray Blix. 1995. Body image of Latinas compared to body image of non-Latina white women. *Health Values: The Journal of Health Behavior, Education & Promotion* 19(6):3–10.

Lovejoy, Meg. 2001. Disturbances in the social body: Differences in body image and eating problems among African American and white women. *Gender & Society* 15(2):239–61.

McIntosh, Peggy. 2000. White privilege and male privilege: A personal account of coming to see correspondences through work in women's studies. In *Gender Basics*, 2nd ed., edited by Anne Minas. Belmont, CA: Wadsworth. (Originally published in 1988 as *White Privilege and Male Privilege: A Personal Account of Coming to See Correspondences through Work in Women's Studies*, Wellesley College Center for Research on Women Working Paper 189, Wellesley, MA.)

McKinley, Nita Mary. 1999. Ideal weight/ideal women: Society constructs the female. In *Weighty Issues: Fatness and Thinness as Social Problems*, edited by Jeffery Sobal and Donna Maurer. New York: Aldine de Gruyter.

Mead, George Herbert. 1934. *Mind, Self, and Society*. Edited by C. W. Morris. Chicago: University of Chicago Press.

Milkie, Melissa. 1999. Social comparisons, reflected appraisals, and mass media: The impact of pervasive beauty images on black and white girls' self-concepts. *Social Psychology Quarterly* 62:190–210.

Mulvey, Laura. 1989. *Visual Pleasures and Narrative Cinema*. Bloomington, IN: Indianapolis University Press.

Pagan, José A., and Alberto Dávila. 1997. Obesity, occupational attainment, and earnings. *Social Science Quarterly* 78:756–70.

Paquette, Marie-Claude, and Kim Raine. 2004. Sociocultural context of women's body image. *Social Science and Medicine* 59(5):1047–58.

Parker, Sheila, Mimi Nichter, Mark Nichter, Nancy Vuckovic, Colette Sims, and Cheryl Rittenbaugh. 1995. Body image and weight concerns among African American and white adolescent females: Differences that make a difference. *Human Organization* 54(2):103–14.

Pope, Harrison G., Jr., Katharine A. Phillips, and Roberto Olivardia. 2000. *The Adonis Complex: The Secret Crisis of Male Body Obsession*. New York: Free Press.

Puhl, Rebecca, and Kelly D. Brownell. 2001. Bias, discrimination, and obesity. *Obesity Research* 9(12):788–805.

Rothblum, Esther D. 1992. The stigma of women's weight: Social and economic realities. *Feminism and Psychology* 2(1):61–73.

Rothblum, Esther D., Carol T. Miller, and Barbara Garbutt. 1988. Stereotypes of obese female job applicants. *International Journal of Eating Disorders* 7:277–83.

Sobal, Jeffery. 2004. Sociological analysis of the stigmatisation of obesity. In *A Sociology of Food and Nutrition: The Social Appetite*, edited by John Germov and Lauren Williams. Oxford: Oxford University Press.

Solovay, Sondra. 2000. *Tipping the Scales of Injustice: Fighting Weight-Based Discrimination*. Amherst, NY: Prometheus Books.

Sprague-Zones, Jane. 1997. Beauty myths and realities and their impact on women's health. In *Women's Health: Complexities and Differences*, edited by Cheryl B. Ruzek, Virginia L. Oleson, and Adele E. Clarke. Columbus: Ohio State University Press.

Sykes, Gresham, and David Matza. 1957. Techniques of neutralization. *American Sociological Review* 22(6):664–70.

Thompson, Becky W. 1992. "A way outa no way": Eating problems among African-American, Latina, and white women. *Gender & Society* 6(4):546–61.

U.S. Department of Health and Human Services (USDHHS). 2001. *The Surgeon General's Call to Action to Prevent and Decrease Overweight and Obesity* (Report). Rockville, MD: Office of the Surgeon General.

Webster, Murray, Jr., and James E. Driskell. 1983. Beauty as status. *American Journal of Sociology* 89(1):140–65.

West, Candace, and Sarah Fenstermaker. 1995. Doing difference. *Gender & Society* 9(1):8–37.

———, and Don H. Zimmerman. 1987. Doing gender. *Gender & Society* 1(2):125–51.

Wolf, Naomi. 1991. *The Beauty Myth*. New York: HarperCollins.

Young, Iris Marion. 1990. *Justice and the Politics of Difference*. Princeton, NJ: Princeton University Press.

16

The Moral Underpinnings of Beauty

A Meaning-Based Explanation for Light and Dark Complexions in Advertising

SHYON BAUMANN

As the last three articles highlighted, disciplines of femininity can focus on many aspects of women's bodies, including breasts, hair, and body size. In "The Moral Underpinnings of Beauty: A Meaning-Based Explanation for Light and Dark Complexions in Advertising," Shyon Baumann turns to an aspect of women's bodies that has received relatively little attention among scholars—or at least among white scholars: skin complexion. Today the manufacture and sale of skin-lightening products have become multi-billion-dollar global industries, and women from around the world consume these products in hopes of attaining brighter, lighter, and whiter skin. Baumann explores the source of women's skin tone ideals and attempts to explain their appeal.

Baumann's content analysis of print advertisements in popular magazines reveals that the skin tone ideal for women is lighter than the ideal for men. This was the case among advertisements in the 1970s and currently, as well as among advertisements featuring either black or white models. Rejecting a biological based argument that these ideals represent evolutionary mechanisms, Baumann argues instead that the observed gender differences in skin tone (particularly for whites) suggest a physical attractiveness ideal that is "submerged." In contrast to "articulated" ideals that are commonly acknowledged within public discourses, "submerged" ideals are less frequently identified and openly discussed. According to Baumann, submerged complexion ideals are tied closely to the link between aesthetics and moral judgment. Specifically, the aesthetic appeal of whiteness and

Reprinted from *Poetics* 36(1), Shyon Baumann, "The Moral Underpinnings of Beauty: A Meaning-Based Explanation for Light and Dark Complexions in Advertising," 2–23, copyright 2008, with permission from Elsevier.

lightness stems from its association with traditional feminine ideals such as innocence, purity, virginity, vulnerability, and delicacy. Baumann's content analysis of a subset of advertisements featuring white women with the lightest and darkest complexions provides further evidence for his theory. He finds that the fairest skin toned women are depicted as reserved, chaste, and proper, whereas the darkest skin toned women are associated with overt sexuality.

. . . In this article I address a question of taste in personal appearance. To speak of taste in appearance is to ask why certain physical characteristics are generally considered more attractive than alternative physical characteristics. Personal appearance is comprised of a vast number of discrete and interrelated physical characteristics. The focus of this article is to explain the dominant tastes in complexion. The empirical question I begin with is, how does the ideal complexion for women compare to the ideal complexion for men, in terms of lightness and darkness of appearance? Through content analysis of advertisements, I find that women are ideally lighter than men. Following this, I address the question of why the ideal complexion for women is lighter than the ideal complexion for men. I first address whether there is convincing evidence that the findings reflect a biological gender difference and conclude that the gender difference in complexions in advertisements cannot be accounted for by biological explanations. I then formulate an alternative explanation grounded in a *meaning-based approach*. This approach differs from most other contemporary sociological analyses of taste because it takes into account the dominant meanings of aesthetic characteristics in order to explain the preference for them. In the case of lightness and darkness, Western culture attributes a set of meanings to each of these traits, and these meanings are gendered in the sense that the meanings of lightness correspond to various dimensions of stereotypically feminine gender roles while the meanings of darkness correspond to various dimensions of stereotypically masculine gender roles. . . .

Advertising and Attractiveness Ideals

Although advertising's ostensible purpose is to sell goods and services, sociologists and communications scholars have identified a latent, secondary role. Schudson (1984, 215), for example, views advertising as "capitalist realism," meaning that advertising "does not claim to picture reality as it is but reality as it should be—life and lives worth emulating." Likewise, Goffman (1979) argues that advertisements should be seen as ritualized displays; they depict idealized social relationships. Rather than showing us how men and women actually behave and appear, advertising shows us how we believe men and women should behave and appear. In order to maximize resonance and appeal with a large audience, advertisements need to accord with widely accepted ideals.

Advertising, then, provides a good opportunity to observe indirectly and to measure widely shared or dominant ideals of the society in which the advertising is distributed. Moreover, much advertising is visual in nature, and much advertising features people. Advertising shows us how people should appear, or what is ideally attractive, even if this is not its manifest function (Pollay 1986).

Physical attractiveness is largely not a matter of choice, but social psychological studies have empirically established that individuals routinely associate a wide range of positive psychological attributes with those whom they judge to be physically attractive (Hosoda, Stone-Romero, and Coats 2003). In the case of physical attractiveness, a "halo effect" (Feeley 2002) means that the evaluation of physical appearance influences the evaluation of other traits. The literature that examines the "what is beautiful is good" phenomenon (Dion, Berscheid, and Walster 1972) has found correlations between ratings of attractiveness and social competence, intelligence, integrity, and general mental health, among other traits. It is not surprising, therefore, that advertisements typically feature attractive models. Given the "halo effect" created by perceptions of attractiveness, attractive models are generally more effective for generating positive responses toward that which is being advertised (Baker and Churchill, 1977; Kahle and Homer, 1985). . . .

Articulated and Submerged Attractiveness Ideals

Ideals regarding physical attractiveness vary between societies as well as between groups within a society. In the United States, as elsewhere, there are *dominant* ideals held by the majority ethnic group, and known to virtually all members of society, regarding a great number of physical characteristics. For example, there are ideals for height, weight, the shape of the nose, the shape of the mouth, the color and positioning of the teeth, the distances between facial parts, and more. At the same time, aesthetic ideals of physical attractiveness have gender-specific dimensions. What is attractive for a man is not necessarily attractive for a woman, and vice versa. Furthermore, some ideals are gendered to the extent that opposite qualities are preferred for each gender (Synott 1987). Oppositional, subcultural, or minority ideals obviously also exist and can differ from the dominant ideals most commonly observed within the beauty ideals of white, mainstream heterosexuals. For readability, the term *ideal* refers in this article to the dominant ideal.

Some physical attractiveness ideals are commonly acknowledged within public discourse where they are regularly *articulated*. The dominant aesthetic preference for low body fat in men and even lower body fat in women is one example. Ample breast size for women is another example. Yet another ideal governs tallness, with ideal height for men exceeding the ideal height for women. Not all people share these ideals, but many openly recognize that they describe how we "should" look.

In contrast, other physical attractiveness ideals are not openly discussed or acknowledged. Rather they are *submerged*, and these ideals are important, yet infrequently identified or studied as an element of aesthetic preferences. While these submerged ideals might be as specific and unforbearing as those that are more consciously held, most of us are not conscious that we have these ideals and that they come into play when we evaluate others' or our own attractiveness. Sometimes an appearance ideal can shift from submerged to articulated when it is discussed by appearance experts (e.g., cosmeticians or plastic surgeons) in the mass media. One example of such an ideal in flux is the notion that for maximum attractiveness the space between one's eyes should be exactly as wide as one eye (Dilio 2005; Habbema 2004). Despite the occasional shift, there are many physical attractiveness ideals that are still largely submerged. The reason for this is that physical appearance has myriad visual components, and this large amount of information is processed by us largely without articulation. We do not consciously acknowledge what we do not articulate. As a consequence, although we can say with certainty whether we find a particular person attractive, we often have difficulty articulating all the reasons behind that finding.

The Complexion Ideal: Evolving, Gendered, and Submerged (for Whites)

The ideal regarding attractiveness of complexion in U.S. society is complicated by its connection to the evolving history of racial prejudice. On the one hand, there is an historical preference for light complexions in the majority white society of the United States. For centuries, the dominant view was that the light skin of Caucasians was more attractive than the darker skin of non-Caucasians. Undoubtedly, this preference was linked to racism and was publicly articulated alongside openly racist attitudes. On the other hand, racial attitudes have evolved in recent decades. Some reports in the popular press have suggested that, though a Eurocentric bias still operates, our conceptions of what is attractive have likewise evolved to become more racially inclusive (Avery 2000; Carr 2002; Sagario 2002). Hence, norms concerning attractive complexions are allegedly changing away from a bias toward lightness.[1] To make matters more complicated, the fashion for tanning has changed over time, creating yet more potential for disagreement over what constitutes an attractive complexion.

To what degree is the complexion ideal articulated in the white majority North American society? I argue that among whites there is no explicitly articulated complexion ideal in contemporary mainstream public discourse. Among African Americans, where complexion is recognized to have important consequences, the preference for a light complexion is to a substantial degree publicly articulated (Breland 1998). Among whites, however, the complexion ideal, and especially its gendered nature, is submerged. The privilege of being racially white renders the significant variation within the category of "white" less consequential than is the case for blacks (see Gullickson 2005; Hill 2000; Hughes and Hertel 1990; Keith and Herring 1991). What is more, because beauty ideals are allegedly becoming more racially inclusive, some ideals inevitably come into conflict, complexion perhaps being one of the clearest examples. The conflicting ideals and varying images of attractiveness shown in the mass media make it difficult for individuals to be able to settle on a clear articulation of a single ideal. Whites, therefore, are less able to articulate what an ideal complexion should look like, and particularly unable to articulate gender-specific ideals.

Because advertising relies on images that embody ideals, it provides an excellent opportunity to observe the ideal complexion in its gendered and racialized variants. Furthermore, because such images are contextualized in a wider advertisement that contains other visual messages, advertisements provide an opportunity to analyze the kinds of messages with which certain complexions co-vary. This co-variation provides evidence for understanding how different physical appearance characteristics are understood to have distinct meanings, and how these meanings are gendered.

Data

The data come from advertisements in nine popular magazines: *People*, *Time*, and *Newsweek* (general interest magazines), *Maxim* and *Esquire* (magazines targeting men), *Vogue* and *Cosmopolitan* (magazines targeting women), and *Ebony* and *Essence* (magazines targeting a black audience). Issues between July of 2003 and May of 2004 were randomly selected. The unit of analysis is the person depicted, not the advertisement, and so the eventual sample size represents the number of individuals appearing in advertisements, with each individual representing a separate record in the data. Advertisements were coded only if they were larger than 2 square inches in size, in color (not black and white),[2] and featured at least one person in the foreground (in focus). People out of focus or in the background were disregarded. In addition to the magazine in which the advertisements were placed, the other independent variables are sex, race, and age. Gender proved readily codable, with the very rare cases of indeterminate gender excluded from analysis (two cases). Race, however, proved slightly more difficult to code. There is no practical way to ascertain the "real" gender or race of the models in advertisements. This difficulty notwithstanding, the objective here is to observe the gender and racial identity that *seem to be put forth* in the advertisements. Even this objective, however, was not always possible to attain as visual cues to race in models' faces were sometimes highly ambiguous (about 3 percent of models). These cases were dropped from the analysis. . . . Because of the stark under-representation of models from other racial categories, . . . analysis only of blacks and whites was possible. . . . Children were excluded from the analysis because it is unclear that aesthetic standards and gender roles as they apply to adults would apply equally to children.

Although previous studies of complexion have dealt exclusively with skin tone, I argue that there is good reason for employing a broader conception of complexion as including both skin and hair tone. This study has three dependent variables: skin tone, hair tone, and a composite measure of complexion comprised of the addition of skin and hair tone. I contend that measuring both skin and hair tone provides a better measure of the overall appearance of lightness or darkness. This article's focus on taste in lightness or darkness of complexion warrants as complete a measurement of lightness or darkness as possible.

The dependent variables of skin tone and hair tone were coded according to a ten-point scale, with 1 being lightest and 10 being darkest. Coders used a pallet of gradations in skin tones and another pallet of gradations in hair tone, matching the tones in the ads to the closest possible tones in the pallets. Each model was coded independently, according only to the pallet and not with respect to other models in the same or in other advertisements. Skin tone was judged according to the predominant tone present in the face, while hair tone was judged according to the predominant tone present in the hair.[3] The composite measure of complexion is the addition of the hair and skin tones, with 2 being the lightest possible composite complexion and 20 being the darkest possible composite complexion. Following the exclusions described previously, there were 2,133 individuals coded from 1,508 advertisements. [Interrater agreement was measured by the Kappa statistic and fell within standard guidelines.] . . .

Complexion Findings

. . . Results are not presented according to age or magazine because these variables had no recognizable influence on complexion [even among magazines aimed at African Americans]. Regarding skin, the lightest color on the palette, 1, is almost purely white, while the darkest color of 10 is a very dark brown. Regarding hair, the palette ranges from a platinum blond color to black. In addition to the results for skin and hair, a composite measure of overall complexion is reported. The composite measure is the simple addition of skin and hair tone results for each person and ranges from 2 to 20. [Sample sizes vary for each racial-gender category.]

Regarding white women, the average skin tone is a very light 2.8, and hair tone averages out to a middling 5.0. The averages conceal a wide range of tones for skin and hair. Although the wide range of white women's hair tones might be expected, the wide range of skin tones of white women is more surprising. Although racially white, these women's skin can appear as dark as 8 (often achieved through the use of shadows or other circumstances where lighting is minimized). The average skin tone for white men is a fairly light 3.3 while the average hair tone is a somewhat dark 6.3. Just as with women, the averages conceal a wide range of tones, and white men's skin was also rated as dark as 8. Most importantly, the gender comparison reveals that white men tend to be presented with darker complexions than white women. The gender differences in both hair and skin tones are statistically significant at the 0.000 level. The composite measure, in particular, reveals the strength of this trend, and the gender difference is likewise significant at the 0.000 level.

Turning to the results for blacks, as could be expected, black men and women have darker skin, hair, and overall complexions than white men and women. [Skin tone averages for black men and black women are, respectively, 8.1 and 7.2; hair tone averages for black men and black women are, respectively, 9.7 and 8.8.] Of greater interest, however, is the gender difference that reappears. For skin, hair, and the composite measure black men appear in darker tones than black women, and the differences are each significant at the 0.000 level. [Composite averages are 9.7 for white men, 7.8 for white women, 17.8 for black men, and 16.0 for black women.] Thus, there is a gender gap in skin and hair tone for both blacks and whites.

Because whites and blacks are analyzed separately, these gender differences cannot be the result of the differential representation of racial groups by gender. Rather, what we see is that women and men differ in their average lightness or darkness according to a consistent pattern for both blacks and whites. The numbers point to trends that are subtle but certainly noticeable to anyone who pays attention to how men and women are portrayed in advertisements.

Are these trends representative of a single point in time, or do they represent more durable gender differences? . . . To address this possibility [that gender difference in complexion norms is a contemporary phenomenon], I collected and analyzed a second sample of magazine advertisements from 1970.[4]

The first point to make is that advertisements in 1970 popular magazines overwhelmingly feature white models. Only 8 of the 268 people coded were non-white (7 black, 1 Hispanic). Therefore, I compare only white men and women. In comparison with the data from 2003 and 2004, both men and women have darker complexions in advertisements in 1970. [Skin tone averages are 3.7 for white men and 2.9 for white women; hair tone averages are 7.7 for white men and 5.3 for white women; and composite averages are 11.4 for white men and 8.3 for white women]. It is beyond the scope of this article to explain these rather small differences between 1970 and 2003–2004.[5] What is relevant, however, is that the same pattern of gender differences is found in both time periods. White men have darker average skin tone, hair color, and overall complexion than white women in 1970 [and these differences are statistically significant]. . . .

Complexion and Biological Gender Differences

. . . Has the research measured not simply an appearance ideal, but also an objective, biological difference between men and women? Do men across races have darker complexions than women? If this is the case, then these data would be inadequate for establishing that there is a gender difference in complexion ideals.

A body of research in physical anthropology is concerned with understanding the evolutionary mechanisms that have created the wide range of skin tones found between human populations. Within this literature, empirical evidence on skin pigmentation, as measured through machines that detect light reflectance, has been collected for populations from around the globe. One interesting finding is that most of the studies that included a record of the sex of subjects find that females do tend to have lighter skin than males from the same populations (Jablonski and Chaplin 2000; Madrigal and Kelly 2006). These studies were generally carried out over the course of the last four decades.

An implication of this body of research, then, is that the observed skin tone gender differences in advertisements reflect simple biological gender differences. There are reasons to be wary of this interpretation, however. One reason for caution is that other, more recent research has found no significant sex differences in the lightness of skin (Shriver et al. 2003; Wagner, Parra, Norton, Jovel, and Shriver 2002). These authors note that while most prior studies have found significant sex differences, it is difficult to assess whether prior studies controlled for differing activity patterns and clothing customs between the sexes, and they suggest that this could explain the pattern found in prior studies, as men in many societies have typically spent more time outdoors.

A second reason to doubt that the different complexions of women and men in advertising reflect only a biological difference is that the size of the difference found in advertising is much larger than the difference reported in the physical anthropological studies. Tegner (1992) notes that the studies of skin pigmentation generally report that females' skin is 2 percent to 3 percent lighter than males'. In contrast, in the sample of advertisements in this study, the skin of white females is 15.2 percent lighter than the skin of white males, and the skin of black females is 11.1 percent lighter than the skin of black males. The magnitude of these differences cannot be explained by biological differences. . . .

Meanings, Morals, and Aesthetics

. . . The meaning-based approach to understanding complexion ideals can advance our knowledge of the cultural forces causing this differential and provide a fuller explanation of this phenomenon. According to this approach, the average gender difference in complexion arises from the close connection between what "lightness" means and what behavior is valued in women, and the close connection between what "darkness" means and what is valued in men.

Physical lightness and darkness are aesthetic characteristics that, perhaps better than any other aesthetic characteristic, exemplify the link between aesthetic and moral judgments. The concepts of lightness and darkness have strong associations with a variety of qualities that have moral connotations. Associations with whiteness or lightness include youth, innocence, purity, virginity, vulnerability, and delicacy. Associations with blackness or darkness include threat, aggression, virility, mystery, villainy, and danger. Lightness and darkness together compose a stable, clear, and well-known cultural dichotomy. Evidence for the nature of this dichotomy can be found throughout our culture. Dyer (1997, 58) notes that, indeed, "the *Oxford English Dictionary* gives as the seventh meaning of white both 'morally and spiritually pure' and 'free from malignity . . . esp. as opposed to something that is characterized as black.'"

Considering the dominant meanings of lightness and darkness, it seems reasonable to argue that women are sometimes held to higher standards of lightness than are men because the meaning of lightness coincides with our definition of the appropriate role of women in society. As women are held to an aesthetic double standard, *they are simultaneously held to a moral double standard regarding precisely those attitudes and behaviors most closely connected to the aesthetic characteristics in question.* Those attitudes and behaviors frequently concern sexual activity. For example, women are held to different standards regarding their virginity, innocence, purity, and their willingness to engage in sexual activity (Aubrey 2004; Foschi 2000, 35)—and these are precisely the qualities invoked by an aesthetic of lightness. Women are rewarded for exemplifying these attitudinal and behavioral qualities, such as chastity and innocence, just as they are rewarded for exemplifying the aesthetic characteristic that symbolizes them.

The meaning-based approach to understanding complexion differences explains why women have fairer complexions than men in advertisements on average. In general, advertisements conform to rather than subvert dominant gender roles. But the approach is also flexible enough to explain the wide variation in women's complexions in advertisements. A meaning-based approach leaves room to interpret women's darker complexions in advertisements as instances when the message of the advertisement involves not women's purity, innocence, or delicacy, but rather women's sexuality or "impurity." One empirical implication of the meaning-based approach, then, is that fairer complexions among women in advertisements are associated with conservative gender role messages, while darker complexions among women in advertisements are associated with greater sexualization. The following section tests for this implication.

Sexualization and Complexion: A Comparison of Fair and Dark White Women

A meaning-based approach to understanding complexion differences predicts the conditions under which advertisements will tend to portray women with fairer complexions—namely, when the advertisement emphasizes the woman's purity and delicacy rather than her active sexuality. Through an analysis of a subsample of advertisements, I find evidence in support of the meaning-based approach to understanding gendered complexion differences. This evidence comes from a content analysis of two groups of advertisements: fifty unique advertisements featuring white women with the lightest complexions in the sample and fifty unique advertisements featuring white women with the darkest complexions in the sample. In this case, the number of advertisements is equal to the number of people in each group.[6] The meaning-based explanation for complexion differences posits that women are ideally lighter in complexion than men because this lightness is representative of ideally feminine moral traits and behavior. If this perspective is accurate, then such moral attributes and behavior should be more prominent on average in advertisements with the fairest women compared to advertisements with women with the darkest complexions. A comparison between these two groups of advertisements provides a test of the explanation.

What evidence exists within the advertisements to link light complexions with innocence, purity, and delicacy? Table 16.1 presents the results of a

TABLE 16.1 Characteristics of Advertisements with White Women with 50 Lightest and Darkest Complexions

Characteristics	Lightest	Darkest	Significantly different (one-tailed test)
State of undress			
Bared midriff	3	20	***
Bared thighs	14	16	
Bared shoulders	20	31	*
Bared feet	0	4	*
Visible cleavage	9	16	
Implied to be naked	0	4	*
Provocatively dressed			
Wearing a bra or similar top without a shirt	2	13	***
Wearing underwear or bikini bottom	2	7	*
Conservatively dressed			
Wearing long sleeves	18	13	
Wearing a jacket	11	7	
Wearing a turtleneck	3	0	*
Wearing long pants	11	6	
Sexual signals			
Hair to shoulders or beyond	20	29	**
Wet	0	5	*
Closed eyes	2	8	*
Caressing an object	4	11	*
In bed	2	2	
Mouth in contact with an object	0	3	*

(*Continued*)

TABLE 16.1 (*Continued*)

Characteristics	Lightest	Darkest	Significantly different (one-tailed test)
Suggestive positioning			
Reclined	3	13	***
Legs spread widely	3	5	
Feet visibly off the ground	2	6	
Suggestions of propriety			
Child present	1	1	
Eye contact with audience	36	24	**
Standing upright	16	11	
Smiling	10	11	
Head/shoulders only	10	3	*
Relationship to men			
Alongside a man	8	10	
No physical contact with man present	4	3	
Casual physical contact with man	2	0	
Intimate physical contact with man	2	7	*
Relationship to women			
Alongside a woman	9	3	*
No physical contact with woman present	2	2	
Casual physical contact with woman	7	1	*
Intimate physical contact with a woman	0	0	
Consumer context			
Advertisement for alcohol	2	7	*
Advertisement in a men's magazine	4	9	
Advertisement for tanning products	0	1	
General context			
Outdoor setting	5	20	***
All white background	20	3	***

Note: ***$p < 0.001$; **$p < 0.01$; *$p < 0.05$.

manifest content analysis that compares the two groups of advertisements in terms of objectively codable characteristics. The first column shows the total number of the lightest women possessing a characteristic, and the second column shows the total number of the darkest women possessing a characteristic. The third column contains the results of difference of proportions tests.[7]

Compared to women with the fairest complexions, women with the darkest complexions are in an advanced state of undress. Although not every difference in proportions achieves statistical significance, each point of comparison is in the expected direction. Given the relatively small sample size, the consistency with which the differences appear in the expected direction should be given weight as supporting evidence. The women with the darkest complexions are also more likely to have a bared midriff, and only they are shown with bared feet and are implied to be totally nude, strategically covered to avoid being entirely nude. The darkest complected women are also likely to be provocatively dressed, wearing a bra or bra-like article of clothing such as a bikini top, and underwear or similar article of clothing such as a bikini bottom. In contrast, the lightest complected women are more likely to be conservatively dressed. Although most of the measures narrowly miss statistical significance, they all point in the expected direction.

The darkest complected women are more likely to have hair that reaches their shoulders or beyond. As Synott (1987, 384) notes, long hair symbolizes both femininity and sexiness within Anglo-American culture. Wetness has an erotic symbolism in our culture (Ingham 2002), and there again the darkest complected women are more likely to be wet in advertisements. In addition to having closed eyes, the darkest complected women were more likely to be caressing or cradling an object, using their fingertips with their fingers extended to lightly touch, hold, or outline an object, a sexualized and non-utilitarian form of touching (Goffman 1979, 29).

The darkest complected women were much more likely to be reclined, a position with an association with sexual activity. In contrast, the lightest complected women were more likely to make eye contact with the audience and to have only their face or face and shoulders depicted. Previous research has documented that such depictions generate an impression of competency in comparison to whole-body depictions (Schwarz and Kurz 1989).

Although only a minority of each group was shown alongside a man, it is the nature of the relationship between the woman and the man that exhibits the greatest difference. The darkest complected women were more likely to have intimate (kissing, hugging, touching of head or face) contact with a man. In contrast, the fairest complected women were more likely to appear alongside another woman, with casual physical contact or none at all. This difference speaks to a tendency for some of the fairest complected women to be presented in a way that evokes chastity and the protective presence of another woman. Some of the darkest complected women, however, were presented in a manner that either strongly connoted sexual contact or was overtly depicting sexual contact.

The final coding categories relate to the context of the women's portrayals. The darkest complected women were more likely to be in advertisements for alcoholic beverages. One interpretation of this difference is that advertisers frequently link alcoholic consumption with sexual activity or sexually charged situations, and the submerged complexion ideal of a dark complexion "looks right" for such ads. The darkest complected women were also more likely to be shown outdoors, the majority of which were rural or natural settings. Such settings can contribute to an atmosphere of reduced constraint, supervision, and formality. Although not overtly sexual in themselves, these qualities are more compatible with the suggestion of sexual potential that is present in these advertisements.

The all-white background in which more of the lightest complected women were portrayed, however, contributed to an atmosphere of purity and radiance. The tendency to portray fair women against white backgrounds in advertisements is noted by Redmond (2003, 176), who argues that these "symbolically loaded white settings . . . connote ideas of purity and innocence and radiance."

The overall picture generated by the manifest content analysis of the subsample of advertisements is that the fairest complected women tend to be portrayed in less overtly sexualized ways than are the darkest complected women. Both groups are conventionally attractive, with every woman being a thin, young adult. But we see here a strong correspondence between an aesthetic characteristic and an implied set of moral traits: fairness in complexion is associated with a presentation of more reserved, chaste, and proper women. The results support the meaning-based explanation of the gendered pattern of complexion differences.

A final comparison based on a qualitative analysis of themes and moods in the advertisements also supports the meaning-based explanation. A subjective assessment of the depiction of women in the advertisements reveals that the darkest complected women were more frequently presented as overtly sexual. For example, some of the women in this group modeled lingerie (in a women's magazine) or wore revealing clothes in advertisements for electronics or furniture (in men's magazines) while wearing an expression of arousal, with mouth slightly ajar and looking away from the camera. An advertisement for electronics features a nearly nude woman with the caption "All your favorite turn-ons." Another advertisement from this group was for an alcoholic beverage and included the caption "Forbidden pleasures are frequently the most enjoyable." Yet another advertisement features a woman lifted by a man on a dance floor. She is smiling broadly with her legs wrapped around his waist. She is wearing a cowboy hat, blue jeans, and cowboy boots, giving the impression of riding him. She is also wearing a bikini top, and he has an alcoholic beverage in his hand.

While the fairest complected women were sometimes portrayed as sultry, sexy, and aggressively sexy, such scenes were less frequent and more tempered. More common among the fairest women were portrayals of friendliness, happiness, and honesty. Such qualities were conveyed in an advertisement for an animal adoption league, in which a smiling, fully clothed woman cuddles a lap dog. Also common was an expression of primness that was nearly totally absent from the group of darkest complected women. Primness was conveyed largely through facial expression, with mouth closed and unsmiling, chin up, and looking into the camera with an expression of judgment or a hint of defiance. Finally, the fairest complected women were more frequently depicted in ways that subtly suggested wealth and privilege. This suggestion was delivered predominantly through the clothing that the women wore. The fairest complected women were more likely to model expensive designer clothing and boutique labels such as Chanel and Versace. Moreover, when the advertisement was not for clothing, the fairest complected women were more likely to be wearing expensive-looking clothing. The association with wealth and privilege contributes to an atmosphere of propriety and autonomy among the fairest complected women, an atmosphere less compatible with objectification.

These results support a link between aesthetic traits and moral codes. The women whose *complexions* are most strongly ideally feminine are the same women whose *implied behaviors and identities* are most strongly ideally feminine. The meaning-based explanation to the aesthetic preference for fair women receives strong support from a comparison which serves as a test case for the explanation.

Lightness and Gender in Popular Culture

Additional support for the meaning-based explanation for gendered complexion differences can be found in numerous examples throughout our culture. Baker-Sperry and Grauerholz (2003) note in their study of the prevalence of beauty ideals in fairy tales that there is often a link between goodness, beauty, and lightness on the one hand, and evilness, ugliness, and darkness on the other. Lightness and darkness might be denoted by complexion or by other means, such as the good daughter being [named Snow White or] showered with gold and the bad daughter showered with pitch that can never be removed. Consider also the symbolism of one of Western culture's most important rituals—the heterosexual wedding. Typically, the man is in a black tuxedo and the woman is in a white dress. Attractiveness ideals regarding complexion, then, are in line with a wider gestalt of gender and lightness or darkness. . . .

Conclusion

. . . A caveat is required regarding the interpretation of the moral codes embodied in these advertisements. On the one hand, prior research has established that Western culture has traditionally judged women negatively for overt expressions of sexual desire or sexual availability, ranging from gendered epithets such as "whore" or "slut" to biases about a lack of competence or intelligence. On the other hand, contemporary Western culture has moved toward greater acceptance of women's sexuality, and so the sexualization of darker complected women in the advertisements may be reflecting and reinforcing a morally neutral depiction of women's sexuality. However, while there is no denying that multiple interpretations of the signals in the advertisements are possible, I argue that there is a hegemonic interpretation, which I have explored in this article. The connection between an aesthetic of lightness and moral evaluation is not the only interpretation, but it draws on the continued inequality of sexual standards for men and women (Crawford and Popp 2003; Marks and Fraley 2006; Milhausen and Herold 1999; Milhausen and Herold 2001) as well as on the dominant understandings of the meanings of lightness and darkness.

The subject of tanning presents an interesting complication for the analysis of complexion ideals. On the one hand, I argue that the ideal complexion for women is fairer than is the ideal complexion for men. On the other hand, many white women tan in order to darken their complexion. Does the phenomenon of tanning negate the connection between moral and aesthetic preferences? Furthermore, are women who tan resisting the social control of beauty standards? The meaning-based approach to explaining the aesthetic preference for fairness in women's complexions suggests an alternative understanding of the meaning of tanning. Prior work has demonstrated that women tan primarily in the pursuit of beauty (Garvin and Wilson 1999; Murray and Turner 2004). However, it is the ***kind*** of beauty they pursue that is key to understanding why a preference for tanning among some women can exist alongside a preference for fairness for women. Rather than a denial of feminine identity or of beauty standards, tanning suggests that beauty ideals are complex and multi-faceted; they contain multiple points of idealization linked with different meanings, even meanings that are held in tension like lightness/darkness. This meaning-based interpretation allows us to analytically move beyond a simplistic, monochromatic notion of beauty ideals, and recognize that tanning is part of the idealization of feminine beauty associated with darkness; it conveys vitality, exposure, sexuality, and experience rather than overtones of purity, delicacy, and innocence. In other words, the link between aesthetic and moral preferences is not broken with tanning, but instead a different link is highlighted, along with the complexity of beauty ideals. It should be noted, however, that tanning is by no means the dominant ideal for women as depicted in magazine advertisements; paler skin than men is dominant, and only a minority of women appears as tanned. . . .

Future research should examine the extent to which these findings hold for media images in non-Western cultures. There is a growing literature that documents the problem of skin bleaching or whitening in many countries. Charles's (2003) study on the self-esteem of Jamaicans who bleach their skin notes that the practice is much more prevalent among women. Japanese culture also finds white skin more attractive than dark skin, with a far greater expectation for whiteness among women than among men (Ashikari 2005). The same gendered preference for whiter skin has been documented in Kenya (England 2004), Brazil (Telles 2004, 193) and in India (Pearson 2004). In each instance, there is a preference for fairness among both sexes, though the preference is stronger for women. There is some evidence that this preference for fairness predates colonialism—for example, the preference for fairness in India is related to the caste system. It stands to reason, however, that such preferences at the least would have been exacerbated by colonialism, and the resulting global prevalence of an Anglo-European beauty ideal based on an idealized fair complexion. Moreover, multinational corporations are contributing to the problem through aggressive marketing of skin lightening products. . . .

Notes

1. Leeds Craig's (2002) work on black women and beauty standards documents the emergence of new aesthetic standards for personal appearance that came along with the "black is beautiful" movement of the 1960s. Leeds Craig (2002, 18) argues, however, that the effects of this movement were "only temporary and within limits," and the Eurocentric ideal is still dominant. In earlier work, Leeds (1994) presents interview data wherein young, black women express a tension between wanting to valorize darker skin and responding to the dominant standard that dark skin is unattractive.
2. This exclusion was necessary because it was not possible to reliably code the dependent variables when advertisements were not in color.
3. Hair tone was sometimes unobservable, for example if a model wore a hat. For this reason, sample sizes vary between analyses for skin and for hair. People who were depicted in advertisements with predominantly or completely grey hair were excluded from the analysis because grey hair has a clear symbolic and actual relationship with age, thereby obscuring and aesthetically overriding its importance as light or dark. The pallets used for coding are available from the author upon request.
4. The sample is composed of advertisements appearing in *Esquire*, *Life*, *Time*, and *Vogue* magazines. These magazines respectively target men, a general audience, and women. Several months were covered within each magazine so that every month in 1970 is represented. The year 1970 is an appropriate comparison because it balances a need to sample from a distant time period with a need for access to advertisements in color. The use of color in magazine advertisements grew gradually in the middle of the twentieth century so that by 1970 a substantial portion of advertisements were printed in color (although fewer than half of the advertisements were in color in the magazines I examined).
5. It is tempting to speculate that fashions for fairness in white people have changed over time. Of the 268 people in the sample, 22 were excluded from the analysis due to unobservable hair color. However, it is also possible that the complexion scores are darker in 1970 because the pages of the magazines have darkened with age. Such a phenomenon cannot, however, explain the observed gender differences in 1970.

6. There were two fairly complected women who were omitted from the analysis because they appeared in the same advertisement as another of the most fairly complected women. This achieved the goal of coding women in unique advertisements to maintain the independence of each data point. To reach the sample size of fifty, the next two most fairly complected women in the sample were chosen. No substitutions were necessary for the darkest complected women.
7. A one-tailed test is used to measure significance because I have directional hypotheses regarding the differences between the two groups.

References

Ashikari, Mikiko. 2005. Cultivating Japanese whiteness: The "whitening" cosmetics boom and the Japanese identity. *Journal of Material Culture* 10:73–91.

Aubrey, Jennifer Stevens. 2004. Sex and punishment: An examination of sexual consequences and the sexual double standard in teen programming. *Sex Roles* 50:505–14.

Avery, Nicole Volta. 2000, May 5. The changing face of fashion: A broader cultural complexion drives diversity in today's advertising. *The Detroit Free Press.*

Baker, Michael J., and Gilbert A. Churchill, Jr. 1977. The impact of physically attractive models on advertising evaluations. *Journal of Marketing Research* 14:538–55.

Baker-Sperry, Lori, and Liz Grauerholz. 2003. The pervasiveness and persistence of the feminine beauty ideal in children's fairy tales. *Gender & Society* 17(5):711–26.

Breland, Alfred. 1998. A model for differential perceptions of competence based on skin tone among African Americans. *Journal of Multicultural Counseling and Development* 26(4):294–311.

Carr, David. 2002, November 18. On covers of many magazines, a full racial palette is still rare. *The New York Times.*

Charles, Christopher A. D. 2003. Skin bleaching, self-hate, and black identity in Jamaica. *Journal of Black Studies* 33:711–28.

Crawford, Mary, and Danielle Popp. 2003. Sexual double standards: A review and methodological critique of two decades of research. *Journal of Sex Research* 40(1):13–26.

Dilio, Dino. 2005. All about eyes. *Cosmetics* 33(2):18–19.

Dion, Karen, Ellen Berscheid, and Elaine Walster. 1972. What is beautiful is good. *Journal of Personality and Social Psychology* 24:285–90.

Dyer, Richard. 1997. *White.* New York: Routledge.

England, Andrew. 2004, August 17. Cosmetics industry cashes in where fairer equals better: In Kenya, women queue to buy lightening creams that damage skin, writes Andrew England. *Financial Times* 9.

Feeley, Thomas Hugh. 2002. Comment on halo effects in rating and evaluation research. *Human Communication Research* 28:578–86.

Foschi, Martha. 2000. Double standards for competence: Theory and research. *Annual Review of Sociology* 26:21–42.

Garvin, Theresa, and Kathleen Wilson. 1999. The use of storytelling for understanding women's desires to tan: Lessons from the field. *Professional Geographer* 51(2):296–306.

Goffman, Erving. 1979. *Gender Advertisements.* Cambridge, MA: Harvard University Press.

Gullickson, Aaron. 2005. The significance of color declines: A re-analysis of skin differentials in post–civil rights America. *Social Forces* 84(1):157–80.

Habbema, Loek. 2004. Facial esthetics and patient selection. *Clinics in Dermatology* 22:14–17.

Hill, Mark E. 2000. Color differences in the socioeconomic status of African American men: Results of a longitudinal study. *Social Forces* 78:1437–60.

Hosoda, Megumi, Eugene F. Stone-Romero, and Gwen Coats. 2003. The effects of physical attractiveness on job-related outcomes: A meta-analysis of experimental studies. *Personnel Psychology* 56:431–462.

Hughes, Michael, and Bradley R. Hertel. 1990. The significance of color remains: A study of life chances, mate selection, and ethnic consciousness among black Americans. *Social Forces* 68:1105–20.

Ingham, John M. 2002. Primal scene and misreading in Nabokov's *Lolita. American Imago* 59:27–52.

Jablonski, Nina G., and George Chaplin. 2000. The evolution of human skin coloration. *Journal of Human Evolution* 39:57–106.

Kahle, Lynn R., and Pamela M. Homer. 1985. Physical attractiveness of the celebrity endorser: A social adaptation perspective. *Journal of Consumer Research* 11:954–61.

Keith, Verna M., and Cedric Herring. 1991. Skin tone and stratification in the black community. *American Journal of Sociology* 97(3):760–78.

Leeds Craig, Maxine. 2002. *Ain't I a Beauty Queen: Black Women, Beauty, and the Politics of Race.* New York: Oxford University Press.

Leeds, Maxine. 1994. Young African-American women and the language of beauty. In *Ideal of Feminine Beauty: Philosophical, Social, and Cultural Dimensions*, edited by Karen A. Callaghan. Westport, CT: Greenwood Press.

Madrigal, Lorena, and William Kelly. 2006. Human skin-color sexual dimorphism: A test of the sexual selection hypothesis. *American Journal of Physical Anthropology* (published online in advance of print: www.interscience.wiley.com).

Marks, Michael J., and Chris R. Fraley. 2006. Confirmation bias and the sexual double standard. *Sex Roles* 54(1/2):19–26.

Milhausen, Robin R., and Edward S. Herold. 1999. Does the sexual double standard still exist? Perceptions of university women. *Journal of Sex Research* 36:361–368.

________. 2001. Reconceptualizing the sexual double standard. *Journal of Psychology and Human Sexuality* 13:63–83.

Murray, Craig D., and Elizabeth Turner. 2004. Health, risk, and sunbed use: A qualitative study. *Health, Risk & Society* 6(1):67–80.

Pearson, Beth. 2004, May 10. Where the formula for a good job is simply skin deep; Sales of skin-lightening products are booming in the east. But will it lead to a better life for women? *The Herald (Glasgow)* 10.

Pollay, Richard W. 1986. The distorted mirror: Reflections on the unintended consequences of advertising. *Journal of Marketing* 50:18–36.

Redmond, Sean. 2003. Thin white women in advertising: Deathly corporeality. *Journal of Consumer Culture* 3:170–90.

Sagario, Dawn. 2002, December 29. Interracial couples becoming more common: The "Halle Berry" syndrome, education boost acceptance. *The Seattle Times.*

Schudson, Michael. 1984. *Advertising, the Uneasy Persuasion: Its Dubious Impact on American Society.* New York: Basic Books.

Schwarz, Norbert, and Eva Kurz. 1989. What's in a picture? The impact of face-ism on trait attribution. *European Journal of Social Psychology* 19:311–16.

Shriver, Mark D., Esteban J. Parra, Sonia Dios, Carolina Bonilla, Heather Norton, Celina Jovel, Carrie Pfaff, Cecily Jones, Aisha Massac, Neil Cameron, Archie Baron, Tabitha Jackson, George Argyropoulos, Li Jin, Clive J. Hoggart, Paul M. McKeigue, and Rick A. Kittles. 2003. Skin pigmentation, biogeographical ancestry, and admixture mapping. *Human Genetics* 112:387–99.

Synott, A. 1987. Shame and glory: A sociology of hair. *British Journal of Sociology* 38:381–413.

Tegner, Eva. 1992. Sex differences in skin pigmentation illustrated in art. *American Journal of Dermatopathology* 14(3):283–87.

Telles, Edward E. 2004. *Race in Another America: The Significance of Skin Color in Brazil.* Princeton, NJ: Princeton University Press.

Wagner, Jennifer K., Esteban J. Parra, Heather L. Norton, Celina Jovel, and Mark D. Shriver. 2002. Skin responses to ultraviolet radiation: Effects of constitutive pigmentation, sex, and ancestry. *Pigment Cell Research* 15:385–90.

17

Reclaiming the Female Body

Women Body Modifiers and Feminist Debates

Victoria Pitts

A generation ago, women's decisions about shaping and marking their bodies focused on meeting cultural norms through weight control, hairstyling, makeup, and other culturally approved means. These days, however, many women have embarked on "body projects"—conscious and sometimes long-term strategies to alter their bodies and selves—that in some instances reject *cultural norms.*

As Amy C. Wilkins described in her article earlier in this volume, second-wave feminists (especially radical feminists) often focused on the social forces that constrained women's lives and that made sexuality dangerous. They often stressed the ways in which women were either socialized or coerced into manipulating their bodies to meet physically and emotionally damaging cultural norms.

In contrast, third-wave feminists more often have emphasized female agency and sexual pleasure, and so have celebrated various forms of body modification as individual choices and individual sources of pleasure (including sexual pleasure). Similarly, postmodern and post-essentialist feminists (groups that overlap with third-wave feminists) reject the idea that any action (such as tattooing) or category (such as woman) has one essential meaning, and instead argue for recognizing the multiple and competing meanings that different individuals find in all aspects of social life. Consequently, they, too, typically argue that even the most extreme forms of body modification, such as facial tattooing and scarification, may serve for some individuals as empowering forms of resistance against gender norms.

In "Reclaiming the Female Body: Women Body Modifiers and Feminist Debates," Victoria Pitts explores these competing interpretations of women's embodied experiences through her analysis of extreme body modification. As she shows, Western culture regards such body modification as abject (that is, as breaking such deep-seated norms regarding the body that those modifications are regarded as degraded and debased). Nevertheless, individuals choose body modification in part because they recognize it will place them in a liminal position (that is, poised between two positions—the person they were and the person they want to become—in the same way that a girl at puberty is poised between girlhood and adulthood). As Pitts illustrates, women who choose body modification often believe that it has helped them take control of their lives and bodies. At the same time, Pitts argues, women's decisions about body modification do not solely indicate individual agency, since these decisions are products of specific social contexts. Moreover, regardless of why women choose body modification, they cannot control how others interpret and react to it, nor use it to create any wider social change. Thus, Pitts's analysis highlights the benefits and the limits of this type of embodied resistance.

. . . Although feminists have largely agreed that the disciplining and normalization of the female body through sexualized, normalized beauty ideals has been damaging to women, we have famously disagreed over how women can assert control over their own bodies. Radical feminists like Dworkin, Catherine MacKinnon, and others have depicted body alterations, even deviant ones, as instances of the patriarchal mistreatment of women's bodies. For MacKinnon, the sexualization of the female body, often achieved through adornments and body modifications, is the height of gender inequality. As she puts it,

> So many distinctive features of women's status as second class—the restriction and constraint and contortion, the servility and the display, the self-mutilation and requisite presentation of self as a beautiful thing, the enforced passivity, the humiliation—are made into the content of sex for women.[1]

In this view, body modifications represent both patriarchy's willingness to make literal use of the female body as well as women's psychic internalization of its aims. Women's willingness to happily endure pain to shape the body, she and Dworkin argue, reflects women's self-abnegation in patriarchal cultures.[2] Along with cosmetic surgery, Chinese foot binding, diet regimes, sadomasochism, and other painful or difficult practices, women's tattoos, piercings, scars, and brands have been described by radical feminists as representing women's "[self-] hatred of the flesh."[3] Even though the most provocative of new subcultural body mod practices usually have the effect of distancing women from Western beauty norms rather than bringing them closer, critics have likened the practices to mutilation. Informing this depiction of women's body modifications as self-objectifying or mutilative is a view that the female body should be "spared," to use Dworkin's term, interference, alteration, and, most certainly, pain.

The "sex wars" of the 1980s foreshadowed the disagreements over body art a decade later. Debates over sadomasochism (SM) focused on women's agency in relation to sexuality. Radical feminists objected to women's SM and women-made pornography (including women's obscene art). According to Dworkin and MacKinnon, these represented the worst consequences of misogyny—women's internalization and reenactment of patriarchal abuse of the female body. Their rejection of a sexualized, modified female body depended partly on the notion that a pristine, natural, organic body—a body unmolested by culture—would be a primary resource for resisting patriarchy and its use and abuse of female embodiment. Pro-sex and postmodern feminists, on the other hand, celebrated women's sexual deviance, including SM and porn, and argued in essence that women were reclaiming sexuality and desire and rebelling against oppressive prohibitions on female pleasure. . . .

By the 1990s, tattoos on the bodies of young feminists, Riot Grrrls, and others were beginning to be embraced by some postmodern feminists as subversions of "traditional notions of feminine beauty."[4] Other, even less legitimate forms of body modification have also been claimed as practices of female rebellion. Because they violate gender norms, explore taboo aspects of embodiment, and provoke attention, they can be seen as ironic examples of women's "strength and independence," to use Klein's term.[5] Karmen MacKendrick describes the new body art practices as promoting "mischievous" pleasures that appropriate the body from culture. Tattoos, scars, and piercings violate Western body norms. Women who undertake such body modifications are not ignorant of the abjection that they can provoke. Neither, according to MacKendrick, are they unaware of the multiple ways body alteration has usually served patriarchy. Rather, she argues, "the postmodern response on display in modified bodies is fully contextualized, ironically playful, and willfully constructed."[6]

The subcultural discourse also celebrates the practices as empowering. In magazines, ezines, underground films, and in body art studios, the subculture depicts women's body modification as having the potential to signify body reclamation for women, including those who have experienced victimization. In reclaiming discourse, women (and sometimes men) assert that scarification, tattooing, and genital piercing can achieve a transformation of the relationship between self, body, and culture. In contrast to radical feminist criticisms of women's body modification as mutilation, they claim that women's anomalous body projects can provide ritualized opportunities for women's self-transformation and for symbolically recovering the female body. Far from revealing women's self-hatred and lack of self-control, they argue, the practices demonstrate women's assertion of control over their bodies.

Reclaiming the Body

Reclaiming discourse was first articulated in print in the highly popular book *Modern Primitives* in the late 1980s, where women's body piercer Raelyn Gallina suggested that women can alter non-Western, indigenous body modification practices to create meaningful rituals, in particular to symbolically reclaim their bodies from rape, harassment, or abuse. . . . [In this discourse,] reclaiming the body is presented as a process of highlighting the power relations that surround the body, and undergoing painful, often emotional ritual to transform the self–body relationship. . . .

Many of the women I interviewed made use of and contributed to the reclaiming discourse surrounding women's body modification. I describe in detail the interview-gathered stories of Jane and Karen. . . . The women's stories situate reclaiming projects in their larger body-biographies, which often reflect on the impact of sexual violence, beauty norms, and gender relations on their body images and sense of self. I make sense of their reclaiming narratives partly by drawing attention to the ritualized, liminal aspects of the practices they describe. Modifications of the body that open the body's envelope are, from the Western perspective, abject and grotesque, but as the women describe, they also place the body in a physical and symbolic state of liminality and transformation. Later, I interpret these stories through the lens of poststructuralist feminism, which can help highlight their political significance while contextualizing them in larger relations of power.

Karen

Karen was raised in a working-class family, one in which she unfortunately suffered abuse as a young child, and became a single mother in her early 20s. Once on welfare and surviving on various low-wage jobs, including reading meters for the water company and driving trucks, she put herself through night school, and, later, through law school. During this time, she used psychotherapy to address her early victimization. At 24, she had also come out as a lesbian, and in her 30s joined a women's SM organization, where she learned about new forms of body modification. Now in her 40s and a breast cancer survivor, she has worn nipple piercings and sports permanent tattoos and scarifications, and uses reclaiming language to describe their meanings: "they were ways," she argues, "of claiming my body for me."

Karen's breast has been marked with a tattoo in the symbol of a dragon. She explains the dragon tattoo as part of a process of recovering from early victimization and gaining a sense of independence.

> I came out of an abusive childhood. I was sexually abused by an uncle. My family sort of disintegrated when I was five years old . . . my family moved back to Chicago because that's where my mother's family was and we moved in with her parents and I grew up in this extended Italian family. One of my

uncles was a child molester. The dragon was really about finding my way to stand on my own two feet. Finding a way of separating from that extended family and being in the world on my own as a real person.

Karen's experience of abuse is presented as an important aspect of her biography. During her interviews, she also repeatedly describes separating from her parents and extended family as a difficult and important event. Karen presents her separation from the family, which had failed to protect her and later resisted her lesbianism, as an assertion of her own authority over her body. The image of the dragon arrived when one of Karen's girlfriends suggested she visualize a dragon guarding a cave as a process of overcoming fear.

> *Karen*: The purpose of that visualization was to give one an awareness of what they do with fear and how they deal with fear and where their courage comes from. The way I dealt with getting into the dragon's cave was I sat in the dragon's mouth very peacefully and made myself one with the dragon. Some people actually pick up swords and swipe the dragon mightily and others figure ways of getting around it. My way of dealing with it was to make myself one with the dragon and make the dragon become me.
>
> *VP*: What was the dragon for you?
>
> *Karen*: I came out of an abusive childhood. I was sexually abused by an uncle.

This plan to "make the dragon become me," a strategy of confronting fear imposed on her body by an abusive adult male, was made literal in Karen's decision, a year after graduating from law school, to have the image of the dragon tattooed on her breast. The inscription, she asserts, claims her ownership of her breast, and symbolically dissolves the fear by incorporating it. She also describes her breasts as a focus of unwanted attention and harassment by men:

> So, the dragon was my way of claiming my body, claiming my breasts. Because I [also] grew up having very large breasts and having men ogle me. Being 14 or 15 years old to be walking down the street and have guys drive by and yell, "hey baby." Really ugly things that guys who are out of control do. And it made it really difficult for me to feel comfortable in my body. So having a dragon put on my breast was a way of saying, "this is mine." It was an evolution of that whole process of keeping myself safe and keeping myself whole.

Reclamation of the body, suggests Karen, is effected by self-writing it. Her ogled and uncomfortable breast, once a site of sexual abuse and later of anonymous harassment, becomes less alienating, she seems to suggest, through inscription. Years later, when she is diagnosed with breast cancer, she is upset by the idea of losing the mark: "my one request to the doctor," she says, "was to save the tattoo." Karen perceives her body as recovered through her marking of it. Through the tattoo, the breasts—and by implication the whole body—have been rewritten with new meanings.

Opening the body transgresses Western bodily boundaries. The boundary transgression of body marking is explicit in Karen's description of her scarifications, one of which created a scar in the shape of an orchid. This mark was created by a body mod artist in an event attended by members of her women's SM community, which was sponsoring workshops on body modification. She describes her scarification as modeled after a "Maui form of tattooing . . . using a sharpened shell to do the cut and rub ash into the open cut to make the scarring." The practice was ritualized and, as she describes it, "spiritual."

> What was going on here . . . was about the spirituality of claiming myself. Accepting myself. And that state of concentration, that is about spirit. I think it is the same or similar state that Buddhists, when they spend hours and hours and hours of the state of prayer. It's that place of acceptance and floating and honor. It's very, it's absolutely connected to the spiritual center of myself. . . . I think that people are really afraid of that state of being. It's terrifying to let go of the control that much. It is really about your control over the moment, and simply being in the moment, being one with the moment. Being completely open.

The openness in scarification ritual creates the liminal stage in what Karen, in modern primitivist fashion, considers a rite of passage. In anthropologist Victor Turner's description of indigenous rituals, liminality is the point of transition in ritual, the middle stage between young and old, unsocialized and socialized, pristine and marked. For example, the male undergoing puberty rites is no longer boy, yet neither a man; he is a liminal persona, a transitional person who resides in the margins.[7] Liminality is the temporal and physical space of ambiguity, in which cultural performance or rite is enacted with initiate and audience. The ritual of scarification invites liminality through its opening of the borders of the body.[8] In Karen's marginal, subcultural view of her rite of passage, the female body can be reappropriated through transgressive, self-marking ritual. The opening of the body violates its surface and also, as Karen describes, its former representations. For Karen, ritualized marking symbolically revokes former claims on the body—those of victimization, patriarchy, and control—and so is deeply meaningful.

Nonetheless, Karen's narrative hints at how such meanings cannot be fixed in the culture. In particular, she worries that the recent popularization of body modifications in her West Coast area, especially tattoos and body piercings, dilutes their significance. In her words, "I think it has become a fad and . . . that's not what it is to me. . . . I have managed to keep myself apart from that." Yet conversely, people in mainstream culture can also react with horror: Karen imagines that some would "scream obscenities at us for doing what we're doing.". . .

Jane

Jane describes her body modifications as acts of reclaiming, although unlike Karen, the reclamation is not a response to sexual victimization. But like them, Jane presents her visual modification as an attempt to claim authority over her body and rewrite its identifications. A 39-year-old student of social work who lives alone in a city on the East Coast, Jane has had a large dream-catcher symbol cut across her chest.[9] It reaches up to her neck and down between her breasts. It is about six inches across and about six inches tall. The scar is highly keloided, and it has been injected with blue and purple tattoo ink. The image is startling, and it visually redefines her. Jane describes getting such a radical scar as a way of acknowledging, and rejecting, the pressure of cultural standards of beauty.

> As a child, I was what might be referred to as an ugly ducking. I was freckly, skinny, gawky, flat-chested, you know, all of the things that are not valued in society. I never thought of myself as cute or good-looking and never of course got told I was. . . . I didn't get positive reinforcement for my looks as a youngster, and I've grown up to become relatively attractive. But that's not how I feel about myself, because I have this lifetime of messages that I received from other people that said that I was not attractive. . . .

Jane presents her scar as a resistance against the normative "lifetime of messages" that pressure her to reach the beauty ideal. As well as self-ownership and renegotiated sexuality, beauty is thus a target for reclamation. In similar fashion, Karen had identified beauty as a target for reclaiming. She had picked an orchid as a scar symbol to represent inner beauty:

> The orchid was about beauty. The orchid was about my having felt that I wasn't particularly beautiful . . . the orchid was about claiming my beauty and about saying, I'm not a spectacular looking person but I am beautiful and beauty comes from inside. So, that's how I came to have the orchid.

Like the body modifications of the other women, Jane's was undertaken in the presence of supportive friends and ritualized. After seeing cuttings and brandings at demonstrations sponsored by the local pro-sex feminist bookstore and later on a trip to the West Coast, Jane decided to organize her cutting event with the things and people that, in her words, "meant something to me." She set up her home as a ritual space:

> I personally went around and smudged my house with sage. For Native Americans, sage is an herb that purifies spiritual energy. . . . I had my own candles and oils that have to do with power and protection. I set up the living room; I set up the atmosphere, to be clear and clean.

In a sense, the ritual was also for her about representing bravery.

> I got a [Native American] dreamcatcher. . . . I can say that it would be a real good thing to have dreams. I haven't been able to allow myself to have dreams and wants or whatever for anything, anybody. I've been sort of plodding along in a very protective shell in my life . . . before I got this cutting. . . . I was acknowledging that I was going to open myself up more and did it.

The cutting as she describes it was extremely painful, more so than she had expected, and she decided to forego any other painful modifications in the future. However, she claims not to regret the experience, and explains by comparing her cutting to another painful body project women undertake or endure:

> *VP*: Do you wish it had hurt less?
>
> *Jane*: That's a real hard one, because it's sort of like having a baby. After the baby's born, you don't remember the pain, and you're just euphoric and you've got this new life here, and it was the same kind of experience.

As a physical body, Jane has dis- and re-figured herself. The surface of her upper torso is radically altered. She can feel the new growth: the scar tissue is sensitive, felt from within the body (a slight itching feel), and tactile. The highly prominent modification of her appearance also removes a normative ideal of beauty from possibility. In this way, Jane's transformation of her physical surface body also transforms her communicative body. Even though most of her descriptions of the experience are positive, she describes a shocked feeling at seeing the final result:

> I realized I've got this thing on my body for the rest of my life and said, what the fuck did I do? It's like not only do I have this thing on my body, but I'm going to be a counselor . . . and I have to wear button down shirts. It's really right there and I'm going to have to cover it up.

In subcultural settings, such as at the fetish flea market which attracts other body modifiers, she can "show it off and get all kinds of compliments and attention." In other settings, such as at her field-service placement for her social work training, she perceives showing the mark as inappropriate. She also has no plans to let her mother see it: "My mother has seen my eyebrow piercing, but no, I'm not going to tell her that I've got a cut. . . . It's where I draw the line.". . .

Modified Bodies and Feminist Politics

Feminist disagreements over body modification reflect divergent assumptions about subjectivity, consciousness, and the body. Post-essentialist feminists view female bodies and subjectivity as socially constructed, culturally negotiable, and saturated with power relations. Such perspectives have argued that the body is always *already* inscribed by culture. It is socially controlled and regulated, including through gender socialization and violence, and marked by relations of power. The "normal" body, in this view, is not a biological category but rather an ideological construct that serves economic and familial functions. The female body is prescribed roles and practices that lend apparent biological evidence for normalized female identity, thereby naturalizing gender relations.

From this perspective, anomalous body practices may have the potential, at least theoretically, to radically challenge the gendered roles and practices of embodiment. The rituals I describe above create anomalous bodies, and require the acceptance of moments of bodily uncertainty and ambivalence. In the liminal state of embodiment that they promote, boundaries are erased and redrawn; heterogeneity and contradiction are embraced. Transformations between states in rites of passage place the individual into a position of marginality; the body-subject in the liminal zone manipulates and fluctuates her identity by enacting, to quote Rob Shields in *Places on the Margin*, "a performance supported by social rituals and exchanges which confirm different personas."[10]

Postmodern feminists have recognized the liminal, heterogeneous body-subject—the cyborg—as subversive, largely because it resists the unified, stable, gendered identity enforced in mainstream culture. Liminality might reflect, at least temporarily, a "liberation from regimes of normative practices and performance codes of mundane life," in Shields's terms.[11] As such, it can denaturalize gender categories. The scarred, branded, or tattooed woman may destabilize, in the words of medical sociologist Kathy Davis, "many of our preconceived notions about beauty, identity, and the female body," as well as focus attention on ways in which female bodies are invisibly marked by power, including by violence.[12] Shields writes that marginal bodies also "expose the relativity of the entrenched, universalising values of the centre, and expose the relativism of the cultural identities . . . they have denied, rendered anomalous, or excluded."[13]

Karen's body markings expose stories of sexual victimization, but also symbolically address women's chances to live in bodies as survivors. All the women have created bodies that rewrite notions of beauty and counter, in Jane's words, the "lifetime of messages" that prescribe and normalize beauty regimens. They have marginalized themselves, but questioned the dominant culture's control over their bodily appearance, behavior, and safety. In marking their bodies, they appear to shift both their private self-identifications and their public identities, telling new stories to themselves and others about the meanings of their embodiment. Rather than depicting hopelessness, the practices imply that their body-stories are in flux, opened to the possibilities of reinscription and renaming.

Yet, radical feminists would claim that body modifiers are "not in control" of their decisions, and that the practices themselves are harmful.[14] Some radical feminists, who are also critical of women's SM, have argued that the practices violate the body and reproduce oppressive relations of power by echoing patriarchal violence. Anti-body modification arguments generally either link the technologies themselves to mutilation and pathology or equate women's body modifications with more mainstream cosmetic practices that are seen as objectifying. Radical feminist scholar Sheila Jeffreys, for example, equates SM and body modification (piercing and tattooing) with addictive self-cutting and other self-mutilative practices:

> Some of the enthusiasm for piercing in lesbians, gay men, and heterosexual women arises from the experience of child sexual abuse. Self-mutilation in the form of stubbing out cigarettes on the body, arm slashing and even garroting are forms of self-injury that abuse non-survivors do sometimes employ. . . . Sadomasochism and the current fashionability of piercing and tattooing provide an apparently acceptable form for such attacks on the abused body. Young women and men are walking around showing us the effects of the abuse that they have tried to turn into a badge of pride, a savage embrace of the most grave attacks they can make on their bodies.[15]

This argument asserts that the marked body is injured and attacked, either literally through pain or symbolically through harming the body's appearance. The fact that some of these bodily inscriptions make reference to experiences of victimization has not escaped their critics. While body modifiers themselves suggest that the violated female body can be rewritten in personally and politically meaningful ways, radical feminists argue in contrast that modifying the body is a straightforward replay of that violence. A large part of what is at issue here is the possibility of women's agency, which radical feminists have long argued is hampered by the psychological effects of patriarchy. Following this view, Jeffreys interprets the practices as "signifiers of false-consciousness," a criticism also reiterated in mainstream press accounts of feminist opposition to women's tattooing, piercing, and scarring.[16] . . .

In my view, any critique of women's body practices as inherently deluded and self-hating must reveal and critique its own assumptions of the truth of female embodiment and subjectivity. The arguments radical feminists make against body modification seem to be informed by implicit assumptions about the body as naturally pristine and unmarked. I would argue that these assumptions are difficult to support in the face of our increasing awareness of the ways in which the body is socially constructed and inscribed by gendered relations of power. We have to ask, where is the elusive unmarked female body that represents women's freedom from bodily intervention? It can be found neither in history nor in anthropology; in the lives of contemporary women, it appears not simply as an ideal type but as a myth. One of the powerful messages of radical feminist thinking of the 1970s was that the threat of rape has influenced the lives and bodies of all women. In her reading of these theories of rape, *Rethinking Rape*, Ann Cahill describes how all women's bodies, not just those that have survived sexual assault, can be comported with what she calls a "phenomenology of fear." Women's bodies have been disciplined both to be wary of the possibility of rape or assault in alleys and on dark streets, and also to be weak and vulnerable as a sign of their femininity and beauty. From the perspective of many women who have suffered from victimization or objectification by patriarchal culture, then, the heralding of the unmarked body appears naive and ideological. Should it be pursued for its own sake despite its practical irrelevance? I would argue that women are not choosing whether or not to be modified and marked, but are negotiating how and in what way and by whom and to what effect.

The problems with charges of false consciousness are many, not the least of which is that they presume its counterpart—a proper, "true" consciousness. This now seems unacceptable. Such a notion asserts a singular, universalized, and essentialist version of feminist enlightenment. The extensive deconstruction of such notions in feminist theory in recent years by women of color, "Third World" and transnational feminists, and others whose views and experiences have traditionally been excluded from feminist discourse should give us pause. In these accounts, the wholly knowing feminist consciousness that can manage to achieve the "true" feminist attitude appears as an ideological fiction, much in the way that the wholly natural, pristine body that stands in opposition to culture has been exposed as a myth by post-essentialist feminists. The feminist debates over the universality of rights and feminist consciousness are far from over, but they have brought us at least to an awareness of how diverse are women's understandings of bodily practices, cultural and human rights, agency and radical consciousness. . . .

I would argue, following a post-essentialist, poststructural approach, that there is no universal standard of the body or of feminist subjectivity against which we can measure the actual practices of lived bodies. Rather, we should look to how the practices come to be surrounded and saturated with meaning. This involves examining the discourses deployed by the people who use the practices and those who observe them, as well as critically situating those discourses in socio-political context. Women's subcultural discourses represent marginal ways of knowing and strategizing the meanings of lived female embodiment. Rather than suggesting self-hatred or even indifference to their own victimization, the subcultural discourse of women's body modification, as I have shown here, explicitly identifies empowerment and rebellion against oppression as integral to their body projects.

But subcultural discourses cannot be accepted as transparent, or as the last word on the importance and effects of these practices. We cannot replace a notion of women as wholly unknowing subjects with one of them as all-knowing ones, as Sarah Thorton has pointed out in her discussion of subcultures.[17] Despite what women themselves may want to accomplish with anomalous body projects, I reject an overly liberal interpretation that would overemphasize women's autonomy and freedom in writing their bodies. Women are not individually responsible for situating their practices in all their larger collective and historical contexts, for predicting the political effects of their practices, or even for wholly authoring their meanings. Amelia Jones writes in *Body Art* that "it is often hard to appreciate the patterns of history when one is embedded in them."[18] Thus, body marks cannot be seen as solely ideographic or autobiographical. Marking the body is not a process that involves simply an individual author executing a strategic design that is read in the way she intends by her readers. The process is intersubjective, and, thus, to some extent, out of the hands of women themselves.

The Limits of Women's "Reclaiming"

Following this warning, I want to point out some of the possible risks and limitations of these practices. In my view, even though the practices are in many ways subversive, there are still serious political and strategic limits to women's reclaiming projects as practices of agency. . . .

First, the aim of symbolically recovering the body from victimization is limited by body projects because eventually, the women must stop. Otherwise, the physical effect would be, even by the standards of body modifiers, harmful and not reclaimative. . . .

Second, bodily resistance, as a private practice, may be not only limited, but also limit*ing*. The language of reclaiming, even written on the body, does not imply material reclamation in an objective sense; past body oppression is not reversed, rape culture is not erased. The rebellion offered is symbolic and communicative [but] . . . often hidden from public view. . . .

Finally, even visibility does not necessarily ensure politically radical messages. Despite women's aims to renounce victimization, objectification, and consumerization, the anomalous female body does not escape these pressures. This is evident in some of the appropriations of body modification practices within mainstream culture. These practices, at their most hard-core still highly deviant, undergo changes in meaning as the broader culture adapts to their presence on the cultural landscape. . . .

This problem is also borne out in the commodification of the subcultural female body as an exotic, sexy Other. . . .

The complexity of women's agency in relation to the body exemplified in reclaiming strategies, I think, counters the sense of political certainty that seems to inform some of the radical feminist pronouncements on women's body modification and on the victimization of the female body more generally. It would also resist overly celebratory interpretations that imply that, in postmodern culture, we are all now fully in control of inscribing our bodies, or that view the body as fully unfixed and individually malleable. Women's marked bodies exemplify both the praxis of culturally marginal body projects and the limits of that praxis. As I see it, they highlight the female body as a site of negotiation between power and powerlessness, neither of which are likely to win fully. . . .

Notes

1. Catherine MacKinnon, "Sexuality," in *The Second Wave*, ed. Linda Nicholson (New York: Routledge, 1997), 197.
2. Andrea Dworkin, "Gynocide: Chinese Footbinding," in *Living with Contradictions: Controversy over Feminist Ethics*, ed. Alison M. Jagger (Boulder, CO: Westview Press, 1994).
3. Karmen MacKendrick, "Technoflesh, or Didn't that Hurt?" *Fashion Theory* vol. 2, no. 1 (1998): 81–108.
4. Melanie Klein, "Duality and Redefinition: Young Feminism and the Alternative Music Community," in *Gender Through the Prism of Difference*, ed. Maxine Baca Zinn, Pierrette Hondagneu-Sotelo, and Michael Messner (Boston: Allyn and Bacon, 1999), 452.
5. Ibid., 454.
6. MacKendrick, 1998: 23.
7. Victor Turner, *The Forest of Symbols: Aspects of Ndembu Ritual* (Ithaca, NY: Cornell University Press, 1967), 95.
8. Which places it in "interaction with the world" where it "trangresses its own limits." Bahktin, Mikhail. 1984. *Rabelais and His World*, trans. Helene Iswolsky (Cambridge, MA: Massachusetts Institute of Technology Press).
9. This is a Native American symbol widely recognized in non-native U.S. culture. Jane's choice of the dreamcatcher symbol and her choice of the scarification ritual reflect the neotribal nature of much contemporary body modification.
10. Rob Shields, *Places on the Margin: Alternative Geographies of Modernity* (London: Routledge, 1991), 269. Even in indigenous rites of passage, as Victor Turner describes, marginality is often regarded as polluting or unclean, but the marginal position of the liminal person is necessary for symbolic transformation to become social reality.
11. Ibid., 84.
12. Kathy Davis, "My Body Is My Art: Cosmetic Surgery as Feminist Utopia?" *European Journal of Women's Studies* vol. 4 (1997): 23–38.
13. Shields, 1991: 277.
14. Valeria Eubanks, "Zones of Dither: Writing the Postmodern Body," *Body and Society* vol. 2, no. 3 (1996): 81.
15. Jeffreys 1994: 21, quoted in Nikki Sullivan, "Fleshing Out Pleasure: Canonisation or Crucifixion?" *Australian Feminist Studies* vol. 12, no. 26 (1997): 283–291.
16. Nikki Sullivan, 1997: "Fleshing Out Pleasure: Canonization or Crucifixion" *Australian Feminist Studies* vol.12, no. 26: 3–24.
17. See Sarah Thornton, "The Social Logic of Subcultural Capital," in *The Subcultures Reader*, ed. Ken Gelder and Sarah Thornton (London: Routledge, 1997), 200–211.
18. Amelia Jones, *Body Art: Performing the Subject* (Minneapolis: University of Minnesota Press, 1998), 11.

IV

THE POLITICS OF BEHAVIOR

The final part of this volume looks at a variety of issues linked to women's—and men's—behavior. Each of these issues touches on the question of the social construction of women's bodies, discussed earlier in this volume, and each illustrates how ideas about women's bodies can serve to constrain women's lives and options. Several of the pieces especially focus on how social institutions (such as sport, the state, and religion) affect women's behaviors, bodies, and selves.

The first article, by Susan K. Cahn, "From the 'Muscle Moll' to the 'Butch' Ballplayer: Mannishness, Lesbianism, and Homophobia in U.S. Women's Sport," addresses the experiences of girls and women who participate in sport, illustrating how social stigma against athletic females (including accusations of lesbianism) can discourage girls and women from athletic endeavors. Vivyan C. Adair then writes about the embodied experiences of poor women, including the ways in which their bodies are sometimes treated by the state as essentially public property, in her article "Branded with Infamy: Inscriptions of Poverty and Class in the United States." Following this, Rachel Roth, in "Backlash and Continuity: The Political Trajectory of Fetal Rights," examines how cultural attitudes toward women's lives and bodies are embedded in current controversies over reproductive rights and "fetal rights." In the next article, "*Hijab* and American Muslim Women: Creating the Space for Autonomous Selves," Rhys H. Williams and Gira Vashi consider the multiple meanings of the *hijab* for the identities of young second-generation Muslim women living in the United States.

The final two articles in this part and book look at various forms of violence against women. C. J. Pascoe's "Compulsive Heterosexuality: Masculinity and Dominance," shows how boys' and men's ideas about women's bodies and behavior contribute to sexual harassment, rape, and other forms of coercion and violence directed at girls and women. Finally, in "Being Undocumented and Intimate Partner Violence (IPV): Multiple Vulnerabilities through the Lens of Feminist Intersectionality," Margaret E. Adams and Jacquelyn Campbell examine how the unique social location of undocumented immigrant women make them particularly susceptible to intimate partner violence and health problems.

18

From the "Muscle Moll" to the "Butch" Ballplayer

Mannishness, Lesbianism, and Homophobia in U.S. Women's Sport

SUSAN K. CAHN

In every historical era, some women have desired sexual and romantic relationships with other women. But as Rose Weitz's opening article in this volume described, for most of history, Western societies rarely stigmatized these women or identified them as lesbian. Almost no women had the economic resources needed to survive if unwed, and women's sexuality was rarely taken seriously, and so few even considered the potential sexual aspects of women's relationships with other women.

By the early twentieth century, however, a growing number of women were receiving higher educations, entering professions, or finding other paid work that gave them the ability, should they choose, to live independently of men. From this point on, prejudice and discrimination against lesbians became a powerful social force. This is the backdrop for Susan K. Cahn's article, "From the 'Muscle Moll' to the 'Butch' Ballplayer: Mannishness, Lesbianism, and Homophobia in U.S. Women's Sport."

In this article, Cahn traces the history of women's participation in sport from the early twentieth century through the 1960s. She uses this history to illustrate how attitudes toward women's sport both reflected and reinforced social ideas about proper female sexuality and the proper place of women in American society. Prior to the 1930s, Cahn shows, critics of women's sport argued that participating in sport encouraged unrestrained emotional excitement and exuberant

Susan Cahn, "From the 'Muscle Moll' to the 'Butch' Ballplayer," was originally published in *Feminist Studies*, volume 19, number 2 (Summer 1993): 343–368, by permission of the publisher, *Feminist Studies*, Inc.

physical activity and thus could increase women's heterosexual *desires and activity. Conversely, in later years, critics argued that participating in sport could lead women to become* homosexual *by reducing their attractiveness to men or their interest in heterosexual relationships. In both eras, gendered fears and stereotypes (complicated by racial stereotypes) served to keep women out of sport and to stigmatize those whose interests or appearance did not fit dominant cultural norms.*

Cahn's historical account can help us understand gender inequality in sport participation today. Despite the passage in 1972 of Title IX—a law that requires gender equity in educational programs that receive federal funding—the Women's Sports Foundation reports that girls continue to participate in sports at lower rates than boys. Moreover, by age 14, girls drop out of sports at two times the rate of boys—in part, the Foundation argues, because of discrimination and social stigma against girls who are or are believed to be lesbians.

In 1934, *Literary Digest* subtitled an article on women's sports, "Will the playing fields one day be ruled by amazons?" The author, Fred Wittner, answered the question affirmatively and concluded that as an "inevitable consequence" of sport's masculinizing effect, "girls trained in physical education today may find it more difficult to attract the most worthy fathers for their children" (1934, 43). The image of women athletes as mannish, failed heterosexuals represents a thinly veiled reference to lesbianism in sport. At times, the homosexual allusion has been indisputable, as in a journalist's description (Murray n.d.) of the great athlete Babe Didrikson as a "Sapphic, Brobdingnagian woman" or in television comedian Arsenio Hall's more recent [1988] witticism, "If we can put a man on the moon, why can't we put one on Martina Navratilova?" More frequently, however, popular commentary on lesbians in sport has taken the form of indirect references, surfacing through denials and refutations rather than open acknowledgment. When in 1955 an *Ebony* magazine article on African American track stars insisted that "off track, the girls are entirely feminine. Most of them like boys, dances, club affairs," the reporter answered the implicit but unspoken charge that athletes, especially Black women in a "manly" sport, were masculine manhaters, or lesbians.

The figure of the mannish lesbian athlete has acted as a powerful but unarticulated "bogey woman" of sport, forming a silent foil for more positive, corrective images that attempt to rehabilitate the image of women athletes and resolve the cultural contradiction between athletic prowess and femininity. As a stereotyped figure in U.S. society, the lesbian athlete forms part of everyday cultural knowledge. Yet historians have paid scant attention to the connection between female sexuality and sport.[1] This essay explores the historical relationship between lesbianism and sport by tracing the development of the stereotyped "mannish lesbian athlete" and examining its relation to the lived experience of mid-twentieth-century lesbian athletes.

I argue that fears of mannish female sexuality in sport initially centered on the prospect of unbridled heterosexual desire. By the 1930s, however, female athletic mannishness began to connote heterosexual failure, usually couched in terms of unattractiveness to men, but also suggesting the possible absence of heterosexual interest. In the years following World War II, the stereotype of the lesbian athlete emerged full blown. The extreme homophobia and the gender conservatism of the postwar era created a context in which longstanding linkages among mannishness, female homosexuality, and athletes cohered around the figure of the mannish lesbian athlete. . . .

Amazons, Muscle Molls, and the Question of Sexual (Im)morality

The athletic woman sparked interest and controversy in the early decades of the twentieth century. In the United States and other Western societies, sport functioned as a male preserve, an all-male domain in which men not only played games together but also demonstrated and affirmed their manhood (Dunning 1986; Kimmel 1987; Mangan and Park 1987; Mrozek 1983). The "maleness" of sport derived from a gender ideology which labeled aggression, physicality, competitive spirit, and athletic skill as masculine attributes necessary for achieving true manliness. This notion found unquestioned support in the dualistic, polarized concepts of gender which prevailed in Victorian America. However, by the turn of the century, women had begun to challenge Victorian gender arrangements, breaking down barriers to female participation in previously male arenas of public work, politics, and urban nightlife. Some of these "New Women" sought entry into the world of athletics as well. On college campuses students enjoyed a wide range of intramural sports through newly formed Women's Athletic Associations. Off-campus women took up games like golf, tennis, basketball, swimming, and occasionally even wrestling, car racing, or boxing. As challengers to one of the defining arenas of manhood, skilled female athletes became symbols of the broader march of womanhood out of the Victorian domestic sphere into once prohibited male realms.

The woman athlete represented both the appealing and the threatening aspects of modern womanhood. In a positive light, she captured the exuberant spirit, physical vigor, and brazenness of the New Woman. The University of Minnesota student newspaper proclaimed in 1904 that the athletic girl was the "truest type of All-American coed" (1904–5 Scrapbooks of Anne Maude Butner, Butner Papers, University of Minnesota Archives, Minneapolis). Several years later, *Harper's Bazaar* labeled the unsportive girl as "not strictly up to date" (Mange 1910, 246), and *Good Housekeeping* noted that the "tomboy" had come to symbolize "a new type of American girl, new not only physically, but mentally and morally" (de Koven 1912, 150).

Yet, women athletes invoked condemnation as often as praise. Critics ranged from physicians and physical educators to sportswriters, male athletic officials, and casual observers. In their view, strenuous athletic pursuits endangered women and threatened the stability of society. They maintained that women athletes would become manlike, adopting masculine dress, talk, and mannerisms. In addition, they contended, too much exercise would damage female reproductive capacity. And worse yet, the excitement of sport would cause women to lose control, conjuring up images of frenzied, distraught co-eds on the verge of moral, physical, and emotional breakdown. These fears collapsed into an all-encompassing concept of "mannishness," a term signifying female masculinity.

The public debate over the merits of women's athletic participation remained lively through the 1910s and 1920s. Implicit in the dispute over "mannishness" was a longstanding disagreement over the effect of women's athletic activities on their sexuality. Controversy centered around two issues—damage to female reproductive capacity and the unleashing of heterosexual passion. Medical experts and exercise specialists disagreed among themselves about the effects of athletic activity on women's reproductive cycles and organs. Some claimed that athletic training interfered with menstruation and caused reproductive organs to harden or atrophy; others insisted that rigorous exercise endowed women with strength and energy which would make them more fit for bearing and rearing children. Similarly, experts vehemently debated  whether competition unleashed nonprocreative, erotic desires identified with male sexuality and unrespectable women, or, conversely, whether invigorating sport enhanced a woman's feminine charm and sexual appeal, channeling sexual energy into wholesome activity.

Conflicting opinion on sexual matters followed closely along the lines of a larger dispute which divided the world of women's sport into warring camps. Beginning in the 1910s, female physical educators and male sport promoters squared off in a decades-long struggle over the appropriate nature of female competition and the right to govern women's athletics (Gerber 1975; Himes 1986; Hult 1985). The conflict was a complicated one, involving competing class and gender interests played out in organizational as well as philosophical battles. It was extremely important in shaping women's sports for more than fifty years. Although historians of sport have examined the broad parameters of the conflict, they have paid less attention to the competing sexual perspectives advanced by each side.

Physical educators took a cautious approach on all matters of sexuality, one designed to safeguard vulnerable young athletes and to secure their own professional status as respectable women in the male-dominated worlds of academia and sport. Heeding dire warnings about menstrual dysfunction, sterility, and inferior offspring, educators created policies to curtail strenuous competition and prohibit play during menstruation. They worried equally about the impact of sport on sexual morality. Alleging that competition would induce "powerful impulses" leading girls into a "temptation to excess" and the "pitfall of overindulgence," educators and their allies pressured popular sport promoters to reduce the competitive stimulation, publicity, and physical strain thought to endanger the sexuality of their female charges (Inglis 1910; Paret 1900, 1567; Sargent 1913).

Popular sport organizations like the Amateur Athletic Union [AAU] agreed that unregulated female competition posed psychological and moral dangers. But AAU officials countered protectionist physical education policies with a nationalist, eugenic stance which argued that strenuous activity under proper guidance would actually strengthen reproductive organs, creating a vigorous cadre of mothers to produce a generation of stalwart American sons (e.g., MacFadden 1929; Steers 1932). Although making some concessions to demands for modesty and female supervision, in the long run AAU leaders and commercial sport promoters also rejected educators' emphasis on sexual control. Sponsors of popular sport found that sexual hype, much more than caution, helped to attract customers and mute charges of mannishness. In working-class settings and in more elite sports like swimming, an ideal of the "athlete as beauty queen" emerged. Efforts to present the female athlete as sexually attractive and available mirrored the playful, erotic sensibility present in the broader commercial leisure culture of the early twentieth century (Erenberg 1981; Freedman and D'Emilio 1988; Peiss 1986).

The class and gender lines in this dispute were complicated by overlapping constituencies. Female educators adhered closely to middle-class, even Victorian, notions of respectability and modesty. But their influence spread beyond elite private and middle-class schools into working-class public schools and industrial recreation programs. And male promoters, often themselves of the middle-class, continued to control some school sport and, outside the schools, influenced both working-class and elite sports. Moreover, Black physical educators advanced a third point of view. Although few in number, early-twentieth-century African American physical education instructors generally aligned themselves with popular promoters in favor of competition and interscholastic sports. Yet their strong concern with maintaining respectability created some sympathy for the positions advanced by white leaders of women's physical education (Arnett 1921; Dunham 1924; Ellis 1939; Roberts 1927).

On all sides of the debate, however, the controversy about sport and female sexuality presumed heterosexuality. Neither critics nor supporters suggested that "masculine" athleticism might indicate or induce same-sex love. When experts warned of the amazonian athlete's possible sexual transgressions, they linked the physical release of sport with a loss of heterosexual *control, not inclination.* The most frequently used derogatory term for women athletes was "Muscle Moll." In its only other usages, the word "moll" referred to either the female lovers of male gangsters or to prostitutes. Both represented disreputable, heterosexually deviant womanhood.

By contrast, medical studies of sexual "deviance" from the late nineteenth and early twentieth centuries quite clearly linked "mannishness" to lesbianism, and in at least two cases explicitly connected female homosexuality with boyish athleticism (Chauncey 1989, 90–91; Ellis 1915, 250; Wise 1883, 88).

It is curious then that in answering charges against the mannish Muscle Moll, educators and sport promoters of this period did not refer to or deny lesbianism. However, the "mannish lesbian" made little sense in the heterosexual milieu of popular sports. Promoters encouraged mixed audiences for women's athletic events, often combining them with men's games, postgame dances and musical entertainment, or even beauty contests. The image of the athlete as beauty queen and the commercial atmosphere that characterized much of working-class sport ensured that the sexual debate surrounding the modern female athlete would focus on her heterosexual charm, daring, or disrepute. The homosocial environment of women's physical education left educators more vulnerable to insinuations that their profession was populated by "mannish" types who preferred the love of women. However, the feminine respectability and decorum cultivated by the profession provided an initial shield from associations with either the mannish lesbian or her more familiar counterpart, the heterosexual Muscle Moll.

The Muscle Moll as Heterosexual Failure: Emerging Lesbian Stereotypes

In the 1930s, however, the heterosexual understanding of the mannish "amazon" began to give way to a new interpretation which educators and promoters could not long ignore. To the familiar charge that female athletes resembled men, critics added the newer accusation that sport-induced mannishness disqualified them as candidates for heterosexual romance. In 1930, an *American Mercury* medical reporter decried the decline of romantic love, pinning the blame on women who entered sport, business, and politics. He claimed that such women "act like men, talk like men, and think like men." The author explained that "women have come closer and closer to men's level," and, consequently, "the purple allure of distance has vamoosed" (Nathan 1930). Four years later, the *Ladies Home Journal* printed a "Manual on the More or Less Subtle Art of Getting a Man" which listed vitality, gaiety, vivacity, and good sportsmanship—qualities typically associated with women athletes and formerly linked to the athletic flapper's heterosexual appeal—as "the very qualities that are likely to make him consider anything but marriage" (Moats 1934). Although the charges didn't exclusively focus on athletes, they implied that female athleticism was contrary to heterosexual appeal, which appeared to rest on women's difference from and deference to men.

The concern with heterosexual appeal reflected broader sexual transformations in U.S. society. Historians of sexuality have examined the multiple forces which reshaped gender and sexual relations in the first few decades of the twentieth century. Victorian sexual codes crumbled under pressure from an assertive, boldly sexual working-class youth culture, a women's movement which defied prohibitions against public female activism, and the growth of a new pleasure-oriented consumer economy. In the wake of these changes, modern ideals of womanhood embraced an overtly erotic heterosexual sensibility.

At the same time, medical fascination with sexual "deviance" created a growing awareness of lesbianism, now understood as a form of congenital or psychological pathology. The medicalization of homosexuality in combination with an antifeminist backlash in the 1920s against female autonomy and power contributed to a more fully articulated taboo against lesbianism. The modern heterosexual woman stood in stark opposition to her threatening sexual counterpart, the "mannish" lesbian (Freedman and D'Emilio 1988; Simmons 1989).

By the late 1920s and early 1930s, with a modern lesbian taboo and an eroticized definition of heterosexual femininity in place, the assertive, muscular female competitor roused increasing suspicion. It was at this moment that both subtle and direct references to the lesbian athlete emerged in physical education and popular sport. Uncensored discussions of intimate female companionship and harmless athletic "crushes" disappear from the record, pushed underground by the increasingly hostile tone of public discourse about female sexuality and athleticism. Fueled by the gender antagonisms and anxieties of the Depression, the public began scrutinizing women athletes—known for their appropriation of masculine games and styles—for signs of deviance.

Where earlier references to "amazons" had signaled heterosexual ardor, journalists now used the term to mean unattractive, failed heterosexuals. Occasionally, the media made direct mention of athletes' presumed lesbian tendencies. A 1933 *Redbook* article, for example, casually mentioned that track and golf star Babe Didrikson liked men just to horse around with her and not "make love," adding that Babe's fondness for her best girlfriends far surpassed her affection for any man (Marston 1933, 60). The direct reference was unusual; the lesbian connotation of mannishness was forged primarily through indirect links of association. The preponderance of evidence appears in public exchanges between opponents and advocates of women's sport.

After two decades of celebrating the female collegiate athlete, yearbooks at co-ed colleges began to ridicule physical education majors and Women's Athletic Association (WAA) members, portraying them as hefty, disheveled, and ugly. A 1937 Minnesota *Gopher* yearbook sarcastically titled its presentation on the WAA "Over in No Man's Land." Finding themselves cast as unattractive prudes or mannish misfits, physical educators struggled to revise their image. They declared the muscle-bound, manhating athlete a relic of the past, supplanted by "lovely, feminine charming girls" whose fitness, suppleness, and grace merely made them "more beautiful on the dance floor that evening" (Mooney 1937; Sefton 1937).

Similar exchanges appeared in popular magazines. After *Literary Digest* published Fred Wittner's assertion (1934, 42) that "worthy fathers" would not find trained women athletes attractive mates, AAU official Ada Taylor Sackett issued a rebuttal which reassured readers that because athletic muscles resembled "those of women who dance all night," women in sport could no doubt "still attract a worthy mate" (1934, 43). When critics maligned athletic femininity, they suggested that athletes were literally un-becoming women: unattractive females who abdicated their womanhood and fell under sexual suspicion. When defenders responded with ardent assertions that women athletes did indeed exhibit interest in men, marriage, and motherhood, it suggested that they understood "mannish" to mean "not-heterosexual."

The Butch Ballplayer: Midcentury Stereotypes of the Lesbian Athlete

Tentatively voiced in the 1930s, these accusations became harsher and more explicit under the impact of wartime changes in gender and sexuality and the subsequent panic over the "homosexual menace." In a post-World War II climate markedly hostile to nontraditional women and lesbians, women in physical education and in working-class popular sports became convenient targets of homophobic indictment.

World War II opened up significant economic and social possibilities for gay men and women. Embryonic prewar homosexual subcultures blossomed during the war and spread across the midcentury urban landscape. Bars, nightclubs, public cruising spots, and informal social networks facilitated the development of gay and lesbian enclaves. But the permissive atmosphere did not survive the war's end. Waving the banner of Cold War political and social conservatism, government leaders acted at the federal, state, and local levels to purge gays and lesbians from government and military posts, to initiate legal investigations and prosecutions of gay individuals and institutions, and to encourage local police crackdowns on gay bars and street life. The perceived need to safeguard national security and to reestablish social order in the wake of wartime disruption sparked a "homosexual panic" which promoted the fear, loathing, and persecution of homosexuals (Bérubé 1990; D'Emilio 1983; Freedman and D'Emilio 1988).

Lesbians suffered condemnation for their violation of gender as well as sexual codes. The tremendous emphasis on family, domesticity, and "traditional" femininity in the late 1940s and 1950s reflected postwar anxieties about the reconsolidation of a gender order shaken by two decades of depression and war. As symbols of women's refusal to conform, lesbians endured intense scrutiny by experts who regularly focused on their subjects' presumed masculinity. Sexologists attributed lesbianism to masculine tendencies and freedoms encouraged by the war, linking it to a general collapsing of gender distinctions which, in their view, destabilized marital and family relations (Breines 1986; Penn 1991).

Lesbians remained shadowy figures to most Americans, but women athletes—noted for their masculine bodies, interests, and attributes—were visible representatives of the gender inversion often associated with homosexuality. Physical education majors, formerly accused of being unappealing to men, were increasingly charged with being uninterested in them as well. The 1952 University of Minnesota *Gopher* yearbook snidely reported:

"Believe it or not, members of the Women's Athletic Association are normal" and found conclusive evidence in the fact that "at least one . . . of WAA's 300 members is engaged" (p. 257). And on May 10, 1956, a newspaper account in the *Texan* regarding the University of Texas Sports Association (UTSA) women's sports banquet led off with the headline, "UTSA Gives Awards," followed by a subheading "Gayness Necessary." The second headline referred to a guest speaker's talk on positive attitudes, entitled "The Importance of Being Debonair," but the lesbian allusion was unmistakable and I believe fully intentional.[2]

The lesbian stigma began to plague popular athletes too, especially in working-class sports noted for their masculine toughness. The pall of suspicion did not completely override older associations with heterosexual deviance. When *Collier's* 1947 article (Lagemann) on the Red Heads, a barnstorming women's basketball team, exclaimed "It's basketball—not a striptease!" the author alluded to both the heterosexual appeal and the hint of disrepute long associated with working-class women athletes. But the dominant postwar voice intimated a different type of disrepute. Journalists continued to attack the mannish athlete as ugly and sexually unappealing, implying that this image could only be altered through proof of heterosexual "success."

The career of Babe Didrikson, which spanned the 1920s to the 1950s, illustrates the shift. In the early 1930s the press had ridiculed the tomboyish track star for her "hatchet face," "door-stop jaw," and "button-breasted" chest. After quitting track, Didrikson dropped out of the national limelight, married professional wrestler George Zaharias in 1938, and then staged a spectacular athletic comeback as a golfer in the late 1940s and 1950s. Fascinated by her personal transformation and then, in the 1950s, moved by her battle with cancer, journalists gave Didrikson's comeback extensive coverage and helped make her a much-loved popular figure. In reflecting on her success, however, sportswriters spent at least as much time on Didrikson's love life as her golf stroke. Headlines blared, "Babe is a lady now: The world's most amazing athlete has learned to wear nylons and cook for her huge husband," and reporters gleefully described how "along came a great big he-man wrestler and the Babe forgot all her man-hating chatter" (Andersen 1945; Gallico 1960; Farmer 1947; Martin 1947).

Postwar sport discourse consistently focused on women's sexual as well as their athletic achievements. As late as 1960, a *New York Times Magazine* headline asked, "Do men make passes at athletic lasses?" Columnist William B. Furlong answered no for most activities, concluding that except for a few "yes" sports like swimming, women athletes "surrendered" their sex. The challenge for women athletes was not to conquer new athletic feats, which would only further reduce their sexual appeal, but to regain their womanhood through sexual surrender to men.

Media coverage in national magazines and metropolitan newspapers typically focused on the sexual accomplishments of white female athletes, but postwar observers and promoters of African American women's sport also confronted the issue of sexual normalcy. In earlier decades, neither Black nor white commentary on African American athletes expressed a concern with "mannish" lesbianism. The white media generally ignored Black athletes. Implicitly, however, stereotypes of Black females as highly sexual, promiscuous, and unrestrained in their heterosexual passions discouraged the linkage between mannishness and lesbianism. Racist gender ideologies further complicated the meaning of mannishness. Historically, European American racial thought characterized African Americans women as aggressive, coarse, passionate, and physical—the same qualities assigned to manliness in sport (Carby 1987; Collins 1990; Giddings 1984). Excluded from dominant ideals of womanhood, Black women's success in sport could be interpreted not as an unnatural deviation but, rather, as the natural result of their reputed closeness to nature, animals, and masculinity.[3]

Within Black communities, strong local support for women's sport may also have weakened the association between sport and lesbianism. Athletes from Tuskegee Institute's national championship track teams of the late 1930s and 1940s described an atmosphere of campus-wide enthusiastic support. They noted that although a male student might accuse an athlete of being "funny" if she turned him down for a date, in general lesbianism was not a subject of concern in Black sport circles (personal interviews, Alice Coachman Davis, Lula Hymes Glenn, and Leila Perry Glover 1992). Similarly, Gloria Wilson (pseudonym, personal interview, 1988) found that she encountered far less uneasiness about lesbianism on her Black semipro softball team in the late 1950s and 1960s than she did in the predominantly white college physical education departments she joined later. She explained that the expectation of heterosexuality was ingrained in Black women to the point that "anything outside of that realm is just out of the question." While recalling that her teammates "had no time or patience for 'funnies,'" Wilson noted that the issue rarely came up, in large part because most team members were married and therefore "didn't have to prove it because then, too, their men were always at those games. They were very supportive."

Although Black athletes may have encountered few lesbian stereotypes at the local level, circumstances in the broader society eventually pressed African American sport promoters and journalists to address the issue of mannish sexuality. The strong association of sports and lesbianism developed at the same time as Black athletes became a dominant presence in American sport culture. Midcentury images of sport, Blackness, masculinity, and lesbianism circulated in the same orbit in various combinations. There was no particular correlation between Black women and lesbianism; however, the association of each with mannishness and sexual aggression potentially linked the two. In the late 1950s, Black sport promoters and journalists joined others in taking up the question of sexual "normalcy." One Black newspaper (*Baltimore Afro-American*) in 1957 described tennis star Althea Gibson as a childhood "tomboy" who "later in life . . . finds herself victimized by complexes." The article did not elaborate on the nature of Gibson's "complex," but lesbianism is inferred in the linkage between "tomboys" and psychological illness. This connotation becomes clearer by looking at the defense of Black women's sport. Echoing *Ebony's* avowal (1955, 28, 32) that "entirely feminine" Black female track stars "like boys, dances, club affairs," in 1962 Tennessee State University track coach Ed Temple asserted in the *Detroit News*, "None of my girls have any trouble getting boy friends. . . . We don't want amazons."

Constant attempts to shore up the heterosexual reputation of athletes can be read as evidence that the longstanding reputation of female athletes as mannish women had become a covert reference to lesbianism. By mid-century, a fundamental reorientation of sexual meanings fused notions of femininity, female eroticism, and heterosexual attractiveness into a single ideal. Mannishness, once primarily a sign of gender crossing, assumed a specifically lesbian-sexual connotation. In the wake of this change, the strong cultural association between sport and masculinity made women's athletics ripe for emerging lesbian stereotypes. This meaning of athletic mannishness raises [the] further question what impact did the stereotype have on women's sport?. . . .

Sport and the Heterosexual Imperative

The image of the mannish lesbian athlete had a direct effect on women competitors, on strategies of athletic organizations, and on the overall popularity of women's sport. The lesbian stereotype exerted pressure on athletes to demonstrate their femininity and heterosexuality, viewed as one and the same. Many women adopted an apologetic stance toward their athletic skill. Even as they competed to win, they made sure to display outward signs of femininity in dress and demeanor. They took special care in contact with the media to reveal "feminine" hobbies like cooking and sewing, to mention current boyfriends, and to discuss future marriage plans (Del Rey 1978).

Leaders of women's sport took the same approach at the institutional level. In answer to portrayals of physical education majors and teachers as social rejects and prudes, physical educators revised their philosophy to place heterosexuality at the center of professional objectives. In the late 1930s, they invited psychologists to speak at national professional meetings about problems of sexual adjustment. Such experts described the "types of people who are unadjusted to heterosexual cooperative activity" and warned women in physical education to "develop a prejudice *against* segregation of the sexes" (National Amateur Athletic Federation-Women's Division 1938). Told that exclusively female environments caused failed heterosexual development, physical educators who had long advocated female separatism in sport were pressed to promote mixed-sex groups and heterosexual "adjustment."

Curricular changes implemented between the mid-1930s and mid-1950s institutionalized the new philosophy. In a paper on postwar objectives, Mildred A. Schaeffer (1945) explained that physical education classes should help women "develop an interest in school dances and mixers and a desire to voluntarily attend them." To this end, administrators revised coursework to emphasize beauty and social charm over rigorous exercise and health. They exchanged old rationales of fitness and fun for promises of trimmer waist-lines, slimmer hips, and prettier complexions. At Radcliffe, for example, faculty redesigned health classes to include "advice on dress, carriage, hair, skin, voice, and any factor that would tend to improve personal appearance and thus contribute to social and economic success" (Physical Education Director, no date). Intramural programs replaced interclass basketball tournaments and weekend campouts for women with mixed-sex "co-recreational" activities like bowling, volleyball, and "fun nights" of pingpong and shuffleboard. Some departments also added co-educational classes to foster "broader, keener, more sympathetic understanding of the opposite sex" (Department of Physical Education 1955).[4] Department heads cracked down on "mannish" students and faculty, issuing warnings against "casual styles" which might "lead us back into some dangerous channels" (Ashton 1957). They implemented dress codes which forbade slacks and men's shirts or socks, adding as well a ban on "boyish hair cuts" and unshaven legs. For example, the 1949–50 Physical Training Staff Handbook at the University of Texas stated (p. 16), "Legs should be kept shaved," while restrictions on hair and dress are spelled out in the staff minutes and physical education handbooks for majors at the universities of Wisconsin, Texas, and Minnesota. . . .

Popular sport promoters adopted similar tactics. Martialing sexual data like they were athletic statistics, a 1954 AAU poll sought to sway a skeptical public with numerical proof of heterosexuality—the fact that 91 percent of former female athletes surveyed had married (Andersen 1954). Publicity for the midwestern All-American Girls Baseball League (AAGBL) included statistics on the number of married players in the league. In the same vein, the women's golf tour announced that one-third of the pros were married, and the rest were keeping an eye peeled for prospects who might "lure them from the circuit to the altar" (All-American Girls Baseball League Records, Pennsylvania State University Libraries; *Saturday Evening Post* 1954).

The fear of lesbianism was greatest where a sport had a particularly masculine image and where promoters needed to attract a paying audience. Professional and semipro basketball and softball fit the bill on both accounts. Athletic leaders tried to resolve the problem by "proving" the attractive femininity of athletes. Softball and basketball tournaments continued to feature beauty pageants. Although in earlier times such events celebrated the "sexiness" of the emancipated modern woman, in later decades they seemed to serve a more defensive function. The AAU's magazine, the *Amateur Athlete*, made sure that at least one photograph of the national basketball tournament's beauty "queen and her court" accompanied the photo of each year's championship team. Behind the scenes, teams passed dress and conduct codes. For example, the All-American Girls Baseball League's 1951 Constitution prohibited players from wearing men's clothing or getting "severe" haircuts. That this was an attempt to secure the heterosexual image of athletes was made even clearer when league officials announced that AAGBL policy prohibited the recruitment of "freaks" and "Amazons" (Markey n.d.; Feminine Sluggers 1952).

In the end, the strategic emphasis on heterosexuality and the suppression of "mannishness" did little to alter the image of women in sport. The stereotype of the mannish lesbian athlete grew out of the persistent common sense equation of sport and masculinity. Opponents of women's sport reinforced this belief when they denigrated women's athletic efforts and ridiculed skilled athletes as "grotesque," "mannish," or "unnatural." Leaders of women's sport unwittingly contributed to the same set of ideas when they began to orient their programs around the new feminine heterosexual ideal. As physical education policies and media campaigns worked to suppress lesbianism and marginalize athletes who didn't conform to dominant standards of femininity, sport officials embedded heterosexism into the institutional and ideological framework of sport. The effect extended beyond sport to the wider culture, where the figure of the mannish lesbian athlete announced that competitiveness, strength, independence, aggression, and physical intimacy among women fell outside the bounds of womanhood. As a symbol of female deviance, she served as a powerful reminder to all women to tow the line of heterosexuality and femininity or risk falling into a despised category of mannish (not-women) women. . . .

Notes

I would like to thank Birgitte Soland, Maureen Honish, Kath Weston, George Chauncey, Jr., and Nan Enstad for their criticisms, encouragement, and editorial advice on earlier versions of this essay.

1. Among the works that do consider the issue of homosexuality are Lenskyj (1986), Zipter (1988), and Bennett (1982). On the relationship between male homosexuality and sport, see Pronger (1990).
2. Although the term "gay" as a reference to homosexuals occurred only sporadically in the mass media before the 1960s, it was in use as a slang term among some homosexual men and lesbians as early as the 1920s and quite commonly by the 1940s.
3. Elizabeth Lunbeck (1987) notes a similar pattern in her discussion of medical theories of the "hypersexual" white female. Because psychiatrists assumed that Black women were naturally "oversexed," when defining the medical condition of hypersexuality, they included only young white working-class women whose sexual ardor struck physicians and social workers as unnaturally excessive.
4. For curricular changes, I examined physical education records at the Universities of Wisconsin, Texas, and Minnesota, Radcliffe College, Smith College, Tennessee State University, and Hampton University.

References

Andersen, Roxy. 1945. Fashions in feminine sport. *Amateur Athlete*, March.

———. 1954. Statistical survey of former women athletes. *Amateur Athlete*, September.

Arnett, Ruth. 1921. Girls need physical education. *Chicago Defender*, 10 December.

Ashton, Dudley. 1957. Recruiting future teachers. *Journal of Health, Physical Education, and Recreation* 28 (October):49.

Baltimore Afro-American. 1957. 29 June, Magazine Section, 1.

Bennett, Roberta. 1982. Sexual labeling as social control: Some political effects of being female in the gym. *Perspectives* 4:40–50.

Bérubé, Alan. 1990. *Coming Out Under Fire: The History of Gay Men and Women in World War Two*. New York: Free Press.

Breines, Wini. 1986. The 1950s: Gender and some social science. *Sociological Inquiry* 56 (Winter):69–92.

Carby, Hazel. 1987. *Reconstructing Womanhood: The Emergence of the Afro-American Women Novelist*. New York: Oxford University Press.

Chauncey, George, Jr. 1989. From sexual inversion to homosexuality: Medicine and the changing conceptualization of female deviance. In *Passion and Power: Sexuality in History*, edited by Kathy Peiss and Christina Simmons. Philadelphia: Temple University Press.

Collins, Patricia Hill. 1990. *Black Feminist Thought: Knowledge, Consciousness, and the Politics of Empowerment*. Boston: Unwin Hyman.

D'Emilio, John. 1983. *Sexual Politics, Sexual Communities: The Making of a Homosexual Minority in the United States, 1940–1970*. Chicago: University of Chicago Press.

de Koven, Anna. 1912. The athletic woman. *Good Housekeeping*, August.

Del Rey, Patricia. 1978. The apologetic and women in sport. In *Women and Sport*, edited by Carole Oglesby. Philadelphia: Lea & Febiger.

Department of Physical Education, University of California, Los Angeles. 1955. Coeducational classes. *Journal of Health, Physical Education, and Recreation* 26 (February):18.

Detroit News. 1962. 31 July, sec. 6. p. 1.

Dunham, Elizabeth. 1924. Physical education for women at Hampton Institute. *Southern Workman* 53 (April):167.

Dunning, Eric. 1986. Sport as a male preserve: Notes on the social sources of masculine identity and its transformation. In *Quest for Excitement: Sport and Leisure in the Civilizing Process*, edited by Eric Dunning and Norbert Elias. New York: Basil Blackwell.

Ebony. 1955. Fastest women in the world. June, 28.

Ellis, A. W. 1939. The status of health and physical education for women in Negro colleges and universities. *Journal of Negro Education* 8(January):58–63.

Ellis, Havelock. 1915. *Sexual Inversion*, vol. 2 of *Studies in the Psychology of Sex*. 3rd rev. ed. Philadelphia: F. A. Davis.

Erenberg, Lewis. 1981. *Steppin' Out: New York Nightlife and the Transformation of American Culture, 1890–1930*. Westport, CT: Greenwood Press.

Farmer, Gene. 1947. What a Babe! *Life*, June.

Feminine Sluggers. 1952. *People and Places* 8(12), reproduced in AAGBL Records.

Freedman, Estelle, and John D'Emilio. 1988. *Intimate Matters: A History of Sexuality in America*. New York: Harper & Row.

Furlong, William B. 1960. Venus wasn't a shotputter. *New York Times Magazine*, 28 August.

Gallico, Paul. 1960. *Houston Post*, 22 March.

Gerber, Ellen W. 1975. The controlled development of collegiate sport for women, 1923–36. *Journal of Sport History* 2(Spring):1–28.

Giddings, Paula. 1984. *When and Where I Enter: The Impact of Black Women on Race and Sex in America.* New York: William Morrow & Company.

Himes, Cindy L. 1986. *The Female Athlete in American Society, 1860–1940.* Ph.D. diss., University of Pennsylvania.

Hult, Joan. 1985. The governance of athletics for girls and women. *Research Quarterly for Exercise and Sport*, April:64–77.

Inglis, William. 1910. Exercise for girls. *Harper's Bazaar*, March.

Kimmel, Michael S. 1987. The contemporary "crisis" of masculinity in historical perspective. In *The Making of Masculinities: The New Men's Studies* edited by Harry Brod. Boston: Allen & Unwin.

Lagemann, John Lord. 1947. Red heads you kill me! *Colliers*, 8 February, 64.

Lenskyj, Helen. 1986. *Out of Bounds: Women, Sport, and Sexuality.* Toronto: Women's Press.

Lunbeck, Elizabeth. 1987. "A new generation of women": Progressive psychiatrists and the hypersexual female. *Feminist Studies* 13(Fall):513–43.

MacFadden, Bernard. 1929. Athletics for women will help save the nation. *Amateur Athlete* 4(February–July):7.

Mangan, J. A., and Roberta J. Park, eds. 1987. *From "Fair Sex" to Feminism: Sport and the Socialization of Women in the Industrial and Post-Industrial Eras.* London: Frank Cass.

Mange, Violet W. 1910. Field hockey for women. *Harper's Bazaar*, April.

Markey, Morris. No date. Hey Ma, you're out! 1951 Records of the AAGBL.

Marston, William. 1933. How can a woman do it? *Redbook*, September.

Martin, Pete. 1947. Babe Didrikson takes off her mask. *Saturday Evening Post*, 20 September.

Moats, A. 1934. He hasn't a chance. *Ladies Home Journal*, December.

Mooney, Gertrude. 1937. The benefits and dangers of athletics for the high school girl. Department of Physical Training for Women Records (Health Ed. folder), Box 3R251. Barker Texas History Center, University of Texas, Austin.

Mrozek, Donald J. 1983. *Sport and the American Mentality, 1880–1910.* Knoxville: University of Tennessee Press.

Murray, Jim. No date. 1970s column in *Austin American Statesman*, Zaharias scrapbook, Barker Texas History Center, University of Texas, Austin.

Nathan, George. 1930. Once there was a princess. *American Mercury*, February.

National Amateur Athletic Federation-Women's Division. 1938. Newsletter, no. 79 (1 June 1938), from Department of Women's Physical Education, University of Wisconsin Archives.

Paret, J. Parmley. 1900. Basket-ball for young women. *Harper's Bazaar*, October.

Peiss, Kathy. 1986. *Cheap Amusements: Working Women and Leisure in Turn-of-the-Century New York.* Philadelphia: Temple University Press.

Penn, Donna. 1991. The meanings of lesbianism in post-war America. *Gender and History* 3:190–203.

Physical Education Director. No date. Official Reports, Kristin Powell's collected materials on Radcliffe Athletics, Radcliffe College Archives, acc. no. R87.

Pronger, Brian. 1990. *The Arena of Masculinity: Sport, Homosexuality, and the Meaning of Sex.* New York: St. Martin's Press.

Roberts, Amelia. 1927. Letter to *Chicago Defender*, 12 March, sec. 2, p. 7.

Sargent, Dudley A. 1913. Are athletics making girls masculine? *Ladies Home Journal*, March.

Saturday Evening Post. 1954. Next to marriage, we'll take golf. 23 January.
Schaeffer, Mildred A. 1945. Desirable objectives in post-war physical education. *Journal of Health and Physical Education* 16:446–47.
Sefton, Alice Allene. 1937. Must women in sports look beautiful? *Journal of Health and Physical Education* 8:481.
Simmons, Christina. 1989. Modern sexuality and the myth of Victorian repression. In *Passion and Power: Sexuality in History*, edited by Kathy Peiss and Christina Simmons. Philadelphia: Temple University Press.
Steers, Fred. 1932. Spirit. *Amateur Athlete* October:7.
Wise, P. M. 1883. Case of sexual perversion. *Alienist and Neurologist* 4:88.
Wittner, Fred. 1934. Shall the ladies join us? *Literary Digest*, 19 May.
Zipter, Yvonne. 1988. *Diamonds Are a Dyke's Best Friend*. Ithaca, NY: Firebrand Books.

19

Branded with Infamy

Inscriptions of Poverty and Class in the United States

Vivyan C. Adair

According to philosopher Michel Foucault, premodern societies convinced their members to obey the laws of state and church by branding, cutting, burning, or otherwise gruesomely and publicly marking the bodies of any who broke those laws. These marked bodies thus became "texts" that could be read as one would read a book. In contrast, Foucault argued, modern societies instill obedience through socializing their members to internalize society's rules and to discipline themselves, making harsh punishments unnecessary. Several articles in this volume, such as Sandra Lee Bartky's, have similarly highlighted how contemporary society teaches women to internalize social norms regarding proper feminine appearance.

In "Branded with Infamy: Inscriptions of Poverty and Class in the United States," Vivyan C. Adair examines the stigmatization and control of poor women's bodies through both modern and premodern strategies. Both historically and recently, women have been affected disproportionately by poverty—an observation some scholars have referred to as the "feminization of poverty." According to the U.S. Census, 15.5 percent of women lived in poverty in 2011, compared to 11.8 percent of men.

The effects of poverty (and resultant lack of health care) physically mark the bodies of poor women and their children, in a very "premodern" way. Simultaneously, however, public portrayals of poor women, combined with assumptions

Vivyan C. Adair. 2001. "Branded with Infamy: Inscriptions of Poverty and Class in the United States," *Signs* 27: 451–481. Permission of University of Chicago Press.

about poor women embedded in public policy, socialize all of us to assume that poverty among women—especially if they are nonwhite—results from their own moral and physical failings. As a result, poor women may internalize a sense of shame and so accept their fate and discipline their bodies—a very "modern" type of social control. Nevertheless, Adair argues, poor women still find ways to engage in resistance.

> My kids and I been chopped up and spit out just like when I was a kid. My rotten teeth, my kids' twisted feet. My son's dull skin and blank stare. My oldest girl's stooped posture and the way she can't look no one in the eye no more. This all says we got nothing and we deserve what we got. On the street good families look at us and see right away what they'd be if they don't follow the rules. They're scared too, real scared.
>
> *Welfare Recipient and Activist, Olympia, WA, 1998*

I begin with the words of a poor, white, single mother of three. Although officially she has only a tenth-grade education, she expertly reads and articulates a complex theory of power, bodily inscription, and socialization that arose directly from the material conditions of her own life. She sees what many far more "educated" scholars and citizens fail to recognize: that the bodies of poor women and children are produced and positioned as texts that facilitate the mandates of a didactic, profoundly brutal and mean-spirited political regime. The clarity and power of this woman's vision challenges feminists to consider and critique our commitment both to textualizing displays of heavy-handed social inscription and to detextualizing them, working to put an end to these bodily experiences of pain, humiliation, and suffering. . . .

Over the past decade or so, a host of inspired feminist welfare scholars and activists has addressed and examined the relationship between state power and the lives of poor women and children. As important and insightful as these exposés are, with few exceptions, they do not get at the closed circuit that fuses together systems of power, the material conditions of poverty, and the bodily experiences that allow for the perpetuation—and indeed for the justification—of these systems. They fail to consider what the speaker of my opening passage recognized so astutely: that systems of power produce and patrol poverty through the reproduction of both social and bodily markers.

What is inadequate, then, even in many feminist theories of class production, is an analysis of this nexus of the textual and the corporeal. Here Michel Foucault's ([1977] 1984) argument about the inscriptions of bodies is a powerful mechanism for understanding the material and physical conditions and bodily costs of poverty across racial difference and for interrogating the connection between power's expression as text, as body, and as site of resistance. . . . Particularly useful for feminists has been Foucault's theory that the body is written on and through discourse as the product of historically specific power relations. …

In *Discipline and Punish*, Foucault sets out to depict the genealogy of torture and discipline as it reflects a public display of power on the body of subjects in the seventeenth and eighteenth centuries. In graphic detail Foucault begins his book with the description of a criminal being tortured and then drawn and quartered in a public square. The crowds of good parents and their growing children watch and learn. The public spectacle works as a patrolling image, socializing and controlling bodies within the body politic. Eighteenth-century torture "must mark the victim: it is intended, either by the scar it leaves on the body or by the spectacle that accompanies it, to brand the victim with infamy. It traces around or rather on the very body of the condemned man signs that can not be effaced" ([1977] 1984, 179). For Foucault, public exhibitions of punishment served as a socializing process, writing culture's codes and values on the minds and bodies of its subjects. In the process punishment discursively deconstructed and rearranged bodies.

But Foucault's point in *Discipline and Punish* is precisely that public exhibition and inscription have been replaced in contemporary society by a much more effective process of socialization and self-inscription. According to Foucault, today discipline has replaced torture as the privileged punishment, but the body continues to be written on. Discipline produces "subjected and practiced bodies, 'docile bodies'" (1984, 182). We become subjects not of the sovereign but of ideology, disciplining and inscribing our own bodies/minds in the process of becoming stable and singular subjects. Power's hold on bodies is in both cases maintained through language systems. The body continues to be the site and operation of ideology, as subject and representation, body and text.

Indeed, while we are all marked discursively by ideology in Foucault's paradigm, in the United States today poor women and children of all races are multiply marked with signs of both discipline and punishment that cannot be erased or effaced. They are systematically produced through both twentieth-century forces of socialization and discipline and eighteenthcentury exhibitions of public mutilation. In addition to coming into being as disciplined and docile bodies, poor single welfare mothers and their children are physically inscribed, punished, and displayed as the dangerous and pathological other. It is important to note, when considering the contemporary inscription of poverty as moral pathology etched onto the bodies of profoundly poor women and children, that these are more than metaphoric and self-patrolling marks of discipline. Rather, on myriad levels—sexual, social, material, and physical—poor women and their children, like the "deviants" publicly punished in Foucault's scenes of torture, are marked, mutilated, and made to bear and transmit signs in a public spectacle that brands the victim with infamy.

Text of the Body, Body of the Text: The (Not So) Hidden Injuries of Class

Recycled images of poor, welfare women permeate and shape our national consciousness.[1] Yet—as is so often the case—these images and narratives tell us more about the culture that spawned and embraced them than they do about the object of the culture's obsession. Simple, stable, and often widely skewed cover stories tell us what is "wrong" with some people, what is normative, and what is pathological; by telling us who "bad" poor women are, we reaffirm and reevaluate who we, as a nation and as a people—of allegedly good, middle-class, white, able-bodied, independent, male citizens—are. At their foundations, stories of the welfare mother intersect with, draw from, reify, and reproduce myriad mythic American narratives associated with a constellation of beliefs about capitalism, male authority, the "nature" of humans, and the sphere of individual freedom, opportunity, and responsibility. These narratives purport to write the story of poor women in an arena in which only their bodies have been positioned to "speak." They promise to tell the story of who poor women are in ways that allow Americans to maintain a belief in both an economic system based on exploitation and an ideology that claims that we are all beyond exploitation.

These productions orchestrate the story of poverty as one of moral and intellectual lack and of chaos, pathology, promiscuity, illogic, and sloth, juxtaposed always against the order, progress, and decency of "deserving" citizens. Trying to stabilize and make sense of unpalatably complex issues of poverty and oppression and attempting to obscure hegemonic stakes in representation, these narratives reduce and collapse the lives and experiences of poor women to deceptively simplistic dramas, which are then offered for public consumption. The terms of these dramas are palatable because they are presented as simple oppositions of good and bad, right and wrong, independent and dependent, deserving and undeserving. Yet as a generationally poor woman I know that poverty is neither this simple nor this singular. Poverty is rather the product of complex systems of power that at many levels are indelibly written on poor women and children in feedback loops that compound and complicate politically expedient readings and writings of our bodies.

I am, and will probably always be, marked as a poor woman. I was raised by a poor, single, white mother who had to struggle to keep her four children fed, sheltered, and clothed by working at what seemed like an endless stream of minimum-wage, exhausting, and demeaning jobs. As a child poverty was written onto and into my being at the level of private and public thought and body. At an early age my body bore witness to and emitted signs of the painful devaluation carved into my flesh; that same devaluation became integral to my being in the world. I came into being as a disciplined body/mind while at the same time I was taught to read my abject body as the site of my own punishment and erasure. In this excess of meaning the space between private body and public sign was collapsed. . . .

Indeed, poor children are often marked with bodily signs that cannot be forgotten or erased. Their bodies are physically inscribed as "other" and then read as pathological, dangerous, and undeserving. What I recall most vividly about being a child in a profoundly poor family was that we were constantly hurt and ill, and, because we could not afford medical care, small illnesses and accidents spiraled into more dangerous illnesses and complications that became both a part of who we were and written proof that we were of no value in the world.

In spite of my mother's heroic efforts, at an early age my brothers and sister and I were stooped, bore scars that never healed properly, and limped with feet mangled by ill-fitting, used Salvation Army shoes. When my sister's forehead was split open by a door slammed in frustration, my mother "pasted" the angry wound together on her own, leaving a mark of our inability to afford medical attention, of our lack, on her very forehead. When I suffered from a concussion, my mother simply put borrowed ice on my head and tried to keep me awake for a night. And when throughout elementary school we were sent to the office for mandatory and very public yearly checkups, the school nurse sucked air through her teeth as she donned surgical gloves to check only the hair of poor children for lice.

We were read as unworthy, laughable, and often dangerous. Our schoolmates laughed at our "ugly shoes," our crooked and ill-serviced teeth, and the way we "stank," as teachers excoriated us for our inability to concentrate in school, our "refusal" to come to class prepared with proper school supplies, and our unethical behavior when we tried to take more than our allocated share of "free lunch." Whenever backpacks or library books came up missing, we were publicly interrogated and sent home to "think about" our offenses, often accompanied by notes that reminded my mother that as a poor single parent she should be working twice as hard to make up for the discipline that allegedly walked out the door with my father. When we sat glued to our seats, afraid to stand in front of the class in ragged and ill-fitting hand-me-downs, we were held up as examples of unprepared and uncooperative children. And when our grades reflected our otherness, they were used to justify even more elaborate punishment that exacerbated the effects of our growing anomie.

Friends who were poor as children, and respondents to a survey I conducted in 1998, tell similar stories of the branding they received at the hands of teachers, administrators, and peers. An African-American woman raised in Yesler Terrace, a public housing complex in Seattle, Washington, writes:

> Poor was all over our faces. My glasses were taped and too weak. My big brother had missing teeth. My mom was dull and ashy. It was like a story of how poor we were that anyone could see. My sister Evie's lip was bit by a dog and we just had dime store stuff to put on it. Her lip was a big scar. Then she never smiled and no one smiled at her cause she never smiled. Kids call[ed] her "Scarface." Teachers never smiled at her. The principal put her in detention all the time because she was mean and bad (they said).

And a white woman in the Utica, New York, area remembers:

> We lived in dilapidated and unsafe housing that had fleas no matter how clean my mom tried to be. We had bites all over us. Living in our car between evictions was even worse—then we didn't have a bathroom so I got kidney problems that I never had doctor's help for. When my teachers wouldn't let me go to the bathroom every hour or so I would wet my pants in class. You can imagine what the kids did to me about that. And the teachers would refuse to let me go to the bathroom because they said I was willful.[2]

Material deprivation is publicly written on the bodies of poor children in the world. In the United States poor families experience violent crime, hunger, lack of medical and dental care, utility shut-offs, the effects of living in unsafe housing and/or of being homeless, chronic illness, and insufficient winter clothing (Edin and Lein 1997, 224–31). According to Jody Raphael of the Taylor Institute, poor women and their children are also at five times the risk of experiencing domestic violence (2000).

As children, our disheveled and broken bodies were produced and read as signs of our inferiority and undeservedness. As adults our mutilated bodies are read as signs of inner chaos, immaturity, and indecency as we are punished and then read as proof of the need for further discipline and punishment. When my already bad teeth started to rot and I was out of my head with pain, my choices as an adult welfare recipient were either to let my teeth fall out or to have them pulled out. In either case the culture would then read me as a "toothless illiterate," as a fearful joke. In order to pay my rent and to put shoes on my daughter's feet I sold blood at two or three different clinics on a monthly basis until I became so anemic that they refused to buy it from me. A neighbor of mine went back to the man who continued to beat her and her scarred children after being denied welfare benefits when she realized that she could not adequately feed, clothe, and house her family on her own minimum-wage income. My good friend sold her ovum to a fertility clinic in a painful and potentially damaging process. Other friends exposed themselves to all manner of danger and disease by selling their bodies for sex in order to feed and clothe their babies.

Poverty becomes a vicious cycle that is written on our bodies and intimately connected with our value in the world. Our children need healthy food so that we can continue working; yet working at minimum-wage jobs, we have no money for wholesome food and very little time to care for our families. So our children get sick, we lose our jobs to take care of them, we fall deeper and deeper into debt before our next unbearable job, and then we really cannot afford medical care. Starting that next minimum-wage job with unpaid bills and ill children puts us further and further behind so that we are even less able to afford good food, adequate child care, health care, or emotional healing. The food banks we gratefully drag our exhausted children to on the weekends hand out bags of rancid candy bars, hot dogs that have passed their expiration dates, stale broken pasta, and occasionally a bag of wrinkled apples. We are either fat or skinny, and we seem always irreparably ill. Our emaciated or bloated bodies are then read as a sign of lack of discipline and as proof that we have failed to care as we should.[3]

Exhaustion also marks the bodies of poor women in indelible script. Rest becomes a privilege we simply cannot afford. After working full shifts each day, poor mothers trying to support themselves at minimum-wage jobs continue to work to a point of exhaustion that is inscribed on their faces, their bodies, their posture, and their diminishing sense of self and value in the world. My former neighbor recently recalled:

> I had to take connecting buses to bring and pick up my daughters at childcare after working on my feet all day. As soon as we arrived at home, we would head out again by bus to do laundry. Pick up groceries. Try to get to the food bank. Beg the electric company to not turn off our lights and heat again. Find free winter clothing. Sell my blood. I would be home at nine or ten o'clock at night. I was loaded down with one baby asleep and one crying. Carrying lots of heavy bags and ready to drop on my feet. I had bags under my eyes and no shampoo to wash my hair so I used soap. Anyway I had to stay up to wash diapers in the sink. Otherwise they wouldn't be dry when I left the house in the dark with my girls. In the morning I start all over again.[4]

This bruised and lifeless body, hauling sniffling babies and bags of dirty laundry on the bus, was then read as a sign that she was a bad mother and a threat that needed to be disciplined and made to work even harder for her own good. Those who need the respite less go away for weekends, take drives in the woods, take their kids to the beach. Poor women without education are pushed into minimum-wage jobs and have no money, no car, no time, no energy, and little support, as their bodies are made to display marks of their material deprivation as a socializing and patrolling force.

Ultimately, we come to recognize that our bodies are not our own, that they are rather public property. State-mandated blood tests, interrogation of the most private aspects of our lives, the public humiliation of having to beg officials for food and medicine, and the loss of all right to privacy, teach us that our bodies are only useful as lessons, warnings, and signs of degradation that everyone loves to hate. In "From Welfare to Academe: Welfare Reform as College-Educated Welfare Mothers Know It," Sandy Smith-Madsen describes the erosion of her privacy as a poor welfare mother:

> I was investigated. I was spied upon. A welfare investigator c[a]me into my home and after thoughtful deliberation granted me permission to keep my belongings. Like the witch hunts of old, if a neighbor reports you as a welfare queen, the guardians of the state's compelling interest come into your home and interrogate you. While they do not have the right to set your body ablaze on the public square, they can forever devastate heart and soul

> by snatching away children. Just like a police officer, they may use whatever they happen to see against you, including sexual orientation. Full-fledged citizens have the right to deny an officer entry into their home unless they possess a search warrant; welfare mothers fork over citizenship rights for the price of a welfare check. In Tennessee, constitutional rights go for a cash value of $185 per month for a family of three. (2003, 185)

Welfare reform policy is designed to publicly expose, humiliate, punish, and display "deviant" welfare mothers. "Workfare" and "Learnfare"—two alleged successes of welfare reform—require that landlords, teachers, and employers be made explicitly aware of the second-class status of these very public bodies. In Ohio, the Department of Human Services uses tax dollars to pay for advertisements on the side of Cleveland's RTA buses that show a "Welfare Queen" behind bars with a logo that proclaims "Crime does not pay. Welfare fraud is a crime" (Robinson 1999). In Michigan a pilot program mandating drug tests for all welfare recipients began on October 1, 1999. Recipients who refuse the test lose their benefits immediately (Simon 1999). In Buffalo, New York, a county executive proudly announced that his county would begin intensive investigation of all parents who refuse minimum-wage jobs that are offered to them by the state. He warned: "We have many ways of investigating and exposing these errant parents who choose to exploit their children in this way" (Anderson 1999). In Eugene, recipients who cannot afford to feed their children adequately on their food stamp allocations are advised through fliers issued by a contractor for Oregon's welfare agency to "check the dump and the residential and business dumpsters" in order to save money (Women's Enews 2001b). In April 2001, Jason Turner, New York City's welfare commissioner, told a congressional subcommittee that "workplace safety and the Fair Labor Standards Act should not apply to welfare recipients who, in fact, should face tougher sanctions in order to make them work" (Women's Enews 2001a). And welfare reform legislation enacted in 1996 as the Personal Responsibility and Work Opportunities Reconciliation Act (PRWORA) requires that poor mothers work full-time, earning minimum-wage salaries with which they cannot support their children. Since these women are often denied medical, dental, and child-care benefits and are unable to provide their families with adequate food, heat, or clothing, through this legislation the state mandates child neglect and abuse. The crowds of good parents and their growing children watch and learn.

Reading and Rewriting the Body of the Text

The bodies of poor women and children, scarred and mutilated by state-mandated material deprivation and public exhibition, work as spectacles, as patrolling images socializing and controlling bodies within the body politic. . . .

Spectacular cover stories of the "Welfare Queen" play and replay in the national mind's eye, becoming a prescriptive lens through which the American public as a whole reads the individual dramas of the bodies of poor women and their place and value in the world. These dramas produce "normative" citizens as independent, stable, rational, ordered, and free. In this dichotomous, hierarchical frame the poor welfare mother is juxtaposed against a logic of "normative" subjectivity as the embodiment of dependency, disorder, disarray, and otherness. Her broken and scarred body becomes proof of her inner pathology and chaos, suggesting the need for further punishment and discipline.

In contemporary narratives welfare women are imagined to be dangerous because they refuse to sacrifice their desires and fail to participate in legally sanctioned heterosexual relationships; theirs is read, as a result, as a selfish, "unnatural," and immature sexuality. In this script, the bodies of poor women are viewed as being dangerously beyond the control of men and are as a result construed as the bearers of perverse desire. . . . They are understood and punished as a danger to a culture resting on a foundation of inviolate male authority and absolute privilege in both public and private spheres.

William Raspberry frames poor women as selfish and immature, when in "Ms. Smith Goes after Washington," he claims, "Unfortunately AFDC [Aid to Families with Dependent Children] is paid to an unaccountable, accidental and unprepared parent who has chosen her head of household status as a personal form of satisfaction, while lacking the simple life skills and maturity to achieve love and job fulfillment from any other source. I submit that all of our other social ills—crime, drugs, violence, failing schools are a direct result of the degradation of parenthood by emotionally immature recipients" (1995, A19). Raspberry goes on to assert that, like poor children, poor mothers must be made visible reminders to the rest of the culture of the "poor choices" they have made. He claims that rather than "coddling" her, we have a responsibility to "shame her" and to use her failure to teach other young women that it is "morally wrong for unmarried women to bear children," as we "cast single motherhood as a selfish and immature act" (1995, A19). . . .

Poor women and children's bodies, publicly scarred and mutilated by material deprivation, are read as expressions of an essential lack of discipline and order. In response to this perception, journalist Ronald Brownstein of the *Los Angeles Times* proposed that the "*Republican Contract with America*" will "*restore* America to its path, *enforcing* social *order* and common *standards* of behavior, and replacing *stagnation* and *decay* with *movement* and *forward* thinking *energy*" (1995, A1; emphasis added). In these rhetorical fields poverty is metonymically linked to a lack of progress that would allegedly otherwise order, stabilize, and restore the culture. What emerges from these diatribes is the positioning of patriarchal, racist, capitalist, hierarchical, and heterosexist "order" and movement against the alleged stagnation and decay of the body of the "Welfare Queen."

Race is clearly written on the body of the poor single mother. The welfare mother, imagined as young, never married, and black (contrary to statistical evidence) is positioned as dangerous and in need of punishment because she "naturally" emasculates her own men, refuses to service white men, and passes on—rather than appropriate codes of subservience and submission—a disruptive culture of resistance, survival, and "misplaced" pride to her children (Collins 2000).[5] In stark contrast, widowed women with social security and divorced women with child support and alimony are imagined as white, legal and propertied mothers whose value rests on their abilities to stay in their homes, care for their own children, and impart traditional cultural mores to their offspring, all for the betterment of the dominant culture. In this narrative welfare mothers have only an "outlaw" culture to impart. Here the welfare mother is read as both the product and the producer of a culture of disease and disorder. These narratives imagine poor women as a powerful contagion capable of infecting, perhaps even lying in wait to infect, their own children as raced, gendered, and classed agents of their "diseased" nature. In contemporary discourses of poverty, racial tropes position poor women's bodies as dangerous sites of "naturalized chaos" and as potentially valuable economic commodities who refuse their "proper" roles. . . .

These representations position welfare mothers' bodies as sites of destruction and as catalysts for a culture of depravity and disobedience; in the process they produce a reading of the writing on the body of the poor woman that calls for further punishment and discipline. In New York City, "Workfare" programs force *lazy* poor women to take a job—"any job"—including working for the city wearing orange surplus prison uniforms picking up garbage on the highway and in parks for about $1.10 per hour (Dreier 1999). "Bridefare" programs in Wisconsin give added benefits to *licentious* welfare women who marry a man—"any man"—and publish a celebration of their "reform" in local newspapers (Dresang 1996). "Tidyfare" programs across the nation allow state workers to enter and inspect the homes of poor *slovenly* women so that they can monetarily sanction families whose homes are not deemed to be appropriately tidied. "Learnfare" programs in many states publicly expose and fine *undisciplined* mothers who for any reason have children who do not (or cannot) attend school on a regular basis (Muir 1993). All of these welfare reform programs are designed to expose and publicly punish the *misfits* whose bodies are read as proof of their refusal or inability to capitulate to androcentric, capitalist, racist, and heterosexist values and mores.

Resisting the Text: On the Limits of Discursive Critique and the Power of Poor Women's Communal Resistance

Despite the rhetoric and policy that mark and mutilate our bodies, poor women survive. Hundreds of thousands of us are somehow good parents despite the systems that are designed to prohibit us from being so. We live on the unlivable and teach our children love, strength, and grace. We network, solve irresolvable dilemmas, and support each other and our families. If we somehow manage to find a decent pair of shoes, or save our food stamps to buy our children a birthday cake, we are accused of being cheats or living too high. If our children suffer, it is read as proof of our inferiority and bad mothering; if they succeed, we are suspect for being too pushy, for taking more than our share of free services, or for having too much free time to devote to them. Yet, as former welfare recipient Janet Diamond says in the introduction to *For Crying Out Loud*: "In spite of public censure, welfare mothers graduate from school, get decent jobs, watch their children achieve, make good lives for themselves. Welfare mothers continue to be my inspiration, not because they survive, but because they dare to dream. Because when you are a welfare recipient, laughter is an act of rebellion" (Dujon and Withorn 1996, 1).

Foucault's later work acknowledges this potential for rebellion inherent in the operation of power. . . . As Lois McNay points out, [Foucault shows us how] "repression produces its own resistance: 'there are no relations of power without resistance; the latter are all the more real and effective because they are formed right at the point where relations of power are exercised'" (1993, 39). . . .

Yet here we also recognize what McNay refers to as the "critical limitations" of Foucault and of post-structuralism in general. For although bodily inscriptions of poverty are clearly textual, they are also quite physical, immediate, and pressing, devastating the lives of poor women and children in the United States today. Discursive critique is at its most powerful only when it allows us to understand and challenges us to fight together to change the material conditions and bodily humiliations that scar poor women and children in order to keep us all in check.

Poor women rebel by organizing for physical and emotional respite and eventually for political power. My own resistance was born in the space between self-loathing and my love of and respect for poor women who were fighting together against oppression. In the throes of political activism (at first I was dragged blindly into such actions, ironically, in a protest that required, according to the organizer, just so many poor women's bodies) I became caught up in the contradiction between my body's meaning as a despised public sign and our shared sense of communal power, knowledge, authority, and beauty. Learning about labor movements, fighting for rent control, demanding fair treatment at the welfare office, sharing the costs, burdens, and joys of raising children, forming food cooperatives, working with other poor women to go to college, and organizing for political change became addictive and life-affirming acts of resistance. Through shared activism we became increasingly aware of our individual bodies as sites of contestation and of our collective body as a site of resistance and as a source of power. . . .

In struggling together we contest the marks of our bodily inscription, disrupt the use of our bodies as public sign, change the conditions of our lives, and survive. In the process we come to understand that the shaping of our bodies is not coterminous with our beings or abilities as a whole. Contestation and the deployment of new truths cannot erase the marks of our poverty, but the process does transform the ways in which we are able to interrogate and critique our bodies and the systems that have branded them with infamy. As a result these signs are rendered fragile, unstable, and ultimately malleable.

Notes

This essay is dedicated to poor women around the world who struggle together against oppression and injustice. With thanks to Margaret Gentry, Nancy Sorkin Rabinowitz, Sandra Dahlberg, and the reviewers and editors at *Signs*. And as always, for my mother and my daughter.

1. Throughout this essay I use the terms *welfare recipient* and *poor working women* interchangeably because as the recent Urban Institute study made clear, today these populations are, in fact, one and the same (Loprest 1999).
2. Unpublished survey, December 1998, Utica, New York.
3. Adolescent psychologist Maria Root claims that a beautiful or "fit" body becomes equated with "purity, discipline—basically with goodness" (DeClaire 1993, 36).
4. Unpublished survey, June 1998, Seattle, Washington.
5. In the two years directly preceding the passage of the PRWORA, as a part of sweeping welfare reform, in the United States the largest percentage of people on welfare were white (39 percent), and fewer than 10 percent were teen mothers (U.S. Department of Health and Human Services 1994).

References

Anderson, Dale. 1999. County to investigate some welfare recipients. *Buffalo News*, 18 August, B5.

Brownstein, Ronald. 1995. Latest welfare reform plan reflects liberals' priorities. *Los Angeles Times*, 24 January, A6.

Collins, Patricia Hill. 2000. *Black Feminist Thought: Knowledge, Consciousness, and the Politics of Empowerment*. New York: Routledge.

DeClaire, Joan. 1993. Body by Barbie. *View*, October, 36–43.

Dreier, Peter. 1999. Treat welfare recipients like workers. *Los Angeles Times*, 29 August, M6.

Dresang, Joel. 1996. Bridefare designer, reform beneficiary have role in governor's address. *Milwaukee Journal Sentinel*, 14 August, 9.

Dujon, Diane, and Ann Withorn. 1996. *For Crying Out Loud: Women's Poverty in the United States*. Boston: South End.

Edin, Kathryn, and Laura Lein. 1997. *Making Ends Meet: How Single Mothers Survive Welfare and Low-Wage Work*. New York: Russell Sage.

Foucault, Michel. (1977) 1984. Discipline and punish. In *The Foucault Reader*, edited by Paul Rabinow, 170–256. New York: Pantheon.

Loprest, Pamela. 1999. Families who left welfare: Who are they and how are they doing? Urban Institute, Washington, DC, August, B1.

McNay, Lois. 1993. *Foucault and Feminism: Power, Gender, and the Self*. Boston: Northeastern University Press.

Muir, Kate. 1993. Runaway fathers at welfare's final frontier. *New York Times*, 19 July, A2.

Raphael, Jody. 2000. Saving Bernice: Women, welfare and domestic violence. Presentation at Hamilton College, May 23, Clinton, New York.

Raspberry, William. 1995. Ms. Smith goes after Washington. *Washington Post*, 1 February, A19.

Robinson, Valerie. 1999. State's ad attacks the poor. *Plain Dealer*, 2 November, B8.

Simon, Stephanie. 1999. Unlikely support for drug tests on welfare applicants. *Los Angeles Times*, 18 December, A1.

Smith-Madsen, Sandy. 2003. From welfare to academe: Welfare reform as collegeeducated welfare mothers know it. In *Reclaiming Class: Women, Poverty and the Promise of Education in America*, edited by Vivyan Adair and Sandra Dahlberg, 160–86. Philadelphia: Temple University Press.

U.S. Department of Health and Human Services. 1994. An overview of entitlement programs. Washington, DC: U.S. Government Printing Office.

Women's Enews. 2001a. Civil rights bad for welfare moms. Mailing list, available on-line at http://www.womensenews.org, May 4.

———. 2001b. Oregon to women on welfare: Dumpster dive. Mailing list, available on-line at http://www.womensenews.org, May 5.

20

Backlash and Continuity

The Political Trajectory of Fetal Rights

RACHEL ROTH

As Rose Weitz's opening article pointed out, throughout history, the law has typically regarded women's bodies as men's property—a legal philosophy that has often fostered violence against women. "Backlash and Continuity: The Political Trajectory of Fetal Rights," by political scientist Rachel Roth, also looks at how cultural attitudes about women's bodies become inscribed in law and restrict women's lives. Roth provides an overview of the history and current status of reproductive rights law, and shows how earlier struggles over abortion have led to the increasing acceptance of the idea of "fetal rights." This idea, she argues, has served more to punish women for nontraditional behavior than to protect their children, while reinforcing the idea that women's bodies are and should be public property.

Roth's article makes it clear that U.S. law and culture consistently have placed the greatest emphasis on restricting reproductive rights among poor and minority women, whether through forced rape under slavery, involuntary birth control for women on welfare, or arrests of pregnant women who use "crack" cocaine but not those who use powerful sedatives.

Poor and minority women also continue to have much less access than do other women to high-quality contraceptives (e.g., pills versus condoms). At the same time, the financial, emotional, and practical dislocations caused by poverty make it more difficult for poor and minority women to use contraception consistently, resulting in higher rates of unwanted [illegible] Consequently, these women have higher rates of abortion than do [illegible] even though governmental restrictions such as mandated wa[illegible] before abortion, combined with the dramatic decline in the availab[illegible] abortion providers, has made it far more difficult for poor and minority women to obtain abortions.

. . . In 1973 the *Roe v. Wade* decision legalizing abortion created new conditions for women's autonomy, provided a legal framework for thinking about fetuses, and realigned abortion politics by satisfying many people working for abortion reform while galvanizing the fetal rights movement in opposition. . . .

The creation and promotion of fetal rights [that is, the idea that fetuses have rights separate from those of the pregnant woman] in situations besides abortion has led to a highly demanding set of expectations about how women ought to behave during pregnancy for the sake of their fetuses. Disseminated through popular media, advice books directed at women, and legal scholarship, these expectations politicize pregnancy itself. In other words, it is not just the decision whether to continue a pregnancy but the entire period of pregnancy that has come under political scrutiny.

The Abortion Connection

Roe v. Wade was a tremendous victory for women: The nation's highest court legalized abortion across the country, granting women the authority to decide whether to carry a pregnancy to term. In many parts of the United States women had access to hospital abortions before World War II. After the war hospital abortions fell sharply as the medical establishment narrowed the health indications for abortion and state laws continued to permit abortion only to save women's lives. Many women who were able to obtain abortions had to agree to a "package deal" of simultaneous sterilization (Solinger 1993). Other women lived in communities where skilled illegal abortionists ran thriving practices, operating under a tacit agreement with law enforcement: no death, no intervention. But their availability, too, dropped after the war (Solinger 1994). The Supreme Court's decision in 1973 thus gave women a new power over their reproductive lives, one that ended the need to resort to dangerous back-alley abortions and also the humiliation of trying to secure permission for an abortion from all-male hospital committees in those states that had liberalized their abortion laws (Kaplan 1995). . . .

Roe v. Wade established a three-part framework of "separate and distinct" competing interests and set up a particular formula for balancing those interests. During the first trimester of pregnancy, a woman's fundamental privacy right encompasses her decision to terminate a pregnancy without state interference. Women obtain at least 90 percent of abortions within the first three months. . . . During the second trimester, the state may regulate abortion in ways reasonably related to its compelling interest in protecting women's health. The Court found that a woman's privacy right is not absolute, and so after viability, during the final trimester, the state may regulate and even prohibit abortion to further its compelling interest in "the potentiality of human life," except where abortion is necessary to preserve a woman's life or health.

The Court also ruled that a fetus is not a person within the meaning of the Fourteenth Amendment. This ruling is consistent with the AngloAmerican legal tradition of treating a fetus as part of a pregnant woman, not as a separate entity with rights of its own. . . .

In response to *Roe v. Wade*, the anti-abortion movement has sought to establish rights for fetuses in a vast array of contexts. Its fundamental goal is to abolish abortion, something it has sought by resisting the reform efforts of the 1960s and by pursuing a "human life amendment" to the Constitution, the appointment of federal judges who disagree with *Roe*, and policies at the state and federal level that interfere with abortion. Unable to achieve this bedrock goal, the movement has successfully limited women's access to abortion services while also shaping the cultural and political terrain for other fights over fetal rights. Some organizations, such as the Chicago-based Americans United for Life, lobby for both parental consent laws and homicide laws that endow fetuses with independent rights. Although these groups tend to support anything that would enhance the legal status of fetuses, some are concerned that criminalizing behavior during pregnancy will backfire by encouraging women to have abortions. . . .

In 1992 the Supreme Court reconsidered its decision in *Roe v. Wade* and replaced the trimester framework with an "undue burden" standard in *Planned Parenthood v. Casey*. *Casey*'s undue burden standard recasts the state's interests, holding that the state has a profound interest in protecting fetal life throughout pregnancy, not just at the point of viability. The state can therefore enact obstacles to abortion as long as they are not so substantial as to be unduly burdensome. Pennsylvania's mandatory twenty-four-hour waiting period after a state-scripted counseling session designed to discourage abortion passed this test. Although it still requires a significant interpretive leap to read these restrictions on women's ability to terminate a pregnancy as permitting restrictions on their conduct during pregnancy, *Casey* creates a new point of departure for analyzing fetal rights claims, one that is arguably more favorable to those claims. . . .

The Historical Connection

. . . Fetal rights politics is continuous with a long history of reproductive politics in the United States. Reproductive control of women has taken many forms. On plantations, slave owners and overseers wielded tremendous power over female slaves and their families by raping women and deciding whether to sell off their children (Davis 1983; Roberts 1991). In the nineteenth century, all states passed laws making abortion a crime (Petchesky 1984). Around the time criminalization was consolidated, campaigns against "vice" successfully restricted women's access to birth control devices and information that might have reduced the need for abortion (Gordon 1976; McCann 1994). The eugenics movement succeeded in institutionalizing and sterilizing masses of "unfit" persons, ranging from developmentally disabled individuals to sexually promiscuous women (May 1995; McCann 1994). The legacy of sterilization abuse continued throughout the twentieth century, shifting primarily to African American, Native American, and Puerto Rican women (Davis 1983; Lopex 1993; May 1995). In Puerto Rico, women have been the subjects of contraceptive experimentation as well as of aggressive sterilization policies; more than one-third of all Puerto Rican women have been sterilized (Davis 1983; Lopez 1993). The stigma associated with out-of-wedlock births operated as an effective mandate for white women to relinquish their children in the years following World War II (Solinger 1992).

Ever since abortion was legalized in 1973, Congress and a majority of state legislatures have enacted barriers to access, including spousal consent, parental consent for minors, public funding cuts, and mandatory waiting periods. Courts have upheld many of these measures. The anti-abortion movement has become emboldened in the past decade, with groups such as Operation Rescue staging mass demonstrations outside health clinics to intimidate women seeking abortions. In the climate of accelerating violence, scores of clinics have been bombed, torched, or vandalized, and many people have been injured and even killed escorting women to clinics and working in them. Consequently, it is harder and harder for women in many parts of the country to find anyone willing to provide abortion services where they live. Poor women dependent on government assistance have much higher rates of sterilization than other women (Petchesky 1984, 180). The federal government subsidizes sterilization costs for Medicaid recipients, but not abortion, constraining poor women's reproductive choices (see Petchesky 1984 on the Hyde Amendment).

Women's rights advocates have been actively challenging the social relations of reproduction since at least the 1840s, when white, middleclass women first called for "voluntary motherhood" (Gordon 1982). The demand for voluntary motherhood was part of a larger movement for women's rights that valued motherhood but recognized that women would not be able to exercise their hard-won political rights if they were incessantly burdened by pregnancy and childrearing. The voluntary motherhood movement promoted women's right to decide when to become pregnant, giving women the right to refuse their husbands' sexual advances (Gordon 1982). Early twentieth-century feminists continued the demand for motherhood on women's terms but added a positive sexual dimension. Where their Victorian counterparts had advocated abstinence and refuge from predatory male lust, these activists, including Crystal Eastman, Emma Goldman, and the young Margaret Sanger, demanded birth control, claiming for women a lust of their own (Eastman 1978, 1920).

A contemporary illustration of reproductive politics is the way Norplant, the first major new contraceptive device to hit the U.S. market in more than twenty years, quickly played into class, race, and gender politics. Norplant is a 99-percent-effective hormonal contraceptive that lasts five years when surgically implanted under a woman's skin. Approved by the U.S. Food and Drug Administration in December 1990, Norplant immediately became a proposed means of legal and economic coercion. Within the first month of its availability, an editorial in the *Philadelphia Inquirer* called for implanting all welfare mothers with the device, and a judge in California made Norplant a condition of probation for a woman who pled guilty to child abuse. Legislatures quickly entertained measures to give AFDC [Aid to Families with Dependent Children, commonly known as *welfare*] recipients cash bonuses for using Norplant or to make it a condition of receiving benefits; some considered establishing mandatory Norplant as a condition of probation for women convicted of child abuse or drug possession (Mertus and Heller 1992, 362–67). These proposals raise serious constitutional concerns, including equal protection, because men are nowhere subjected to similar treatment and because African American women rely disproportionately on welfare for support. The health implications of coercing Norplant use are especially troubling for African American women, who are more likely to have high blood pressure, diabetes, and heart disease, all of which contraindicate Norplant (Mullings 1984; Mertus and Heller 1992, 360). Finally, in 1993, the Michigan legislature earmarked $500,000 to distribute Norplant in family-planning clinics. The program's champion, Senator Vern Ehlers, described it as "totally voluntary" but added that the program targets prostitutes, drug addicts, and teenage mothers. Ehlers explained that the Norplant program was "developed strictly on the standpoint of rights—every child has a right to be born normally" (*State Legislatures* 1993). Rather than facilitating women's right to control their fertility, Ehlers sees the Norplant funding as safeguarding fetal rights. [Ed: Because of lawsuits, health concerns, and other problems, Norplant was taken off the market in the United States in 2002; another contraceptive implant, Implanon, is now available.] . . .

Current struggles over fetal rights fit into this political history. Ultimately, it should be clear that the debate about fetal rights is not so much about fetal personhood as it is about women's personhood. Notice the dehumanizing language that fetal rights advocates commonly use to describe pregnant women: Women are called "maternal hosts" and even the "fetal environment" (Raines 1984; Blank 1993). Pregnant women's drug use is referred to as "gestational substance abuse," an expression that reduces women to incubators (Flannery 1992; Lowry 1992). These advocates also describe pregnant women's bodies as inanimate objects: The title of a scholarly article calls the "maternal abdominal wall" a "fortress" against fetal health care (Phelan 1991). In his role as "lawyer for the fetus," the public guardian in Chicago asked the court to order a pregnant woman to submit to a cesarean against her will. He argued in court that the judges had to decide whether the fetus is "a real life form being kept prisoner in a mother's womb" (quoted in Terry 1993, A22). This language makes two things clear: that pregnant women are not considered full-fledged human beings, but merely better or worse vessels for fetuses, and that the pregnant woman's body, once thought of as a nurturing sanctuary, is now often seen as a form of solitary confinement for the fetus.

Politicizing Pregnancy

The experience of pregnancy today, at least among middle- and higher-income women, is governed by doctors' appointments, expert advice books, and classes, as well as cultural norms about the ever-narrowing bounds of appropriate behavior that affect all pregnant women. Pregnant women are told what to eat, how to exercise, when to stay in bed, and whether to work or have sex. Lisa Ikemoto calls this "the code of perfect pregnancy" (1992).

Helena Michie and Naomi Cahn argue that middle-class women internalize the code by consuming advice books that teach them to police their own conduct, while the state polices poor women, disciplining them and sending a symbolic message to all others. They deftly reveal the way the best-selling "yuppie bible" *What to Expect When You're Expecting* constructs an autonomous fetus who monitors and ultimately effaces the pregnant reader, ironically producing a "homeless fetus, a baby without walls," even as it is deeply invested in domesticity (Michie and Cahn 1997, 31). . . .

Moving beyond exhortation to enforcement, a Boston-area health club owner canceled a woman's membership when she became pregnant. The member was a longtime bodybuilder and was consulting with her obstetrician about her training activities. The owner hinted at fears of liability should the bodybuilder injure herself, but she told a reporter that she didn't understand why a "mother" would want to burn calories or "overheat." Renee Solomon interprets these remarks as evidence of the owner's sense of entitlement to replace her client's motivations with her own sense of concern for the fetus (1991, 421). This sense of entitlement to make unilateral decisions for pregnant women politicizes disagreements over fetal health in a way that simply giving unsolicited advice does not. . . .

. . . [Similarly, legal scholar] John Robertson argues that women have both legal and moral duties to protect the fetus. Because his scholarship has been so influential, it is worth considering in some detail. Robertson situates his argument for controlling pregnant women and for punishing those who do not comply within the context of a sweeping defense of procreative freedom. He does this by distinguishing between the right to procreate, which he supports, and women's "right to bodily integrity *in the course of* procreating," which he does not (Robertson 1983, 437; emphasis in original).

In his most famous declaration, Robertson claims that "once she decides to forgo abortion and the state chooses to protect the fetus, the woman loses the liberty to act in ways that would adversely affect the fetus" (p. 437). Put somewhat differently, he says, "Although she is under no obligation to invite the fetus in or to allow it to remain, once she has done these things she assumes obligations to the fetus that limit her freedom over her body" (p. 438).

The loss of freedom that pregnant women experience under Robertson's scheme is almost total. He argues that women can be compelled to take medication or submit to surgery on the fetus as well as to be force-fed in the case of anorexia, to be civilly committed to an institution in the case of mental illness, or to be subjected to any other intervention that poses "reasonable" risks to their health and safety (pp. 444–47). Decisions about where to give birth (home or hospital), how to give birth (vaginally or by cesarean), and whether to submit to electronic fetal monitoring, episiotomy, or other procedures should be subordinated to expert opinion about the "child's well-being" (pp. 453–58). Robertson also asserts that the state may validly prohibit women's use of alcohol, tobacco, and drugs, as well as their employment in potentially harmful workplaces (pp. 442–43). . . .

According to Robertson, if women choose not to exercise their constitutionally protected right to have an abortion, then they become liable for less than perfect outcomes of their pregnancies. The meaningfulness of women's "choices"—in the case of a poor woman, for instance, whose state Medicaid program does not pay for abortions—or the timing of women's decisions to carry to term is ultimately irrelevant, because women are held accountable for their actions from the moment of conception. Robertson retreats from his claim that a woman's "obligations to the fetus arise only after she has already exercised her procreative rights by choosing to bring the child into the world," arguing later that a woman who has not yet made up her mind "should have a duty to avoid the harmful activities in case she decides not to abort. Similarly, she should be penalized for failing to use a fetal therapy before viability, so that the infant will be healthy if she decides to go to term. If she does not want the therapy, her choice will be to abort or to risk the penalty" (pp. 442, 447, n129).

Under this regime, women have no room for error or indecision. Robertson's attitude toward women is nothing short of callous and, if implemented as policy, would probably result in women feeling pressured to abort pregnancies they would rather bring to term, for fear of the consequences. Waxing philosophical, Robertson concludes that freedom "provides meaning only through the acceptance of constraint" (p. 464). For some reason, this applies only to women. . . .

. . . [In sum,] as fetuses attain independent legal status, women are finding themselves not only erased as important social beings but also disenfranchised as people entitled to fair, equal treatment. New fetal rights claims get layered on top of older moral claims and increasing cultural demands, all in a context in which pregnancy is highly medicalized, enhancing professional and state authority over women. . . .

Note

1. Susan A. Cohen, 2008. "Abortion and Women of Color: The Bigger Picture." *Guttmacher Policy Review*, vol. 11, no. 3(2008):1–12.

References

Blank, Robert. 1993. *Fetal Protection in the Workplace: Women's Rights, Business Interests, and the Unborn*. New York: Columbia University Press.

Davis, Angela. 1983. The legacy of slavery: Standards for a new womanhood; Rape, racism, and the myth of the black rapist; and Racism in the reproductive rights movement. In *Women, Race, and Class*. New York: Vintage Books.

Eastman, Crystal. 1978. Birth control in the feminist program (1918) and Now we can begin (1920). In *Crystal Eastman on Women and Revolution*, edited by Blanche Wiesen Cook. Oxford: Oxford University Press.

Flannery, Michael. 1992. Court-ordered prenatal intervention: A final means to end gestational substance abuse. *Journal of Family Law* 30:519–604.

Gordon, Linda. 1976. *Woman's Body, Woman's Right: A Social History of Birth Control in America*. New York: Penguin Books.

———. 1982. Why nineteenth-century feminists did not support "Birth control" and twentieth-century feminists do: Feminism, reproduction, and the family. In *Rethinking the Family: Some Feminist Questions*, edited by Barrie Thorne and Marilyn Yalom, 40–53. White Plains, NY: Longman.

Ikemoto, Lisa. 1992. The code of perfect pregnancy: At the intersection of motherhood, the practice of defaulting to science, and the interventionist mindset of law. *Ohio State Law Journal* 53:1205–1306.

Kaplan, Laura. 1995. *The Story of Jane: The Legendary Underground Feminist Abortion Service*. New York: Pantheon Books.

Lopez, Iris. 1993. Agency and constraint: Sterilization and reproductive freedom among Puerto Rican women in New York City. *Urban Anthropology* 22(3–4):299–323.

Lowry, Susan Steinhorn. 1992. The growing trend to criminalize gestational substance abuse. *Journal of Juvenile Law* 13:133–43.

May, Elaine Tyler. 1995. *Barren in the Promised Land: Childless Americans and the Pursuit of Happiness*. Cambridge, MA: Harvard University Press.

McCann, Carole. 1994. *Birth Control Politics in the United States, 1916–1945*. Ithaca, NY: Cornell University Press.

Mertus, Julie, and Simon Heller. 1992. Norplant meets the new eugenicists: The impermissibility of coerced contraception. *Saint Louis University Public Law Review* 11:359–83.

Michie, Helena, and Naomi Cahn. 1997. *Confinements: Fertility and Infertility in Contemporary Culture*. New Brunswick, N.J.: Rutgers University Press.

Mullings, Leith. 1984. Minority Women, Work, and Health. In *Double Exposure Women's Health Hazards on the Job and at Home*, edited by Wendy Chavkin, chap. 6. New York: Monthly Review Press.

Petchesky, Rosalind. 1984. *Abortion and Women's Choice: The State, Sexuality, and Reproductive Freedom*. Boston: Northeastern University Press.

Phelan, Jeffrey. 1991. The maternal abdominal wall: A fortress against fetal health care?" *Southern California Law Review* 65:461–90.

Raines, Elvoy. 1984. Editorial comment to Ronna Jurow and Richard H. Paul, Cesarean delivery for fetal distress without maternal consent. *Obstetrics & Gynecology* 63(4) (April):598–99.

Roberts, Dorothy. 1991. "Punishing drug addicts who have babies: Women of color, equality, and the right of privacy," *Harvard Law Review* 104:1419–1482.

Robertson, John. 1983. Procreative liberty and the control of conception, pregnancy, and childbirth. *Virginia Law Review* 69:405–64.

Solinger, Rickie. 1992. *Wake Up Little Susie: Single Pregnancy and Race before "Roe v. Wade."* New York: Routledge.

———. 1993. "A complete disaster": Abortion and the politics of hospital abortion committees, 1950–1970. *Feminist Studies* 19(2):241–68.

———. 1994. *The Abortionist: A Woman against the Law*. New York: The Free Press.

Solomon, Renee. 1991. Future fear: Prenatal duties imposed by private parties. *American Journal of Law and Medicine* 17(4):411–34.

State Legislatures. 1993. Norplant approval in Michigan unmarred by controversy 19(5):7.

Terry, Don. 1993. Illinois is seeking to force woman to have cesarean. *New York Times*, 15 December, A22.

21

Hijab and American Muslim Women

Creating the Space for Autonomous Selves

Rhys H. Williams and Gira Vashi

According to the Pew Research Center, about 700,000 Muslim women live in the United States, over a third of whom report that they always wear a headcover or hijab *in public. The* hijab *is a headscarf that covers a woman's head, hair, neck, and ears, but leaves the face uncovered. Since 9/11 it has become a visible and controversial symbol of Muslim identity. Feminist scholars have debated whether the* hijab *should be, on the one hand, vilified as a symbol of women's oppression or, on the other hand, defended as a form of resistance against Western hegemony and the commodification of women's bodies. Disagreements about veiling revolve in part around the question of whether women who veil are exercising agency or exhibiting false consciousness (that is, they have been misled about their own interests and subordination). Understanding these debates requires examining the meanings of the* hijab *for Muslim women themselves. In "*Hijab *and American Muslim Women: Creating the Space for Autonomous Selves," Rhys H. Williams and Gira Vashi do just this. Using interview data and ethnographic observations, they explore the meanings of the* hijab *for college-age, second-generation Muslim Americans.*

According to Williams and Vashi, there are two important cultural contexts for understanding the meanings of the hijab*. First, American equal rights discourses emphasize liberty and equal treatment, including gender equality. Second, embedded in American cultural discourses are critiques of cultural decadence, including American materialism, individualism, and sexual openness.*

Rhys H. Williams and Gira Vashi, "*Hijab* and American Muslim Women: Creating the Space for Autonomous Selves," *Sociology of Religion*, 2007, 68(3), 269–287, by permission of Oxford University Press.

To make sense of these two distinct sets of cultural messages, young Muslim Americans, Williams and Vashi maintain, engage in "cultural work" that enables them to negotiate competing values.

For example, in contrast to arguments that construct the hijab *as a symbol of inequality and oppression, young Muslim Americans point out that different does not necessarily mean unequal, that Islam in some ways elevates women's position, and that Islam also mandates rules of modesty for men. Williams and Vashi also illustrate how, for Muslim women, the* hijab *has multiple meanings, which enables them to foster a Muslim American identity. At times, the* hijab *is about interpersonal issues such as public reputation, social ostracism, and group inclusion. At other times, it symbolizes modesty and piety, grants moral authority among peers, and enables young women to negotiate generational differences with their parents. Finally, as Williams and Vashi acknowledge, the* hijab *serves as a potential fashion statement.*

As increasing numbers of Muslims live in the United States, and as Islam becomes increasingly visible as a public religious presence in what is still a Christian-majority country, many Islamic religious practices are being adopted, adapted to, and abandoned by American Muslims. This is particularly true for first- and second-generation Muslims from traditionally Islamic societies such as Pakistan or Egypt. Some of these adaptations make Muslims more like the American majority in speech, dress, and cultural folkways. Other adaptations call attention to differences between Muslims and other Americans, particularly native-born Christians.

A visible and often controversial difference is the *hijab*, the headscarf that covers a woman's head, hair, neck, and ears—leaving only the face showing.[1] Many, but not all, Muslims consider wearing *hijab* theologically mandated. Many second-generation young women in the United States choose to wear *hijab*—often when they are in college and sometimes over their parents' objections. Drawing on the extant sociological literature, interviews, and ethnographic observations, we address the practice of wearing *hijab* by young Muslim American women.[2] We consider the context in which it is worn, the meanings it has for young women, and the consequences they see it having for their lives. . . .

Women and Traditional Religion

One way to frame the question about *hijab* and college-age women in the United States is to place it within the recent literature about women and traditional forms of religious practice. Scholars such as Davidman (1991) and Griffith (1998) have investigated why some upwardly mobile, achievement-oriented, American-born women voluntarily join religions that protect a traditional gender order. The feminist critique of religious patriarchy that emerged in the 1960s and early 1970s has become well known in American culture, and as a general rule Americans prize individual autonomy and release from external obligations or coercion. Given that college-educated, often middle-class women are generally immersed in modernist social and cultural worlds, the attraction to traditionalist religion seems to need explaining. Neither a straight interest-based answer (Marxian or rational-choice), nor a cultural assimilationist argument provides a coherent answer.

One persuasive answer regarding women and traditional religion has come from the study of white and black evangelical Protestant women (e.g., Griffith 1998; Lawless 1983). These scholars argue, with some variation, that women find themselves in a man's world in most of our societal institutions. This is particularly true for working-class women who have more limited professional or mobility opportunities, but it applies to all women. One institution in this man's world where women can exercise some control and autonomy and can gain some recognition for their efforts is religion. Religious organizations become relatively free spaces for women. Men may control the top leadership positions, and there may be restrictions on women's participation. Nonetheless, women actually run many religious institutions in practice, and they thereby become spheres of female empowerment and solidarity (cf. Warner 1993, 1045).

Our research with young Muslim women who are active in their religion, both those who wear *hijab* and some who do not, suggests that these women would find interest-based answers to be missing a crucial dimension. Also, they probably would not endorse in its entirety the empowerment answer. Indeed, they would—and sometimes did—object to even framing the question in terms of "modern" women and "traditional" religion. These women are the daughters of immigrants and practice a minority religion in a country that does not understand it. They live in a city (and most attend college) where social, religious, and ethnic diversity is widespread and obvious. And they are at a stage of life where self and group identities are often in the foreground of consciousness and social life (see Peek 2005). We argue that donning *hijab* is a practice that allows young women to create some cultural space for themselves—it is a part of a larger identity project by second-generation Muslim young people to negotiate their dual identities as Muslims and Americans and gives them the opportunity to be part of both worlds.

Methods and Data

. . . We gathered data through several methods. First we draw on data gathered under the auspices of the Youth and Religion Project (YRP), co-directed by R. Stephen Warner and Rhys H. Williams. The YRP used individual and focus group interviews, site visits at religious organizations and institutions, and visits with families from a sample that included white, black, and Latino Christians, Muslims, and Hindus. . . . These data were collected primarily from 1998–2001, although some follow-up visits and conversations occurred in late 2001 and early 2002.

The second data source is an interview-based project spun off from the YRP. The second author interviewed forty Muslim women ages 18 to 25, three-fourths of whom attended college. These interviews, conducted in 2001–2002, focused specifically on the meanings of and decision to wear or not wear *hijab*. Half of these women were *hijabis* (those who wear *hijab*), and many were recruited through MSA [Muslim Student Association] organizations (at more than one university in our metropolitan area).

Many of the women we encountered are from Indian or Pakistani families—or in the shorthand we often heard, they are ethnically "Indo-Pak." Others were ethnically Arab. Occasionally, we encountered Euro-American converts to Islam, but none of our individual interviewees was African American (one member of the focus group was black) or Asian. Some came from middle-class homes, often with one or more parents who are professionals and had been in this country for some time. Others came from lower-middle-class households, and had arrived in the United States more recently. Most of the young women we met and talked to were from the city of our research site [a midwestern metropolitan area] and lived in ethnically dense neighborhoods near other Muslims. . . .

The Cultural Contexts

Two cultural contexts are significant for understanding young Muslim Americans and *hijab*: American emphasis on "equal rights," and contemporary critiques of the moral status of American culture. We unpack each in turn.

Equality is a core American value, frequently expressed by the term *equal rights*. The dominant American cultural interpretation of equal rights has two parts. First is that rights involve liberty from the control of external, especially institutional, authorities, and that these rights are the inalienable property of individuals. One is an individual, and is free, to the extent that one can make autonomous, individual decisions. Social obligations are legitimate only to the extent that they represent a contract between equal, consenting individuals (see Bellah, Madsen, Sullivan, Swidler, and Tipton 1985; Bromley and Busching 1988; R. Williams 1995).

The second dimension of equal rights is the notion of treating all people the same. According to this interpretation of equal rights, responding to gender inequality means dismantling barriers to women in public life, organizational memberships, economic opportunity, and the like, especially through legal challenges. Many such challenges have been successful. Accompanying these changes in women's legal and institutional statuses has been a degree of cultural androgyny, such as women wearing pants and playing sports, as well as the relaxation (though not elimination) of sexual double standards. Given these two interpretative themes of what constitutes equal rights—individualism and equal treatment—many Americans view any outward manifestations of difference as inequality.

The notion that difference is an indicator of inequality is most publicly institutionalized in the 1954 *Brown v. Board of Education* Supreme Court decision, which held that separate is inherently unequal. That framework shaped the public's understanding of the civil rights movement and the second wave of the women's movement. Thus, "gender neutrality" has emerged as the cultural frame to solve the problem of gender inequality; it has achieved legitimacy as the culturally appropriate way to relate to individuals—both socially and politically (see G. Williams and R. Williams 1995). Equal rights as gender neutrality rejects any institutionally authorized sanctioning of behavior that separates the sexes or that applies to men and women differently.

Given this assumption, it is not difficult to see that *hijab*, in and of itself, can be considered a manifestation of inequality—women wear it, but men do not. In addition, the American media are full of stories about women's oppression in Islam, such as the prohibition on women's driving in Saudi Arabia and the Taliban's vicious treatment of women in Afghanistan. Operating from this perspective, many Americans do not understand why second-generation Muslim American women wear *hijab*. It seems to many Americans to be an open admission of second-class status (this is not only a U.S. problem, see Shakeri's 1998 analysis of Canada).

The second context in which second-generation Muslim women operate is the widespread debate and critique of American culture now current in media and politics. This includes critiques of American culture's materialism, individualism, and sexual openness. The critique is not limited to Muslims, but is common among both Muslim religious leaders and laity. During our fieldwork and interviews, we heard many criticisms of American society and culture, from its reliance on credit cards and personal debt, to its elevation of work and career achievement above family. Respondents often combined the defense of Islam's views on gender with a discussion of the problems of modernity, the threat of carnality to moral purity, and a rehearsal of the social problems in the United States that are allegedly caused by moral breakdown. In this frame, the idea of equal rights as promoting individualism is seen as one source of society's problems.

However, when the issue is gender and *hijab*, the heart of the Islamic critique of contemporary American society seems to be a basic distrust of human nature and its ability to resist sexual impulses. For example, we attended a summer camp run for youth at a local *masjid* [mosque]. According to one of the male speakers, himself in his mid-20s, making a presentation at the camp to high school–age males, "whenever a man and a woman are alone in a room together, there is always a third figure present, *shatan* [Satan]." Field notes from the same camp session on relations between men and women, but from a different speaker, reveal:

> You know what this means: You see some girl wearing little more than a handkerchief for a dress, and the guy in us (we're all guys) says, "wow!" That's natural. We're human. But after that one look, we look away, because Allah has something better for us, paradise, not hell.

Fear of untrammeled sexuality appeared in a number of different settings. Many of these concerns focused on the threat to women from men's inability to control their sexual desires (cf. Read and Bartkowski 2000). However, in a number of talks we heard, the attention centered on the threat women pose to the moral purity of men. In either formulation, American society's sexualized culture appears as a significant problem for Muslims and a threat to society's well-being.

Thus, college-aged American Muslims have access to two distinct streams of cultural messages—equal rights vs. cultural decadence—that in many ways paint opposite portraits of what are the normatively appropriate relationships between men and women. As Ajrouch (2004) documents, this produces a contested space for ethnic, religious, and gender identity development. Ajrouch's respondents felt particularly caught between what they called the "boater" culture of their immigrant parents, and "white" culture of the United States. . . .

Cultural Work and the Religious Response

American Muslims, especially young people born in the United States, are aware of the conventional American assumptions about women's inequality in Islam (e.g., Hasan 2000). Further, college-age young people are in a period in the life course where issues of dating, romance, love, and sex are salient for people of all cultural and religious backgrounds. The distance between the practices and values of first-generation immigrants (our respondents' parents' generation) regarding sex and marriage and the so-called mainstream American culture of sex and romantic love is too wide to be ignored.

As a result, young Muslims in America are constantly engaged in the cultural work of trying to figure out appropriate gender practices for their situation. In our research, we heard formal presentations on Islamic dating and marriage practices and informal discussions on appropriate ways to behave toward men and women. We attended workshops on Muslim parenting and read literature on what is permissible and forbidden for men and women to do. One major theme of these various settings and media was a denial that women's inequality was intrinsic to Islam. In almost every discussion of Islam, gender, or family that we heard in the course of this research, Muslim speakers (both male and female) went out of their way to claim "in Islam, women have equal rights," or "men and women are different, but that does not mean unequal." Some of these claims may have been for the authors' benefit—non-Muslims openly engaged in research. But we take as significant how often our respondents went out of their way—often completely unprompted—to make this point.

Several of our respondents clarified to us that equality as sameness was not how Islam views gender, but rather, that Islam emphasizes "equity." Equity was then interpreted in terms of complementarity of needs, functions, and contributions (cf. Bartkowski and Read 2003). This formulation includes a degree of essentialism that is often connected to biology, sexual drives, and the basic distrust of human nature and its ability to resist sexual impulses that we noted earlier.

Other respondents provided us with rationales for their understanding of women's equity in that they claimed women actually had an advantaged position, in some respects, as compared to men. For example, one respondent noted to us that in Islam, women are allowed to keep their own money, whereas the money men earn is the family's money and must support the household. In addition, a male elder from a *masjid* explained that, unlike in the West, women in Islam had never been considered "chattel" property (his term) and thus their issues were not the same as Western women's. Whether that claim is true is less relevant to our case than the way it demonstrates that Muslims in America are acutely aware of the clash between their practices and many Americans' notions of equal rights. We also note that these are not Victorian separate spheres arguments, because nothing in them necessarily mandates that women should remain only in the private domain of home and family. These claims were often articulated to us by women who are themselves creating very public, career-oriented lives.

Another example of the cultural work being done by American Muslims comes from a long evening's discussion of Islamic marriage practices, presented as one class in a series of talks geared for young people and held at a *masjid* (also in attendance were a significant number of people who looked more like parents than singles). The lecturer, an out-of-town sheikh who was an invited speaker, discussed courtship and marriage practices using the language of "rights" and "choice," repeatedly emphasizing that women as well as men are allowed to choose their partners. He questioned the wisdom of arranged marriages, claiming that without a chosen relationship, built on love, respect, and observance of Islam, a marriage could not be happy (note that "happiness" as a criterion for a good marriage was important). Arranged marriages, he claimed, were part of Arab and Pakistani culture, not Islamically prescribed. We found it significant the extent to which the sheikh put Islamic practices in the United States within the language of choice and rights. Following is a passage, quoted from the first author's field notes, where the sheikh was discussing how men and women could begin to evaluate potential marriage partners:

> A man can look at his prospective wife. This is unavoidable in the U.S. Since one will be "living with the choice for the rest of life" it is important that one look at one's spouse first. And, this should/can be done without her parents' permission. One can look at a young woman on the streets or in public. Indeed, one should look before one gets serious—it is important to protect the other's feelings, so that one does not reject them in a face-to-face meeting (say at the family house, etc.; that kind of rejection can be very painful to the young woman and her family).

Most of the lecture was from a male perspective—the sheikh often stumbling a bit to keep women's concerns in mind—but the framing was choice, rights, and equality.

Finally, at several points Muslims emphasized to us, and we observed, that there are definite rules of modesty for men as well—concern about moral purity and sexual control are not directed solely at women. In some discussions at the MSA at a local university we heard claims by young women that men, as well as women, should wear *jilbab* (a full length, long-sleeved robe)—thus rejecting the Western custom of pants. This was, in effect, a protest against a modesty double standard, as well as against dominant American norms of attire. Similar claims are evident in Hasan's (2000) book and among Ajrouch's (2004) respondents.

Young men themselves often emphasize the importance of their own modesty. At one work-service day attended by the first author, groups of young Muslims (males and females working in separate groups) were painting, collecting litter, and planting grass and flowers in an impoverished neighborhood. Quoting from field notes from that day:

> Near the end [of the post-prayer lecture] was an admonition to the women working to keep their *hijabs* buttoned completely and to the men to have their shirts tucked in as they worked. He [the Imam] said, "men, we don't need to see your backs!" I did notice that while many of the . . . [male] volunteers had on t-shirts, they were generally t-shirts whose sleeves hung all the way to the elbow. None had on shorts or sleeveless tee/tank tops.

Male modesty in appearance was a point made a number of times in the functions we attended. Indeed, several observations in the first author's field notes from various site visits note that the author was dressed slightly "immodestly"—khakis and short sleeve, open-collared shirts—as compared to the Muslim men in the draping *shalwar kameez* clothing of South Asia or others in Western dress, but with their long-sleeve shirts buttoned all the way to the wrists and the neck.

Religion and Culture

All of these examples point to ways in which Muslim Americans deal with the tension between dominant American constructions of equal rights, gender, and the status of women. The second generation is clearly working to find a "negotiated order" (Maines and Charlton 1985) in gender matters. They often have concerns about American culture, but they cannot accept the traditional restrictions that many associate with Arab or Pakistani culture. They need to figure out how to be co-workers with professionals of the opposite sex and to find marriage partners without the arranged customs their parents may have used.

We found one particular discursive claim used by many American Muslims, both male and female, to deal with the cultural and potential logical tensions they face. Warner, Martel, and Dugan (2001) call this Islam's "Teflon construction." That is, things that are objectionable, or that are seen as restraining, unfair, or unwise, are deemed to be aspects of "culture" and can be jettisoned without damaging the purity of Islamic truth. Bad things slide off the "true Islam" as if it were coated with Teflon. Further, many respondents said that Islam should be purged of cultural pollutions; for example, some interviewees told us that Islam in America is "liberated" (one used that term) from the problems of Middle Eastern and other traditional cultures. Thus, the necessary reality of Islam in America—that it must adapt to a much different cultural environment from which it emerged—is turned into a virtue. . . .

Hijab and American Muslim Women

. . . Many of the women we talked to made a conscious decision to wear *hijab*; for some of our respondents this decision was not made until they were in college (see similar evidence in Schmidt 2004, 101, 105–10). The decision was presented to us as having a number of dimensions, although it invariably involved a sense of religious obligation. A keyword in many of the explanations was "modesty." Revealing too much of the body endangers the moral status of both men and women. *Hijab* helps protect women from men and men from women. These discussions of modesty often occurred in all-male settings, or when men spoke to gatherings of men and women at a meeting or at *Jummah* (midday Friday) prayer.

Interestingly, in many of the notes gathered by the second author and other female research assistants, the discussions of *hijab* among young women themselves were often less about modesty and moral purity than about other interpersonal issues. Perhaps the modesty angle is so obvious to young women it need not be mentioned in all-female discussions, but our field notes and experiences did not report the types of fire and brimstone speeches and warnings of moral danger among young women that we witnessed regularly among young men. Rather, many discussions among young women were more about visibility, social ostracism, and public reputation. One young woman told the second author, "If I don't wear the *hijab* the Muslim girls [at the MSA] will not acknowledge me." Another said, "I don't like [her college's] MSA because all the girls want you to wear the *hijab* or else they are rude to you," indicating the peer pressure and social expectations involved. Other dimensions of identity also intersect with religion for these second-generation youth in their cultural identity work. The first author's field notes from various MSA functions, such as potluck meals (not prayer services), indicate that a significant minority of the young women were uncovered—often seven or eight among the thirty-odd women there. When asked about this, one Arab informant replied that the ones without the *hijab* were definitely "Indo-Pak," as "no Arab girl would be uncovered."

Several women mentioned the benefit of gaining more respect from men after starting to cover. One meaning of respect in this case may be discouraging unwelcome flirting or sexual attention. It is not hard to imagine that women who cover are much less likely to be hit on by non-Muslim, or even Muslim, men. Such overt signs of piety help remove ambiguity from new social settings. Others may well react to a covered woman differently, and co-religionists who may be present can react to such visible piety to help divert people from temptation. Women in *hijab* instantly signal who they are and what group they identify with, making clear their religious and community connections. Schmidt (2004) reasons that young women who wear *hijab* are more likely to be granted religious and moral authority among peers, particularly among groups such as an MSA, and thus taken more seriously. Similarly, Ajrouch's (2004) respondents held higher behavioral expectations for covered women because of their easily visible claims to piety. We often heard women say they monitored their own behavior when wearing *hijab* because "you represent Islam" to others.

Emphasizing differences from non-Muslims is one key to understanding the identity functions of *hijab*. However, the young women we encountered were not all facing the same situations in college or vis à vis their families. Some came from families where their mothers did not cover; others came from families who worried about their daughters being alone among nonbelievers and exposed to big-city temptations. There are multidirectional pressures, and simultaneous negotiations involved, but despite varying logics, wearing *hijab* is a viable way of dealing with many of them. As with any social practice or embodied symbol, different people had different rationales for its use, and any given person often had more than one reason.

For many, wearing *hijab* and being involved in Islamically oriented organizations provide a way to escape parental authority and supervision, at least temporarily. These are very public young women, who drive around the city to various events, organize meetings of MSA and other religiously related groups, and plan for graduate school and careers. One local MSA itself recognizes this and offers workshops on things such as self-defense (showing the expectation that women would be without male escorts in many settings) and applying to medical school (one flyer noted explicitly "sisters are encouraged to attend").

A couple of the women provided an account of *hijab* that emphasized the way in which it provides some insulation from the restrictions that might otherwise accompany their status as unmarried women. Their families often had traditional gender ideas and regarded their young women protectively. And yet, the young women want to take advantage of what America can offer them, and still consider themselves good Muslims. Wearing *hijab*, an outward, public display of piety and religious identity, can finesse the constraints that conservative gender roles might impose upon them. One young woman who did not cover told the second author, "If I wore the *hijab* I would be able to do so much more." *Hijab* is so symbolically loaded and so legitimate within the Islamic community—as is involvement in Islamic organizations and the women's attention to their own religious education—that the women are insulated (at least to some degree) from reactionary backlash from Muslim men or other women (such as their mothers) protecting a traditional gender order. In another example, one interviewee suggested that other women on her campus often wore *hijab* just to be able to "date" without repercussions (although we note that she did not mean "date" the way most native-born middle-class Americans would define the term). Similarly, while many of our respondents could not imagine themselves marrying someone about whom their parents disapproved, they also did not anticipate an arranged marriage of the type so many of their parents had. *Hijab* carves out a cultural space for young Muslim women to live lives that their mothers could barely have imagined (see a similar theme in Cainkar 1996 and Read and Bartkowski 2000) and still to be publicly Muslim.

Alternatively, other young women are trying to achieve some distance from their assimilating, Westernized parents, or are from areas in which there are very few Muslims at all. They come from situations in which they and their families were reasonably well-integrated into non-Muslim communities. Often the women in their family of origin did not cover, except when in the mosque. In establishing their own identities, these women are often resisting assimilationist pressures from their families. Their arrival at college was their first experience with all-Muslim circles of friends. They began to wear *hijab* as an expression of a Muslim identity-in-formation (on their way to what Peek [2005] would call a "declared identity"),[3] as well as trying to fit in with a new crowd of friends. These women are creating identities that are distinct from their more Americanized families and that offer their own forms of autonomy. For example, one woman explained that going to college, meeting more Muslims, and continuing to learn more about her religion persuaded her to begin to cover: "It wasn't really taught to me. My mom doesn't wear it, my grandma doesn't wear it. No one wears it. But I found out—I researched, I talked to people—just one day it hit me and I decided to wear it."

Another young woman, whose friendship circles were all Muslim, related that she began to wear *hijab* in college, even over her parents' objections. She grew up in a mid-sized community in a state without a significant Muslim population, and her physician parents felt *hijab* to be unnecessary. Thus, *hijab* helps negotiate the generational difference with parents—establishing a distinct identity—as well as the difference with non-Muslim society. Many young American Muslims have experiences and knowledge that differ widely from that of their parents, whose social and cultural lessons are not very relevant to them. Many young people report that their parents—while culturally traditionalist—are lax or secularized in their religious practice. Consider this excerpt from a young woman:

> My parents, my family has always been Muslim by culture which I mean . . . is not always very valid because I don't believe that . . . that God considers you a Muslim or a Christian or a Jew based on your blood or . . . something that you inherit. I believe . . . you have to make a conscious decision. And so, at first, I think my parents were Muslim by culture . . . [I]t wasn't until

> much later in life—my mother didn't begin covering until probably in her early 30s . . . I started [at] 16, 17 years old. And this is something—this is a general thing in any Muslim family. So I think there's been like a, you know, a rise in awareness, Islamic awareness, in my own generation compared to my parents' generation.

Note her emphasis on individual choice and conscious decision as the essence of authentic religious commitment. Also, how she separates what is "religious"—and thus a true aspect of Islam—from what is "cultural" and to be examined, evaluated, and perhaps discarded. By her account, her mother began covering about the same time she did—but she presents this as a trend that is going from the second generation to their parents' generation, rather than vice versa. This young woman is becoming an American in her approach to chosen, voluntaristic religiosity, and still preserving a distinctly Muslim identity, visibly proclaimed with *hijab.*

In effect, these young women are using *hijab* as a cultural resource to give some substantive meaning to their contentions that difference does not necessarily mean inequality. In the process, they are creating practical dimensions of an American Islam. As Read and Bartkowski (2000) also show, these young women are active agents and are able, to some degree, to create their own lives. *Hijab* helps them do so, while also keeping them anchored in a traditional identity and avoiding potential anomie.

Fashion as an Autonomous Dynamic

We have presented the decision to wear *hijab* as one of identity development and the re-orientation of college-aged women from their families to their peer groups. However, we want to note that wearing *hijab* has a fashion dynamic that cannot be fully accounted for by religious motivations or social, ethnic, or class backgrounds. Lieberson (2000) charts what he calls the independent cycle of fashion as a social phenomenon in its own right. We call upon that now because, in our view, it is also indisputable that along with its religious and social meanings, *hijab* is a fashion statement. Schmidt (2004, 105–10) refers to the *jilbab* and *hijab* as an "informal dress code" among the Muslims she met. In our experience, girls and young women talk about *hijab* with each other as if they were talking about their clothes from the mall. Further, the ways in which they wear *hijab*, for example, the different ways in which it is wrapped about the head and draped down over the shoulders, is subject to fashion, innovation, and trend. Young women experiment with different styles, teaching them to and learning them from their sisters and peers.

Further, as more and more young women wear *hijab*, others are now starting to wear the *jilbab*, the full-length robe. We have observed some women taking it a step further and wearing the *nikab* that covers their face. Part of this seems to be a dynamic where demonstrating one's piety may require ever-increasing steps in order to distinguish oneself from the many others who are beginning to adopt the symbol. Paradoxically, as is the case with the display of many symbols, this increasing demonstration of piety is simultaneously a dimension of fitting in with religiously identified peer groups even as it distinguishes identity and status. Thus, while this increasing covering is on one level about religion, it is also the case that religion is just the substantive content with which statements of personal identity and social distinction are being made. We have not pursued these last observations systematically, but they do make sense of some of the internal personal and social dynamics we have observed within Islamic schools, *masjids*, and student organizations. . . .

Notes

1. There is no uniformly accepted set of terms for the clothing/covering we discuss here. Mernissi (1987) notes that the Qur'anic text in which *hijab* is used refers to a curtain used to separate the Prophet and his wife from some wedding guests in Medina, and thus the term refers to a boundary that segregates and protects. She is critical of the interpretations of the term *hijab* that have made it a veil worn by women alone. Roald (2001, 260) agrees that *hijab* is not a technically accurate rendering of "veil" from Qur'anic Arabic, but is critical of Mernissi's (1987; 2003) and Ahmad's (1992) readings of the pertinent Qur'an and *hadith* passages for being selectively feminist. Roald also notes that *jilbab*, another word in the Qur'an, is a vague term that connotes a one-piece garment, which often includes the face covering, but not always. Roald (2001, 262–63) provides a variety of regional variations in the terms used to describe Muslim women's clothing. We will follow the conventions of current American scholarship—and the informants from our research—in using *hijab* to refer to the scarf that covers head, hair, neck, and ears, but leaves the face uncovered, *jilbab* to mean the one-piece full-length robe-like dress that does not necessarily cover the head, and *nikab* to refer to the face covering. When the English word "veil" is used in general conversation or media, the reference could be to various clothing items and leaves unclear whether the face is covered. However, when the young women we interviewed referred to "covering," they almost invariably meant wearing the *hijab* headscarf, usually without the *nikab*.
2. In this article we use the terms "American Muslims" and "Muslim Americans" interchangeably. However, we note a difference in implications. The connotation of the former term is that "Muslim" is the main identity, and "American" is the qualifier adjective. We heard this term often from our respondents and found it in the "how to" literature on Islamic parenting and families (e.g., Hasan 2000); it indicates that those involved are working to create an American version of Islam. However, doing research within the United States involves studying people who are almost all "Americans," and thus the qualifying adjective (the hyphenated identity) is "Muslim," as it might be Italian-, Irish-, or Jewish-Americans.
3. In her study of the events of 9/11, Peek (2005) distinguishes between "chosen" and "declared" identities, the latter being an intensification of self-identity following a crisis. Our impression was that we saw fewer *hijabis* immediately post-9/11, but we do not believe this changes the fundamental dynamic we report here.

It seems to us that, while not as traumatic as a public crisis such as 9/11, many young people's encounter with diversity and alternative social identities at college or in a metropolis, followed by finding a comfortable peer group, can result in something that approximates the sense of an emphatic declared identity.

References

Ahmad, Leila. 1992. *Women and Gender in Islam.* New Haven: Yale University Press.

Ajrouch, Kristine J. 2004. Gender, race, and symbolic boundaries: Contested spaces of identity among Arab American adolescents. *Sociological Perspectives* 47:371–91.

Bartkowski, John P., and Jen'nan Ghazal Read. 2003. Veiled submission: Gender, power, and identity among Evangelical and Muslim women in the U.S. *Qualitative Sociology* 26:71–92.

Bellah, Robert N., Richard Madsen, William Sullivan, Ann Swidler, and Steven Tipton. 1985. *Habits of the Heart.* Berkeley: University of California Press.

Bromley, David G., and Bruce C. Busching. 1988. Understanding the structure of contractual and covenantal social relations: Implications for the sociology of religion. *Sociological Analysis* 49(S):15–32.

Cainkar, Louise. 1996. Immigrant Palestinian women evaluate their lives. In *Family and Gender among American Muslims*, edited by B. Aswad and B. Bilge. Philadelphia: Temple University Press.

Davidman, Lynn. 1991. *Tradition in a Rootless World.* Berkeley: University of California Press.

Griffith, Marie R. 1998. *God's Daughters.* Berkeley: University of California Press.

Hasan, Asma Gull. 2000. *American Muslims: The New Generation.* New York: Continuum.

Lawless, Elaine J. 1983. The power of women's speech in the Pentecostal religious service. *Journal of American Folklore* 96:434–59.

Lieberson, Stanley. 2000. *A Matter of Taste.* New York: Oxford University Press.

Maines, David R., and Joy C. Charlton. 1985. The negotiated order approach to the study of social organization. In *Foundation of Interpretive Sociology: Original Essays in Symbolic Interaction*, edited by H. Farberman and R. Perenbanaygam. Greenwich, CT: JAI Press.

Mernissi, Fatima. 1987. *Women & Islam: An Historical and Theological Enquiry.* Oxford: Basil Blackwell.

______. 2003. *Beyond the Veil: Male-Female Dynamics in Muslim Society.* Rev. ed. London: Saqi Books.

Peek, Lori 2005. Becoming Muslim: The development of a religious identity. *Sociology of Religion* 66:215–42.

Read, Jen'nan Ghazal, and John P. Bartkowski. 2000. To veil or not to veil? A case study of identity negotiation among Muslim women in Austin, Texas. *Gender and Society* 14:395–417.

Roald, Anne Sofie. 2001. *Women in Islam: The Western Experience.* London: Routledge.

Schmidt, Garbi. 2004. *Islam in Urban America: Sunni Muslims in Chicago.* Philadelphia: Temple University Press.

Shakeri, Esmail. 1998. Muslim women in Canada: Their role and status as revealed in the *hijab* controversy. In *Muslims on the Americanization Path?* edited by Y. Haddad and J. Esposito. New York: Oxford University Press.

Warner, R. Stephen. 1993. Work in progress toward a new paradigm for the sociological study of religion in the United States. *American Journal of Sociology* 98:1044–93.

Warner, R. Stephen, Elise Martel, and Rhonda E. Dugan. 2001. *Catholicism Is to Islam as Velcro Is to Teflon: Religion and Ethnic Culture among Second Generation Latina and Muslim Women College Students.* Paper presented to the Midwest Sociological Society, St. Louis.

Williams, Gwyneth I., and Rhys H. Williams. 1995. "All we want is equality": Rhetorical framing in the father's rights movement. In *Images of Issues*, 2nd ed., edited by J. Best. New York: Aldine de Gruyter.

Williams, Rhys H. 1995. Constructing the public good: Social movements and cultural resources. *Social Problems* 42:124–44.

22

Compulsive Heterosexuality

Masculinity and Dominance

C. J. Pascoe

No analysis of women's bodies would be complete without a discussion of how men think about and treat women's bodies. This is the topic tackled in "Compulsive Heterosexuality: Masculinity and Dominance" by sociologist C. J. Pascoe. Earlier in this volume Karin A. Martin explored how preschools teach young girls and boys to "do gender" or to engage in "gender performativity" (i.e., to present their bodies as "properly" masculine and feminine in their interactions with others). Pascoe shows us one of the long-term consequences of this socialization. As she describes, male high school students repeatedly demonstrate their heterosexuality and dominance over girls' bodies as a means of claiming masculine power and identity for themselves. Pascoe describes these actions as "compulsive heterosexuality" because they seem almost obligatory for most young men in most social circles. Only by repeatedly performing *masculinity will others acknowledge them as masculine and will they be confident of their own masculine identity. Any boy who fails to do so risks being placed in what Pascoe describes as the* abject fag *position (that is, being labeled as incompetent at masculinity and thus experiencing extremely high social stigma).*

As Pascoe shows, the rituals of compulsive heterosexuality require young men to sexualize and dominate young women's bodies, through actions that are sometimes violent or near-violent. Yet these actions are almost never punished by the schools. Meanwhile, girls' options for responding to boys' behavior are limited, since the main way that girls can obtain power or status is through gaining male attention. Thus, boys' actions reinforce their own status as subjects who actively control their own fate while reinforcing girls' status as objects for boys to enjoy or use.

. . . The public face of male adolescence is filled with representations of masculinity in which boys brag about sexual exploits by showing off a girl's underwear (as in the 1980s film *Pretty in Pink*), spend the end of their senior year talking about how they plan to lose their virginity (*American Pie*), or make cruel bets about who can bed the ugliest girl in the school (*She's All That*). In many ways, the boys at River High, [a suburban middle-class high school in north central California where I observed and interviewed students for 18 months,] seemed much like their celluloid representatatives. . . . Heterosexual innuendoes, sexual bravado, and sexual one-upmanship permeated primarily male spaces. . . . But boys' talk about heterosexuality reveals less about sexual orientation and desire than it does about the centrality of the ability to exercise mastery and dominance literally or figuratively over girls' bodies (Wood 1984). . . . Engaging in very public practices of heterosexuality, boys affirm much more than just masculinity; they affirm subjecthood and personhood through sexualized interactions in which they indicate to themselves and others that they have the ability to work their will upon the world around them. . . .

Compulsive heterosexuality[1] is the name I give to this constellation of sexualized practices, discourses, and interactions. . . . Practices of "compulsive heterosexuality" exemplify what Butler (1995) calls "gender performativity," in which gender "is produced as a ritualized repetition of conventions . . ." (p. 31). Compulsive heterosexuality is not about desire for sexual pleasure *per se*, or just about desire to be "one of the guys"; rather, it is "an excitement felt as sexuality in a male supremacist culture which eroticizes male dominance and female submission" (Jeffreys 1998, 75). Indeed, ensuring positions of power entails boys' constant "recreation of masculinity and femininity" through rituals of eroticized dominance (Jeffreys 1998, 77). Looking at boys' ritualistic sex talk, patterns of touch, and games of "getting girls" indicates how this gender inequality is reinforced through everyday interactions. Taken together, these ritualized interactions continually affirm masculinity as mastery and dominance. By symbolically or physically mastering girls' bodies and sexuality, boys at River High claim masculine identities. . . .

Getting Girls

. . . Rituals of getting girls allowed boys to find common ground in affirming each other's masculinity and positioned them as subjects who had a right to control what girls did with their bodies. A close examination indicates that rituals of "getting girls" relied on a threat of sexualized violence that reaffirmed a sexualized inequality central to the gender order at River High.

On Halloween, Heath arrived at school dressed as an elf carrying a sprig of mistletoe and engaged in a fairly typical ritual of getting girls. He told anyone who would listen that an elf costume was a brilliant idea for Halloween because "it's the wrong holiday!" We stood by his friends at the "water polo" table who tried to sell greeting cards as a fundraiser for the team. Heath attempted to "help" by yelling at girls who passed by, "Ten dollars for a card and a kiss from the elf! Girls only!" Girls made faces and rolled their eyes as they walked past. Graham walked up and Heath yelled to him, arms outstretched, "Come here, baby!" Graham walked toward him with his hips thrust forward and his arms open, saying, "I'm coming!" and quickly both of them backed away laughing. Graham challenged Heath's kissing strategy, saying that the mistletoe sticking out of his green shorts wouldn't work because it wasn't Christmas. Heath, to prove his point that mistletoe worked at any time of the year, lifted the mistletoe above his head and, moving from behind the table, walked up to a group of girls. They looked at him with a bit of trepidation and tried to ignore his presence. Finally one acquiesced, giving him a peck on the cheek. Her friend followed suit. Heath strutted back to the table and victoriously shook hands with all the boys.

Heath, in this instance, became successfully masculine both through . . . [emphasizing he was kissing girls only] and through "getting girls" to kiss him. Graham then congratulated Heath on his ability to overcome the girls' resistance to his overtures. This sort of coercion, even when seemingly harmless, embeds a sense of masculinity predicated upon an overcoming of girls' resistance to boys' desire (Hird and Jackson 2001). Indeed, if one of the important parts of being masculine, as stated by the boys earlier, was not just to desire girls, which Heath indicated through his "girls only" admonition, but also to be desired by girls, Heath demonstrated this in a quite public way, thus ensuring a claim, at least for a moment, on heterosexuality.

While the boys laughed and celebrated Heath's triumph of will, the girls may not have had the same reaction to his forced kisses. In a study of teenagers and sexual harassment, Jean Hand and Laura Sanchez (2000) found, not surprisingly, that in high school girls experienced higher levels of sexual harassment than boys did and were affected more seriously by it. The girls in their study described a hierarchy of sexually harassing behaviors in which some behaviors were described as more problematic than others. The girls overwhelmingly indicated that being kissed against their will was the worst form of sexual harassment, rated more seriously than hearing boys' comments about their bodies or receiving other types of unwanted sexual attention.

Of course, it is unlikely that boys, or girls, would recognize these sorts of daily rituals as sexual harassment; they are more likely seen as normal, if perhaps a bit aggressive, instances of heterosexual flirtation and as part of a normal adolescence (Stein 2002). In fact, I never saw a teacher at River recognize these seemingly flirtatious interchanges as harassment. In auto shop, Tammy, the only girl, often faced this sort of harassment, often at the hands of Jay, a stringy-haired white junior with a pimpled face. One afternoon he walked up to Tammy and stood behind her deeply inhaling, his nose not even an inch away from her hair. Clearly uncomfortable with this, she moved to the side. He asked her if she was planning to attend WyoTech (Wyoming Technical College, a mechanic school), and she responded, "Yes." He said, "I'm going too! You and me. We're gonna be in a room together." He closed his eyes and started thrusting his hips back and forth and softly moaning as if to indicate that he was having sex. Tammy said, "Shut up" and walked away. Used to this sort of harassment, she had developed a way of dealing with such behavior. But no matter how many times she dismissed him, Jay continued to pepper her with sexual innuendoes and suggestive practices.

Both Jay's and Heath's behaviors show how heterosexuality is normalized as a sort of "predatory" social relation in which boys try and try and try to "get" a girl until one finally gives in. Boys, like Jay, who can't "get" a girl often respond with anger or frustration because of their presumed right to girls' bodies. Marc reacted this way when a girl didn't acknowledge his advances. As usual, he sat in the rear of the drama classroom with his pal Jason. A tall, attractive blonde girl walked into the room to speak to Mr. McNally, the drama teacher. As she turned to leave the class, Marc, leaning back with his legs up on the chair in front of him and his arm draped casually over the seat next to him, yelled across the room, "See you later, hot mama!" Jason, quickly echoed him, yelling "See you later, sweet thing." She didn't acknowledge them and looked straight ahead at the door as she left. Marc, frustrated at her lack of response, loudly stated, "She didn't hear me. Whore." Instead of acknowledging that not getting her reflected something about his gender status, he deflected the blame onto her. . . .

Getting, or not getting, girls also reflects and reinforces racialized meanings of sexuality and masculinity. Darnell, [an] African American and white football player, . . . [was] pacing up and down the stairs that line the drama classroom. He yelled across the room to me "there's just one thing I hate! Just one thing I hate!" Shawna, an energetic, bisexual African American sophomore, and I simultaneously asked, "What's that?" Darnell responded, frustrated, "When mixed girls date white guys! Mixed girls are for me!" Shawna attempted to interrupt his rant, saying, "What if the girl doesn't want to date you? Girls have a say too." Darnell responded, not in as much jest as one might hope, "No they don't. White boys can date white girls. There's plenty of 'em. They can even date black girls. But mixed girls are for me." Darnell's frustration reflects a way in which racialized, gendered, and sexual identities intersect. While he felt that he had a claim on "getting girls," as a "mixed" guy he saw his options as somewhat limited. Girls and girls' bodies were constructed as a limited resource for which he had to compete with other (white) guys.

Touching

Just as same-sex touching puts boys at risk for becoming a "fag" [the epithet used constantly by boys to denigrate any "unmasculine" behavior], cross-sex touching affirms heterosexuality and masculinity. "The use of touch (especially between the sexes)" maintains a "social hierarchy" (Henley 1977, 5). In general, superiors touch subordinates, invade their space, and interrupt them in a way that subordinates do not do to superiors. At River High masculinity was established through gendered rituals of touch involving boys' physical dominance and girls' submission.

Girls and boys regularly touched each other in a way that boys did not touch other boys. While girls touched other girls across social environments, boys usually touched each other in rule-bound environments (such as sports) or as a joke to imitate fags. While boys and girls both participated in cross-sex touching, it had different gender meanings. For girls, touching boys was part of a continuum of cross-sex and same-sex touching. That is, girls touched, hugged, and linked arms with other girls on a regular basis in a way that boys did not. For boys, cross-sex touching often took the form of a ritualistic power play that embedded gender meanings of boys as powerful and girls as submissive, or at least weak in their attempts to resist the touching. Touching, in this sense, becomes a "kinesic gender marker" producing masculinity as dominance and femininity as submission (Henley 1977, 138). . . .

Touching rituals ranged from playfully flirtatious to assaultlike interactions. Teachers at River never intervened, at least as far as I saw, when these touching interactions turned slightly violent. In her study of sex education practices in high school, Bonnie Trudell (1993) noted that teachers don't or won't differentiate between sexualized horseplay and assault among students. I also never saw administrators intervene to stop what were seemingly clear violations of girls' bodies. While these sorts of touching interactions often began as flirtatious teasing, they usually evolved into a competition that ended with the boy triumphant and the girl yelling out some sort of metaphorical "uncle."

Darnell and Christina, for instance, engaged in a typical touching ritual during a morning drama class. The students had moved into the auditorium, where they were supposed to be rehearsing their scenes. Christina, a strikingly good-looking white junior with long blonde hair, donned Tim's wrestling letterman's jacket. Darnell asked her if she was a wrestler. In response she pretended to be a wrestler and challenged him to a wrestling match. They circled each other in mock-wrestling positions as Darnell, dressed in baggy jeans and a T-shirt, yelled, "I don't need a singlet to beat you, lady!" She advanced toward Darnell, performing karate kicks with her legs and chops with her arms. Darnell yelled, "That's not wrestling!" and grabbed her torso, flipping her flat on her back. She pulled him down and managed to use her legs to flip him over so that he ended up underneath her on his back while she straddled him, sitting on his waist. Graham yelled out, watching in fascination,

"What is going on?!" Many of the students had gathered around to watch and laugh at the faux wrestling match. Finally Darnell won the match by picking Christina up and throwing her over his shoulders. He spun her around as she squealed to be put down.

The general pace and sequence of this interaction were mirrored in many boy-girl touching rituals. Boys and girls antagonized each other in a flirtatious way. The flirtatious physical interaction escalated, becoming increasingly violent, until a girl squealed, cried, or just gave up. This sort of daily drama physically engendered meanings of power in which boys were confirmed as powerful and girls as weak.

While the "wrestling incident" between Darnell and Christina expressed seemingly harmless notions of dominance and submission, other "touching" episodes had a more explicitly violent tone. In this type of touching the boy and the girl "hurt" each other by punching or slapping or pulling each other's hair until in the end the girl lost with a squeal or scream. Shane and Cathy spent a large part of each morning in government class beating up on each other in this sequence of domination. While it was certainly not unidirectional, the interactions always ended with Cathy giving up. One of the many instances in which Cathy ended up submitting to Shane's touch began when Shane "punched" Cathy's chin. Cathy, trying to ignore the punch, batted her eyelashes and in a whiny voice pleaded, "Take me to In and Out for lunch." In response Shane grabbed her neck with one hand and forehead with the other, shoving her head backward and forward. Cathy squealed, "You're messing up my hair!" As he continued to yank her head around, Cathy tried to do her work, her pen jerking across the page. While this sort of interaction regularly disrupted Cathy's work and actually looked exceedingly painful, she never seriously tried to stop it. When I asked Cathy why they interacted like that, she answered, "He has always been like that with me. We used to have a class right on the other side of that wall together, and he always beat me in there, too. I don't know. He just beats on me." Her response echoed Karin Martin's (1996) finding that adolescent girls, especially working-class girls, don't have a strong sense that they control their own bodies. While some girls, such as Shawna, were able to assert subjectivity and deny the primacy of boys' desire—as when she confronted Darnell's "Mixed girls are for me!" comment—not all girls felt entitled to or expressed alternative definitions of gender. It may be that Shawna, with her baggy pants, hip-hop style, and "tough girl" demeanor, found it easier to confront Darnell than did a normatively feminine girl like Cathy, whose status depended on her electability to the homecoming court. Cathy's affectively flat response to my question revealed that she simply didn't have access to or couldn't express her own bodily needs, desires, and rights.

Interactions such as the one between Cathy and Shane rarely drew the notice of teachers (except to the extent that the two were disrupting class time), most likely because these encounters were read as harmless flirting. But in the larger context of the school's gender and sexual order they reflected a more serious pattern in which both heterosexuality and masculinity presumed female passivity and male control. River boys often physically constrained girls in a sexual manner under the guise of flirtation. For instance, in the hallway a boy put his arms around a girl as she was walking to lunch and started "freaking" her, rubbing his pelvis against her behind as she walked. She rolled her eyes, broke away, and continued walking. What really undergirded all of these interactions is what some feminists call a "rape paradigm," in which masculinity is predicated on overcoming women's bodily desire and control. A dramatic example of this "rape paradigm" happened between classes during passing period. Walking between government and drama classes, Keith yelled, "GET RAPED! GET RAPED!" as he rhythmically jabbed a girl in the crotch with his drumstick. She yelled at him to stop and tried to kick him in the crotch with her foot. He dodged and started yelling, "CROTCH! CROTCH!" Indeed, the threat of rape was what seemed to underlie many of these interactions where boys repeatedly showed in cross-gender touching that they were more physically powerful than girls. . . .

Girls Respond

Girls frequently colluded in boys' discourses and practices of compulsive heterosexuality. When interacting with boys, many girls emphasized their own sexual availability or physical weakness to gain and maintain boys' attention. Because a girl's status in high school is frequently tied to the status of the boys she dates, this male erotic attention is critical. Of course, gender practices like this are not limited to teenagers. Grown women "bargain with patriarchy" by submitting to sexist social institutions and practices to gain other forms of social power (Kandiyoti 1988).

The day before winter break, I handed out lollipops shaped like Christmas trees and candy canes to thank students for their help with my research. In government class Cathy took a Christmas tree lollipop, tipped her head back, and stuck the long candy down her throat, moaning as if in ecstasy. Jeremy and Shane laughed as Cathy presumably showed off her roomy mouth or throat and her lack of a gag reflex, both highly prized traits by boys when receiving "blow jobs." Cathy responded with a smirk, "I don't think I'm *that* good." The group laughed at her conclusion. It seems that the social power girls gained from going along with this behavior was more than they gained by refusing. A way to gain male attention and thus in-school status was to engage in these boys' discourses and practices about sexuality.

This approach, illustrating sexual prowess, was danger laden for girls at River and is dangerous for teenage girls in general as they tread the shifting and blurry boundary between sexy and slutty (Tanenbaum 1999). To negotiate this boundary, girls invoked a variety of gender strategies. Some, like Cathy, promoted their own sexual prowess or acted as if the boys' comments were compliments; others suffered quietly; and some actually responded angrily, contradicting boys' claims on girls' sexuality. Teresa, like most girls, quietly put up with boys' daily practices of compulsive heterosexuality. She was one of the few girls who had enrolled in the weight-lifting class. While she told me that she signed up for weight lifting because "I like to lift weights," she continued by saying she didn't like exercising in a class with all boys. "It's really annoying because they just stare at you while you lift. They just stare at you." Like many girls, she quietly put up with this treatment. I didn't see her confronting any of the boys who stared at her.

Other girls developed a more defensive response, though not one couched in feminism or in opposition to sexism. In auto shop Jay expressed frustration about his upcoming eighteenth birthday, saying that soon he couldn't "have sex with girls younger than eighteen. Statutory rape." He continued angrily (presumably referring to his rape charge), "Younger girls, they lie, stupid little bitches." He laughed, "God, I hate girls." He saw Jenny, the female student aide in the class, look at him as he said this. So he looked directly at her and said loudly, "They're only good for making sandwiches and cleaning house. They don't even do that up to speed!" She just looked at him and shook her head. Brook, another auto shop student, said to me, "Write that down!" Jay continued to harass Jenny by throwing licorice at her and yelling, "I agree, her sister is a lot hotter!" Jenny looked at him and shook her head again. Jay commanded, sitting back and folding his arms, "Make me a sandwich!" At first she ignored him with a "whatever." Then Jenny carried back the licorice he threw at her and dumped it on him. Jay responded dismissively, shaking his head and muttering, "Fucking crybaby." In this instance Jenny both acquiesced to and resisted Jay's sexist treatment. She sort of ignored him while he made blatantly sexist remarks and tried to get even with him by dumping licorice on him. Like the girl who tried to fight back as she was being jabbed in the crotch with a drumstick, Jenny developed an off-the-cuff response to let the boys know she didn't appreciate their sexism.

Other girls, like Cathy, seemed flattered by boys' behavior, responding with giggles and smiles. In the drama class Emir . . . "flirted" regularly with two girls, Simone and Valerie, throughout the class period. He made kissing motions with his lips, ran his tongue slowly over his teeth, and lustfully whispered or mouthed comments such as "Come on, baby. Oooh baby. Yeah, I love you." The girls responded with laughs and giggles, occasionally rolling their eyes in mock frustration. Other girls frequently adopted the smile and giggle strategy. While I interviewed Darnell, he yelled at a passing girl that he liked her "astronaut skirt." She laughed and waved. I asked him what "astronaut skirt" meant, and he explained, "Oh, it's just a little joke. That's an astronaut skirt 'cause your butt is outta this world." As Nancy Henley (1977) points out, this giggle and smile response signifies submission and appeasement, usually directed from a lower- to a higher-status person.

Though most girls submitted to this sort of behavior, not all of them did. . . . The most apparent resisters were the girls in the Gay/Straight Alliance. . . . But even girls without an espoused political orientation sometimes rejected boys' control of girls' bodies. In the hallway, for instance, Jessica stood behind Reggie as he backed up and rubbed his behind into her crotch. In response, she smacked him hard and he stopped his grinding. Similarly, in the weight room, Teresa sometimes resisted in her own way. Reggie once said to her, "When we gonna go and have sex? When we gonna hit that?" Teresa responded with scorn, "Never!" and walked away. This, unfortunately, happened more rarely than one would hope.

I'm Different from Other Guys

Thus far this chapter has focused on boys who treated girls as resources to be mobilized for their own masculinity projects, but not all boys engaged in practices of compulsive heterosexuality at all times. Most boys engaged in these sorts of practices only when in groups, and some boys avoided them in general.

When not in groups—when in one-on-one interactions with boys or girls—boys were much less likely to engage in gendered and sexed dominance practices. . . .

When alone some boys were more likely to talk about romance and emotions, as opposed to girls' bodies and sexual availability. . . . [In addition,] . . . on another occasion I heard a boy, in a group of other boys, refuse to engage in practices of compulsive heterosexuality by claiming that he couldn't talk about his girlfriend [in derogatory, sexualized terms]. A boy probably could not have argued that talking this way about girls was derogatory on principle without claiming he was speaking about a girlfriend.

Other boys who refrained from participating in these sorts of conversations frequently identified as Christian. . . . Christian boys at River High had institutional claims on masculinity such that they didn't need to engage in the sort of intense interactional work that Kimmel (1987) claims is characteristic of contemporary "compulsive masculinity." As a result, unlike nonreligious boys, they did not need to engage in the continual interactional repudiation of equality with girls. Their respective religions buttressed male power through their teachings such that the interactional accomplishment of masculinity was less central to their identity projects. Thus the Christian boys at River may have been less interactionally sexist, but their investment in gender difference and gender inequality was little different from that of the other boys at River. . . .

Females are the Puppets

> At a country square dance a few years ago I saw an offensive game between two men on opposite sides of a square, to see who could swing the women hardest and highest off the ground. What started out pleasantly enough soon degenerated into a brutal competition that left the women of the square staggering dizzily from place to place, completely unable to keep up with what was going on in the dance, and certainly getting no pleasure from

> it. The message that comes through to women in such physical displays is: you are so physically inferior that you can be played with like a toy. Males are the movers and the powerful in life, females the puppets.

It is heartbreaking, thirty years after Nancy Henley (1977, 150) wrote this passage, to document the continuing centrality of what she called "female puppetry" to adolescent masculinity. Like these square-dancing men, boys at River High repeatedly enforced definitions of masculinity that included male control of female bodies through symbolic or physical violence. . . .

Just as in the square dance that Henley described, girls' bodies at River High provided boys the opportunity to demonstrate mastery and dominance. These practices of compulsive heterosexuality indicate that control over women's bodies and their sexuality is, sadly, still central to definitions of masculinity, or at least adolescent masculinity. By dominating girls' bodies boys defended against the fag position, increased their social status, and forged bonds of solidarity with other boys. However, none of this is to say that these boys were unrepentant sexists. Rather, for the most part, these behaviors were social behaviors. Individually boys were much more likely to talk empathetically and respectfully of girls. Even when they behaved this way in groups, boys probably saw their behavior as joking and in fun (Owens et al. 2005). Maintaining masculinity, though, demands the interactional repudiation of this sort of empathy in order to stave off the abject fag position. It is precisely the joking and sexual quality of these interactions that makes them so hard to see as rituals of dominance. . . .

Note

1. This is not to say that similar enactments of dominance and control don't occur among gay men. But such behavior is out of the scope of this study, since there were not enough self-identified gay boys at this school from which to draw conclusions about the way sexual discussions and practices interacted with masculinity for gay boys.

References

Butler, Judith. 1995. "Melancholy gender/refused identification." In *Constructing Masculinity*, edited by Maurice Berer, Brian Wallis, and Simon Watson, pp. 21–36. New York: Routledge.

Hand, Jeanne Z., and Laura Sanchez. 2000. "Badgering or bantering? Gender differences in experience of, and reactions to, sexual harassment among U.S. high school students." *Gender & Society* 14(6):718–46.

Henley, Nancy. 1977. *Body Politics: Power, Sex, and Nonverbal Communication.* Englewood Cliffs, NJ: Prentice Hall.

Hird, Myra J., and Sue Jackson. 2001. "Where 'angels' and 'wusses' fear to tread: Sexual coercion in adolescent dating relationships." *Journal of Sociology* 37:27–43.

Jeffreys, Sheila. 1998. "Heterosexuality and the desire for gender." In *Theorising Heterosexuality*, edited by Diane Richardson, pp. 75–90. Buckingham, England: Open University Press.

Kandiyoti, Denise. 1988. "Bargaining with patriarchy." *Gender & Society* 2(3):274–90.

Kimmel, Michael S. 1987. "The cult of masculinity: American social character and the legacy of the cowboy." In *Beyond Patriarchy: Essays by Men on Pleasure, Power, and Change*, edited by Michael Kaufman, pp. 235–49. New York: Oxford University Press.

Martin, Karin. 1996. *Puberty, Sexuality and the Self: Girls and Boys at Adolescence.* New York: Routledge.

Owens, Laurence, Rosalyn Shute, and Philip Slee. 2005. " 'In the eye of the beholder . . .': Girls', boys' and teachers' perceptions of boys' aggression to girls." *International Education Journal* 5:142–51.

Stein, Nan. 2002. "Bullying as sexual harassment." In *The Jossey-Bass Reader on Gender in Education*, edited by S. M. Bailey, pp. 209–28. San Francisco: Jossey-Bass.

Tanenbaum, Leora. 1999. *Slut! Growing up Female with a Bad Reputation.* New York: Seven Stories Press.

Trudell, Bonnie Nelson. 1993. *Doing Sex Education: Gender Politics and Schooling.* New York: Routledge.

Wood, Julian. 1984. "Groping towards sexism: Boy's sex talk." In *Gender and Generation*, edited by Angela McRobbie and Mica Nava, pp. 54–84. London: MacMillan.

23

Being Undocumented and Intimate Partner Violence (IPV)

Multiple Vulnerabilities through the Lens of Feminist Intersectionality

MARGARET E. ADAMS AND JACQUELYN CAMPBELL

The 2010 National Intimate Partner and Sexual Violence Survey *(published by the Centers for Disease Control and Prevention) reports that over a third of U.S. women will experience rape, physical violence, and/or stalking by an intimate partner in their lifetime. As Margaret E. Adams and Jacquelyn Campbell point out in their article, "Being Undocumented and Intimate Partner Violence (IPV): Multiple Vulnerabilities through the Lens of Feminist Intersectionality," these experiences are even more common among the 3.2 million undocumented immigrant women living in the United States.*

In this final article of this book, Adams and Campbell examine, from a public health perspective, how undocumented immigrant women are particularly vulnerable to experiencing IPV. They frame this investigation using a feminist theory of intersectionality originally generated by black feminist writers such as Patricia Hill Collins. Intersectionality theory maintains that factors such as gender, ethnicity, and immigration status interact and create multiplicative effects for self-identity and life outcomes. Adams and Campbell show how these women are often isolated and economically, socially, and psychologically dependent on their partners. They also possess limited English language skills, along with a lack of knowledge of legal rights and services available to IPV survivors. These factors are then compounded by the constant—and realistic—fear of deportation.

Margaret E. Adams and Jacquelyn Campbell. 2012. "Being Undocumented and Intimate Partner Violence (IPV): Multiple Vulnerabilities Through the Lens of Feminist Intersectionality," *Women's Health & Urban Life* 11(1): 15–34. Reprinted by permission of University of Toronto.

According to Adams and Campbell, U.S. immigration law further endangers abused undocumented immigrant women who are married to U.S. citizens by placing the women's legal status almost totally in their husbands' hands. Although legal reforms enacted in the Violence Against Women Act permit abused women to apply for legal residency on their own, many emotional, financial, and logistical obstacles remain. Moreover, turning to the legal system for help can still place an undocumented immigrant woman at risk of deportation.

Fear of deportation also deters women from turning to healthcare services, leading to myriad adverse health effects. The frequent everyday stress of living in a country without documentation contributes to "allostatic load," a body's stress response to ongoing exposure to environmental challenges that can physically damage the body if hyperarousal becomes chronic. In light of these multiple vulnerabilities, Adams and Campbell outline several important areas of intervention including education, documentation assistance, advocacy and policy, awareness, and research.

One in ten women in the United States (U.S.) is an immigrant (Glass, Annan, Bhandari, and Fishwick 2011). Out of the total foreign-born population in the U.S., 26 percent are undocumented; almost half of those undocumented individuals—about 41 percent—are women (Passel, Capps, and Fix 2004). All told, there are about 3.2 million undocumented women living in the U.S. today (ibid). Their documentation status, coupled with their race, ethnicity, and gender, makes them particularly vulnerable to violence.

The population of undocumented immigrants living in the U.S. constitutes a significant and growing public health sector. Pushed and pulled by a combination of political and economic forces such as poverty, economic opportunities, political instability, and the loss or gain of family ties, increasingly significant numbers of people are entering the U.S. illegally each year (Erez, Adelman, and Gregory 2009). This population is both underserved in health care and at risk for Intimate Partner Violence (IPV) (Berk and Schur 2001; Bustamante et al. 2010; Glass et al. 2011). . . .

Violence against women is one of the most common victimizations experienced by immigrants (Erez et al. 2009; Raj and Silverman 2002), regardless of documentation status. Research indicates that the incidence of domestic violence in immigrant women, both documented and undocumented, far outstrips that experienced by the general U.S. population. While the lifetime prevalence of domestic violence in the general U.S. population is estimated at 22 percent to 25 percent (Breiding, Black, and Ryan 2008; Tjaden and Thoennes 2000), one survey of Latina immigrants found a lifetime prevalence for intimate partner violence more than twice that high (Moynihan, Gaboury, and Onken 2008). IPV against immigrant women has reached what some researchers are calling "epidemic proportions" (Raj and Silverman 2002, 367). The same trend is visible in other countries, although not in all settings (Hyman, Forte, Du Mont, Romans, and Cohen 2006; Schei et al. 2012).

IPV is a global health and social problem. It occurs in all countries and across economic, social, religious, and cultural groups (Glass et al. 2011).

Significant negative economic as well as negative health consequences to individuals, families, communities, and societies have been documented as resulting from IPV (WHO 2005). The high rate of IPV seen in immigrant populations is not a function of culture so much as it is a function of socioeconomic marginalization. Thus, while IPV *may appear* more prevalent in immigrant populations for "culturally innate" reasons, research shows that differences in IPV by race and ethnicity often decrease or disappear when socioeconomic status is included in the analysis (Glass et al. 2011; Menjívar and Salcido 2002). While this sort of analysis has not been frequently conducted in samples of immigrant women, as a highly marginalized population immigrant women are exposed to far more factors contributing to IPV than nonimmigrant women (Amanor-Boadu, Messing, Stith, Anderson, O'Sullivan, and Campbell 2012).

Immigrant women without documentation are at an even higher risk for violence than those with legal status. Those without documents—people known derisively in the U.S. by hate-speech labels like "illegals"—are among the most socially, economically, and legally marginalized in U.S. society, and subsequently the most vulnerable. Their lack of documentation defines their experience and is a pivotal factor in their risk for IPV. More than cultural issues or language barriers, an individual's immigration status is emerging as "the most significant factor in determining how, or even if, domestic violence is addressed when it occurs in immigrant families" (Earner 2010, 288).

An Unseen Class

. . . [Undocumented immigrant women] are, by nature, an unseen class . . . [and] studying a population that necessarily flies under the radar is not easy. . . . When attention *has* been given in research, advocacy, and services to IPV in immigrant populations, the diversity within immigrant groups is often overlooked, particularly differences in class, the lowest of which being the undocumented (Glass et al. 2011). As in most scholarship, there is an entire segment of immigrant population (such as undocumented workers) that may be discounted as if nonexistent (Glass et al. 2011).

Despite the lack of substantial research on undocumented abused women, the theory of feminist intersectionality (Glass et al. 2011; Kelly 2009) is particularly applicable to them. . . .

Feminist Theory of Intersectionality

The theory of feminist intersectionality, originally generated by black feminist writers in the 1980s (Collins 1986; hooks 1984; Sokoloff 2005), recognizes that "oppressed groups and individuals live at the margins of society with inequitable access to resources resulting in societal inequities and social injustice. The negative effects on health from belonging to more than one oppressed group are multiplicative and unique" (Kelly, Gonzalez-Guarda, and Taylor 2011, 76). This theory of intersecting, oppressive factors yielding multiplicative, negative effects has been used by an expanding circle of researchers and applied to theories addressing both the impacts of immigration status and the epidemiology of IPV.

An ethnogender perspective or intersectionality approach to studying IPV in populations of immigrant women—for a moment, setting aside the issue of documentation status—gives equal importance to both gender inequality and racial/ethnicity discrimination, or "dual subordination" (Glass et al. 2011; Kelly 2009). Intersectionality theory asserts that the intersection of gender, race, and ethnicity, as well as the cultural differences and alienation experienced by immigrants, compound each other and become important criteria for the social construction of identity and marginalization (Glass et al. 2011). Regardless of the class to which the woman belongs in her home country, she faces subordination not only as a woman but also as a minority woman in a foreign land. Socialization into the often rigid gender norms of one's home country, combined with the lack of institutional support in a foreign land due to alien status, exposes immigrant women to dual marginalization (Glass et al. 2011). The effect of these multiple forms of marginalization is not additive but multiplicative, with each added factor exacerbating the others.

Analytically, immigration status can be separated out as yet another category of intersectionality (Erez et al. 2009). This third factor places undocumented immigrant women in a category of triple marginalization. "*Immigrant*," Erez says, is "a separate and multiplicative aspect of identity, violence, and oppression" (ibid, 33); thus, being undocumented puts women in a position of still *more* vulnerability. Rather than considering immigration status as a variable or static category within race, we consider immigration as part of the multiple grounds of identity shaping the woman's experience of domestic violence. The combined factors of gender, race/ethnicity, and lack of legal documentation compound and increase the woman's disenfranchisement. . . .

Multiple Barriers to Help-Seeking

Extricating oneself from an abusive relationship is an incredibly complex and difficult proposition for any woman, one with emotional, financial, logistical, health, and security-related barriers; leaving is neither a simple nor a safe choice for many (Kelly et al. 2011). It is important to note that in addition to all the existing barriers to accessing services that are experienced by all victims of abuse, the plight of abuse victims is greatly exacerbated if they are immigrants, and even more so if they have arrived in the U.S. illegally (Moynihan et al. 2008). Immigrant women *with* documentation are often economically, socially, and psychologically dependent on their spouses and their families; this increases the women's risk of experiencing IPV, a risk that is further compounded by their equally restricted access to needed resources for increasing safety while in the relationship and when leaving the abusive partner (Glass et al. 2011). Living as an immigrant *without* legal documentation dramatically exacerbates both that dependence on the partner and the extremely limited access to safety-securing resources.

Many immigrant women, both with and without legal status in their country of residence, have left their entire social support systems behind in their countries of origin, furthering their emotional, social, and psychological reliance on their partners. Abusers actively exploit this reliance and use it to further isolate women. The abuser's coercive control, the woman's limited language skills, and lack of knowledge of legal rights and services available for IPV survivors all serve to deepen the isolation of immigrant women (Glass et al. 2011). Isolation techniques include restricting their contact with family both in the U.S. and in their country of origin, as well as prohibiting friendships with "Americans" (Raj and Silverman 2002). Many abusers will increase immigrant women's insecurities about their ability to function in U.S. society without their spouses by demeaning women based on their limited English and their lower levels of acculturation, education, or work skills (Raj and Silverman 2002).

Further exacerbating the barriers faced by abused immigrant women, both documented and undocumented women may lack information that legal recourse for IPV exists. Studies consistently report that immigrant and refugee women of all legal statuses who are abused are often completely unaware of the domestic violence services in their communities, or that laws exist that may protect them from abuse, especially as there frequently are few or no laws against IPV in their countries of origin (Moynihan et al. 2008; Raj and Silverman 2002). Husbands/partners are likely to be themselves ignorant of the domestic violence laws in the U.S., and if they are aware of such legislation give women incorrect information about it (Moynihan et al. 2008). Finally, even if women are aware of the illegality of IPV in the U.S., many women (regardless of documentation status) do not seek help because of shame, stigma attached to abuse, fear of the abuser, and/or cultural expectations of maintaining familial harmony (Glass et al. 2011).

Research conclusively demonstrates that abused immigrant women with and without documentation are less likely than nonimmigrant abused women to seek both informal (e.g., social support) and formal (e.g., medical and legal services) help for IPV (Berk and Schur 2001; Bustamante et al. 2010; Menjívar and Salcido 2002; Raj and Silverman 2002; Wood 2004). Even when women do overcome some of the barriers described previously, help-seeking continues to be limited by the systemic biases and discrimination often faced by these individuals, which are embedded in and exacerbated by the challenges they face as refugee and immigrant women (Moynihan et al. 2008).

For immigrant women who are undocumented and/or legally dependent on their partner for residence, all of these isolating factors are greatly exacerbated by the constant fear of deportation. Immigration status places women on a social hierarchy that directly affects their vulnerability to abuse: for undocumented immigrant women, deportation is a constant threat that batterers can use against them (Moynihan et al. 2008; Raj and Silverman 2002). What is more, for many undocumented women, the threat of deportation is not only for themselves, but for undocumented family members who the abuser may also threaten to report to immigration authorities.

The threat of deportation is not an idle one. Abusive partners have been known to keep, destroy, or threaten to destroy partners' immigration documentation, placing immigrant women at risk for removal (Raj and Silverman 2002). Abusive partners have also been reported to actually start deportation proceedings themselves, sometimes accusing a woman of marriage fraud to escape prosecution for abuse or to get an advantage in divorce or custody proceedings (Raj and Silverman 2002). Some women have been taken back to their countries of origin by batterers "under the pretext of a family trip" and left there without resources or support to return (Raj and Silverman 2002, 381). Importantly, fear of being returned to the country from which they fled is a powerful force in not seeking or even exploring avenues for help (Moynihan et al. 2008).

Without any form of identification, undocumented immigrant women are often unable to secure employment and, if employed, may not be able to keep any of their wages. Some undocumented women without legal work papers are simultaneously abused and/or exploited by their employers (Moynihan et al. 2008). Those who are in the U.S. on temporary work visas must maintain their sponsored employment to remain in the country. Batterers have been reported to disrupt and threaten immigrant women's jobs, not only undermining their ability to remain employed but, for some, their ability to remain in the U.S. (Raj and Silverman 2002).

IPV, Immigrants, and the Legal System: Where the Ball Got Dropped

The criminalization of domestic violence in the U.S. was the hard-won result of the efforts of the battered woman's movement (Erez et al. 2009). That said, feminist criminologists, their cross-disciplinary associates, and others have been part of a growing critique of the "limits or unintended effects of the criminalization of domestic violence" (ibid, 33). Most notably, U.S. reliance on the state for women's safety has left immigrant women without citizenship status largely unprotected (Bhuyan 2008; Erez et al. 2009). Furthermore, U.S. immigration law endangers abused immigrant women by giving near total control over the women's legal status to the sponsoring spouse, "replicating the doctrine of coverture . . . [which], in effect, identifies the married couple as a single legal entity, within which the husband has control over the property and body of the wife and their children" (Erez et al. 2009, 36). Women who immigrate as wives of U.S. citizens, legal permanent residents (LPRs), diplomats, students, or workers are legally dependent on others to sponsor, pursue, and complete their visa petitions. This legal dependency intensifies gendered inequality, creates new ways for men to abuse and control their intimate partners, and entraps abused women (ibid). The Violence Against Women Act (VAWA) legal reforms instituted in 1994 served to relieve some of the legal and economic dependencies imposed on abused and undocumented immigrant women, but not all.

The VAWA legal reforms (see Table 23.1) include self-petition, which lets an abused spouse apply for a green card on his or her own; cancellation of removal, which lets an abused spouse who has already been subjected to removal proceedings request to remain in the U.S.; the U-visa, which lets a victim of crime (including domestic violence) who has been helpful to its investigation or prosecution apply for a nonimmigrant visa and work permit; and access to public benefits such as food stamps (Erez et al. 2009). Obstacles to obtaining these protections remain, in particular "the complex nature of legal qualifications, including who is eligible to apply for which form of legal relief, and meeting the threshold required to demonstrate having been subjected to battery or extreme cruelty" (ibid, 37). Add to these obstacles the post-9/11 processing delays in visa applications and the increasingly exclusionist laws that are the consequence of widespread U.S. anti-immigrant sentiment, and the resulting situation is one in which the implementation of these legal protections becomes almost prohibitively difficult.

Barriers for women's self-petitioning under VAWA are emotional, financial, and logistical in nature (Ingram et al. 2010). In a recent qualitative study conducted by Ingram and colleagues (2010), six major aspects of preparing the VAWA self-petition were identified by petitioners as extremely difficult: (1) having to provide a personal statement of the abuse, (2) the insecurity of the process, (3) confusion regarding the self-petition process, (4) the amount of evidence required to demonstrate eligibility, (5) the length of time a self-petitioner has to wait for employment authorization and subsequent financial hardship, and (6) immigration law penalties (Ingram et al. 2010). Being forced to relive the experience through personal statements, having to come up with extensive documentation to prove the severity of their abuse, and waiting for months (or longer) without any security that the outcome of the petition would be positive were all deeply stressful for VAWA self-petitioners. Just being able to continually file the necessary paperwork presented many challenges; for women seeking refuge in temporary shelters or in other locations, the issue of having a permanent address for the duration of the petition was deeply problematic. Transience, frequently experienced by women fleeing from an abuser, makes changing immigrant status logistically impossible

TABLE 23.1 Violence against Women Act (VAWA) Legal Reform Provisions

SELF PETITION: Allows immigrant survivors of domestic violence and their children to obtain lawful permanent residence without the cooperation of their documented spouse/parent.

Those Eligible to File:

Spouse: You may file for yourself if you are, or were (within 2 years of filing), the abused spouse of a U.S. citizen or lawful permanent resident (LPR).

(*Continued*)

TABLE 23.1 (***Continued***)

Parent: You may file for yourself if you are the parent of a child who has been abused by your U.S. citizen or LPR spouse.

Child: You may file for yourself if you are an abused child under 21, unmarried and have been abused by your U.S. citizen or LPR parent.

What does a person need to prove for a VAWA self-petition?

- Spouses must file their application within two years of a final divorce;
- The abuser is a U.S. citizen or LPR, or has lost status within the two years prior to the filing of the application;
- The petitioner resided in the United States with the citizen or LPR spouse or parent;
- The petitioner was battered or subjected to extreme cruelty during the marriage;
- The petitioner is a person of good moral character; AND
- The petitioner married her spouse in good faith.

CANCELLATION OF REMOVAL: VAWA cancellation of removal is available to an immigrant survivor who is already in deportation proceedings. The same three categories of people eligible for Self Petition (see above) are also eligible to file for Cancellation of Removal.

What does a person need to prove a VAWA cancellation of removal?

- Has lived in the United States continuously for 3 years immediately preceding filing the application for cancellation of removal;
- Was subjected to battering or extreme cruelty by her spouse while in the United States and is determined to be of "good moral character."
- Is currently deportable. She will not be eligible for cancellation if she is deportable for marriage fraud, certain criminal convictions or because she is a threat to U.S. national security, AND
- She or her child, in the opinion of the Attorney General, would suffer extreme hardship if deported.

  A parent of a child abused by an LPR or USC parent may self petition or apply for cancellation of removal under VAWA, *if she/he is the spouse of the abusive parent.* The non-abused parent can also include other children as derivatives, even if the children are not related to the LRP or USC abuser.

U-VISA: These visas are available to survivors of crime (U-Visa).

What does a person need for a U-Visa?

- Show that she has suffered "substantial physical or mental abuse" as the result of a form of criminal activity (or "similar" activity), *including domestic violence.*
- Show that she possesses information concerning the criminal activity, AND
- Provide a certification from a federal, state or local law enforcement officer, prosecutor or judge or authority investigating the criminal activity designated in the statute that certifies that the victim has been helpful, is being helpful or is likely to be helpful in the investigation or prosecution of the crime.

For more information on VAWA, 1994: go to http://www.uscis.gov/portal/site/uscis/

when a steady residence is needed for the extensive paperwork to be processed over time (Raj and Silverman 2002).

Each year, hundreds of thousands of women enter the U.S. as spouses of U.S. citizens or legal permanent residents (LPR) (INS 1997; Monger and Yankay 2011), coming to the U.S. with significant disadvantages in social status and resources compared with their male partners (Raj and Silverman 2002). In the absence of VAWA protection, control over their documentation status is solely in the hands of the spouse. If the marriage dissolves prior to the immigrant spouse obtaining permanent residency status, the immigrant spouse will remain undocumented and can be deported as an illegal alien. Furthermore, if the U.S. citizen or LPR spouse opts not to file for permanent residency status on their spouse's behalf, in the absence of VAWA protection, the immigrant spouse cannot attain legal immigration status, thus maintaining dependence on the batterer. Disturbingly, 72 percent of citizen and LPR spouses do not file immigration papers for their wives (Dutton, Orloff, and Hass 2000; Raj and Silverman 2002).

Underlying all of these barriers is the reality that approaching the legal system for help can be incredibly daunting to the immigrant whose primary goal is to avoid contact with this system so as to avoid deportation. Women in countries in which there are no laws against IPV are often able to rely on religious, traditional, and societal institutions for protection. As these kinds of protections are rarely in place in the U.S., abused immigrant women are often at a loss as to where they can turn for help (Raj and Silverman 2002). In addition, immigrant women often fear the police, given that the police in many of their countries of origin are hostile and even dangerous to women and/or perceived as corrupt forces of oppressive governments (Wessel and Campbell 1997).

Social Services and Compounding Barriers

As the debate on immigration intensifies in the U.S., the response in the political arena has placed emphasis on passing increasingly stringent controls on access to social benefits based on immigration status—creating what Earner describes as "a sort of negative immigrant policy whose intended outcome is, presumably, to make it difficult for immigrants, specifically the undocumented, to stay and hopefully, make them go back to wherever they came from" (Earner 2010, 289). This kind of thinking presumes that undocumented immigrants are single people, when in fact, like most adults, they form families (Earner 2010).

For undocumented immigrant families as a whole, the unintended consequences of limiting access to social benefits are enormous and include increasing economic hardship, inadequate food, lack of access to health care, and increased stress. These are the very risk factors often identified as correlating with increases in family violence (Earner 2010). In this way, the cycle of risk and vulnerability perpetuates: Undocumented women are restricted from access to help by the very policies that simultaneously make them more likely to experience IPV. This chain of events can quickly spiral into family disintegration and negative health outcomes as curtailed access to public benefits and social services for the undocumented leads to further impoverished families without safety nets (ultimately leading to the involvement of public child welfare services).

In a recent study by the Urban Institute, it was clear that immigrant populations, despite eligibility and need, did not access services that would ameliorate problems such as lack of access to food and health care. This could effectively place children of undocumented mothers at risk and bring the attention of public child welfare services (Capps et al. 2002; Earner 2010; Passel et al. 2004). These restrictive policies are becoming increasingly widespread as initiatives at the state level are simultaneously seeking to restrict undocumented immigrants' access to state-funded benefits and services, including developing the type of legislation which could restrict immigrant women's access to basic domestic violence services such as shelters and counseling (Earner 2010).

Undocumented women fear that if they ask for help, healthcare or social service providers will turn them in for deportation; even abused immigrant women with legal status feel vulnerable to deportation for themselves or their families should they seek help (Raj and Silverman 2002), an impression that is the result of both misinformation and an overall culture of fear. Furthermore, many states' mandatory arrest policies in domestic violence cases result in the arrest of both the male perpetrator and female victim. Subsequently, immigrant women seeking police help for abuse may also risk their own deportation if convicted through this process.

Other service-related barriers to seeking help include lack of outreach to immigrant communities on behalf of domestic violence services, lack of accessible or culturally relevant services, and language barriers (Raj and Silverman 2002). Some shelters have already denied immigrant women access by requiring proof of citizenship or English fluency for entry, despite the fact that this denial of services is a violation of federal law (Ganatra 2001; Raj and Silverman 2002).

Biological Effects of Being Undocumented: Stress and Allostatic Load

In a research study done by McGuire and Georges (2003) exploring the qualitative experiences of women immigrants, most women in the study identified lack of legal documentation as "a major and overriding concern that influenced their thoughts about seeking health care and complicated their lives with fear" (p. 190). Simply living day-to-day without legal status within a country is a great source of anxiety and fear. The direct, negative health impacts of the stress of being undocumented are twofold. First, undocumented women are much less likely to seek any kind of health care, both because of cost and because of fear of being reported. As a source of prolonged stress, lack of documentation can exacerbate health risks because of other variables such as affordability, accessibility, acceptability, knowledge, cultural views and practices, and willingness to seek care. Second, in keeping with the recent research on the concept of allostatic load, the stress itself of being undocumented—a "major and overriding" source of concern and fear—takes a very real, direct physical toll (McGuire and Georges 2003, 190). This concept of allostatic load has been used in nursing and other disciplines since the 1990s to examine the direct effects of stress on the human body. The frequent activation of the body's stress response, while essential for managing acute threats, can physically damage the body if hyperarousal becomes chronic. The accumulation of biological risk associated with persistent hyperarousal is applicable to the lives of many immigrants, even those *with* documentation; this state of hyperarousal is deeply intensified by being "an illegal" (McGuire and Georges 2003).

When discussing the biological impact of distress, it is important to note how crucial the element of time can be, in the sense that undocumented women who might suffer from chronic conditions like anemia or type-2 diabetes, or preliminary, early, or curable stages of cancers such as cervical dysplasia carry elevated risk if they do not or are unable to access available health services for early detection (Coker, Bond, Madeleine, Luchok, and Pirisi 2003; McGuire and Georges 2003). The longer women endure these stressors, and the fewer levels of prevention they have access to, the more at risk for serious negative health effects they become. Even further compounding these risks is the loss of future Social Security benefits and better economic security, given the well-acknowledged association between poverty and health risk (McGuire and Georges 2003).

The level of stress that undocumented immigrants live with should not be underestimated. For these women, their documentation status dominates their entire lives. Being undocumented "renders the immigrant a 'persona non grata,' one who has no official right to exist within the political-legal-geographic boundaries of the country in which they live" (McGuire and Georges 2003, 191). Understandably, the greatest hope of the undocumented women studied by McGuire and Georges was that they would "someday qualify to legalize their status either through an amnesty program as occurred last in 1986, or through grown citizen children (a very long wait)" (ibid, 191).

When this stress is combined with the equally all-consuming stress of living in an abusive relationship, the potential for serious negative health consequences rises dramatically. Viewed through the lens of intersectionality, an undocumented abused woman's risk for severe negative health effects via allostatic load are further amplified: She is dealing with the stress of abuse, the stress of the constant threat of deportation, and the stress inherent in being socially subjugated by merit of gender, race, and nationality. All of these factors interact and compound each other to add to health-crippling stress; again, the effect of the intersection of these factors is multiplicative, rather than additive.

Implications for Healthcare Providers and Social Service Providers

. . . Healthcare and social service providers need to be deeply engaged with this issue [domestic violence] and aware of the many factors compounding it. One of the biggest barriers to help is lack of awareness and education on potential legal protections available to women (namely, VAWA). Well-informed clinicians and social service providers can provide that education. Clinicians can also play a key role in providing one of the biggest requirements for VAWA petitions: the documentation of abuse. For undocumented immigrant women *not* eligible for legal protections such as VAWA, providers need to understand the vulnerable position these women are in and try to reach out to them regardless of citizenship status.

Undocumented immigrant women and children are in danger of being abused, have little or no protection from their abusers, and have little or no ability to seek help (Moynihan et al. 2008). . . . Here we outline several areas of intervention.

Patient Education: A major constraining factor preventing abused immigrant women from accessing help is the "lack of awareness of available IPV services, lack of culturally or linguistically competent IPV services, and lack of awareness of IPV as a legal issue for which they can receive assistance" (Raj and Silverman 2002, 385). For example, few women are aware of the existence of VAWA. Education has always been a primary healthcare concern; when victims of IPV lack awareness of their options, as is often the case, patient education is more important than ever. If and when these women enter the healthcare system, school system, or any other place where healthcare or social service providers practice, all efforts should be made to build awareness and assist women and children in accessing services. Access to the opportunity of provider-patient interaction—and, especially for the undocumented, to medical care at all—is very dependent on the ability of abused immigrant women to seek treatment (which is often compromised by the abuser's unwillingness to let the victim, or her children, see a medical provider) (Moynihan et al. 2008). Every effort should be made to encourage potential patients to seek treatment. . . .

Documentation: The biggest and most difficult hurdle for many women in petitioning for VAWA protection is getting a good, clear paper trail of their abuse. Of critical importance is the documentation of battering or other "extreme cruelty" perpetrated on the abused woman. This is an excellent area for clinicians, who are able to identify and assess this form of victimization, to make a critical contribution (Moynihan et al. 2008). Obtaining the necessary evidence to demonstrate eligibility for VAWA is both overwhelming and difficult, and has been identified as one of the major obstacles to VAWA (Ingram et al. 2010). As Bhuyan (2008) noted, "proving you are a good (enough) victim" (p. 162) is a central and problematic part of the VAWA self-petitioning process. The easier and less painful we can make this process, the better. Documentation of the abuse that has occurred should record what the victim says in quotation marks, specifying dates of particular episodes of violence, and recording any evidence of violence (e.g., describing "old" bruises or bruises in various stages of healing, or entering on a body map notation of injuries and what date they occurred) (Laughon, Amar, Sheridan, and Anderson 2011). These medical records are admissible as evidence in legal proceedings, including VAWA hearings.

Advocacy and Policy: [In February 2013, the U.S. House of Representatives passed a bipartisan Senate version of the VAWA, which was then signed into law by President Barack Obama.] . . . Despite all of its logistical shortcomings, VAWA is still an excellent protection and far better than nothing at all. All health practitioners in the U.S. can and should be involved in advocating for its renewal whenever it comes up. Further recommendations for policy should include not only the renewal of VAWA, but the serious reevaluation of some of the elements of the VAWA process already addressed in this article that hinder the acquisition of VAWA protection. For all policy makers in every country, certain realities of IPV need to be considered in the implementation of legal provisions like VAWA which are meant to protect abused women: transience, security, clarity, time, children, and limiting the amount of repeated trauma that abused immigrant women experience should all be taken into account. Beyond VAWA, there is a great need for advocacy on behalf of these vulnerable individuals in U.S. society. The testimony of professionals who are privy to a unique and powerful perspective regarding the public health crises of the undocumented, such as healthcare workers, could greatly contribute to improving legal protections. From their position as routine witnesses to the unnecessary hardships suffered by undocumented women, healthcare workers can consistently and persistently direct their support for an amnesty to their legislators in Congress. Furthermore, agency policy can be shaped by advocating for outreach to immigrant women irrespective of documentation (McGuire and Georges 2003, 192).

Awareness: There is a great deal of ignorance and even more misconceptions in U.S. society about undocumented immigrants, who they are, and the obstacles they face. Spreading awareness about this population, among coworkers as well as in the community at large, should be a priority for the thoughtful individual engaged with this issue. It is critical that we understand this population's abundance of health-related vulnerabilities. It is also important to be aware of some of the traumatic experiences many undocumented immigrants have already faced. While undocumented immigrants come from many parts of the world, a large proportion of them come into the U.S. via our southern border with Mexico—a border that has been identified as "the most violent border in the world between two countries not at war with one another" (McGuire and Georges 2003, 192). It is rare that an individual who has crossed into the U.S. illegally via this pathway has not experienced some kind of trauma; the increased militarization and rampant human rights violations contribute to a growing public health problem, and the potential that undocumented immigrants will demonstrate symptoms of post-traumatic stress [disorder] as a result of their crossing is high. Talking about the issue with co-workers and the IPV advocacy community is very important.

Research: Data regarding the healthcare needs of the undocumented immigrant populations in America has been difficult to uncover and may not have been collected on a regular basis, for obvious reasons. More research is necessary to determine the best possible interventions. For example, we know that cultural competency on the part of IPV outreach is an issue; however, culturally appropriate interventions have not been designed and widely tested. More exploration of this topic is greatly needed. Furthermore, more research on the topic of how documentation status affects overall health is needed to better design policies and interventions for this population. Through the voices of undocumented women, we are beginning to see specialized knowledge with implications for women's and family health and social justice. . . .

References

Amanor-Boadu, Y., J. T. Messing, S. M. Stith, J. R. Anderson, C. S. O'Sullivan, and J. C. Campbell. 2012. Immigrant and nonimmigrant women: Factors that predict leaving an abusive relationship. *Violence Against Women* 18(5):611–33.

Berk, M. L., and C. L. Schur. 2001. The effect of fear on access to care among undocumented Latino immigrants. *Journal of Immigrant and Minority Health* 3(3):151–56.

Bhuyan, R. 2008. The production of the "battered immigrant" in public policy and domestic violence advocacy. *Journal of Interpersonal Violence* 23:153–70.

Breiding, M. J., M. C. Black, and G. W. Ryan. 2008. Prevalence and risk factors of intimate partner violence in eighteen U.S. states/territories, 2005. *American Journal of Preventive Medicine* 34:112–18.

Bustamante, A. V., H. Fang, J. Garza, O. Carter-Pokras, S. P. Wallace, J. A. Rizzo, and A. N. Ortega. 2010. Variations in healthcare access and utilization among Mexican immigrants: The role of documentation status. *Journal of Immigrant Minority Health*, published online, pp. 1–10. http://www.ncbi.nlm.nih.gov/pmc/articles/PMC3256312/.

Capps, R., L. Ku, M. Fix, C. Furgiuele, J. S. Passel, R. Ramchand, S. McNiven, D. Perez-Lopex, E. Fielder, M. Greenwell, and T. Hays. 2002. *How are immigrants faring after welfare reform? Preliminary evidence from Los Angeles and New York City—Final report.* Washington, DC: The Urban Institute.

Coker, A. L., S. M. Bond, M. M. Madeleine, K. Luchok, and L. Pirisi. 2003. Psychosocial stress and cervical neoplasia risk. *Psychosomatic Medicine* 54:644–51.

Collins, P. H. 1986. Learning from the outsider within: The sociological significance of black feminist thought. *Social Problems* 33(6):S14–S32.

Dutton, M., L. E. Orloff, and G. A. Hass. 2000. Characteristics of help-seeking behaviors, resources, and service needs of battered immigrant Latinas: Legal and policy implications. *Georgetown Journal on Poverty Law and Policy* 7:245–305.

Earner, I. 2010. Double risk: Immigrant mothers, domestic violence and public child welfare services in New York City. *Evaluation and Program Planning* 33:288–93.

Erez, E., M. Adelman, and C. Gregory. 2009. Intersections of immigration and domestic violence: Voices of battered immigrant women. *Feminist Criminology* 4(1):32–56.

Glass, N., S. L. Annan, T. B. Bhandari, and N. Fishwick. 2011. Nursing care of immigrant and rural abused women. In *Family Violence and Nursing Practice*, edited by J. Humphreys and J. C. Campbell. New York: Springer.

Ganatra, N. R. 2001. The cultural dynamic in domestic violence: Understanding the additional burdens battered immigrant women of color face in the U.S. *Journal of Law in Society* 109:118–19.

hooks, B. 1984. *Feminist theory: From margin to center.* 2nd ed. Cambridge, MA: South End Press.

Hyman, I., T. Forte, J. Du Mont, S. Romans, and M. M. Cohen. 2006. The prevalence of intimate partner violence in immigrant women in Canada. *American Journal of Public Health* 96:654–59.

Ingram, M., D. J. McClelland, J. Martin, M. F. Caballero, M. T. Mayorga, and K. Gillespie. 2010. Experiences of immigrant women who self-petition under the Violence Against Women Act. *Violence Against Women* 16:858–80.

INS (Immigration and Naturalization Services). 1997. *Immigration in Fiscal Year 1995* (Report No.6). Washington, DC: Author.

Kelly, U. 2009. Integrating intersectionality and biomedicine in health disparities research. *Advances in Nursing Science* 32(2):E42–E56.

Kelly, U., R. M. Gonzalez-Guarda, and J. Taylor. 2011. Theories of intimate partner violence. In *Family Violence and Nursing Practice*, edited by J. Humphreys and J. C. Campbell. New York: Springer.

Laughon, K., A. Amar, D. Sheridan, and S. Anderson. 2011. Legal and forensic nursing responses to family violence. In *Family Violence and Nursing Practice*, edited by J. Humphreys and J. C. Campbell. New York: Springer.

McGuire, S., and J. Georges. 2003. Undocumentedeness and liminality as health variables. *Advances in Nursing Science* 26(3):185–95.

Menjívar, C., and O. Salcido. 2002. Immigrant women and domestic violence: Common experiences in different countries. *Gender & Society* 16(6):898–920.

Monger, R., and J. Yankay. 2011. *Annual Flow Report: U.S. Legal Permanent Residents: 2010.* Retrieved July 28, 2011 from http://www.dhs.gov/xlibrary/assets/statistics/publications/lpr_fr_2010.pdf.

Moynihan, B., M. T. Gaboury, and K. J. Onken. 2008. Undocumented and unprotected immigrant women and children in harm's way. *Journal of Forensic Nursing* 4:123–29.

Passel, J. S., R. Capps, and M. Fix. 2004. Undocumented immigrants: Facts and figures. *Urban Institute Immigration Studies Program.* Retrieved April 5, 2011 from http://www.urban.org/publications/1000587.html.

Raj, A., and J. Silverman. 2002. Violence against immigrant women: The roles of culture, context and legal immigrant status on intimate partner violence. *Violence Against Women* 8:367–98.

Schei, B., M. Laanpere, A. M. Wangel, G. Lindmark, N. Nyström, U. Hogberg, K. Wijewardene, K. Karmacharya, I. Harstad, P. Rishal, R. Lund, R. Emmelin, A. K. Myhre, and B. Rostad. 2012. *The BIDENS study: Violence against women and women's health in the Baltic.* Manuscript submitted for publication.

Sokoloff, N. J. 2005. *Domestic violence at the margins: Readings on race, class, gender, and culture.* New Brunswick, NJ: Rutgers University Press.

Tjaden, P., and N. Thoennes. 2000. Prevalence and consequences of male-to-female and female-to-male intimate partner violence as measured by the National Violence Against Women survey. *Violence Against Women* 6(2):142–61.

Wessel, L., and J. C. Campbell. 1997. Providing sanctuary for battered women: Nicaragua's casas de la mujer. *Issues in Mental Health Nursing* 18:455–76.

Wood, S. M. 2004. VAWA's unfinished business: The immigrant women who fall through the cracks. *Duke Journal of Gender Law and Policy* 11:141–55.

WHO (World Health Organization) 2005. *Multicountry Study on Women's Health and Domestic Violence: Summary report on prevalence, health outcomes and women's responses.* Geneva: World Health Organization.

Appendix

Discussion Questions

PART I: THE SOCIAL CONSTRUCTION OF WOMEN'S BODIES

Chapter 1. "A History of Women's Bodies" by Rose Weitz

1. Weitz identifies three ideas about women's bodies that recur consistently in Western history (i.e., women bodies are inferior to men's, are men's property, and are sexual threats). How have these ideas restricted women's lives in the past? Currently? How do they affect women of different social groups (e.g., lesbian women, women of color, and working-class women)?
2. What is the role of feminism and the feminist movement, both historically and today, in challenging men's control over women's bodies? In challenging cultural assumptions about women's bodies?
3. Throughout history women have tried to take control over their own bodies and have met with backlash for doing so. What form does this backlash take today?

Chapter 2. "Believing Is Seeing: Biology as Ideology" by Judith Lorber

1. Lorber discusses how female athletes sometimes "do athlete" on the court, but "do woman" off the court. How do other women who challenge gender binaries—such as soldiers or business executives—"do gender" on a daily basis to "apologize" for their violations of gender norms? When and how do you "do gender"? Are there times when you consciously try *not* to "do gender"?
2. How does *belief* in biological sex differences result in biological sex differences?
3. What physical structures, aside from Lorber's examples of tables and bathrooms, assume a male physiological norm? What are the consequences of these physical structures for women?

Chapter 3. "Becoming a Gendered Body: Practices of Preschools" by Karin A. Martin

1. Martin argues that the gendering of children's bodies sets the stage for further gendering of bodies throughout the life course. How does your childhood socialization continue to affect your relationship with your body? How has the media reinforced or challenged ideas about female and male bodies that you learned as a child?
2. Martin's study focuses on female teachers in mostly secular schools. What similarities and differences might you find if you did the same research but studied male teachers, ethnic minority teachers, or teachers in a religious school? Why?
3. What changes can schools implement to encourage less gender-biased teacher–children interactions?

Chapter 4. "Medicalization, Natural Childbirth, and Birthing Experiences" by Sarah Jane Brubaker and Heather E. Dillaway

1. How do meanings of the terms *natural* and *medical* vary by time and place, as well as across social groups?
2. How does problematizing the conceptual dichotomy of "natural" and "medical" illuminate other medicalized phenomena such as female sexual "dysfunction," menopause, and premenstrual syndrome?
3. Taking into consideration differences by race/ethnicity, socio-economic background, maternal health status, etc., what strategies can birthing women and their advocates use to increase women's agency?

Chapter 5. "Foucault, Femininity, and the Modernization of Patriarchal Power" by Sandra Lee Bartky

1. Can a woman's focus on her physical appearance be simply a matter of individual expression, or is it always a form of discipline?
2. Bartky maintains that the disciplines that construct a feminine body are not race and class specific. Nevertheless, do some groups of women (e.g., lesbian women, women of color, or working-class women) have a greater or lesser stake in conforming to hegemonic body ideals compared to others? Why? Do all women gain equally from their attempts to meet body ideals?
3. If the "disciplinary power that inscribes femininity on the female body is everywhere and … nowhere," how can these powers be challenged? What would resistance look like?

Chapter 6. "Integrating Disability, Transforming Feminist Theory" by Rosemarie Garland-Thomson

1. How can feminist scholars incorporate lessons from disabilities studies to better understand the politics of women's bodies?

2. Garland-Thomson observes that disability is the most human of experiences because, if we live long enough, we are all affected by it. How can this observation be reconciled with the ongoing disciplining, exclusion, and lack of tolerance of disabled bodies, and human diversity in general?
3. According to Garland-Thomson, the commercial realm can potentially offer useful feminist images to challenge narrow depictions of disabled individuals. Alongside the disabled fashion models she suggests, what might these images look like? Consider paraplegic actress Ellen Stohl's attempt to affirm her sexuality through a *Playboy* spread. How are these depictions both liberating and oppressive?

PART II. THE POLITICS OF SEXUALITY

Chapter 7. "Breasted Experience: The Look and the Feeling" by Iris Marion Young

1. In light of the dominant phallocentric culture that constructs women's breasts as sexual objects, how can women reclaim this highly signified part of their bodies, as their own and as a potential source of pleasure? Do you think this would be easier for lesbian women? Why or why not?
2. How do meanings, including the objectification, of women's breasts change across life stages (e.g., in puberty, during pregnancy and lactation, and at menopause)? How do women cope with this objectification? What are the consequences of these strategies for women's lives?
3. Young uses the Madonna–whore dichotomy to explain the scandalous views of women's nipples. While cleavage is good, she says, nipples are forbidden as they show the breasts as active zones of eroticism. What counterarguments or alternative perspectives might also account for society's approach to women's nipples?

Chapter 8. "Daring to Desire: Culture and the Bodies of Adolescent Girls" by Deborah L. Tolman

1. According to Tolman's research, how does social context affect how urban and suburban girls respond to their sexual desires? What other factors might impact how girls relate to and respond to their sexual bodies?
2. Tolman argues that our cultural story about adolescent girls and sexuality essentially assumes that they want only intimacy and relationships, not sex. Yet many now argue that the media is constantly sexualizing girls, at younger and younger ages. How, if at all, can this cultural story be reconciled with rampant media depictions of adolescent girls' sexuality, and observations that girls are sexualized at increasingly young ages?

3. How do girls attempt to experience sexual pleasure while also protecting themselves from dangers such as disease, pregnancy, and physical violence? What factors make it difficult for them to do so?

Chapter 9. "A Tale of Two Technologies: HPV Vaccination, Male Circumcision, and Sexual Health" by Laura M. Carpenter and Monica J. Casper

1. How do both old and new medical technologies reproduce meanings of gender and sexuality? How can medical technologies be used to subvert traditional gender relations and create new understandings about women's sexual lives?
2. How have the politics of hygienic containment positioned some groups as Others? What are the implications of such politics?
3. How can Carpenter and Casper's findings inform or challenge state policies such as mandatory vaccinations in public schools?

Chapter 10. "'Get Your Freak On': Sex, Babies, and Images of Black Femininity" by Patricia Hill Collins

1. In terms of both form and consequences, how are the controlling and objectifying images of black women in the new racism similar to older forms of overt racism? How do they differ?
2. Hill Collins seems ambivalent regarding whether black women who use the term *bitch* are participating in their own subordination or are resisting oppression. How have black women attempted to reclaim this term, and to what degree is this reclamation successful?
3. What role, if any, should black men play in creating and supporting positive and diverse images of black women?

Chapter 11. "Brain, Brow, and Booty: Latina Iconicity in U.S. Popular Culture" by Isabel Molina Guzmán and Angharad N. Valdivia

1. How does the commodification of Latina icons in popular culture harm Latinas specifically, as well as women and the Hispanic community generally? Is there an upside to commodification?
2. Molina Guzmán and Valdivia discuss how constructions of "tropicalism" mark Latina bodies as sexually desirable Others. How are other ethnic minority women (e.g., Asian American women) similarly or differently constructed and commodified?
3. How are the experiences of the three women discussed in this article different from those of Jennifer Hudson, Rihanna, or other black actresses and singers?

Chapter 12. "'So Full of Myself as a Chick': Goth Women, Sexual Independence, and Gender Egalitarianism" by Amy C. Wilkins

1. To what degree do Goth sexual norms reflect mainstream sexual norms? If forms of gender subversion are evident in Goth subcultures, to what degree do they influence dominant norms about sexuality and gender structures more broadly?
2. Wilkin describes how some Goth women who do not conform to narrow hegemonic beauty norms dress in a highly sexualized manner at the Haven. How are these forms of dress an empowering "statement of female choice"? How do they reproduce traditional gender constructs?
3. How do Goth sexual norms increase women's power and agency? How do they restrict it?

PART III. THE POLITICS OF APPERANCE

Chapter 13. "Designing Women: Cultural Hegemony and the Exercise of Power among Women Who Have Undergone Elective Mammoplasty" by Patricia Gagné and Deanna McGaughey

1. Gagné and McGaughey argue that women choose to have cosmetic surgery, but that their choices are limited by the social context in which they live. In your opinion, are women who have cosmetic surgery free actors making rational choices, victims of a system that forces their hands, or somehow both?
2. How does cosmetic surgery reinforce hegemonic beauty norms? How does it reinforce sexism, ableism, ageism, heterosexism, racism, and classism?
3. How does cosmetic surgery help women? How does it hurt them? How does it affect women who do not use cosmetic surgery?

Chapter 14. "Women and Their Hair: Seeking Power through Resistance and Accommodation" by Rose Weitz

1. According to Weitz, how do women seek power through their hair using traditional and nontraditional strategies? What are the limitations of these strategies?
2. If a woman dyes her hair blonde in order to marry a wealthy man, is it resistance, accommodation, or both? If a woman gets a "power cut" to get a high-level professional job, is that resistance, accommodation, or both?
3. Weitz maintains that all strategies women use to gain power through their hair contain some elements of accommodation. For example, in the long run even Afros, dreadlocks, and asymmetrical haircuts became simply fashion choices. Is resistance through hair as a medium possible?

Chapter 15. "Navigating Public Spaces: Gender, Race, and Body Privilege in Everyday Life" by Samantha Kwan

1. What are other forms of body privilege aside from weight-based privilege? How do they lead to similar or different forms of body consciousness and body management? In general, how is body privilege similar to or different from privilege based on other advantaging systems (e.g., male privilege, white privilege, or heterosexual privilege)?
2. Alongside gender and race/ethnicity, how do social identifiers such as age, ability, and/or sexual orientation affect experiences of body privilege?
3. What changes would lead to a society where body privilege is not a privilege but "simply part of the normal civic and social fabric" where all bodies can navigate their daily lives comfortably?

Chapter 16. "The Moral Underpinnings of Beauty: A Meaning-Based Explanation for Light and Dark Complexions in Advertising" by Shyon Baumann

1. How does Baumann account for women's lighter skin tone ideal (compared to men)? Can other physical attractiveness ideals be explained using Baumann's theory?
2. Aside from the heterosexual wedding symbolism and fairy tale images he discusses, what examples in popular culture support Baumann's theory? What are some examples that challenge his lightness-goodness and darkness-badness links?
3. Can Baumann's explanation of gendered skin tone ideals explain the use of skin-lightening products by women across the globe? How might his theory need to be revised in light of racial/ethnic diversity in an international context?

Chapter 17. "Reclaiming the Female Body: Women Body Modifiers and Feminist Debates" by Victoria Pitts

1. How do the arguments about body alterations (including "deviant" alterations) made by radical feminists differ from those made by postmodern feminists? How does each group approach body modification, agency, and structure?
2. What are the advantages, as well as the limitations, of using body modification as a means of "reclaiming" one's body?
3. Do tattooed, scarred, and pierced bodies effectively challenge social ideas about beauty and about gender?

PART IV. THE POLITICS OF BEHAVIOR

Chapter 18. "From the 'Muscle Moll' to the 'Butch' Ballplayer: Mannishness, Lesbianism, and Homophobia in U.S. Women's Sport" by Susan K. Cahn

1. How does Cahn explain why Americans shifted from believing that participating in sport increased women's *heterosexual* desire to believing that participating in sport could increase women's *homosexual* desires?
2. Cahn notes that African American women were once less likely to be labeled as lesbians than white women, because of historical racial stereotypes of *all* African American women as aggressive, coarse, and physical. Are white and non-white women athletes currently portrayed differently in popular media and discussion? Does the sport a woman plays affect how or if she is stereotyped?
3. Cahn observes how some women adopt an "apologetic stance" toward their athletic skill. How do women athletes nowadays exhibit this "feminine apologetic"? How do sports organizations and the sports media "apologize" on their behalf?

Chapter 19. "Branded with Infamy: Inscriptions of Poverty and Class in the United States" by Vivyan C. Adair

1. In contrast to ideal "normative" citizens, how are the bodies of poor women constructed as pathological, dangerous, and undeserving? How are these constructions gendered?
2. How does a lack of medical care, as well as other forms of material deprivation, physically mark poor women's bodies?
3. How are poor women's bodies treated as if they are not their own, but rather, as Adair puts it, "public property"? What strategies do poor women use to reclaim their bodies and resist inscriptions of their bodies as marked Others?

Chapter 20. "Backlash and Continuity: The Political Trajectory of Fetal Rights" by Rachel Roth

1. How have states and other social institutions attempted to control the reproductive rights of women, both historically and today?
2. How have attempts to control women's reproductive freedom differently affected single versus married women, poor versus middle-class women, and white versus minority women?
3. How will pregnant women be affected if our society adopts the language of "fetal rights"? How might non-pregnant women be affected?

Chapter 21. "*Hijab* and American Muslim Women: Creating the Space for Autonomous Selves" by Rhys H. Williams and Gira Vashi

1. Williams and Vashi maintain that young Muslims living in the United States negotiate two cultural contexts (i.e., equal rights versus cultural decadence). How does the current political, economic, and social climate influence this group's cultural and identity work, as well as the meanings of the *hijab*?
2. Williams and Vashi's study focuses on young, educated Muslim Americans. How are their findings relevant to other Muslim American women, such as those who are older or are less socio-economically privileged?
3. Williams and Vashi maintain that, despite its religious and social meanings, the *hijab* is a fashion statement. How is the *hijab*, as a fashion statement, similar to or different from other fashion garments and accessories, religious or not?

Chapter 22. "Compulsive Heterosexuality: Masculinity and Dominance" by C. J. Pascoe

1. How do the boys Pascoe observed enact compulsive heterosexuality through their everyday interactions with girls? How is compulsive heterosexuality reinforced outside the school by other institutions such as sport, family, and the media?
2. Why and how do girls collude in boy's discourses and practices of compulsive heterosexuality?
3. Pascoe maintains that teachers typically dismiss boys' physical aggression against girls as simply normal, harmless flirting. What are the consequences of teachers' inaction? What would a teacher training program that would make teachers more likely to intervene, and to intervene effectively, look like?

Chapter 23. "Being Undocumented and Intimate Partner Violence (IPV): Multiple Vulnerabilities through the Lens of Feminist Intersectionality" by Margaret E. Adams and Jacquelyn Campbell

1. How does a lens of intersectionality shed light on the intimate partner violence experienced by undocumented immigrants, as well as other forms of violence against women?
2. To what extent are women more likely than men to experience allostatic load because of their material and social circumstances? How can the concept of allostatic load be applied to understand women's experiences beyond intimate partner violence?
3. Aside from those suggested by Adams and Campbell, what are some strategies that can be implemented to prevent and address IPV among undocumented immigrant women?